Education
and
Community

A Radical Critique
of Innovative Schooling

Donald W. Oliver

Harvard University

𝔐𝔠𝔠𝔲𝔱𝔠𝔥𝔞𝔫 𝔓𝔲𝔟𝔩𝔦𝔰𝔥𝔦𝔫𝔤 ℭ𝔬𝔯𝔭𝔬𝔯𝔞𝔱𝔦𝔬𝔫
2526 Grove Street
Berkeley, California 94704

Library of Congress Catalog Card Number 76-2114
ISBN 0-8211-1406-9

Printed in the United States of America

To Pauline

without whose love and companionship this book would have been completed a year earlier

Preface

The initial premise of this book is that there is a crisis of will in the education professions, as well as the helping professions generally, because of a loss of faith in the liberal vision of the modern democratic society. Traditionally, these professions have been built on psychological theories which provide guides for the improvement, correction, or growth of individual human beings. The theories have been (and are being) applied to curriculum reform, teacher training, the upgrading and humanization of supervisors and the process of supervision, the process of administration, and the like. They run all the way from mechanistic statements about the nature of man (e.g., Skinner) to humane and sentimental statements stressing personal autonomy and self-actualization (e.g., Rogers and Maslow). Beneath the application of these theories, however, is a technological model of progress. One creates a model of change; one applies it to individuals or institutions; one evaluates it to establish a "data base"; one then corrects the model and goes through the process a second time (the "double loop"), etc. It is a straightforward research and development paradigm borrowed from the industrial revolution.

With this approach to social change, one does not usually look at the society as a whole, or the community, or the neighborhood. One looks at individual humans (i.e., clients) and the corporate institutions within which they behave and are managed. One assumes that through gradual increments of behavior change managed by scientists and technicians some diffuse whole called "society" will get better and better.

We believe that the inability of the helping professions to act constitutes a loss of faith in this model of social change. Although the modern helping professional continues to proliferate and be affluent, he does not really resolve the fundamental problems of the larger society. Crime increases. Violence increases. Inequality of the most blatant sort persists. Honesty in politics deteriorates. The alienation of the old and the young, the halt and the blind, grows. Clearly, the incremental mechanistic theory of social progress, based on the monitoring of social institutions by social scientists and helping professionals, is in a good deal of trouble. It is the thesis of this book that this model of social amelioration is, in the long run, ineffective for two reasons: it operates out of a wrong-headed theory of human nature; and it requires an intrinsically exploitative mode of "helping."

The theory is wrong-headed because it assumes that various primitive aspects of man's nature can be successfully extinguished or reconstructed. These aspects include, for example:

1. The need for small communities (bands, tribes, villages, neighborhoods, etc.) as sources of support which stand midway between the intimate and volatile nuclear family and the work-oriented corporation;

2. The need for a concrete (perhaps magical) religio-philosophical meaning system which explains the various mundane requirements of life; and

3. The need for validation and acceptance of the broad diversity of types (in age, sex, temperament, status, etc.) commonly found in human communities.

The modern professional is prone to say that man's need for community can be fulfilled by the humanization of corporate life (e.g., make schools more informal and personal), or by providing therapy and counseling to make sick families well; his need for religious meaning can be fulfilled by giving him maximum choices among all meaning systems and letting each individual make his own commitments; his need for understanding the value and worthiness of diversity can be transformed into a commitment to the equality and perfection of each individual. Hence, diversity will no longer be a problem. We think these premises and the policies which follow from them simply do not work. For a great variety of reasons—suggested in the book—man's need for community will not go away; it cannot be replaced by other social forms or the transformation of the nuclear family and corporation. Man cannot simply "choose" among religio-philosophical meaning systems and then commit himself to one, because the processes of choice and commitment are intrinsically antithetical. And the notion that all humans can be raised to some common level of intellectual, moral, esthetic, and social maturity is refuted by so much anthropological and historical evidence that it defies common logic. Societies are built on the premise of human diversity and difference rather than the premise of literal equality and uniformity.

It is the thesis of this book that the central problem of education is *not* how to create humane organizations, or how to provide people with the capacity to create their own individual meaning systems, or how to create fully mature individuals (although there is nothing intrinsically wrong with any of these goals). Rather the problem is one of creating balance between the primal and modern aspects of human community, systems of thought, and personality. This means creating balanced participation among primal social forms (family and community) and the modern social form of the corporate organization; creating a balance between an ultimate sense of religio-philosophical meaning and the skeptical sense of choices we associate with "scientific thinking"; and creating a balance between efforts to maximize the potential development of each individual and recognizing the necessity and value of diversity among humans, even in such sensitive areas as intelligence, motivation, and social responsibility.

We concede that this book paints reality with very broad and perhaps superficial strokes. Even saying that there is "a central problem in education" is presumptuous. But the methodology of the book—the breadth of its speculations—is intentional. From Skinner to Piaget to John Holt education is frought with fragmentary theories and schemes which attempt to repair one human frailty at a time. Education is, in fact, in desperate need of metatheories, overarching ways of looking at things that can plausibly push in the direction of realistic appraisals of man's requirements and potentialities for decent if not utopian living. We hope that presenting what we call an "evolutionist perspective" (i.e., working toward a more reasonable balance between the primal and modern tendencies in man) will demonstrate, if not the necessity of a radical reorientation in the way helping professionals look at their work, at least the necessity of a philosophical debate at this level of theory and meaning.

Such theories must take some kind of ethical stand about how they see the quality of life for man on this planet. This is discussed in chapters 2 and 3. They must deal specifically with a more sophisticated and complex way of construing issues of quality of life than simple economic upgrading. This question is explored in chapters 4 and 5 and examined further in chapters 6-8. They must also show positive instances of the relationship between the quality of social and communal life and the quality of education and schooling. This is illustrated in chapters 9 through 15.

This book is, therefore, concerned with both methodology and substance. The methodology is synthetic and broad. It works toward the development of metatheory. The substance has to do with the major facets by which one views man-in-community and possible relationships between education and community within this broader view. It is our hope that the book might provide a new conceptual basis for a social studies and humanities curriculum.

Donald W. Oliver

Contents

Introduction

1

Community and Educational Reform

    This book is an attempt to link and relate three concepts: education, community, and quality of life. Our essential thesis is that education has become an increasingly narrow concept virtually synonymous with managed instruction: that the relative narrowness with which we conceive of education is no accident but has evolved within a society that itself is highly managed and specialized, in the interest of efficiency—even to the point where it would destroy smaller, less organized patterns of human intercourse that commonly take place in neighborhoods or "microcommunities."

    An underlying premise behind this conclusion is that there are fundamentally two very different systems of sociality wherein groups of humans can engage in ordered, meaningful, and peaceful intercourse. One system may be termed roughly the "corporate organization," which is an extension of the traditional human work group. It is certainly as old as the Egyptian pyramids, but has taken on

An earlier version of this chapter appeared in *The National Elementary Principal* 54, no. 4 (March/April 1975).

dramatic new significance when coupled with modern technology. Modern sociology has, in fact, patterned its positive view of development, cultural evolution, and progress after this technological-organizational model. In simplest terms, the theory is that division of labor (both with respect to machines and people) in which the requirements of work (or "production") are broken into finer and finer interrelated parts leads to increased efficiency. This in turn requires specialized machines, specialized tasks, and specialized workers. To do this, however, one must carry out the rational analysis of a system of production and the precise planning of the interrelationship of each function.

The other system we would call "community." It is complex and highly organized, but the organization evolves out of a mixture of trial and error events over a long period of time, often at an unconscious level of deliberation and culture building. In a rough way, the distinction between these two systems of sociality correlates with Redfield's distinction between the moral and the technical order.

Technical order and moral order name two contrasting aspects of all human societies. The phrases stand for two distinguishable ways in which the activities of men are co-ordinated. It refers to the organization of sentiments into judgments as to what is right. Describing how the division of labor puts an organization of society based on occupation and vocational interests in place of an older kind of organization of society, Park contrasts these newer ties, based on common interests with "forms of association like the neighborhood, which are based on contiguity, personal association, and the common ties of humanity." The division of labor modifies this older moral order. Here we will extend the significance of the phrase, and make it cover all the binding together of men through implicit convictions as to what is right, through explicit ideals, or through similarities of conscience. The moral order is therefore always based on what is peculiarly human —sentiments, morality, conscience—and in the first place arises in the groups where people are intimately associated with one another. . . . We may conceive of the moral order as equally present in those societies in which rules for right conduct among men are supported by supernatural sanctions and in those in which the morality of human conduct is largely independent of the religion (in the sense of belief and cult about the supernatural). "Moral order" includes the binding sentiments of rightness that attend religion, the social solidarity that accompanies religious ritual, the sense of religious seriousness and obligation that strengthens men, and the effects of a belief in the invisible beings that embody goodness. . . .

By a corresponding extension of another and more familiar term, all the other forms of co-ordination of activity which appear in human societies may be brought together and contrasted with the moral order under the phrase "the technical order." The bonds that co-ordinate the activities of men in the technical order do not rest on convictions as to the good life; they are not characterized by a foundation of human sentiments; they can exist even without the knowledge of those bound together that they are bound together. The technical order is that order which results from mutual usefulness, from deliberate coercion, or from the mere utilization of the same means. In the technical order men are bound by things, or are themselves things. They are organized by necessity or expediency. Think, if you will, of the orderly way in which automobiles move in response to the traffic light or the policeman's whistle, or think of the flow of goods, services, and money among the people who together produce, distribute, and consume some commodity such as rubber. (1953, p. 2021)

We assume that in modern society there is an *overextension* of the technical order as a primary basis for the ordering and maintenance of human groups, that is, bringing together people for reasons of efficiency, expediency, convenience, and economic growth. The essence of the problem is that man evolved within bands and tribes, the integrity and meaning of which were based on a moral order. The technical order, however, demands a level of conceptual intelligence bonded to underlying sentiments of universal morality that are not common to all men (or to most men). Complex cosmopolitan societies are therefore always split between an elite, including a ruling class and the retinue of "professionals" who assist the ruling class, and the common folk. What is increasingly apparent is that the common folk do not "rise" to a level of conceptual intelligence which would make them comfortable in an atomized society wherein bands and tribes based on a moral order have all but disappeared. There is a constant effort to recreate village life within cities; or to pretend that whole nations are nothing more than folksy communities (e.g., Nazi Germany). And the elite carries on a constant battle to cosmopolitanize the folks, to teach them an abstract ethical, economic, and political system which will allow them to cope with the problems of the technical order. (And increasingly the elite feels guilty and ashamed of its privileged status.)

We assume that there are, therefore, serious problems in maintaining a society based so heavily on a technical order. These problems might be summarized as: (1) The inevitability of a class-caste system of stratification consisting of a highly privileged ruling class which benefits most from the technical order; a retinue of meritocratic professionals who have considerable affluence, but who must work to make the system go; a large "middle class" which substitutes material advantages for community and pays a large price in compulsory and relatively meaningless work; and a relatively large class of "defectives" or expendibles who cannot work, but must be supported in some marginal way, either in ghettos or custodial institutions. (2) The general stress and insecurity on all humans within the society because they are deprived of the unconditional emotional support of a primary community. In some sense, all are expendible. (3) The ennui and emptiness that develops within people's lives, especially the lives of both the affluent and expendible classes, as they discover that status, convenience, and material affluence as well as secular intellectual and artistic expression will not satisfy the human longing to search for ultimate meaning. This ultimate meaning must come from a moral order by communal rituals. (Ironically, ennui and emptiness can be temporarily assuaged by giving the folk classes the same privileges that have led the elite to its sense of boredom and loss of meaning.)

While one might give a much more highly differentiated list of problems associated with the technical order, we assume that those listed here are sufficiently serious to warrant some kind of radical reconsideration of how they might be ameliorated. The most common possibilities for such amelioration are suggested below:

1. One can assume that the more virulent influence of the corporate organization (and its underlying type of culture, i.e., the technical order) can be "tamed" by building strong alternative primary group relationships in each person's life (e.g., families, therapy groups, recreation groups, the YMCA). One can then tolerate the highly instrumental part of one's corporate life because one has the support and integrity of a set of primary relationships. We are skeptical of this mode of reform (although we think it common today), because of the tremendous emotional pressure it places on a limited set of primary relationships. It is likely that the anxiety people feel over their adequacy or effectiveness in corporate life spills over into primary relationships, where individuals cannot really conceive of themselves as having intrinsic worth. In other words, relatively transient albeit primary relationships do not have the force to balance the pressure of a corporate identity. The nuclear family is too fragile and emotionally charged to deal with the competency requirements of corporate settings—in school, jobs, etc.

2. A second mode of reform is to modify the corporation as a social form wherein welfare mechanisms and insurance can replace communal primary group relationships (day care centers in the business or factory, medical clinics, etc.); and where primary group mechanisms are built into the lifestyle of the corporation (bowling clubs, libraries, dining halls, etc.). This approach is apparently common in Japan. We are skeptical of this approach because it still assumes a monolithic, highly ordered, and managed environment with a level of security and predictability that is difficult for most humans to endure. Nor do either of these first two modes of reform resolve problems of loss of ultimate meaning, or what to do with the "expendible classes."

3. A third possibility for reform is to work toward some balance between the two very different human systems: the corporate context based on the technical order and the community context based on the moral order. Our thesis is that modern people should have the option of living not simply in isolated families linked to corporate service agencies (schools, police, shopping centers, etc.), but that they should have available the possibility of living within real neighborhoods. We obviously support this mode of reform, but understand that its feasibility and development present a host of problems, the most serious of which is determining what would be the cohesive basis of such neighborhoods. We know that ethnic neighborhoods still exist; that they tend to be based on shared language (in the midst of a dominant second language); a shared church affiliation; a shared sense of turf. How to go about creating a sense of neighborhood where there is no such common culture is a difficult question.

Social Reform and the Schools

Mirroring possible approaches toward general reform in the larger society are specific possibilities for reform in the schools. One approach is to make more humane and socially comfortable that corporate institution called school. Or one can attempt to rebuild or retrieve that missing or dying social form called small community or neighborly group within and around the school. Unless these two approaches are separated, one tends to think in very confused terms about the topic of education and community. For if we begin with the problem of "communitizing schools," that is, making schooling more informal, humane, and socially comfortable, our focus is not really on community at all, but only on introducing certain additional qualities into that corporate institution called school. And if we are fundamentally interested in rebuilding small, holistic social units of neighborhood scale (say five hundred to five thousand people), we soon see the school is likely to be a destructive or disruptive influence with little or no regard for the integrity of such outside parochial units. The busing movement*, for example, is explicitly concerned with orienting children outside of their neighborhoods. Of course, our essential question underlying both approaches is whether the common school can be "humanized" to the point of replacing the old neighborhood to provide the kind of support that humans have sought after, and found in the small community, for most of their evolutionary history.

Unfortunately, this issue is rarely posed. Enlightened school leaders are ordinarily engaged in quite a different struggle: preventing the straightforward, efficiency-oriented corporate types, such as school board members, educational consultants, and conservative teachers, from blocking even the simplest and most obvious kinds of reforms required for a decent corporate school environment.

Such reform efforts are obviously good, obviously beneficial. Of course there should be a greater variety of "real life" community activities and more different kinds of adults around the school. Everything possible should be done to build a genuine partnership between clients (parents and children) and professionals. The people should feel the school is theirs as a social institution; they should help build it, help equip it, help run it, and participate in its operation. These are characteristics of any humane corporate institution.

It is our position, however, that conditions of genuine community cannot be met within the school for a variety of reasons, two of which we shall suggest here. First, the public school is a pluralistic institution that must find ways of celebrating commonalities across subcultures and minimizing the particularities of subcultures that evolve out of individual neighborhoods or communities. The pressure on the school is to draw the individual away from the parochialness and the specialness of family, social background, religion, dialect—

---

*Busing is here used to mean transportation in consolidated and regionalized school districts as well as an instrument for desegregation.

anything that might make one seem odd or unusual in the mainstream of cosmopolitan life. (At best, of course, an individual might be "bicultural.") The mission of the school is to create a single, cohesive society, emphasizing what is common to modern man (his capacity for intelligent coping), rather than supporting the great plurality of habits and rituals characteristic of subcultures or subsocieties.

But small communities and their subcultures are held together precisely by their parochial characteristics, which leads to the "we-they" distinction, the sense that one is a member of an ingroup that has a particular history, a particular set of heroes, a particular set of opinions and myths about the most fundamental human questions: Where did the earth come from? Where did man come from? What is the meaning of sexuality and reproduction? Why do humans grow old and die? Is man fundamentally good or evil? The school must either avoid these questions as too controversial and leave them to be resolved by each individual in his own special way, or it must treat them as secular, scientific problems that are to be answered by scholars and scientists. Since such questions cannot be worked through within the limits of science and without an act of faith, and since the school has no mandate to generate such meaningful faith, the fundamental issues on which we must agree for a sense of community cannot really be adequately treated in the school.

Conditions of genuine community cannot be met within the school for a second reason as well. And that is that small communities or neighborly places characteristically include a broad range of diverse humans (babies, adults, old people; the lazy, the aggressive; the trained, the untrained; etc.) who interact within relatively fluid contexts to allow for the natural evolution of interdependent coalitions. The places of community can be street corner hang-outs, sewing groups in living rooms, church fairs, baseball in vacant lots. Some of these contexts are specifically organized; others simply emerge. They tend to produce substantial order as well as a set of productive relationships without a great deal of pressure from formal rules or sanctions or explicit management. Neither families nor schools have the fluidity of settings or diversity of people to allow these arrangements to evolve. Such evolution requires a social unit that is larger and less intimate than the family; one that is geographically stable; one that is under less pressure than the corporate school to work at systematic tasks and produce results. In short, it requires a community. Because the school stands somewhat between the family and the more standard corporate organizations, it can accept the limited task of preparing the young to enter into and cope with corporate life by imitating it in school; or it can accept this task along with a more complex responsibility—that of relating to and supporting other primary institutions in the society that have more realistic potential for becoming or maintaining themselves as neighborly places.

We believe that communitarian educators must come to see that pursuing social reform or improving the quality of life through something called "community" cannot be done simply by humanizing corporate welfare institutions. It requires, rather, that we distinguish between two fundamentally different lifestyles and opt for a radical shift in the way we live. The distinction between the two is perhaps most clearly described if we first consider the following settings within which we spend our time:

—Organized corporate work settings;

—Organized corporate social welfare settings (hospitals, schools, clinics, old age homes, homes for the retarded and the mentally ill, etc);

—Family settings;

—Semiformal, special interest gatherings for work, recreation, and sociality (chess clubs, choral societies, health spas, etc.);

—General communal or neighborly places with diffuse interests and goals (churches, fraternal lodges, the YMCA, etc.).

In a conventional modern lifestyle, people are first segregated according to their capacity and competence to cope with or without support. If they need support, they are placed in a social welfare setting for treatment or, more usually, custodial care: children are placed in school; the mentally retarded are placed in training schools; and so on. If people can cope, they spend their lives centrally committed to an organized work setting. Unless they are employed in one of the helping professions, they are generally free from responsibility to attend to or care for the incompetent. They rest within the haven of the family and regenerate strength to return to the work setting, and if they have special motivation or a high activity level, they fulfill special interests and the need for personal growth in semiformal, special interest gatherings.

One can describe an alternative communitarian lifestyle, in

which one's commitment to the corporate work setting would be reduced. There is concomitantly a substantial press toward increasing the significance of the neighborly place, which then absorbs some of the activities that would normally occur as social welfare, in the family, or in the special interest gatherings.

Social reform for the conventional modern lifestyle is generally limited to humanizing corporate and custodial work settings, as well as upgrading the professional competence of teachers, social workers, and child care specialists. Social reform for the communitarian life-style, however, requires us to integrate to a larger extent what are commonly private family or special interest gatherings into trans-family or communal relationships.

One strength of the communitarian lifestyle mode of reform over other efforts to relate education and community is its potential power to deliver social welfare services. This range of services—those related to "incompetent" people, such as small children, the men-tally retarded, the alcoholic and neurotic, the insane, and the aged—is now provided in corporate welfare institutions that are always in a state somewhere between brutality and reform. There is now consid-erable agreement that the reform of social welfare services requires radical decentralization, the return of "incompetents" to the local community, and their reintegration with "normal" people who can cope for themselves and give aid and succor to others.

The basic problem in this proposal is simply that the majority of the competent adults are apparently already overburdened coping with their corporate and family responsibilities. One can speculate, however, that there are increasing numbers of adolescents, young adults, and old people who are excluded from the corporate context by unemployment or underemployment (for example, students and homemakers) or who participate minimally in nuclear family settings (for example, ummarried college students). Such people find them-selves not only excluded, but alienated—partly because being produc-tive is inextricably associated with earning money. To cite just one instance, women are considered more productive as clerks at a check-out counter than as shoppers, because one activity earns a paycheck while the other does not, although the one activity is certainly as critical to the economy as the other. These people have great poten-tial in delivering social welfare services within the community.

Building Communitarian Settings versus
Communitizing the School

We can attempt to improve society by humanizing or "communitizing" corporate institutions, including those that have traditionally provided basic welfare services (schools, prisons, clinics, and so on); or we can attempt to build or strengthen more highly integrated, transfamily, communitarian settings. Conservatively, these might be institutions such as the local church parish or fraternal order; radically they might be intentional communities or radical residential schools.

Common efforts to revitalize local neighborhoods include food co-ops, neighborhood day care, and the community-school movement. Despite these efforts, few institutions seem to have the stability or ideological base that might allow individuals or families to extricate themselves from their tendency to live isolated and private lives. One possible exception is, perhaps, the local church.

Traditional places of worship have been heavily supported by kinship ties: parental concern that their children have the experience of religious education; the celebration of traditional holidays and rituals that punctuate the seasons (Christmas, Passover, Thanksgiving) or mark one's human career (baptism, bar mitzvah, marriage). More dynamic churches and synagogues have added programs that tend to be educational or cultural in nature. Skills in the arts and crafts are taught or shared; local or visiting musicians, poets, writers, and puppeteers present programs for the entertainment or uplifting of the congregation. Discussion groups are sometimes formed, either to share common interests or to institute some needed social action.

While it is difficult to generalize about the quality of experiences shared by members of a local parish, there is little doubt that churches and synagogues have been deeply troubled, both financially and programmatically, by the increasing influences of privatism and occupational mobility. Older ministers and parishioners often reminisce about the days when a dozen or so families or sets of relatives filled the church. Now the pews are occupied by older people whose families have moved away and younger families who are passing through from one job to another, on the way up. These two groups tend to be separated from one another. The older people may mourn the loss of roots and kinship and for this reason often envy the younger families, who in turn see their involvement in the church as a gesture toward conventional religion or spiritual transcendence. Often neither group feels any pressing responsibility outside its own private relationship to the church.

Some religious institutions are little more than mourning grounds for the rituals and celebrations that once gave Americans a sense of tradition and rootedness; others simply provide a context for token gestures toward bringing up children in a Christian or Jewish way. There are, however, vigorous congregations whose members see the church or synagogue as a central institution for raising the spiritual and social quality of their lives. But as most professional clergy and active lay people will attest, there are all too few of them.

One central challenge of genuine reform is how to build a relationship between the school as a corporate service agency and the local church or synagogue which has the potential of being an authentic neighborly place. There are two major requirements for building such a coalition. First, there must be professional commitment by both educators and religious leaders to collaborate and redefine the responsibilities each might take toward the education of people in the local neighborhood. And second, there must be a fundamental alteration in the modern lifestyle.

It is unlikely that these conditions can or will be met, partly because they are contrary to larger and more substantial forces in the society, but specifically because they are contrary to the narrower interests of competitive status-oriented educators. Building the type of communitarian institutions suggested here (in churches, private schools, or intentional communities) would reduce the power and significance of the local school and the educational establishment that supports and is supported by it. Hopefully, however, school administrators, teachers, and board officials who have worked to expand the responsibilities and powers of the schools will, at some point, realize that the communal unit from which a great many basic human needs must be met is not a bureaucratically organized, well-managed corporate institution such as the modern school, but rather a more fluid family-oriented institution such as the local parish. And with this realization might come experiments—not in communitizing schools and related corporate institutions—but rather in building communitarian institutions which might take some of the destructive pressure off the schools.

Conclusion

The burden of this book is to critique the limitations of the modern "two context life," that is, a life spent mainly in the nuclear family and the corporate organization. Our assumption is that we must build a third context, a transfamily community-oriented context, concerned less with the promotion of *individual growth* and more with improving the quality of collective primary group life. This suggests that members of the various helping professions (especially educators) might well reorient their lives away from efforts to separate themselves from the common people by developing new specialities, new training, new and more esoteric processes of credentialing. Instead, they might well allocate more of their energies toward relating informally to primary institutions, such as churches or social clubs, and help build networks of sociality based on kinship and friendship. While such people are less likely to climb the ladder of professional success and attain regional or national visibility and recognition, they might, in the long run, have a greater chance of maintaining their own sense of moral integrity and personal worth.

Reference

Redfield, Robert. *The Primitive World and its Transformations.* Ithaca, N.Y.: Cornell University Press, 1953.

PART I

Ethical Bases for the Anaylsis of Education and Community

2

Competing Ideological Forces in the Struggle for Communitarian Reform

A Second Lens from Which To View Efficiency and Accountability in Education

A central quality of "modern society" is a view of reality in which we come to see as quite natural the increasing differentiation and specialization of its various parts resulting in a larger, more efficient, and complex whole. We then take for granted that human activities, including those of an essentially "helping" nature such as teaching the young or healing the ill or caring for the aged, are to be carried on within specialized segregated institutions. We assume that these institutions will be run by professionals, and that defects or problems within such institutions can be adequately construed or managed *within the framework of the single activity itself.*

Reprinted by permission from *Social Forces and Schooling*, edited by Nobuo Kenneth Shimahara and Adam Scrupski (New York: David McKay, 1975).

Improvement or "reform" in the teaching of the young is seen as quite a separate issue from the problems we have in caring for infants or the aged, the way we treat the mentally ill, the boredom and tediousness of factory work, poverty and violence in the inner city ghettos, or boredom of adolescents and housewives in the affluent suburbs. Progress in teaching the young is translated into improving the efficiency, the order, and morale of those who inhabit schools. This can be done by such devices as creating new curriculum; constructing and using behavioral objectives; developing more sophisticated methods of testing and evaluation; finding less stressful and more regularized methods of disciplining and controlling children and youth; and making more efficient the process of managing and using teachers, buildings, books, courses, school buses, and the whole apparatus we now call "schooling." Callahan (1962, p. 180), for example, documents the explicit use of the business metaphor applied to American schools in the early part of this century.

The men who were leaders in educational administration in the period from 1910 to 1918 . . . represented a new type of school administrator. . . . To a man they were able, energetic, and practical, and, to an amazing degree they represented in their interests and actions the dominant tendencies in American life in the first decades of the twentieth century. They not only manifested a great interest in and admiration for businessmen and industrialists, but they resembled these men in their behavior. They were active in introducing and using business and industrial procedures and terminology in education, and they centered their attention almost exclusively upon financial, organizational, and mechanical problems.

The contemporary controversy over the issue of "accountability"—whether or not individual teachers should be rewarded or penalized on the basis of test performances of their students—suggests that the "cult of efficiency" is still very much alive.

Within the past few years, however, a central premise of modern society itself—the premise that most of us should spend most of our time in highly specialized managed institutions separated from the common life of a human community—has come under reexamination. From the radical perspective, efforts to reform or improve the teaching of the young consist of minor variations on a common theme: How can some humans be more efficiently trained to carry out tasks that are structured and assigned by other humans? In more general societal terms the theme includes such elements as creating a national or corporate consciousness which increasingly tears apart

any remaining fabric of common community life (e.g., neighborhoods, ethnic clubs, local church parishes, small family businesses)
on the one hand while on the other isolating and individuating persons or nuclear families so they can function efficiently as competitive mobile interchangeable parts striving to succeed within the national economic arena. The goal of the overall system is a balance
between corporate *efficiency* and *stability* based on meritocratic
stratification and segregation. In sociological terms, an underlying
central goal of schooling is to preselect and stratify children to make
success and failure within the system seem reasonable, justified, and
personally earned.

One of these radical critics, Michael Katz, is a student of the
historical process in the nineteenth century during which schools
became corporate institutions. He suggests that there were, in the
early years of the Republic, a variety of competing models of schooling. These he conceptualizes and labels as paternalistic voluntarism
(the charitable rich voluntarily civilizing the indigent poor); democratic localism (decentralized neighborhood schools); corporate voluntarism (e.g., private academies and schools); and the public bureaucracy. From casual observation it is clear that Katz's democratic
localism was the model of schooling linked to neighborhoods and
small towns—something akin to groups of people sharing a common
life. It is also clear which model became dominant in the twentieth
century. Katz (1971, p. 3) summarizes his conclusions:

There are no effective alternatives in American life. . . . There is only one way to
grow up in America if one wants to eat regularly, to be warm, and not to be
harassed by the police. For the vast majority there is only one place to go to
school, and that place is the same nearly everywhere.

Nor is the school unlike its surrounding institutions. As Katz
adds, "There is one city, one mode of production, one road to
power. And there is little freedom" (1971, p. 7).

Regardless of rationales or apologies given by professional educators for the monolithic quality of their contemporary institutions,
most practices of modern schooling make a good deal of sense within
the framework of this kind of radical criticism. For example:

—Mass psychological testing and evaluation procedures are simply analogies to industrial quality control. Humans, like prod-

ucts, are valued for common uniform qualities. Testing is also a quick and efficient way to teach people their "place."

—Requiring teachers to draw up teaching units, lesson plans, or make explicit behavioral objectives are methods for training teachers and students that they are accountable to the larger society in concrete utilitarian terms.

—The stress on learning disabilities and remedial reading for "slow" children are ways of teaching them early that they are defective and can be corrected only by specialized professionals who have a body of esoteric knowledge and special skills.

—The coalition between educational specialists in the universities and commercial publishing companies leads teachers to believe that there are uniform materials and methods to carry out a professional public responsibility. The notion that the unique relationship between a teacher and a child or a teacher and a community has value (other than as a means toward uniform goals) then seems at best trivial, at worst wasteful.

—Educational hierarchies come to mirror corporate hierarchies with managers at the top (in consort with technical or scientific specialists). Teachers are seen as the "workers" who are organized for purposes of efficient production. Team teaching or the "house system" simply creates another layer in the hierarchy.

The radical twist in the above statements describing examples of modern practice or reforms in schooling is not simply a set of barbs aimed at bureaucratic excesses in corporate institutions. The critical attitude toward modern schooling is based on a fundamental disillusionment with the level of planning, control, management, and stratification that seem required to make what we euphemistically call "modern civilization" function. And beyond this is a growing suspicion that modern man, with all his planning and managing and intervening and evaluation and feedbacks, is not on some linear road to progress and perfection, but rather is increasingly anxious and alienated from a variety of circumstances "primitive men" and "peasants" took for granted: unconditional acceptance by small communities of humans who share a common life, a sense of relatedness if not harmony with one's natural surroundings, and a sense that the human career is punctuated by meaningful rituals and celebrations even for the aged and the dead.

The suspicions and skepticisms directed toward the rational planners and managers is based first on the rediscovery by some of us of what is perhaps the most obvious characteristic of the species, one that is constantly emphasized in literature, mythology, and religion: the paradoxical and contradictory qualities in man's nature; the sense of a species suspended and uncompleted. One need only observe, for example:

—Man has an incredible capacity to plan, to organize, to create a social and technical world of his own choosing, yet social relationships and technology seem constantly to flow of their own force in their own direction, mostly out of human control.

—Man has an awareness that he is separate from his social and natural environment—a narcissistic sense of his own separate being. Yet as he moves toward a greater sense of individuality he is haunted by the fear of loneliness and alienation.

—As far as we can tell, individual humans have exhibited differences in talent and temperament, differences in styles of loving and working: some exploitative and aggressive; some passive and receptive; some generous and supportive; some reflective and innovative; some stingy and retentive. Yet we resist in the most agonizing way to accept diversity and variety as "normal." We must search constantly for the perfect specimen as well as for educational techniques for creating it.

—Humans often yearn for freedom, freedom from the bonds of ascribed statuses of occupation, social class, religion, kinship groups, national groups; yet at the same time we yearn for "home"—neighborhood or village, the family, the religion, the tradition that will support and protect us from freedom.

—Man commonly believes that his senses and the rational processes by which sense information is made comprehensible will allow him to fully know the world. Yet he is plagued by an uneasiness that there are forces and realities which can be understood only dimly; and he seeks to build uncertain bridges of faith to cross over into these other realities.

One underlying basis of such human contradiction and paradox is man's multilayered nature. On one level he shares with his mammalian relatives very similar physiological metabolic limits and requirements. He has little control over an autonomic nervous system, which regulates his need for air, water, nutrition, exercise, warmth, and rest. At a second level, he has a set of biosocial characteristics some of which he shares in modified and attenuated ways with other primate relatives, for example, male-female bonding, mother-child bonding, male dominance, the tendency to associate in small bands, the tendency toward social hierarchy. While the environment that allows man to meet his biosocial requirements seems less rigidly defined than conditions for metabolic regulation, there seems little doubt that the needs are real, that conditions required for social caring and trust, for example, are as essential to human life as water or food. The disintegration of a single organism occurs relatively quickly when metabolic requirements are not met; the disintegration of human societies and consequently of individual humans may take several generations when biosocial needs are not adequately met.

On a third level are strata of thought and emotion which are not only *adaptive* in that they allow man to construe and respond to the world in some systematic way; they also establish needs, requirements, and limits in their own right. In a rough way we might identify three such strata: unconscious dreaming or imaging; conscious concrete representation of reality; and finally, hypothetical formal reasoning. On the level of the unconscious, man relates to his needs in the phenomenal world through images and metaphors which are revealed only through inference from myths, totems, pictures, dreams, music, drama, and dance. For example, mother = earth; fire = life or sex; dry wood = tradition and continuity. (We assume that one takes seriously the work of Freud, Jung, and Lévi-Strauss.) At the level of concrete representation, man has the capacity to construe the world with diagrams and language reflecting the simple logic of time, space, and movement. At the hypothetical level, he has the capacity to create science and philosophy; to analyze and describe his environment in very abstract ways, and to analyze and describe the complex logic of such descriptions. The problem for *Homo sapiens* is that elements of a human lifestyle or whole lifestyles themselves which would integrate and nourish the various levels of human personality simultaneously are only weakly connected or patterned by instinct.

Man thus runs the risk of creating lifestyles that may be consistent with one aspect of human nature and yet stifle another, for example, thinking in conceptual, analytic, instrumental terms may enhance his ability to create technology—to cope with the requirements of metabolic comfort and survival; yet the emphasis he places on "scientific thinking," technology, and work may inhibit his ability to maintain, "realize," or express his primitive connectedness with his natural environment, that is, his ability to be "superstitious" and experience the presence of other living and nonliving forms who have shared his environment throughout his evolutionary development.

Our argument in simplest form is that *Homo sapiens* evolved over a period of millions of years, and that within each of us is a complex of social needs and requirements along a continuum from primitive to modern which make demands, often conflicting demands, on individuals and societies alike. We would speculate, for example, that one of the more stable and pressing of these primitive demands for most humans is that they live within "bands" or small communities (see Service 1971). The concomitants of band life are many. For example:

—Commitment to the full range of humans who are born in and live within the band is taken for granted; the aged, the halt, and the lame are cared for. (It is difficult for humans to allow members of their own band with whom they have direct personal contact to starve or otherwise to suffer.)

—It is difficult for centralized elites to control the band, at least from within, since the essential humanity—its weakness and strength—of all is obvious and visible. Powerful elites require social distance to legitimize their demands.

—The various functions that human societies must perform for survival tend to be integrated around a common culture or meaning system. Human attachment and caring, work, celebration, relaxation, decision making, and conflict resolution tend to be woven together with symbol, ritual, and religion.

—The small nuclear family is less significant and less critical as a necessary base from which the quality of all other human relationships must flow. Extended kinship relationships allow for a great range of social affiliations very early in life.

—Although the individual may choose to venture forth and leave the band, there is always the sense that one will be sheltered and accepted somewhere.

—A great variety of human differences must be accepted and used within the culture, or at least tolerated, since it is intolerable to segregate or banish individuals except under the most unusual circumstances.

It is obvious that a large number of these characteristics is negated or reversed for modern man, who spends the majority of his life either in impersonal corporate groups or in the highly charged intimate nuclear family. For example:

—Commitment to other humans outside of the small nuclear family is difficult except on a *quid pro quo* contractual basis. The aged, the lame, and the halt are cared for in corporate institutions under contract with the government or relatives.

—Invisible, often inaccessible elites make the important decisions for the society.

—Pluralities of cultures, religions, and meaning systems are encouraged, since this allows none to be seen as genuinely true or sacred.

—Human differences are generally seen as negative and not accepted; all aspire to have those characteristics perceived to be common to the elite: youthful maturity, physical attractiveness, the capacity to cope competently and aggressively, intellectual brightness, the flexibility to move about socially and geographically.

Our assumption is that this dramatic reversal or negation of man's more primitive lifestyle without any fundamental, biologically based adaptive change in the species is not possible without substantial stress. This stress, described psychologically as alienation and societally by a host of "ills" or problems (e.g., crime, poverty, racism, absenteeism from work, communication gaps, brutalization in custodial institutions), must be meaningful within some ideological framework. The ideology of modern man we could call utilitarian perfectionism—the belief that the purpose for which the planet was created is the comfort, convenience, and perfection of the human species and that man's maximal comfort and convenience can be attained through large, highly differentiated social organizations (e.g., nations, corporations, factories) arranged to fit the requirements of complex technology.

It is our contention that this ideology is inadequate if not dangerous because it underestimates or discounts the more primitive needs of the human species; that continued educational development based on its premises will inevitably exacerbate rather than ameliorate the human condition on the planet; that the first order of business for philosophers, educators, and social scientists is to work toward a more adequate ideology, which better accounts for our current knowledge about the full range of human needs. And the first step in this venture is to understand better how deeply we are embedded in the myth of utilitarian perfectionism by comparing it with a more accurate and beneficial myth—what we shall call "evolutionism" or "communitarianism."

The Ideological Choice

The ideological content of utilitarian perfectionism is succinctly summarized by Stuart Hampshire:

Utilitarianism has always been a comparatively clear moral theory, with a simple core and central notion, easily grasped and easily translated into practical terms. Its essential instruction goes like this: when assessing the value of institutions, habits, conventions, manners, rules, and laws, and also when considering the merits of individual actions or policies, turn your attention to the actual or probable states of mind of the persons who are, or will be affected by them. That is all you need to consider in your assessments. In the final analysis, nothing counts but the states of mind, and perhaps, more narrowly, the states of feeling, of persons; or, more generously, of sentient creatures. . . . From this moral standpoint, the whole machinery of the natural order, other than states of mind, is just machinery, useful or harmful in proportion as it promotes or prevents desired states of feeling.

For a utilitarian, the moral standpoint, which is to govern all actions, places men at the very center of the universe, with their states of feeling as the source of all value in the world. If the species perished, to the last man, or if the last men became impassible and devoid of feelings, things would become cold and indifferent and neutral, from the moral point of view; whether this or that other unfeeling species survived or perished, plants, stars and galaxies, would then be of no consequence. (1973, p. 26)

The utilitarians, having placed the maximization of man's plea-sure and the minimization of his suffering as central considerations about quality of life, are then more or less compelled to posit some-thing qualitatively "special" about man as a species.

. . . even if the transcendental claims of Christianity have been denied, any seri-ous thought about morality must acknowledge the absolute exceptionalness of men, the unique dignity and worth of this species among otherwise speechless, inattentive things, and their uniquely open future. (Hampshire 1973, p. 26)

The second view—call it "evolutionism"* or more narrowly communitarianism—takes off from a very different set of premises. The initial unit of moral consideration is not man set in the Garden with dominion over the plants and animals; it is the universal space and immense time in which energy, matter, and life exist and have existed on this planet. It generally views as moot whether or not any particular direction of evolution is positive, negative, or neutral. It assumes that life evolved from nonlife; man and insects evolved from simpler life forms, but would hold that neither is in any state of near-perfection blessed with a purposeful creator-protector. Over thou-sands and millions of years nonlife forms evolve—mountains, rivers,

---

*Since this term is perhaps used in a novel way here, I would associate the position described generally with the writing of such men as G. Gaylord Simpson and Loren Eiseley. The specific position described is, of course, my own. The position is clearly not to be associated or confused with cultural evolutionists who construe human history as progressive development.

continents, and oceans; likewise, life forms come and change and go. Turtles and cockroaches and moss have been on the planet a long time and are likely to be here a long time; man has been on the planet a relatively short time and is likely to be here but a short time. Although he is clever in adapting through technology to a variety of climatic and ecological conditions, he is genetically unstable and extremely vulnerable to small changes in atmospheric radiation.

So the first major point of difference in viewpoint is in the way utilitarian perfectionists and evolutionists see human life and the relative importance of man's place on earth. Utilitarians place man at the center of things; evolutionists place man within a broad framework of time and space and see him as sharing the planet with or simply "living among" other forms of life and nonlife.

The evolutionist operates from a dual perspective: (1) that of the human species who has a conscious or unconscious bias toward creating the conditions which meet his own particular metabolic, biosocial, and intellectual-emotional requirements; and (2), the "friends of earth" perspective: the point of view which values the historical-geological continuity of living and nonliving forms on the planet. Each perspective has its own particular moral basis, although they are clearly related.

From the bias of *Homo sapiens* the evolutionary moral imperative is that man fulfill as best he can the underlying potential of his nature. This is, in fact, little different from a simple utilitarian position, since human fulfillment presumably leads to maximal pleasure and minimal suffering. Only when utilitarianism embraces a single-minded liberal perspective positing man as a totally flexible and hence perfectable species deserving unique and special moral consideration do we see it as a wrongheaded and dangerous ideology. There is no essential contradiction between an evolutionary and utilitarian position as long as the latter will grant the multileveled and paradoxical characteristics of man which complicate considerably how one construes "pleasure" and "suffering." Only when utilitarianism denies or diminishes in importance man's fundamental biological, biosocial, and unconscious needs and limitations (e.g., his mortality, the fragility and suffering of the physical body, the sense of loneliness and social loss when loved ones depart or die, the agonizing responsibility the strong feel for the infirm) do the two ideologies clash sharply.

The evolutionist assumes, moreover, that it is only when man gives due weight to the limits of his own nature—when he sees his own nature as continuous with and embedded within the evolution of a broader planet and universe—that he will embrace the more universal principle of historical-geological continuity.* That is, if one projects the condition of the planet from past to future, the evolutionist assumes that deliberate human efforts to create radical or massive shifts in the geological or biological continuity of the planet are likely to be harmful. For man lives within such a complex and interdependent web of relationships with living and nonliving forms which have evolved over billions of years that any substantial interference with these relationships is likely to be destructive. One can, of course, argue that man's obsessive development and use of technology and social organization to transform the planet for his purposes is also the product of "natural evolutionary forces." We would have to assert that if one places value on forces which enhance geological or biological continuity, man seems to be an evolutionary mistake. In his exceptional case we would assert that modern man is a threat to the continuity of other living and nonliving forms on the planet, just as a small number of cancer cells are potentially a threat to the living out of a normal existence of the whole organism from which the cancer cells evolved.

The doctrine of evolutionary continuity set forth here suggests that we take a major leap of faith by committing ourselves to a view of human life circumscribed by two conditions: (1) the *pace of time* over which the planet has evolved (four to five billion years), including a deep reverence for the living and nonliving forms which have evolved during that period; and (2) the view of the planet *as an interrelated whole,* including a sense of the complexity among all the forms of matter and energy which exist on and surround the planet. From these premises we would argue, for example, that the extinction of a species because of gradual climatic changes on a continent (e.g., the Pleistocene extinction of the woolly mammoth in North America) is morally neutral, whereas the slaughter of the American bison during the nineteenth century by Europeans was a massive

---

*That some men have the capacity to place the interests of other forms of existence above their own is, of course, another paradox of the human condition.

crime against nature, against the planet, as well as against other people (i.e., the American Indian).

Change and Progress. A second major consideration in comparing the utilitarian-perfectionist and evolutionist orientations toward social amelioration is man's attitude toward change and progress. For the utilitarian, in Hampshire's words:

> both emotional sensitiveness and intelligence in the calculation of consequences can be expected to multiply and increase, as moral enlightenment spreads and as standards of education improve, into an indefinite and open future. In this future there will be less avoidable waste of human happiness, less considered destruction of positive and valued feelings, as the human sciences develop and superstitions become weaker and softer. The story of the past—this is the assumption—is essentially the story of moral waste, of a lack of clear planning and contrivance, of always repeated losses of happiness because no one methodically added the emotional gains and losses with a clear head and undistracted by moral prejudices. The modern utilitarian policy makers will be careful social economists, and their planning mistakes will be progressively corrigible ones; so there is no reason why there should not be a steadily rising balance of positive over negative feelings in all societies that have a rational computational morality. A new era of development is possible, the equivalent in morality of high technology in production. (1973, p. 26)

The evolutionist sees change initially in terms of geological and biological evolution, both of which seem largely out of man's control. The earth's orbit around the sun, the rise of mountains, the separation of continents, the covering of continents by sheets of ice, the creation and extinction of forms of life describe neither progress nor loss; only change. The notion that more complex and highly differentiated forms of life are somehow morally or functionally superior to "lower" forms seems simplistic and naive. They certainly seem less durable. So when the evolutionist arrives on the scene of ongoing human societies, he sees remarkable similarities and commonness in the behavior of humans. He sees the myth of progress in centralized complex societies as seductive and illusory. He sees the most obvious differences across modern and primitive human societies as technological, not as a gradation of underlying qualities of human feeling, motivation, happiness, or moral superiority.

The utilitarian sees progress as civilization; he sees civilization as the development of man's "higher" capacities: literacy; contractual or legal modes of social relating; complex technology based on principles of science; centralized highly organized modes of social work and aesthetic achievement (e.g., symphony orchestras or cinema).

Conversely, the evolutionist who emphasizes the necessity for balance between the "higher" human capacities common to civilization and the more primitive needs of his biosocial and unconscious personality is more alarmed than impressed by the one-sided gains of human social and technological engineering. The evolutionist assumes that the various layers of human personality must be nourished by concrete elements of lifestyle; that when man's life no longer allows him to express or work through his various needs and strivings, he tends to become alienated or disconnected from parts of self. In summary the evolutionist would speculate that civilization runs the constant threat of alienating or separating man (or any species)* from the basic conditions within which he evolved or adapted to cope for his own survival. If one asks, to what is man supposedly "connected," a variety of conditions can be cited:

1. The geological circumstances characteristic of the planet—sun, light, water, soil, wood, seasons, cold, fire, etc.—and man's relatedness to these conditions (the need for water; the use of energy represented by fire) that have borne a direct relationship to his evolution and survival.

2. Flora and fauna on which human life depends and the biological relatedness of man with other forms of life.

3. The process of growth and aging and death for man and for other living organisms.

4. The process of coping for food, water, warmth, shelter, safety; the sense of competency in solving problems of coping.

5. The sociality involved in kinship relationships—family, bands, clans as well as feelings of antipathy toward outsiders and outgroups.

6. The sense of territory—the security that comes with familiarity not only with social group but with geographic surroundings.

7. The sense of history—the security that comes with knowing the past out of which one's own life (and the lives of ancestors) evolved.

---

*Note the behavior of animals in a zoo.

8. Orderliness in social existence, which comes with the sense of shared obligations and responsibility; the relationship between places in the social hierarchy and age, competence, and experience.

9. The sense of fatefulness and unpredictability as it relates to suffering, joy, and the range of human experience.

10. The obvious diversity within the species in age, sex, temperament, competence, physical strength, beauty, etc.

For the evolutionist there is always the precarious balance: man must remain connected to his geological and biological past, yet he has unusual flexibility. He constantly dreams of some trick of training, invention, or insight that will allow him to transcend either his biological or his primitive biosocial heritage. So quality of life for the evolutionist must be construed not simply as preventing alienation, but rather as establishing a tolerable balance between evolutionary connectedness and the sense of hope, freedom, or destiny which characterize his flexibility.

The utilitarian is little prone to ask about the extent to which the human species needs to remain connected with any evolutionary past. Man is thought to be unique among life forms in that he is free to invent his own cultural rules rather than remain enslaved to instinct. His faith in his own *freedom* is seemingly validated by the technology, organizational ability, and political power acquired by groups of men who have come to believe in it. Modern utilitarian man is bound and determined that he can rid himself of his evolutionary limits—that he can place himself in a linear track to progress now and, in the end, attain his own perfection.

Human Institutions. "Primitive," "village," or preindustrial urban societies which have traditionally lived by evolutionist principles have been extinguished or are being rapidly transformed by utilitarian man. Fewer and fewer people are permitted to live in a neighborhood or village culture in *dignity*—even, as Paul Goodman said, to be decently poor. Neighborhood-village life is in a constant state of siege. While industrial-urban-village-agricultural complexes did in fact coexist for substantial periods of time to provide a link with man's social and natural evolutionary past, this no longer seems possible. A new ideological and structural force has emerged which subsumes agricultural life, village-neighborhood life, and the city, transforming all in its own service. The force and form has various names: the industrial state, technopolis, the purposive-rational society. It has a multiplicity of facets: the consolidation of smaller political units into large units called nation-states; massive use of inanimate machines which free man from dependence on human or animal energy; transportation of natural resources across great land masses to meet the needs of the new technology; the broad-scale use of rationally ordered human relationships (bureaucracy) to manage the new technology and the larger political units; the fragmentation of towns and preindustrial cities into specialized functions with utilitarian efficiency the major criterion for the "success" of a function; the fragmentation of human behavior into specialized human roles centered mainly around work in highly specialized settings; family life in small transitory nuclear units, the location and quality of which is determined largely by the nature of one's work; the exploitation of both living and nonliving elements in nature as objects to serve man's pleasure; and finally, the exploitation of man himself to serve the requirements of the corporate and technological structures he himself has created.

The evolutionist views such a transformed world with alarm, predicting that post-industrial societies will decline and decay because they alienate man from primordial social and environmental conditions that are critical to nourish the full range of human personality. He sees the kind of primary group support represented by the extended family, by semipermanent sodalities or work parties, by small community neighborhood or village life, for example, as essential for the emotional well-being of most humans. He sees the integrative basis of social life in the corporate organization—the open contract where the individual freely negotiates conditions of work, love, consumption, recreation, and celebration—as a luxury purchased at the price of personal insecurity and the brutalization of others. A good many humans simply cannot cope or are prevented from coping with such a choice-oriented society: housewives isolated with small children; alcoholics; people living in inner-city ghettos; those institutionalized in rest homes, prisons, schools, and mental hospitals. Moreover, he sees the tension between cosmopolitan culture based on the lifestyle of the open contract and the village culture based on the lifestyle of the traditional neighborhood as a permanent source of conflict for the species (e.g., in medieval Europe or colonial America). In recent history, the dominant cosmopolitan culture has responded to this tension by continuing to destroy neighborhood life, and assuming that "villagers" could be reeducated away from their sense of alienation. Alienation, like any other psychic condition, is presumed by utilitarian man to be amenable to rational human control.

Two Meanings of Human Rationality. The shift that takes place when we move from a village-city complex to a technopolitan society is radical to the core. It universalizes and merges sacred and secular standards of "life success" into a single monolithic goal: useful economic activity. As Gouldner points out, historically the economic utilitarian standard of "human worth" as a legitimizing criterion for station and privilege is associated with the rise of the so-called middle class and the decline of aristocratic-feudal arrangements (at least in the West). Utilitarianism as a quasi-religious belief systems carries with it a great deal of complex baggage we are only now coming to understand. The most radical shift is the way we see man himself.

In large reaches of our society and particularly in the industrial sector, it is not man that is wanted. It is, rather, the function he can perform and the skill with which he can perform it for which he is paid. If a man's skill is not needed, the man is not needed. If a man's function can be performed more economically by a machine, the man is replaced. . . . The useless qualities of persons are either unrewarded or actively punished should they intrude upon the employment of a useful skill . . . just as there is the unemployed man, there is also the unemployed *self.* Because of the exclusions and devaluations of self fostered by an industrial system oriented toward utility, many men develop a dim sense of loss, for the excluded self, although muffled, is not voiceless and makes its protest heard. They feel an intimation that something is being wasted, and this something may be nothing less than their lives. (Gouldner 1970, pp. 73-74)

The *utilitarian-perfectionist view of man* along with its faith in the value and *necessity of rapid technological growth* have now merged into a single world view. Instead of beginning with man and his needs, we begin with the requirements of a self-generating technology and corporate-organizational form, and then seek to shape man to fit that environment. *Rational control of the means for doing* becomes the end itself.

In Habermas's terms:

The institutionalized growth of the forces of production following from scientific and technical progress surpasses all historical proportions. From it the institutional framework draws its opportunity for legitimation. The thought that relations of production can be measured against the potential of developed productive forces is prevented because the existing relations or production present themselves as the technically necessary organizational form of a rationalized society.

Here "rationality," in Weber's sense, shows its Janus face. It is no longer only a critical standard for the developmental level of the forces of production in relation to which the objectively superfluous, repressive character of historically obsolete relations of production can be exposed. It is also an apologetic standard through which these same relations of production can be justified as a functional institutional framework. Indeed, in relation to its apologetic serviceability, "rationality" is weakened as a critical standard and degraded to a corrective within the system: what can still be said is at best that society is "poorly programmed." At the stage of their scientific-technical development, then, the forces of production appear to enter a new constellation with the relations of production. Now they no longer function as the basis of a critique of prevailing legitimations in the interest of political enlightenment, but become instead the basis of legitimation. *This* is what Marcuse conceives of as world-historically new. (1970, pp. 83-84)

Habermas then quotes Marcuse:

In this universe, technology also provides the great rationalization of the unfreedom of man and demonstrates the "technical" impossibility of being autonomous, of determining one's own life. For this unfreedom appears neither as irrational nor as political, but rather as submission to the technical apparatus which enlarges the comforts of life and increases the productivity of labor. Technological rationality thus protects rather than conceals the legitimacy of domination and the instrumentalist horizon of reason opens on a rationally totalitarian society. (1970, p. 84)

Understanding the role of technology in modern society requires clarification of various ambiguities in the term "rational." In the Weberian sense, rationalism fuses three concepts: (1) instrumental-purposive work-oriented man, (2) the universal scientific characteristics of technology, and (3) organized social labor directed toward the use of technology. When man is behaving in a purposeful way, channeling his energy toward visible or publicly describable goals, he is rational. When he creates or invents tools to facilitate the attainment of visible public goals, he is rational. When he organizes and manages other men in instrumentally efficient ways, he is rational. Only when these senses of rationality are fused into a world view and become the primary purpose and exclusive meaning of rational behavior do we have what Marcuse calls a "totalitarian society." Modern man is so committed to the view that rational men must live in a highly structured society organized around and consuming in socially productive corporate organizations set up to operate efficient technical apparatus that alternative world views seem as unrealistic or romantic utopias.

As Habermas suggests, the critical deficiency in this view of rationality is that it excludes a complex set of elements that we believe are fundamental to any healthy or decent human society. Those elements we have associated with alienation and connectedness. They have to do with functions such as spontaneous human bonding (love, friendship, caring) as well as the creation of informal consensual norms within group life, norms or standards which evolve out of the basic fact of sharing a common life. In short, the function of man most susceptible to the more limited sense of "rational" implied in rational-purposive behavior is work; other functions such as various kinds of bonding, play, human ritual and celebration require a broader meaning of the term or much of what humans find meaningful comes to be construed as irrational, nonrational, or even irrelevant.

The Helping Professional. The evolutionist sees the stresses in the lifestyle of utilitarian man as caused by alienation from the more primitive elements in the human community and personality. Man becomes alienated from *meaningful work,* for example, when its connection with communal needs or visible survival press is obscured by technology, specialization, and excessive leisure. Man becomes alienated from his normal *social impulses* when "purposeless" or nonwork activities such as play, gossip, ritual, and active celebration are discouraged because they conflict with the efficiency and structure of organized work. Man becomes alienated from his normal tendencies toward *cooperation and generosity* when the dependent and less competent among him are segregated and isolated so that he may not expend economically useful energy becoming emotionally or personally involved with them.

The utilitarian assumes that these various social stresses can be resolved by the same approach that caused them: the application of systematic rational thought to social action, that is, by the further use of science and technology—practical intelligence. Alienation from meaningful work may be cured, for example, by requiring very little

human work—work is automated. "Nonwork" can take the form of
formal recreation, sensitivity classes, etc., and becomes "work" for
those who direct and manage such activities. The generous human
impulse is institutionalized in the form of "helping professions." Specialized professionals (doctors, psychologists, group leaders, pastoral
counselors, teachers, social workers, lawyers, nurses, etc.) are trained
to care for and hopefully "cure" or ameliorate the suffering of the
exceptional people, in other words, those who cannot cope with
alienation from meaningful work, reduced support from primary
communal groups, or the guilt caused by an overly exploitative and
affluent lifestyle. Quite logically, the utilitarian criterion by which
the helping professional is judged is not the quality of his concern or
compassion or generosity. It is the same as for any specialized professional: the extent to which he can make the noncoper—his clients,
students, or patients—effective, useful functionaries as either producers or consumers.

To attain legitimacy, the helping professional has developed
elaborate theories and research methodologies to give the appearance
of participating in the same scientific enterprise that characterizes
other sectors in the economy. Medicine is the prototype. It has a
sophisticated division of labor: chemicals and professional techniques
are developed in research laboratories; medicines and hardware developed in the laboratory are then manufactured in factories, sold by
salesmen, prescribed and administered by physicians, and sold in
commercial drug and supply stores. Other helping professionals seek
to legitimize their work in similar ways. Psychiatrists administer therapy created and tested in research settings in universities and mental
hospitals. Educational research and development centers develop,
test, and prescribe school organizational plans (open classrooms,
team teaching), personnel training procedures, and curricula. This research and development is often based on elaborate theories which
suggest how individuals and organizations can be made to function
more efficiently.

In the past twenty years, for example, education has stumbled
through one utilitarian-perfectionist school of thought after another:
Skinnerian behaviorism; Bruner and the teaching of the disciplines;
Rogers, Maslow, and the so-called third force of psychology; and
more recently the developmental psychologists inspired by Piaget
and Kohlberg. Each grasps one element of human potential and ex-
plodes it into a comprehensive theory of schooling.

How does the helping professional who sensitively attends to an inner calling toward social amelioration, who feels some special responsibility to help others, deal with the utilitarian trap within which he now finds himself? We would argue that one can come to terms with the futility and destructiveness of the helping professions as they are now commonly practiced only by a basic reassessment of the utilitarian-perfectionist doctrine, a doctrine which now looks at only *one part of the human condition:* man's capacity to conceptualize purposefully and manipulate his social and physical environment to satisfy his short-run appetites. This reassessment, we would argue, should move us in the direction of an evolutionary viewpoint which stresses (1) the limits placed on man by his need to remain connected to those primordial conditions within which a substantial part of his moral, intellectual, and physical nature evolved; and (2) the often paradoxical or contradictory relationship between man's more "primitive" self and his self-conscious, reflective, directed self. The paradox can only be taken seriously, moreover, when we recognize that his primitive needs are not to be stigmatized as "lower" or morally inferior. The need of most humans, for example, for social attachments to quasi-permanent primary community life must not be seen as the negative end of ideologically loaded dimensions such as tradition-freedom, rigidity-flexibility. Man can no more tolerate extreme freedom than suffocating tradition.

Utilitarianism, Community, and School Reform

We see models and justifications of various proposals for school reform as inextricably linked to which of the two visions of society one carries in one's head, or, for those who apprehend both models, the relative weight given the two visions. For the devout utilitarian the road to progress is straightforward and consists of making schooling more efficient and effective. For example:

1. Pushing teachers toward the use of explicitly stated behavioral objectives.
2. Development of formulas to justify relative cost benefits for various school programs.
3. Development of curriculum models along with teacher training experts (or consultants) who will install such models whenever and wherever wanted.

4. Vocational education reform construed as training and channeling students with various talents into the most appropriate job
slots in the economy.

5. Ever-increasing specialization of job functions: creating new
curriculum departments for effective education or value clarification;
creating new coordinators to integrate increasing numbers of specialists.

6. Devotion to highly specialized educational research which
will answer critical questions relating to efficient instruction and administration (e.g., group size, methods of presenting material, various
systems for teaching reading or math).

7. Development of complex systems models to describe the educational process, usually involving complex loops, feedbacks, evaluation procedures, etc.

For the utilitarian with humanist tendencies educational reform
is more complicated. Like the straight utilitarian, he sees the process
of modern schooling as essentially necessary and correct. But he has a
vague and uneasy sense that things aren't quite what they should be.
He reads such dissenting "anarchist" literature as Paul Goodman or
Michael Katz and catches a glimpse of alternative visions. He comes
to see the corporate school as too specialized, too formal or impersonal, too large, too regimented, too task-oriented, too meritocratic,
too bureaucratic, too separated from the "community," and searches
for palliatives for each of these shortcomings. For example:

—If schools are too specialized, teams of specialists can work
together. Subject-matter specialists can create core curriculum,
student services personnel (psychologists, guidance counselors,
teachers, administrators) can work as teams to deal with troubled children and adolescents. Walls between the specialties can
be lowered as long as one doesn't give up one's sense of being a
specialist.

—If schools are too formal and impersonal, they can be made
informal and more impersonal. Call teachers by their first
names. Give students flexible assignments and have them discuss
work options with the teacher. Have subject matter teachers
play softball with the students at the lunch break. Go on weekend retreats and sit around campfires rapping together.

—If schools are too large, break them into smaller units: institute the house system, increase the importance of homerooms and call them "family groups." Have teams of four or five teachers work with a hundred students and really get to know them.

—If schools are too regimented, eliminate the bells (or substitute chimes for bells), institute flexible scheduling or "arena scheduling" (where students get the chance to choose the time of day or the teacher who will administer Algebra I).

—If schools are too merit-conscious, substitute written evaluations for letter grades; or institute special curricula for the mediocre losers so they feel that they are being given special attention to remedy their lack of intellectual brightness.

—If schools are too task-oriented, institute the open campus so kids can wander about casually during "study periods," or play cards, or simply sit around and talk.

—If schools are too bureaucratic, give greater support to the student council or create special teacher task forces so everyone can have some say in running the school.

—If schools are too separated from the "community," or from the parents, institute a voluntary teacher-aid plan, put parent monitors on the school buses, have more PTA meetings; or send students into the community to participate in work-study programs.

Public school systems as well as private schools have implemented various comprehensive versions of these reforms, commonly called "alternative schools." It is our experience that more radical alternative schools, those which have begun with the premise that an "evolutionist" or communitarian culture will *evolve* from the needs and requirements of individuals sharing a common environment, common work, and common problems, have had very rough going. The following scenario is not unusual. One of the first "crises" in such schools is the dual problem of class attendance on the one hand and groups of kids hanging around doing nothing on the other. If one observes carefully the "hanging around" phenomenon, it tends to become increasingly regularized: friendship groups are formed; a limited set of activities come to characterize the different groups (e.g., playing cards, gossiping, eating, horseplay, record playing); territories are selected by different groups for different activities (corridors, empty work space, toilets). As this happens the class attendance or "cutting" problem becomes more serious. There is, then, a direct confrontation between the new and somewhat unstable beginnings of a communitarian culture (one might characterize it as a street culture) and the managed classroom culture. Teachers, administrators, and the more task-oriented responsible students tend to see the nascent street culture as "wasting time," at best; and as adolescents on the brink of orgiastic sex and violence, at worst. The crisis is resolved in a variety of ways, but the common result is to abolish the free time or unused space which supports the newly developing "street life," or, more accurately, "corridor life."

The high mortality rate of communitarian alternative schools is perhaps superficially caused by ambivalent adults (parents and teachers) and youngsters who are initially committed to the freedom of each to choose his own education, or to the pluralistic goal of allowing a variety of subcultures to emerge which suit the needs and temperaments and talents of different kinds of students. These hopes and visions, however, are soon challenged either by students' and parents' realistic fear of failure, or by outside pressures to meet standardized goals of conventional utilitarian institutions. The school is pressed to show that students are reading at grade level, that students can get into good colleges, or that the school will not become immersed in legal troubles because it harbors truants, drug users, or allows smoking on school grounds. These pressures are commonly handled by inefficient group-decision-making processes, which outstrip the ability of the school to cope, until finally everyone gives in to a more managed system in the hope of getting back to work. So ends an agonizing drama.

From our perspective, the most serious problem for communitarian alternative schools, however, is *not* the pressure to be accountable according to utilitarian standards, for example, reading scores, college admissions, truancy. (Obviously, a great many conventional schools are failing miserably by these standards, but they persist.) The most serious problem is that settings that characterize communitarian cultures or institutions require conditions that are *generally unavailable for any kind of modern schooling,* for example, the sharing of honest work, a broad mix of people of all ages and temperaments, or the sharing of a common religion or cultural tradition. The following illustrations should amplify and clarify this point.

Age and Sex Diversity. Natural communities normally contain the full range of ages and both sexes. Out of this diversity commonly evolves various coalitions; for example, women of childbearing age, girls, and babies; young adolescent boys; older adolescent boys and mature men; old people and young children. We would speculate that these coalitions might be considered "natural" in the sense that they are self-selected and produce consensual (noncoerced or explicitly managed) order as a basis for work, recreation, celebration, and shared experience. Such coalitions evolve, presumably, out of mutual benefits for individuals, members of groups, and the community as a whole. Girls gain status and a sense of adulthood by caring for young children, which frees adult women to talk or work nearby. The high activity and risk-taking physical acting-out of younger adolescent boys is drained away safely by their self-segregation. (Women, younger children, and old people are protected from the latent sadism of the boys by the older adolescents who have settled into more symbolic and less overt demonstrations of sex and aggression.)

Old people have a number of unique resources. Their presence tends to enhance peace and order, both because of their slow pace and because they are the focus of a large number of kinship bonds which can demand a good deal of paternal or maternal respect. Because of their long memories, they are the repository of the history of the group and have the leisure to care for, tell stories to, and indulge young children. Such coalitions tend to produce substantial order as well as a set of productive human relationships without a great deal of hassle over the need for formal rules or explicit sanctions for their enforcement. Modern schools consisting largely of children *or* adolescents and young or middle-aged adults provide little basis for such coalitions.

Temperamental Diversity, Cooperative Activity, and Division of Labor. Human communities carry on a variety of social functions which normally demand a diversity and range of talent and leadership. The great majority of activity requires a combination and integration of planning and symbolic manipulation as well as physical activity and routine (e.g., carpentry, cooking, farming, sports, dance). Human activity tends to be cooperative and division of labor tends to evolve on the basis of natural diversity in temperament and talent.

But most modern schooling, especially for older children and young adults, has neither the time, the imagination, nor the flexibility to have work parties engage in meaningful activities which combine symbolic planning, trial-and-error experimentation, physical effort, and routine, and which can draw upon diverse temperamental potential of a variety of humans. Schooling is largely sedentary manipulation of symbols (with activity breaks), in which human diversity in talent and motivation is looked upon as a problem—for all students are pursuing uniform goals. Those who can do the assigned tasks well are rewarded; those who do them poorly are encouraged to emulate those who do them well. Those who find the tasks too complex, meaningless, or repetitive are given remedial training.

Building a Common Culture To Describe a Common Life. Culture is a set of beliefs, rules, and images at least partly shared by groups of humans who also share a common life. The beliefs, rules, and images must be meaningfully interpreted at various levels of abstraction. In a highly segregated and fragmented society, where much of the work is invisible or infrequently seen or experienced by those who do not actually do it, there is, in fact, little common life; there can therefore be little common positive culture. (There are a number of shared prohibitions and sanctions, made highly visible by mass media, e.g., crime, police, detectives, and lawyers disseminated by novels, movies, comic books.)

Since there is little common shared life, the only culture modern man can construct must be highly complex and abstract. One can describe society in such abstract terms as industrial production, assembly line, advertising, marketing, distribution, consuming, recreation, housing, marriage, family, and the like; but the categories mean very different things for the gas station attendant, the corporation lawyer, or the welfare mother. Schooling exists, presumably, to transmit (or to operate within the framework of) a common culture. But if that culture, in order to be "common," must be stated in highly abstract and complex terms, it is available only to those who can think in complex and abstract ways. For other kinds of humans who tend to "think" visually, kinesthetically, or who are just plain simple and more concrete, there can be no common culture except as a set of transitory fragments (TV ads, popular songs, images of political leaders, etc.). And education without a sense of a common life and a common culture to reflect that life and give it meaning is either motivated out of instrumental self-interest or obedience to authority. A voluntary noncoerced community requires that there be meaningful senses of work, celebration, decision making, suffering, and the like which can be shared by all. In a society in which many of these relationships are either invisible or trivial, meaningful culture and hence meaningful schooling cannot exist without coercion or extrinsic rewards.

We see alternative schools failing for two reasons. First, their inventors are ambivalent and draw back when the risks of downward social and educational mobility become apparent from the unsettling anarchy that erupts as the constraints of a managed system are removed. But more importantly, alternative schools are unable to meet the complex conditions of community (e.g., availability of natural coalitions, visible division of labor, the sharing of a common life along with a set of religious myths to give that common life meaning) from which a new basis for order might evolve. The schools are still locked into a level of specialization (i.e., education is seen as a function to be segregated from the rest of the society) that makes a sense of the common life impossible.

The point is that one does not create "community" with superficial or transitory devices such as confrontation groups or weekend camping trips. One does not create community by calling one another by their first names or giving students and parents more control over curriculum or the selection of teachers. One simply tinkers with the structure of a managed system.

The Viability of "Community" as an Approach to Educational Reform

The most radical approach to communitarian educational reform is the creation of intentional communities. Such communities have a somewhat dreary record. Those with a strong and demanding religious base (e.g., the Amish, the Hutterites, or the Bruderhof) have the best record of longevity. Those based only on humanistic communitarian concerns seem to fall quickly by the wayside (e.g., Brook Farm of the last century and the countless communes of the last ten years).*

The more communitarian private schools (e.g., Summerhill and its followers) have very limited applicability as models for at least two reasons: they are not economically viable and depend wholly on the good graces of the well-to-do whom they usually serve; and more importantly, they eject those who do not get along—a fundamental violation of one premise of community.

What might be called "educational service communities" which relate to ongoing neighborhoods, towns, or cities would seem to be more hopeful examples of radical communitarian reform.

A good example of this approach is Myles Horton's Highlander Folk School, which has served for the past forty years as an adult residential center in Appalachia for the development of community leaders among school, church, civic, labor, and farm groups, as well as for liberal education. Horton's initial conception of the school is described as follows:

If I understood our purpose correctly, we will all be working at the same job but will be using different approaches. Our task is to make class-conscious workers who envision their roles in society, and to furnish motivation as well as technicians for the achievement of this goal.

In other words, we must try to give the students an understanding of the world in which we live (a class-divided society) and an idea of the kind of world we would like to have. We have found that a very effective way to help students to understand the present social order is to throw them into conflict situations where the real nature of our society is projected in all its ugliness. To be effective, such exposure must be preceded, accompanied by, and followed by efforts to help the observer appreciate and digest what he has seen. This keeps education from getting unrealistic. While this process is going on, students need to be given an inkling of the new society. Perhaps this can be done best by having a type of life that approaches as nearly as possible the desired state. This is where our communal living at the school comes into the picture as an important educational factor. The tie-in with the conflict situations and participation in community life keeps our school from being a detached colony or utopian venture. But our efforts to live out our ideals makes possible the development of a bit of proletarian culture as an essential part of our program of workers' education. (Adams 1972, pp. 516-17)

_____

*The special historical and geographical conditions that have made the kibbutzim endure for two generations are probably not applicable to this country.

Frank Adams summarized Highlander as follows:

Through Highlander's programs, many people have been encouraged to find beauty and pride in their own ways to speak their own language without humiliation, and to learn of their own power to accomplish self-defined goals through social movements built from the bottom up.

People learn of unity by acting in unity. They learn of democracy by acting democratically. And each time they do these things as a result of experiences at Highlander they both renew their capacity to act in these ways again and demonstrate the process of education in action. Talk about this distorts, and is one step removed from the essential element—the people themselves doing. Writing words about the process is two steps removed. Education at Highlander is a synthesis of person, group, time, place, purpose, and problem. (1972, pp. 519-20)

A second example of an educational service community is Synanon (see Yablonsky 1967) and its related offspring (e.g., Daytop in New York; Marathon House in New England). In its early years Synanon was a residential drug rehabilitation community with a strong cultural press toward interpersonal openness and honesty coupled with a complementary press for shared social support and mutual help. Honesty and openness were encouraged if not "forced" on people by the Synanon Game, a variation of the confrontation group. Support and mutual help were given by a close-knit residential lifestyle. Synanon communities are now open to both addicts (for rehabilitation) and nonaddicts who simply want the honesty encouraged by the Synanon Game as well as the support brought about by residential living.

Both Highlander and Synanon have a dual goal: to relate to the outer society in some obvious and constructive way as well as to maintain a sense of integrity within an inner community. The services one might render to a larger society fraught with a host of social diseases take no great imagination. Identifying minimal conditions required to build integrity for the inner community is a more difficult task. As a beginning we would list the following as necessary characteristics for communitarian reform institutions:

1. There must be a *common life*. This means they probably must be residential or quasi-residential and share some of the basic tasks of daily coping (preparing food, eating, housekeeping, etc.) commonly carried out in the nuclear family. The sharp separation

between "home" and "work," between "family group" and "work group" must be reduced.

2. They must include a broad range of *human diversity* along such dimensions as age, sex, temperament, and talent to allow for the natural evolution of interdependent coalitions as well as leadership. The presence of diversity implies that the distinction between professional (or certified) elites and the common people must be minimized. Natural leadership within community must come from both sources.

3. There must be a substantial *reconnection or dealienation of the community with the basics of survival and human sociality* and a move away from living "in one's head." Activities such as gardening, carpentry, and mechanics have to be elevated to the same plane as the high arts or social science. Increased (and legitimate) satisfaction must come from simple and various human activities, such as gossip, storytelling, sports, singing, playing games. The present recreational habits of members of professional elites would have to go (e.g., ski weekends, jet trips) because they are too expensive and too exclusive.

4. Such communities would have to effect a fundamental shift in the modern attitude toward *religious and spiritual commitment.*

The problem of identifying minimum conditions for building community in a utilitarian society is actually *twofold*. One must ask, first, what conditions are necessary to provide the initial social cement to build sustained commitment; and second, what conditions are required to alter personality toward feeling comfortable with communitarian values and life styles. Fromm and Maccoby deal with the latter question in their study of an orphan community in Cuernavaca, Moreles, Mexico. They are interested in the conditions under which boys and girls coming from peasant villages might change their attitudes in essential areas, especially those of cooperation vs. selfishness and suspiciousness. They state:

Following are the most important principles which seem to us to be responsible for making this change possible:

1. *The principle of unconditional acceptance.* No child once accepted in the community is ever expelled, for whatever reason. . . . This situation expresses the principle of motherly love which is unconditional, and which never excludes a child, regardless of what he may have done. . . .

2. This motherly principle of unconditional acceptance is balanced by the paternal principle of demanding from the child *respect* for the rights of others and fulfillment of his obligations to the community in accordance with his age. . . .

3. Another principle which seems to us of great importance is that of the extensive participation of the children, especially the adolescents, in the *management of their own affairs*. Every two weeks a "house director" is appointed in the unit of boys who attend secondary school. . . .

The children cultivate their own vegetable garden and take care of the animals (chickens, cows, ducks, pigs). Aside from cooking, they also bake their own bread.

4. In relation to this, another factor must be mentioned which is crucially important. In spite of the fact that this is a rather large institution, it is conducted in a *nonbureaucratic spirit*. The children are not treated as "objects" to be managed by a bureaucracy, but are loved and cared for as individuals by Father Wasson and his assistants. . . .

5. Another factor of considerable importance is the *degree of stimulation* which the children receive. There is folkloric dance group, a mariachi band (string instruments and trumpets), and children play individual instruments too. . . . The children also learned to make their own costumes. . . . There is a carpentry shop, and there are classes in painting, sculpture, and ceramics. There are good soccer and baseball teams; a library of books and records is being developed. (1970, pp. 214-16)

It should be noted that the orphanage fulfills a number of the conditions we have already cited above: It is residential; it has a broad range of diversity (with the exception that it is all-male); there are a range of dealienating conditions in the environment (e.g., cooking, gardening, carpentry, etc.); there is a rich religious and spiritual life.

Conclusion

The immediate question for individual educators who would take seriously the evolutionist-communitarian position is how to alter a life that is currently overspent coping with the utilitarian pressures of conventional schools. There are a variety of perspectives from which to view one's work in schooling. The utilitarian administrator uses a standard factory model. The school (the plant) produces or refines goods (students) for the community (consumers) using personnel (teachers) and tools (curriculum). Teachers who buy this model then focus on their own ability to administer standard curricula. More circumspect teachers who stand back and view the total institution as a human processing plant are prone to lunge forward and push toward the reform of the institution as a whole.

In this chapter, we are suggesting that redoubling one's efforts to change the basic quality of life within schools as a whole is unlikely to achieve any substantial result. This is not to suggest that one should not try to correct the more obvious indecencies (e.g., requiring passes to go to the toilet). It simply means that schools, as other corporate institutions in the society, have a strong gravitational pull toward being highly managed directed settings. Schools no more have the potential for fulfilling man's basic communitarian needs than businesses or factories.

It is our guess that the most productive role for the teacher is in teaching an evolutionist or communitarian ideology as a basis for an alternate vision of society as well as creating opportunities for students to have positive experiences which would reinforce and be consistent with this vision. These experiences might include, for example, organizing or working in food cooperatives, helping in a parent-run day-care center, working in programs to integrate emotionally disturbed or mentally retarded children into settings with normal children.

Such a vision might be "fitted in" to the curriculum within a great number of standard courses. We might begin by teaching history as the history of the planet, rather than as the history of "civilized" or literate man. We might teach biology with as much awe and respect for the adaptive capacities of the honeybee as we have for man. Or in American history, we might stop glorifying the success of the Constitutional Convention and begin a sober reassessment of what the United States might have been had it remained a continent of small nations. In anthropology, we might stop talking in terms of cultural progress from primitive to modern man and begin to explore positive elements in quality of life for primitive people, peasants, and the people who inhabited pre-industrial cities. In sociology we might begin a serious assessment of the field commonly called "community." And perhaps most of all we should begin to face squarely, as teachers and in what we teach, the implicit and persistent distinction built into most societies between elites and common folk and ask: How can the two groups live among one another in a nonexploitative way, share a common life, and feel a mutual responsibility for a common welfare?

But this is clearly only a first step: to teach young people a different view of the planet, of man in a different kind of society, through words and drama and fragmentary experiences in more communitarian settings. The next step is the creation of fundamentally altered settings where humans can live at least part of their lives as neighbors. It is here that the Highlander Folk School or Synanon may be instructive.

What is presented here is an overall strategy for how a teacher who embraces an evolutionist or communitarian vision of society might spend his or her life. The essence of that strategy is that educators not be seduced into attempting to change the overall tone or structure of the school as an institution (although this is usually the most direct road to "success" and mobility); that they spend their energy in three ways:

1. Revising curricular content so as to stop glorifying the utilitarian perfectionist view of nature, man, and society; and creating a new view of how man might inhabit this planet.

2. Searching for significant, albeit fragmentary, experiences for oneself and for students which would be consistent with the evolutionist-communitarian ideology.

3. And finally, participating in building "neighborhoods" or neighborly places quite apart from the school.

While the creation of these "neighborly" institutions may seem increasingly unfeasible, even far-fetched, one should remember that large, centralized, highly managed, complex societies of the past did not last. They eventually experienced the fatal pains of alienation similar to our own. There is little reason, for example, to think that we shall escape the destiny of an Egypt or a Greece or a Rome. Nor is there any reason to think that there is not some broad historical dialectic in which man plays out the tower of Babel drama. His intelligence and arrogance lead him to the brink of a highly controlled managed society, a society in which the spontaneous roots of small, decentralized tribal cultures are all but snuffed out. And then it all comes crashing down.* The question is not whether we are on some

---

*The dialectical vs. progressive linear themes as interpretations of history have a long and distinguished history. For more recent works supporting the nonlinear, nonprogressive view, the reader is referred to Nisbet 1969 and Muggeridge 1973.

linear track to cultural progress and perfection or whether we are caught up in a dialectical historical process. The evidence is substantially on the side of the latter conclusion. The basic question is how accurately we can identify the locus of historical transition; and whether or not enough of us have the intelligence, the courage, and the spiritual resources to prepare for that point in history.

References

Adams, Frank. "Highlander Folk School: Getting Information, Going Back and Teaching It." *Harvard Educational Review* 42, no. 4 (November 1972): 497-520.

Callahan, Raymond. *Education and the Cult of Efficiency.* Chicago: University of Chicago Press, 1962.

Fromm, Erich, and Maccoby, Michael. *Social Character in a Mexican Village.* Englewood Cliffs, N.J.: Prentice-Hall, 1970.

Gouldner, Alvin. *The Coming Crisis of Western Sociology.* New York: Basic Books, 1970.

Habermas, Jurgen. *Toward a Rational Society: Student Protest, Science, and Politics.* Trans. Jeremy Shapiro. Boston: Beacon Press, 1970.

Hampshire, Stuart. "Morality and Pessimism." *New York Review of Books* (January 25, 1973): 26.

Katz, Michael. *Class, Bureaucracy, and Schools.* New York: Praeger, 1971.

Muggeridge, Malcolm. *Chronicles of Wasted Time.* New York: William Morrow, 1973.

Nisbet, Robert A. *Social Change and History.* Oxford: Oxford University Press, 1969.

Service, Elman. *Primitive Social Organization.* New York: Random House, 1971.

Yablonsky, Lewis. *Synanon: The Tunnel Back.* New York: Penguin, 1967.

3

Quality of Life and Some Further Ideological Distinctions

It is our contention that there exists a crisis in teaching (as well as in the helping professions generally), not because of the apparent inefficiency or ineffectiveness of the schools, but rather because teachers are losing faith in highly managed environments as places where the young are to be educated or "humanized." This is a subset of the more general problem, which is the paradoxical, inconsistent, or incomplete integration of more primitive aspects of the species with the more modern aspects. We suspect that humans can tolerate only limited doses of managed settings along with the heavy doses of conceptual training that go with these settings without serious pathology. It is our contention that as teachers we can respond to this pathology in at least two ways. We can attempt to make people aware of another way of viewing man (loosely called consciousness raising); and we can attempt to build settings wherein the more primitive requirements of human existence can be expressed and related to our modern world. That is, we can create communities where humans spend part of their time sharing a common life, making decisions consensually rather than bureaucratically, building particularistic religious meaning rather than univeralistic scientific meaning, celebrating and participating in games and rituals rather than viewing them as spectators, and learning and doing work that is transparently related to requirements of human survival. In either case, one must face the ethical challenge of the conventional teacher (or citizen) who asks us to justify our grounds for dissent. Why a new consciousness? Why new settings for a common life?

Our response to this challenge depends partly on the ground from which the challenger asks the question. In this respect it is important to distinguish among three very different ethical postures:

1. The genuine cultural relativist who asserts that there is no universal criteria by which one can make quality-of-life judgments—each society is "good" for those who have been conditioned to function within it.

2. The modernist who is willing to make quality-of-life judgments, but largely along a primitive-modern dimension. "Primitive" is associated, for example, with superstition, magical religions, lack of sophisticated technology, highly structured traditional roles, and commitment to a local parochial world view. "Modern" is associated with a universalistic scientific meaning system, a highly technical, specialized, and efficient economy, and maximum opportunity for all to pursue private interests and develop the individual to the fullest level of maturity.

3. The evolutionist who assumes that cultures which are more consistent with underlying tendencies of the species are more likely to be positive; those which are inconsistent with these tendencies are likely to be negative; and when there are conflicting tendencies (e.g., between magical or superstitious thinking and "scientific" thinking) positive culture is that which balances the conflicting tendencies, rather than celebrating the one and attempting to extinguish the other.

The underlying distinction between the evolutionist and the modernist rests mainly on the way each treats conflicts between the primal and modern characteristics of man. The modernist assumes that primal tendencies can either be integrated into the lifestyle or mode of thinking of modern man, or simply sloughed off as obsolete. (For example, superstitious or magical aspects of religion can be reinterpreted as meaningful "symbols" rather than literal truth, or simply rejected as untrue.) The evolutionist assumes that many primitive characteristics of man are, in fact, difficult if not impossible to integrate or reject. He assumes that man is, in a sense, caught or suspended between often conflicting tendencies, for example, he wants stable kinship and communal relationships (a primal need for security) and he wants an atomistic and highly individuated life with maximum freedom and choice. Both the evolutionist and the modernist do, however, believe in better and worse societies. The modernist sees highly developed societies as "progressive"; the evolutionist sees them as deficient in that they suppress basic primal needs and tendencies. Both reject the relativist position, however, in assuming that a viable society is necessarily a "good" society. Both reject the notion that man is totally plastic and can adjust to any environmental or cultural condition, so long as he can survive and procreate. Both assume that there are positive and negative cultures.

We believe there is increasing evidence that one of man's more salient characteristics may be his capacity to survive in misery rather than his ability to slough off negative cultural elements and create positive sociocultural arrangements, that is, arrangements that express an adequate range of his talents and diversity and soften the effects of his weaknesses and contradictions. This is not to deny the unusual degree of human plasticity when compared with other animals on the planet. We would argue, however, that it is far more limited than many social scientists commonly recognize. It is simplistic to assert that man is mainly a culture-building animal while his nonhuman relatives are instinct-driven animals. It is rather that man has available a broader range of behavioral resolutions to meet the press of his primary biological and social instincts. Man's social needs are not unlike those of his primate relatives. But man has secondarily an element of freedom. Not only are there a variety of behavioral modes by which he can successfully fulfill his instinctual needs; he can build destructive or alienating cultures. That is, he can build cultures which meet poorly some needs and which compensate (always inadequately) for deficiencies in some instinctual areas by activity in others. He can compensate for insecure social attachments, for example, by compulsive work. The "trick" that nature has played on man is that since he generally lives in only one culture at a time, his mode of adaptation always seems normal and natural. The suffering caused by destructive elements in a particular sociocultural system seems to him inevitable. When he faces societies different from his own, he concludes that each society must have a culture or a social structure that is "natural" for that society.

But what if we stop confusing societal survival with positive culture? The question then is not whether man can survive under a broad range of conditions—he can live in submarines under the north pole or in igloos on top of the pole. The question is whether it is reasonable to make judgments about the relative quality of various cultural solutions in the variety of societies that man has created, and what is the basis for such judgments. From our point of view it is reasonable to make such judgments on the basis of the evolutionary character of the species itself. Man may well have flexibility to create a range of societies, but some sociocultural elements are more obviously within positive limits set by man's species characteristics, while other elements cause stress or pain because they violate such characteristics. That he survives in the midst of stress or pain does not mean that stressful resolutions of his lifestyle options are better than more positive resolutions.

We know, for example, that various primitive peoples have carried on what Westerners consider brutal activities: Eskimos abandoned the aged; the Chinese, among others, practiced infanticide. Many such practices were institutionalized in response to pressures for survival, but we would still argue that it is contrary to natural human impulses to abandon old people or to kill new-born babies.

The problem, of course, is that as human societies invent new responses to economic or social arrangements which involve less stress, people are caught in the bind between commitment to tradition and innovative solutions to human problems which may be functionally more positive, for the process of change itself involves great stress. And there is the further complication that what appears at first glance as functionally positive may, in the long run, be destructive. (For example, stress caused by discrimination against ethnic or "foreign" neighborhoods has been attenuated by schools pressing toward a universal middle-class consciousness and lifestyle; yet more recently Americans have an increasingly positive assessment of the

value of particularistic communal experience provided by such neighborhoods.)

The fact that human societies are constantly shifting their social
patterns suggests that man senses in some way deficiencies or inadequacies in the success with which his social institutions are meeting
his needs. In Jules Henry's terms:

The lack of specificity of man's genetic mechanisms has placed him in the situation of constantly having to revise his social structures because of their frequent
failure to guide interpersonal relations without tensions felt as burdensome even
in the society in which they originate. Stated another way: because man's genetically determined mechanisms for governing interpersonal relations lack the specificity and the predictability found in lower animals, man, in constructing society, frequently makes choices that create interpersonal situations heavily laden
with stress. Meanwhile, given the necessity of constantly revising his social structures, and given his enormous variability, *Homo sapiens* gropes with his massive
cerebral cortex toward the solution of the variety of interpersonal problems
peculiar to the species and arising under the varying conditions of human life.
Thus, man has been presented with a unique evolutionary task: because his
mechanisms for determining interpersonal relations lack specificity, he must
attempt to maximize social adaptation through constant conscious and unconscious revision and experimentation, searching constantly for social structures,
patterns of interpersonal relations, that will be more adaptive, as he feels them.
Man's evolutionary path is thus set for him by his constant tendency to alter his
modes of social adaptation. Put somewhat in value terms, man tries constantly
to make a better society, i.e., one in which he can feel more comfortable. When
he makes a "mistake," he tries to change. This is one way in which he evolves.
(Henry 1959, pp. 221-22)

If man has the capacity to create new patterns of social interaction in an effort to reduce stress, he is often more inclined to develop new dysfunctional compensatory behavior piled on top of
older inadequacies, rather than abandon the prime cause of the stress
in the first place. In short, it seems very difficult for man to abandon
culture traps once he is caught. Undergoing the insecurity and
trauma required for radical movement toward a culture that is more
consistent with his own nature is often more threatening than ingeni-
ously inventing temporary tricks to ameliorate immediate stress. It is
easier to take drugs which reduce loneliness and boredom, for example, than to create communal institutions which would more naturally generate both security and social stimulation.

In summary, we would respond to the cultural relativist that although man has considerable capacity to bear the stress of going against his natural tendencies, this capacity also allows him to maintain highly dysfunctional cultures when the adaptive reasons have disappeared. Such tolerance for stress is clearly a mixed blessing. If his underlying instinctual nature were more obvious and made more pressing demands (i.e., life and death demands), there might be fewer men on the planet, but they might be considerably happier.

Any nonrelativist position must distinguish between good and bad levels of stress (assuming, perhaps, that moderate stress as a life challenge is desirable) as well as functional and dysfunctional stress, the latter being stress that is unnecessary or is not resolvable over long periods of time. Henderson, for example, distinguishes between natural and artificial stress:

The concept of stress has gained considerable attention in the medical profession as a cause of numerous diseases and an abettor in others. *Type A Behavior and Your Heart* linked stresses of the artificial type with heart disease, the cause of half the adult deaths in America each year (Report of the National Center for Health Statistics, 1974). More technical research in this regard was carried out at the Harvard Medical School by Bernard Lown.

> Results so far have shown that psychological stresses can exert a profound effect on a heart. . . . It is becoming clearer that a major trigger for many serious and abnormal heart rhythms is not the heart but the brain and the central nervous system. (Lawrence K. Altman, "Heart Research Has Key to Fatal Heart Attacks," *New York Times* (November 11, 1973), p. 52)

Hans Selye, who has done more work in the field than anyone, differentiates between good stress and bad stress, the former being the "spice of life" while the latter leaves one with acid feelings of frustration, fear and depression (*Stress Without Distress*, Philadelphia: J. B. Lippincott, 1974). This is an alternative mode of looking at stress that includes a different range of activities.

Quantity as well as quality of stress is significant in the work of Thomas Holmes. His life-change-units suggest the logical direction of *all* stress. Holmes' list includes natural stress items but is heavily weighted to the presence of the controllable artificial factors. The Holmes hypothesis is that an accumulation of 200 or more life-change-units in a single year may be more disruptive than an individual can stand. . . .

How Different Events Cause Stress

Event	*Scale of Impact*
Death of spouse	100
Divorce	73
Marital separation	65
Jail term	63

Event	Scale of Impact
Death of a close family member	63
Personal injury or illness	53
Marriage	50
Fired at work	47
Marital reconciliation	45
Retirement	45
Change in health of family member	44
Pregnancy	40
Sex difficulties	39
Gain of new family member	39
Business readjustment	39
Change in financial state	38
Death of close friend	37
Change to different line of work	36
Change in number of arguments with spouse	35
Mortgage over $10,000	31
Foreclosure of mortgage or loan	30
Change in responsibilities at work	29
Son or daughter leaving home	29
Trouble with in-laws	29
Outstanding personal achievement	28
Wife begins or stops work	26
Begin or end school	26
Change in living conditions	25
Revision of personal habits	24
Trouble with boss	23
Change in work hours or conditions	20
Change in residence	20
Change in schools	20
Change in recreation	19
Change in church activities	19
Change in social activities	18
Mortgage or loan less than $10,000	17
Change in sleeping habits	16
Change in number of family get-togethers	15
Change in eating habits	15
Vacation	13
Christmas	12
Minor violation of the law	11

Source: Adapted from Thomas Holmes and R. H. Rahe, "Life Events Scale." *The Journal of Psychosomatic Research* II: pp. 214-15.

While anthropologists were among the first to recognize the intrinsic meaningfulness and integrity of primitive cultures—and thus

to see relativism as a reasonable ethical posture, they have consistently tortured themselves over the more obvious differences between
primitive and modern man. In dealing with this issue, Redfield
writes:

Writing more than fifteen years later, Kroeber looked again at the questions as to
whether history showed man's progress and found more than Boas had found.
Kroeber states "three approaches that seem to yield at least a partial standard of
what constitutes 'higher' or more advanced culture, apart from mere quantity of
it." One of these three is the cumulative development of technology and science.
The other two standards for judging a culture as "higher" or "more advanced"
according to Kroeber, lead us into recognition of differences between precivilized and civilized peoples with regard to, respectively, the true and the good.
    "The first is the criterion of magic and 'superstition.' " By this Kroeber
means that people who have visions or other experiences that in modern society
are regarded as neurotic or psychotic are in preliterate societies highly valued,
along with the experiences. "Retarded peoples," he writes, "invert the emphasis. . . . To them a child or a hawk or a stone seen or heard in a certain kind of
dream or trance is much more important than a physical child or hawk or stone
that one can touch and handle, because it is the possible source of much more
power." Therefore he concludes, "The bestowal of social rewards for the inability to distinguish subjective experiences from objective phenomena, or for the
deliberate inversion of the two, is a presumable mark of lack of progress." In
these passages Kroeber recognizes a transformation in judgment as to the truth
as precivilized living gave way to civilization. The principle of cultural relativism
leads the anthropologist to look sympathetically at the view that primitive man
takes of these experiences when the anthropologist is attentive to the moral and
religious values that are, for the primitive person, involved in these mistakes of
judgment as to the truth. On the other hand, when the visions and magical beliefs lead to sickness or cruelty, the anthropologist, who is then apt to think that
scientific knowledge is better than magical mistakes, will pass an unfavorable
value judgment on such primitive customs, and perhaps help the administrator to
reduce the sickness or end the cruelty.
    The other criterion for progress which Kroeber finds is even more interest-
ing. He describes this great trend in history as the "decline of infantile obsession
with the outstanding physiological events of human life." The primitive person
allows to obtrude into public recognition and the social order "blood and death
and decay." Kroeber's long list of primitive customs which exhibit this obtrusion
evokes these, to us, disagreeable facts: I do not quote the list here; it includes
blood sacrifice, wearing of skull or jaws by widows, ritual prostitution, and cannibalism. Kroeber reminds us that such practices are not uniformly present in
preliterate societies; rather we have here "a probable tendency that holds good
on the whole or in the long run." (Redfield 1953, pp. 160-61)

Kroeber as well as Redfield are really endorsing the general notion that what is more modern about humans is what is morally

higher and more civilized. This is true for all of Kroeber's criteria. The relationship between technology and modernism is obvious. It is also more modern to think in a highly directed "reality oriented" way; to see dreams and fantasies as more primitive modes of thought, not to be taken seriously. Finally, what Kroeber considers "the outstanding physiological events of human life" are precisely those events which link man to the other biological and geological events of the planet, within which and from which the human species evolved. To lose our fascination for or repress these events is certainly more modern; it may also result in an irreversible loss of connectedness with the larger picture of man's place on the planet.

Evolutionists, Egalitarians, and Developmentalists

There is a critical, if somewhat subtle, transition between the posture of the cultural relativist and that of the liberal utilitarian "modernist," presented by Redfield; it hinges on the concept of *free choice*. When asked quality-of-life questions requiring him to compare one society with another (e.g., the Amish with their modern neighbors), the liberal commonly responds that each society is good for those who live in it. This, of course, is the standard relativist response. When faced with the fact that primitive societies, including both aboriginal groups and intentional agricultural communities, are gradually being destroyed because they cannot compete with modern society, the response is simply that if people freely choose one way of life over another, there is no reason to interfere with that choice. It is precisely on the issue of free choice that liberals tend to split into *egalitarians* and *developmentalists*. The egalitarians see choice as an ethical end; the quality of a society is then determined by actual opportunities for choice that exist. The appropriate metaphor is the supermarket. Quality of life is determined by the extent to which each individual has reasonably equal or adequate access to the goods in the supermarket. Progress equals maximization of consumer choice. For the developmentalist progress relates not only to the material affluence of the society which maximizes choice, but also to the individual capacities of the consumer. In a higher quality society humans will be intellectually more enlightened, aesthetically more sensitive, spiritually more transcendant, and morally more conscientious and responsible. Herein lies the positive justification for destroying or converting primitive peoples; *the people themselves need to be developed.*

For the developmentalist there is an additional issue: the choice of a more mature individual has greater value than the choice of the less mature individual. "Maturity" has both personal and social meaning. On a personal level, it means psychological growth; on a social level it is construed as a type of society characterized by a "developed" or "mature" social, political, and economic system. The psychological meaning of developmentalism is eloquently articulated by Kohlberg and Mayer.

The developmental-philosophic strategy can deal with the ethical question of having a standard of non-relative or universal value and with factual questions of prediction. The concept of developmental, as elaborated by cognitive-developmental theory, implies a standard of adequacy *internal* to, and governing, the developmental process itself. It is obvious that the notion of development must do more than merely define what comes later in time. It is not clear that what comes later must be better. . . .

Cognitive-developmental theory, however, postulates a formal internal standard of adequacy which is not merely an order of events in time. In doing so it elaborates the ordinary-language meaning of the term "development." Webster's Dictionary tells us that to develop means "to make active, to move from the original position to one providing more opportunity for effective use, to cause to grow and differentiate along lines natural of its kind, to go through a process of natural growth, differentiation, or evolution by successive changes." This suggests an internal standard of adequacy governing development; it implies that development is not just any behavior change, but a change toward greater differentiation, integration, and adaptation. Cognitive-developmental psychological theory postulates that movement through a sequential progression represents movement from a less adequate psychological state to a more adequate psychological state. (1972, p. 483)

It should be clear that both *utilitarian modernists* (egalitarians and developmentalists alike) and evolutionists are committed to the notion of social and cultural amelioration. Both believe there are better and worse societies. The fundamental difference is in the criteria applied and the breadth of the human condition each is willing to look at. For the utilitarian, quality of life is defined as maximum choice—either choice generally for the egalitarian or choice by a fully developed or mature human being for the developmentalist. For the evolutionist, quality of life is defined by two sets of criteria: the extent to which culture channels human behavior along lines that are consistent for humans as a species or consistent for the variety of temperaments for individuals; and the extent to which paradoxical or contradictory tendencies are worked out with minimum objective stress and maximum cultural meaning.

Out of this analysis come two areas of fundamental difference between developmentalists and evolutionists. The first relates to the nature of human ontogeny. The developmentalists argue that man is fundamentally a progressive animal, able to integrate earlier forms of primary experience into later forms of mature experience. The evolutionists claim that man is fundamentally a paradoxical animal, who must settle for, at best, an uneasy equilibrium balancing earlier and later forms of experience. One might consider, for example, the extent to which humans are capable of integrating the four kinds of attachment that occur at different points in their career: the child-parent bond that begins at infancy; the work-play-friendship peer bond; the mating bond; and the parent-child bond which begins for the adult when offspring are born. These four kinds of bonding overlap and confound the human psyche in a variety of constructive and destructive ways. In peer friendship relationships children play roles they learn within the child-parent bonding; mating relationships commonly serve the partner in a dual or triple capacity (the husband or wife may be treated as a mate, a parent, or a child). Or an adult may learn a pattern of egalitarian peer relating in a work or play relationship and apply it to relationships with children. Many of the Freudian insights we now take for granted bear on relationships among various layers of affectional bonding which lead to psychic complexity and confusion.

The developmentalist position maintains that all humans have the potential for integrating earlier styles of attachment or affection with later ones so that, in the end, one has a highly differentiated, integrated, and positive style of relating to one's fellow humans. One "gives up" infantile or narcissistic "primitive" forms of relating and "grows up"; one is then able to accept responsible autonomous adult relationships toward children, mates, and other adults.

The evolutionist sees the goal of having everyone arrive at the state of "fully integrated love" unrealistic. The evolutionist assumes that most humans have permanent dependency needs relating back to ontogenetic experiences as well as to archetypes representing early band or tribal life within which the species evolved. We believe it is simply unrealistic to require that most humans fully "grow up." The evolutionist is also more pessimistic about the ability of humans to integrate their lives on a societal or cultural level. He sees the four bonding experiences as in some ways contradictory. The preservation of infantile love needs may, in fact, simply be a dysfunctional evolutionary event which attends the positive consequences of a long childhood. When one looks at the great variety of cultural methods by which affectional (or bonding) confusion is and has been handled by the species, one stumbles only rarely on examples of "fully mature and integrated individuals." This point of conflict between the evolutionists and developmentalists rests on different factual assumptions about the capacity of all humans to be raised to the "higher" or "more adaptive" modes of functioning.

The developmental advocates, while disclaiming any elitism, reveal a commitment to perfectionism which leaves little doubt about who is more perfect and who is less perfect. The more perfect are those who can think and integrate ideas in a more complex and abstract way. (The unstated assumption is, of course, that those who can *think* more competently are also those who can *feel* more competently.) Again, if one looks at the cultural record, one finds little evidence that societies have resolved the problem of training all to the same level of complexity, integration, and competence.

Choice as a Basis for Quality of Life

For the developmentalist, quality of life is based on the two meanings of "modern," modern man and modern society; both converge on the idea of maximum choice. Modern man is one who has the right mix of reflective intelligence and moral sensibility to make reasonable choices for himself and for the human society in which he lives. The developed or mature society is one which can turn out the maximum number of life options. This applies to material goods, social groups, leisure activities, religions, etc. Again, the best metaphor is a supermarket, stocked with an infinite supply of social, aesthetic, material, religious, and affectional goods and services. Here the intelligent (but unique) and affluent citizen can spend his time, energy, and money selecting the life that best meets his own preferences. Each person gives up a part of his life in a highly specialized "economic" activity creating and delivering goods and services to the supermarket, in return for which he lives the life of great choice.

"Problems" are construed mainly in economic terms. What do we do with the people who will not work? What do we do with the people who cannot or will not be trained into the specialized roles required to create the goods and services? What do we do with greedy or unscrupulous producers who turn out shoddy goods or "choices"? What do we do with people who choose shortcuts, that is, steal or cheat to get goods and services without paying at the check-out counter? What do we do with "undeveloped" people?

There are, however, two underlying but obvious ideological biases in the "maximum choice" position, which seems at first glance so open. The first is in the concept of openness itself. To look at life as a series of open choices, or to tolerate or even celebrate rapid change because it makes available new choices, is the basis of an ideology or a concept of "truth." Second, generating new choices inevitably moves in the direction of increasingly complex and sophisticated technology. Bicycles move from one-speed to three-speed to five- and ten-speed. Recreation in general moves from activities such as walking and playing simple games to activities requiring elaborate equipment, such as skiing, motorcycling, boating, and ballooning.

So the ideology of open choice does in fact have fundamental restrictions. First, it presses toward the denial of man's urge for stability and tradition—the choice to have limits of choices—and comes out unequivocally for change and "development" as positive values. Second, it defines development as increasing specialization and integration of functions toward improved adaptation and more versatile coping. Increasing versatility then allows one a wider range of choices. And so the spiral continues.

Human Nature as a Basis for Quality of Life

The evolutionary view of man begins with the assumption that each living form inherits elements characteristic of the larger family or genus of living forms to which it belongs. Each also inherits the more particular elements characteristic of its own species. In our own self-centered way, humans tend to call the more general characteristics we share with other forms of life our "primitive" legacy and the more specific characteristics "modern." While these terms are accurate from the point of view of the time during which the characteristics evolved, they carry unfortunate value connotations. Primitive characteristics are denigrated or denied; modern characteristics are elaborated and nourished. In our perception of our own bodies, for example, we tend to stress our bipedalism and prehensile forelimbs with the opposing thumb, rather than a host of physiological or morphological characteristics we share with other mammals and birds (e.g., our warm-bloodedness and endoskeleton). In making mind-body distinctions, we view the bodily functions (and needs) as more primitive albeit more basic than those of the mind. From an evolutionary point of view, we would argue that one must pay as much attention to the older characteristics of a species as the younger. It appears that modern man's most profound and distressing hang-up is his inability to accept his total evolutionary legacy. The Adam and Eve myth is reflective of this hang-up. Man is presumably alienated from the rest of nature because he knows too much. The question then is whether this knowledge is used to separate him further from nature (through myths of human uniqueness and technology), or whether man's more primitive legacy is respected and accepted as well.

Suppose as evolutionists we begin with a more modest (and perhaps fuller) assessment of man as a species, one that is not concerned with the testing of his ultimate capacity for inventing, creating, or maintaining modern artifacts and culture (e.g., air-conditioned cities under geodesic domes, interplanetary exploration, freezing human corpses to be later cured of malignancy). Rather, we might begin with a view of man that is concerned more with an assessment of his natural tendencies, limits, or contradictions as well as with his natural flexibility and capacity to cope, and assume that any decent society must function within these limits. One need not become a hard-core evolutionist or instinctualist to take such human limitations seriously. One might look, for example, at Anthony Wallace's analysis of man's tendency to work out dominance-submission relationships in characteristic primate fashion:

... let us begin with the trite observations that in the larger primates below man, individuals form strong attachments to one another and to groups, including the community, and that loss of skin contact in infants, and personal attachments and group-membership in adults, is likely to be fatal. In these organizations, dominance is a function of age (adults dominating infants), of gender (males dominating females), and of strength and aggressiveness within male and female groups. It is also apparently linked to sexuality, and the rituals expressive of dominance-and-submission are, in fact, often simulations of sexual approach and of copulation, both heterosexually and homosexually. Normally, a primate troop manages to get along with minimal real fighting because the members are sorted out into a stable dominance order such that each member of a pair of animals, on confrontation, knows and accepts his relative position. Serious challenges to this order, chiefly as a result of the maturation, in-migration, changing alliances, and senescence of individuals, take the form of actual fighting or "agonistic" (threatening) displays. Accidental or trivial challenges elicit irritable responses, but ready ritual submission generally aborts a developing conflict. All animals know, and are capable of relating to others in, both dominant and submissive roles, depending on the circumstances; and dominance is not pressed to the point where any animal is excluded from food, sex, reproduction, or group membership; indeed, male group solidarity may flourish where hierarchy is clear. Social play, in which existing dominance structures are suspended in nonescalating agonistic competition, occurs primarily among the young. Mother-son incest is minimized because it requires behavior that complicates an age-based dominance relationship. Species differ in regard to territoriality and acquisitiveness, but it cannot be said that preoccupation with territoriality and property is a universal primate trait. Destructive aggression between groups is rare or nonexistent. Nor are the lower primates primary carnivores and hunters of other species, although the larger species can and do hunt on occasion.

If one were to use these data as the baseline, then, one would postulate the following fundamental (and very old) pattern for human nature: men are creatures who live most comfortably in small troops and profoundly fear rejection by their group; whose sexual impulses are closely connected with dominance-and-submission impulses in both sexes; who sort themselves out into established dominance hierarchies; who are irritably sensitive to challenges to dominance and respond to such challenges with agonistic displays, but who also are capable of switching to a comfortable and passive submission; who can form close personal attachments to mothers, to children, to leaders, to friends, and to sexual consorts, and who as children enjoy playing at games in which dominance roles alternate.

Now let us suppose that our protohuman creature has a relatively large and perhaps especially efficient brain, enjoys a prolonged infancy and childhood, walks on two feet with hands free, and has fine stereoscopic color vision, and as a result of the superiority of this biological equipment, invents wood, stone, and bone tools, controls fire, develops language, becomes a professional hunter, specializes occupationally, and in the end produces a kind of culture we can call human. What kind of problems of psychodynamics will his desire to maintain this economically advantageous mode of life entail for him?

One obvious problem will be a tendency to find innumerable new and technically inconvenient ways in which dominance can be both exercised and challenged. And along with this, because of the old tie between dominance and sex, will go a sexualizing of these new opportunities for dominance and submission. This tendency will be a problem because the technology, the language, and the specialization of labor will increasingly necessitate the modification of a sexually oriented dominance hierarchy based on simple physical fighting and agonistic display. Hence there will have to be elaborate rules for the compartmentalization of dominance into areas of authority and responsibility based on many criteria of competence, not just irritability and physical strength; a partial separation of dominance from sexuality, by such devices as incest taboos in kinship structures, by taboos on nepotism, and (with an eye to the efficiency of large male organizations) by taboos on or at least careful management of homosexuality; and a prohibition of dominance relations in certain contexts. Many of the creatures will spend much of their time mechanically carrying out instrumental tasks without a satisfying sense of either dominance or submission. Many will feel that they deserve to be dominant but are not permitted to be; many will feel inadequate to maintain the dominance required of them. All this will become a source of innumerable potential frustrations and anxieties that will be the more pervasive the more complex the technology and the social system becomes; fear of loss of social acceptance and of self-acceptability may become chronic. The psychoanalytically described mechanisms of defense, and their institutionalized counterparts in religious belief and ritual, in play, and in the arts, develop to relieve some of this chronic fear; what cannot be handled in these structurally stable compromises produces the symptomatic expressions of anxiety, delusion, "regressive" displays of agonistic and sexual behavior, and all the rest of the disorders we lump together as mental illness, meaningless violence, unreasonable exploitation, and senseless war.

The nuclear problems, for this kind of primate nature, then become first, one of constantly minimizing fear by separating areas of experience and by responding to challenge not with impulsive dominant or submissive actions but on the basis of socially sanctioned calculation, and second, differentiating between dominance-submission relationships that may include explicit sexual aspects and those that may not, irrespective of provocations and solicitations, opportunities and impulses. (Wallace 1970, pp. 132-35)

To look at man as a primate or a particular kind of primate is not to denigrate or diminish him; it is rather to explore within what limits positive culture might be created. From this point of view, positive culture is one which *successfully channels man's natural tendencies or which minimizes the stress of contradictory tendencies; destructive culture is one which violates human tendencies—which then require stressful methods of socialization or direct coercion to obtain compliance with cultural rules.*

From an evolutionary point of view a central question is: What are the constraints and tendencies in man's nature, that is, what "nature" has he inherited through the long process of his evolutionary history?

One has no great problem producing a list of such human characteristics which suggest potential limitations on the range within which constructive culture might be built. The problem, of course, is that we know very little about the range of tolerable stress within any particular characteristic. The following list will, however, at least specify significant areas wherein we might be sensitive to such limits:

1. *Limitations in the way man responds to others within the same physical space.* Density of populations within residential areas; number of people who can work comfortably and cooperatively in a single work setting; density and privacy within households; tendency to protect personal space in face-to-face contacts.

2. *Biological rhythms.* Day-night—work-play-rest cycle; necessity of structure and punctuation within days, weeks, years; tendency to build celebrations related to major geological events (e.g., winter solstice, spring equinox).

3. *Celebration of visible ecological interdependence.* Conscious and unconscious sense of being linked to life chains (e.g., creation of gods, myths, naming of plants and animals, and relating to kinship groups).

4. *Necessity of fulfilling minimal requirements for healthy development.* Body contact and regular feeding relating to trust; protected support and freedom related to autonomy, etc.

5. *Cognitive limitations.* Tendency to construe the world as categories, described with bipolar adjectives; tendency to judge events in terms of a limited number of salient adjectives—strong-weak, active-passive, good-bad, natural-unnatural, etc.

6. *Diversity within the species.* Constructive organization of diverse humans within groups and societies, using talents and needs of individuals to create symbiotic interdependent relationships; negative tendency of one type of human to see other types as outgroup threats, needing to be excluded or remediated (e.g., bright people seeing dull people as needing "education"; adults seeing adolescents as "overactive" and "insensitive"). The most significant and enduring elements of diversity appear to be sex, age (different stages of life-cycle), and various temperamental predispositions. The latter include activity level, level of conceptual brightness, introversion-extroversion, physical strength and agility, and dominance-submission.

7. *Creation of stable role patterns and relationships to reduce ambiguity about expected behavior.* Roles may include kinship relationships (mother, father, uncle), work roles, leadership roles, religious roles, etc.

8. *Placement of roles in a stable status hierarchy based on age, sex, relative importance to survival or happiness of the group, or efficiency* (how well a task is performed).

9. *Creation and maintenance of stable social forms, each of*

which has inherent characteristics. These may include the dyad, nuclear family, extended kinship groups, neighborhood, peer sentiment groups, the city, or bureaucratic organization.

10. *Limited instinctual controls on requirements for the successful resolution of shifts in the life cycle.* These shifts may include, for example, the change from being a play-oriented child to a work-oriented adult; the change from being a sex-oriented adult in a mating relationship to the inclusion of children within that relationship; the shift from being a work-oriented adult to a marginally useful "old person."

11. *The need to fulfill a set of functional requirements within societies without the availability of strong instinctual directives to meet these requirements.* These requirements may include productive work, inclusion within community or group life, a meaningful set of religious beliefs to explain man's place in the cosmos, ritual celebrations to reinforce and "make real" more abstract beliefs, etc.

12. *Self-awareness and the sense of personal freedom and restriction.* This is the ability to separate the self from objects and other selves. It gives one the sense that personal behavior is not somehow inevitably embedded within the fabric of one's surroundings; one has the subjective sense of choice. Humans are constantly tormented either by the sense that they have more choice than they can responsibly handle, or by the sense that they have so little choice that they cannot be fulfilled.

13. *The illusion of unlimited flexibility and choice.* This tendency is expressed in fantasies of Eden or Utopia; the sense that cultures can be invented or managed like beasts or machines; the sense that magical incantations or belief systems can prevent illness, death, loss of loved ones, etc.

14. *The perception of oneself as part of a favored ingroup in contrast to an unfavored outgroup.* Ingroup members are seen as fully human, to be protected from injury and exploitation by other members of the ingroup. Members of outgroups are seen as less than human and therefore are not exempt from injury and exploitation. Humans vary in their conceptual and affective capacity to include increasingly remote groups as part of a human "ingroup." This adds a second source of conflict to human societies: members of ingroups fight over who is to be included in the category "fully human."

15. *Destructive and exploitative relationships.* The strong ex-

ploit the weak; adults exploit young people; old people are discarded; men exploit women.

16. *The overemphasis on technology.* Economic efficiency, the control of physical power, the fulfillment of short-run conveniences and comforts, and technological innovations to achieve all of these are given priority over weaker tendencies. For example:

a. Highly structured work settings such as offices, schools, factories, and stores stifle informal human relating and personal caring as well as the natural discharge of limited amounts of hostility and aggression.

b. Weapons technology neutralizes man's natural inhibition against intraspecific killing.

c. Creation of total man-made environments dulls human sensitivity to ecological interdependence among living and non-living forms on the planet.

d. Population expansion and efficiency in transportation and communication defeat control of ingroup-outgroup aggression and exploitation which was initially controlled through spacial isolation.

e. The problem of future shock: rapid self-generating technological change leads man into extreme relativism, nihilism, and a sense of alienation.

f. Culture shock: population expansion, efficiency in transportation and communication, and efforts by technologically advanced societies to develop "backward" countries all create considerable intercultural anxiety and abrasion, with the persistent threat that one culture or subculture will dominate or subvert another.

17. *Physical and physiological limitations of the human body.* Relative fragility of human body to accidental damage with limited capacity for regeneration and repair; inevitability of aging and death; relatively heavy genetic load (rate of negative mutations); vulnerability to wide range of microorganisms; hazardous and painful childbirth; long period of maturation and development allowing for traumatic physical and emotional accidents when organism is relatively young.

Limits such as those given here suggest criteria by which to assess positive and negative elements in culture. Although they are speculative and general, at least they provide a beginning point from which to climb out of the paralytic condition of cultural relativism or the naivete of developmentalism. At the extremes it would seem that quality-of-life judgments on these dimensions would not be difficult to make. As Redfield puts it:

I am sure that the mores [referring to Sumner's work on folkways] have an easier time making it right for mothers to cherish their children or somebody's children, than they have to make it right for a mother to cherish her child and eat it. The insight we have in condemning as "inhuman" certain extremes of conduct such as the cold cruelty of the Nazis, or cannibalism within the in-group, is an insight into a truth that might perhaps some day be expressed in scientific form: that the rules of conduct, in the societies the world has known so far, have their modality, their tendency toward a very general similar content. (1957, pp. 159-60)

The problem of identifying and agreeing on positive elements of culture is probably considerably more difficult than identifying negative and stressful conditions. For example, it is probably harder to identify the range of positive activities a six-year-old child might engage in to express his natural potentialities than to find agreement on the fact that he or she should not be required to sit quietly for five or six hours a day following highly structured verbal commands to manipulate abstract verbal symbols.

Human Nature and Prestructured Capacities

It should be emphasized that both developmentalists and evolutionists (as opposed to relativists) reject the idea of the human as essentially a plastic culture-building animal who is simply a product of habits he learns from his fellows or from adaptive discoveries he makes *de novo*. Rather, both construe him as having implicitly structured capacities or, as Bidney states, "culture is to be understood primarily as a regulative process initiated by man for the development and organization of his determinate, substantive potentialities" (Bidney 1967, p. 154). The difference between the two ideologies is that the developmentalist sees the structured potentialities as possible of increasingly complex integration to the point where all humans—and human societies—are complete, mature, or fully developed. (These terms have, of course, political connotations as well as technical, economic, and psychological meaning). The evolutionist, on the other hand, sees humans as having a variety of tendencies and often contradictory potentialities (both within individuals and within human societies); he sees culture as a mode of limiting which of these potentialities are allowed expression. Again, in Bidney's words:

> Each type of culture develops certain potentialities of human nature and neglects others. This explains why actual historical man appears to vary with the cultural conditions which affect him and why the modes of behavior and thought of the adherents of one culture often appear so unintelligible to adherents of another. No one culture system completely satisfies all human needs and potentialities; each system has defects corresponding to its virtues. (1967, p. 81)

It is this broader-than-can-be-expressed potential of man that leads to three very different conclusions about whether one can evolve quality-of-life standards for human societies. The relativist assumes that since man expresses himself through a variety of sociocultural systems, one system is as good as another. The developmentalist assumes that when the individual and the society have reached their maximum potential, there will be maximum choice, that is, a wide variety of cultural or subcultural alternatives will be available. The "good society" is one with maximum choice; the good individual is one with the capacity to choose among the broadest range of alternatives. The evolutionist assumes that freedom of choice itself is another human paradox. For to know that one has choice is to weaken one's commitment to social groups, meanings, and a traditional style of life. Quality of life for the developmentalist is maximum choice. Quality of life for the evolutionist is defined as some reasonable balance between the more primitive tendency to define ingroup tradition as the only set of legitimized behaviors versus the tendency to "tolerate" a wide variety of social choices as reasonable, and perhaps even participate in those choices. The way one views language reflects the same conflict in interpretation of quality of life between developmentalists and evolutionists. All humans presumably have underlying potentials for a similar linguistic structure in the nervous system. But various cultures invent languages which differ in relatively superficial ways. Languages are more or less complex and subtle, more or less euphoneous; some allow for more or less precision or vagueness, etc. For the developmentalist, the better developed one's language capacity the more options one has in human expression. Having a large vocabulary and complex syntax is "good." Or one might write prose in English, poetry in Japanese, and sing operas in Italian. The evolutionist assumes, however, that with the richness and variations in choice of language comes a loss of concrete connectedness between sensuous reality and the symbols that describe that reality. When one can name the object designated by a particular word in five languages the shape and sound of the word itself in any one language tends to lose any "magical" or intrinsic association with the object. Nor is this loss trivial, for the connection between sounds, signs, and objects is the stuff of poetry and religion. The metaphor "mother tongue" reflects the importance of this connection.

As these dilemmas illustrate, the problem of imagining positive culture is more complicated than identifying limits in human tendencies and somehow inventing and institutionalizing behavior within these limits. As stressed initially, man has in many domains of behavior a paradoxical and contradictory nature. He wants social stability, he wants disorder and adventure. He wants the security of stable love relationships, yet he wants freedom to change interpersonal affections and commitments. He wants the love and protection of the gods and the temptation of the devil.

Other examples easily come to mind. The human sense of time spans both past and future. We learn from the past to anticipate events in the future and in so doing prepare to cope with them. Adaptive as this capacity is, there are some events or circumstances for which it is difficult to prepare, such as aging and death. Much destructive and futile anxiety is expended focusing on one's own annihilation. Or one might consider man's intimacy or Oedipal hang-up. Warm, highly inclusive parent-child dyads may produce children who experience considerable trauma when faced with the problem of achieving independence and maturity; it is the childhood love experience that allows one to feel great depths of human sensitivity and loneliness. A society such as ours with only one institution to resolve this problem—the recreation of the small, fragile, and transitory nuclear family in which the child later performs the adult role—is bound to have an abundance of people who have a poignant childlike anxiety about being lonely or abandoned, an anxiety that is inevitably projected onto one's own children and so perpetuated.

Constructive cultures somehow thread their way through such contradictions, but never resolve them. There is always stress. One can, for example, build formal mating arrangements by linking two families economically and in so doing provide for greater stability and security. (A house and land might be provided by one family, bride prices might be paid, etc.) Under this condition, individuals of roughly equal wealth tend to mate. Another human tendency, however, is the capacity for romantic love, including a period of mutual infatuation, which may totally disregard the relative economic status of the partners. How does one build mating institutions which will take both human tendencies into account? To build a marriage on the basis of formal economic arrangements may make them less fragile, but it may bring about substantial psychic suffering if it ignores the human potential for infatuation.

In looking at the evolution of a society toward or away from a higher quality of life we would distinguish between what we would call "cultural tuning" and "cultural traps." Cultural tuning suggests that we continuously refine institutions to minimize the stress we feel from imperfections or contradictions in the species. (We might invent marginally dangerous games, such as hockey or rugby, for risk-prone young males, and surrender mortal warfare, although in doing so we deny these males certain "ultimate" emotional experiences related to male bonding and personal sacrifice.) The notion that one can tune a culture so finely that there is no static, or so there are no mixed signals, is certainly naively utopian. But it seems obvious that some cultures are tuned so badly that their inhabitants undergo senseless conflict and stress.

Cultural traps on the other hand are inventions which temporarily compensate for or defend against destructive aspects of existing cultural elements, but in addition either exacerbate negative aspects of existing elements or simply make it more difficult to slough off a destructive element, or both. Examples are relatively easy to come by in modern utilitarian societies. We invent programs of "preparation" or "rehabilitation" for groups of people so they will be better fit to function in the society (young people are institutionalized in school; old people are institutionalized in "homes for the aged"; deviant personalities are institutionalized in prisons or mental hospitals). Segregating "unfit" people until they are somehow corrected (young people by growing up; old people by dying; mental patients often never) avoids the more fundamental problem of how "normal" or competent humans can learn to accept and care for the less able. Thus the idea of preparation and rehabilitation is a trap in that it temporarily justifies segregation, which then becomes a problem as serious in its own right as the problem it was supposed to correct.

Another example is the use of television, which allows people to escape from the stress of a socially monotonous and physically soft life through vicarious participation in the heroic activities of doctors, detectives, and football players. But the time expended watching television may be all that one has with which to deal more constructively with the soft and monotonous lifestyle that is destructive to human existence in the first place.

The paradoxical qualities of much of human nature suggest that the genius of positive culture is not simply building social institutions which are somehow more consistent with natural human tendencies; positive culture is created both by "tuning" dominant institutions to better meet human needs, and also by constructing complementary or compensatory institutions which offer alternative ways of balancing inevitable conflicts and stresses with potential satisfactions.

The problem, of course, is finding criteria by which to distinguish cultural tuning from culture traps. It is often difficult to ascertain in midstream whether one is building around an essentially constructive institution positive alternative institutions which will better handle man's limiting or conflicting tendencies, or whether one is simply investing more deeply in an inadequate or destructive institution.

The effort to institutionalize universal literacy in modern nations is, perhaps, a useful example of the ambiguity between cultural tuning and cultural traps. Children between the ages of about six and twelve are placed under considerable social press to "read at grade level" so that all may share the expression of a significant human personality. For a variety of somewhat mysterious reasons, a sizeable proportion fail to meet the standard. At this point we might ask whether the cultural expectation is wrong; perhaps we should simply assume that many people cannot read well but this will not prevent their living a decent and worthy life; or should we insist that the societal demand be met? Having chosen the latter course, we have now institutionalized remedial reading, which carries with it the connotation that those who cannot read well are defective human beings. The question is: Is remedial reading cultural tuning (a back-up or alternative institution which reduces stress caused by natural human differences)? Or is it a trap? Is remedial reading a destructive institution built on top of an already destructive institution—the rule of universal literacy?

Ideologies and Human Differences

One of the most fundamental paradoxes of the human condition is the species response to diversity. Humans have a strong tendency to make ingroup-outgroup distinctions—to respond to the ingroup with amity and positive concern; to respond to the outgroup with suspicion, hostility, or exploitation. As long as humans were living in small face-to-face bands the ingroup-outgroup distinction was easily made. Although privilege and status might be linked to such fundamental human differences as age, sex, and temperament, all manner of humans would be seen as included within the band, to be treated with a modicum of dignity and respect—to be treated as "human." In complex multiculture societies, however, where privilege, status, and association are based more on meritocratic considerations, stratification occurs and, in the long run, social classes tend toward subcultural homogeneity, often based on shared temperamental characteristics. In a very general way, we might speculate that brighter, more aggressive, more talented, or more creative individuals move toward more privileged and exploitative positions; those who may be bright or talented, but passive, move to the middle; those who are dull and passive end up on the bottom. (This is not to suggest that brightness, creativity, and aggressiveness are the only significant bases of status.) This general tendency is, of course, moderated and adulterated in any single generation by inherited wealth and status, which results in institutionalized privilege and exploitation.

The human then ends up with the rather distressing phenomenon of living in a single society (at least conceptually) where all members have ingroup status, but where members of other social classes often have very different lifestyles, dialects, values, and ways of thinking. This condition muddies considerably who one "instinctively" should treat with ingroup consideration, and who should be treated with outgroup exploitation or indifference.

One mode of adapting to this confusion is the creation of a two-layered society, one with a great variety of "little traditions" set within an all-encompassing "great tradition" (to use Redfield's distinction). Little traditions are those which evolve within small, relatively isolated peasant communities, which also later persist as urban villages. Great traditions evolve within urban centers, where artists, scholars, scientists, merchants, inventors, and kings have the time and the talent to create systematic belief systems, large rational human organizations (e.g., trading companies, manufacturing companies, churches, armies), and elaborate cultural artifacts (e.g., pyramids, cathedrals). Great traditions often evolve from and feed on the creative invention of little traditions. In preindustrial urban societies, the lower classes live within little traditions, the upper classes within a great tradition. Modern social theorists—both egalitarians and developmentalists—see little traditions for the common folk as inextricably linked with parochialism, poverty, and ignorance, and assume that they must be inferior and limited.

Both the radical egalitarian (or socialist) and the liberal developmentalist imagine a classless society (or one with moderately fluid classes), in the one case brought about by political or revolutionary redistribution of power and wealth, in the other case by the uplifting of peasants, workers, and poor through education. The socialist eschews the problem of individual differences by assuming that when the burden of class-consciousness has been removed from social institutions, all will find a place of dignity and worth. The liberal developmentalist does not let the common folk off quite so easily. From his point of view, each must earn his way into bourgeois status by becoming a highly competent, individuated, fully-developed self.

As indicated in the last chapter, the "middle class" historically is a group that is strangely liberated from a sense of any tradition. It arose simultaneously with the massive use of science and technology as modes of ordering and controlling both the natural and social environment. The meaning system used to rationalize and explain its place in the cosmos we have roughly called "utilitarianism." What is historically new is the notion that there need be no stable tradition, little or great. Rapid technological and environmental change require that each individual be capable of making and remaking sense out of an unstable and fragmentary world. For those who founder in this task—who cannot cope without tradition—the developmentalist has an answer. Acting as professional scientists (psychologists, educators, etc.) he will carry out the job of completing the process of development for his intellectually or emotionally deficient brothers.

While the developmentalist would erase those temperamental and intellectual differences (through education), which are a major dynamic in maintaining a class-based society, the evolutionist is inclined to accept the differences as permanently linked to the species, and work toward creating local communities where common folk can live decent and worthy lives. Once one accepts the notion that most humans are not temperamentally capable of becoming the competitive self-centered individuals postulated by the utilitarian ideology or bourgeois culture, the central question becomes one of developing symbiotic nonexploitative and mutually supportive relationships between cosmopolitan elites, the enterprising bourgeois, and the common folk.

The key issues for social theory are then twofold: How can the content of any tradition (little or great) be maintained in the face of a utilitarian perfectionist ideology which reinforces and reflects the value of rapid cultural and technological change? And second, how can neighborhoods and little communities out of which are generated little traditions (and eventually great traditions) marshall the economic and political power to maintain themselves, when their developed bourgeois or elite "friends" see their existence as "cultural deprivation"? The two questions are linked, moreover, for we suspect that it is only when the little traditions and the great traditions have common overarching content (albeit different structural complexity) that one has a society in which the common folk can share in the quality of a great tradition, contribute to it, and be protected from its excesses of power and exploitation.

We now seem to be in an odd transitional period. The "great tradition," at least for Europeans, revolves around a mixture of the classic civilizations of Greece and Rome, Feudalism and Christianity, and the Enlightenment. The content of this great tradition has been undermined by modern utilitarianism. But one hesitates to call utilitarianism a new great tradition, because it celebrates novelty and change, rather than continuity. We would now ask whether or not one can have a tradition based not on a moral order, but on a technical order, that is, on the *process* by which a society provides consumable goods and services. Modern man's faith in science and technology as means for providing new and interesting choices approaches a tradition based on a technical order. The problem is that most people, and in particular the common folk, can participate only in the results of that process, not in the shaping of it, for to do that one must be a specialist—a scientist, engineer, or entrepreneur who directs scientists and engineers.

What we find today is not the generation of vital little traditions, but rather the common folk sharing in indirect and receptive ways in the technical order (watching television; taking fast rides in cars, motorcycles, speedboats; making use of newly developed beauty aids and fashions; listening to very loud music played with electric guitars and amplifiers, etc.). The paradox is that the technical order provides a kind of "instant equality" or democratization of life through technology (e.g., television provides instant access to million dollar drama; automobiles instantly destroy spacial barriers; prefabricated housing interiors instantly provide an attractive environment). The creative forces of the society become highly centralized; very few people are producers; most are consumers. While the keepers of the great tradition have suffered from the onslaught of this kind of creative centralization, it is still possible to listen to church music, attend a little theater production, or visit an art museum. Centers of high culture still abound with creative energy as the affluent search for some balance between celebrating the remnants of the old great tradition and the spate of novel possibilities generated by the modern technological order. (An interesting metaphorical example of this is Burgess's *A Clockwork Orange* in which the hero celebrated sex, sadism, and Beethoven's Ninth Symphony.) The common folks, however, seem to have lost their opportunity for balance.

Perhaps the key to viable little traditions is the role of creative transitional people who are born and raised among common folk. These people can choose to abandon their people and join the affluent elite (it may take two or three generations); they can join the ranks of the bourgeois utilitarian consumers; they can maintain some connection with and leadership for the common folks. Presumably, there might be transitional roles where such people can participate in both great and little traditions. However one makes it possible, the evolutionist assumes that decent societies require that there be vital and constantly evolving little traditions within which common people find a sense of active control over meaning and work in their lives.

Conclusion

The general evolutionary point of view presented here can, we believe, be developed to provide a valid and coherent sense of meaning for contemporary human existence on this planet. To say that it is based on "science" or "social science" is both pretentious and misleading. It is obviously based on a mixture of intuitive assumptions, personal experience, interpretations of social science, and faith. The implications of this position square, we think, more directly with the common experience of human existence than many of the assumptions underlying what we have called modern utilitarianism—assumptions which present science, technology, work, and consumption as means to equalize, perfect, fulfill, and govern man; to place him in dominion over a predictable, orderly, and comfortable environment. At this point we have a clear choice: to work more arduously and compulsively to remediate and repair a social order based on the liberal utilitarian premises; or to stand back and begin anew from a fundamentally different posture. In the following chapters we attempt to do the latter; to suggest a new kind of thinking implied by an evolutionary approach to human society.

References

Bidney, David. *Theoretical Anthropology*. New York: Schocken, 1967.

Henderson, John. "On Quality of Life." Unpublished manuscript, Harvard University.

Henry, Jules. "Culture, Personality and Evolution." *American Anthropologist* 61, no. 2 (April 1959): pp. 221-26.

Kohlberg, Lawrence, and Mayer, Rochelle. "Development as the Aim of Education." *Harvard Educational Review* 42, no. 4 (November 1972): 449-96.

Redfield, Robert. *The Primitive World and its Transformations*. Ithaca, N.Y.: Cornell University Press, 1953.

Redfield, Robert. "The Universally Human and the Culturally Variable." *Journal of General Education* 10, no. 3 (July 1957): 150-60.

Wallace, Anthony F. C. *Culture and Personality* (2nd ed.). New York: Random House, 1970.

PART II

Dimensions of Quality of Life

4

The Potentialities of Human Nature

In this book we are attempting to present a way of looking at the human species which will emphasize criteria for judging quality of life and the evolutionary limitations placed on man in his quest for a positive life. The most basic source of these limitations is in man's nature itself. In a very direct way man's potentialities are limited by the physical equipment that has evolved with him over the millions of years life has been transforming itself on this planet. In a more obvious way this equipment includes prehensile forelimbs, bipedalism, and a highly differentiated central nervous system which is capable of complex information storage and problem-solving. In a somewhat less obvious way, man is a species with a large number of social capacities and tendencies, some of which he shares with his primate neighbors: temporal biological rhythms, the capacity and need for physical and emotional attachments, the tendency to create and teach stable role patterns, the tendency to polarize social life in terms of ingroup-amity—outgroup-enmity, and the need to legitimate social patterns with cultural rules overtly expressed in cognitive statements and symbolic gesture and celebration.

To move directly from statements about human nature—tendencies, capacities, instincts, or the like—to supporting evidence, illustrations, or social implications short circuits a number of significant and clarifying analytic categories. We think that man's nature—both its limits and flexibilities—is expressed in any setting through four channels or subsystems: environment, culture, social structure, and personality (see figure 4.1).

These channels suggest a limited set of structured potentials through which the full range of human possibilities can be described. It assumes, for example, that male-female dyads, nuclear or restricted families, full or extended families, bands or villages are natural human social forms each of which has special limiting characteristics. It is possible to imagine social forms in which males and females relate promiscuously, or adults and young people relate only casually and randomly, or adolescent females direct and control all others. It happens, however, that these structures rarely occur.

We assume that the same kinds of limited possibilities occur for personality, culture, and environment. Regarding personality, for example, Fromm says:

Freud's clinical descriptions of the oral-receptive, oral-exploitative, and anal character seem to us essentially correct and confirmed by experiences in the analysis of individuals, as well as analytical research into the character structure of groups. (Fromm and Maccoby 1970, p. 13)

Freud's classification refers, of course, to only one complex dimension of human personality.

Below we shall suggest subsets within these channels. Conceptually it is important to understand that the channels are present and limiting because of the underlying characteristics of the species. If we hypothesize, for example, with Wallace (1970), that age and sex are related to social hierarchy, we would expect to find this fact represented in social structures (families, communities); in culture (beliefs about who is in authority); in personality (some types would be predisposed in voice, gesture, and manner to express dominant behavior; some types would be predisposed to express submissive behavior); as well as in the way technology is organized. Furthermore, it is critical

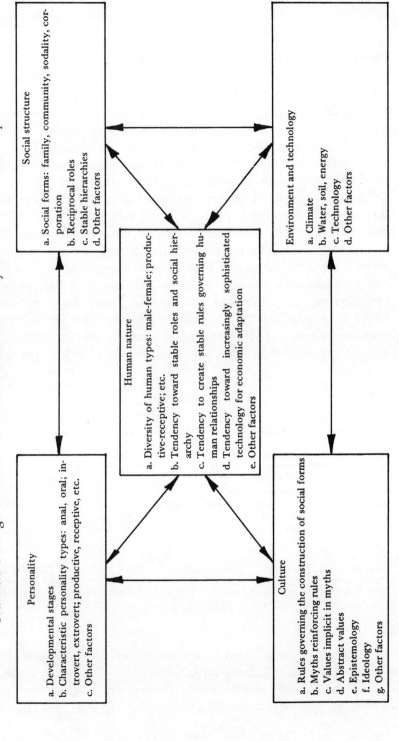

Figure 4.1

Channels Through Which the Limits and Potentialities of Human Nature Are Expressed

Social structure

a. Social forms: family, community, sodality, corporation
b. Reciprocal roles
c. Stable hierarchies
d. Other factors

Environment and technology

a. Climate
b. Water, soil, energy
c. Technology
d. Other factors

Human nature

a. Diversity of human types: male-female; productive-receptive; etc.
b. Tendency toward stable roles and social hierarchy
c. Tendency to create stable rules governing human relationships
d. Tendency toward increasingly sophisticated technology for economic adaptation
e. Other factors

Personality

a. Developmental stages
b. Characteristic personality types: anal, oral; introvert, extrovert; productive, receptive, etc.
c. Other factors

Culture

a. Rules governing the construction of social forms
b. Myths reinforcing rules
c. Values implicit in myths
d. Abstract values
e. Epistemology
f. Ideology
g. Other factors

to understand, as the above example suggests, that the channels through which human tendencies are expressed are interrelated—not independent. Social structures must take account of variations in personality; culture tends to reinforce social structure; human technology demands certain types of social structures, and so on. High quality of life presumably occurs only when the channels are related in complex ways, for example, when there are sufficiently varied social forms (including diverse and reciprocal social roles) to include the full range of human personality types; when the culture is loose enough to accommodate this diversity but defined enough to give direction and meaning to people's lives; when technology has created sufficient economic wherewithal to meet minimal human needs, but not impose overwhelming amounts of alienating machinery (e.g., factories, office buildings) on human lives. These distinctions are, of course, commonly made by social systems analysts. (See, for example, Parsons 1971.) Parsons attempts to link *subsystems* through which human behavior is channeled with *functional requirements* of human societies. His classic set of analytic relationships is summarized in table 4.1. Our own analysis suggests that there is no

Table 4.1
Parsons' Paradigm

	Subsystems	Primary function	Structural components	Aspects of developmental process
Social	Societal community	Integration	Norms	Inclusion
Cultural	Pattern maintenance	Pattern maintenance	Values	Value generalization
Personality	Polity	Goal attainment	Collectivities	Differentiation
Behavioral organism	Economy	Adaptation	Roles	Adaptive upgrading

Source: Adapted from Talcott Parsons, *The System of Modern Societies* (Englewood Cliffs, New Jersey: Prentice-Hall, 1971): pp. 6, 11.

intrinsic relationship between specific functional requirements of a society—economics (adaptation), politics (decision making), ideology (belief and values)—and the societal subsystems discussed here. That is, we do not see human adaptation, for example, as intrinsically linked or parallel with only the economic system (what we would call environment and technology).

Environment and Technology

A basic limiting factor in human society is the level of support offered by the environment and the extent to which environment has or can be adapted by technology for human survival and comfort. What man needs for survival is, of course, problematical, but there are obvious necessities: food, air, water, shelter, and usually external energy in the form of domestic animals, wind and water power, fossil fuels, etc. Beyond these environmental or material requirements, what man calls poverty is somewhat relative to what his neighbor has. It is clear, for example, that the early Eskimos lived on the margin of successful adaptation. Minor changes in environmental pressures or technology might lead to extinction or to a serious depletion of the population. (Their loving abandonment of old people is legendary.) It is difficult to argue, however, that the Eskimo had a lower quality of life than, for example, Banfield's Italian peasant who probably had less environmental pressure (Banfield 1958). The peasant of Montegrano lives in a marginal environment.

If all the measures that have been suggested here [for improving the standard of living] were pursued actively and effectively, there would be no dramatic improvement in the economic position of the village. . . . Under the best of circumstances, it will be a very long time before the people of Montegrano have enough to eat. (p. 166)

But at least as important as the stark environmental pressures are the relative standards of the "good life" which the peasant has in his head.

By the standards of the larger society, the peasant's work, food, and clothing all symbolize his degradation. It is on this account, as much as for biological reasons, that he finds them unsatisfying and even hateful. Italians attach great importance to being mannerly (*civile*); the peasant feels that he is the very opposite: association with earth and animals, he thinks, has made him dirty and animal-like. . . .

La miseria, it seems safe to conclude, arises as much or more from social as from biological deprivations. (p. 65)

Technology is currently seen as the destiny and salvation of man's ills, on the one hand, and the undermining of more primitive conditions for a decent and humane life on the other. There is little doubt that man has the capacity to create destructive, ugly, and demeaning technology, just as he has the capacity to create destructive culture or sadistic personality. Moving from intuitive quality-of-life judgments regarding environment and technology to systematic or persuasive criteria, however, is difficult. The Goodmans (1960, p. 171) deal with this issue:

SOME ELEMENTARY PRINCIPLES FOR THE MORAL SELECTION OF MACHINES

1. Utility (functionalist beauty)
2. Transparency of operation
   A. Repairability by the average well-educated person (freedom)
   B. Constructivist beauty
3. Relative independence of machine from non-ubiquitous power
4. Proportion between total effort and utility (neo-functionalist beauty)

Mumford makes a similar search for standards by which to judge not only the quality but the limits of technology. He sees the positive limits in terms of what he calls "dynamic equilibrium."

Dynamic equilibrium, not infinite progress, is the mark of the opening age: balance, not rapid one-sided advance: conservation, not reckless pillage. The parallel between neolithic and neotechnic times holds even here: for the main advances which were consolidated in neolithic times remained stable, with minor variations within the pattern, for between 2500 and 3500 years. Once we have generally reached a new technical plateau we may remain on that level with very minor ups and downs for thousands of years. What are the implications of this approaching equilibrium?

First: equilibrium in the environment. This means first the restoration of the balance between man and nature. The conservation and restoration of soils, the re-growth wherever this is expedient and possible, of the forest cover to provide shelter for wild life and to maintain man's primitive background as a source of recreation, whose importance increases in proportion to the refinement of his cultural heritage. . . .

Second, equilibrium in industry and agriculture. . . .

This state of balance and equilibrium—regional, industrial, agricultural, communal—will work a further change within the domain of the machine itself: a change of tempo. . . . It is not the absolute speed assumed by any part of the machine system that indicates efficiency: what is important is the relative speed of the various parts with a view to the ends to be accomplished: namely, the maintenance and development of human life. (1963, pp. 431-32)

Both the quality and quantity of man's control over his natural environment are complex and debatable issues. What seems clear, however, is that modern societies often use technology and create environments with little or no regard for the requirements of man's underlying nature, aside from what seems comfortable or convenient in the most superficial way. One might entertain with some certainty, for example, the principle (as the Goodmans suggest) that technology which obscures or denies man's biological self is potentially dangerous and destructive. Seeing food only in its frozen or canned state obscures our absolute dependence on the sun for food; having waste products carted away in trucks or flushed down toilets and drains obscures the fact that we are intrinsically involved in a critical life-sustaining ecological chain. This latter illusion Slater calls the Toilet Assumption.

Prior to the widespread use of the flush toilet all of humanity was daily confronted with the immediate reality of human waste and its disposal. They knew where it was and how it got there. Nothing miraculously vanished. Excrement was conspicuously present in the outhouse or chamber pot, and the slops that went out the window went visibly and noticeably into the street. . . .

Our ideas about institutionalizing the aged, psychotic, retarded, and infirm are based on a pattern of thought that we might call the Toilet Assumption—the notion that unwanted matter, unwanted difficulties, unwanted complexities and obstacles will disappear if they are removed from our immediate field of vision. (1970, p. 15)

It is our position that there are environments and technology which are more and less consistent with underlying human requirements in much more profound ways than the superficial principles of comfort and convenience. The convenience of the garbage disposal and the flush toilet, for example, might well be weighed against the alienation caused by man living with the illusion that he has no waste products at all.

More important than simple statements we make about the material environment alone is the differential power of control over environment and technology various groups within the society exercise and for whose benefit that power and control are used. This, of course, is the thrust of Marxist thinking. The life one can imagine is a function of the material surroundings within which one finds oneself. Marx imagined beyond his immediate surroundings into a projective history, a history which had less to do with the tyranny of technology and the human systems which manage them and more to do with who had the power to control and benefit from the blessings of technology.

More recent analysts of postindustrial society seriously challenge the assumption that science and technology are value free—that it is only how humans use them that gives them normative significance. It is important to distinguish here between simplistic materialism—the idea that man is simply a conditioned product of his material surroundings—and the Faustian idea that man can be seduced into styles of life which emphasize materialism, consumerism, greed, and alienation from his natural sense of human sociality, cooperation, and relatedness to other forms of life and the broad conditions that sustain them. Man's vulnerability to seduction by technological and political power is perhaps the most serious threat to a decent quality of life in the contemporary world. From an evolutionary point of view, the problem is that man has never developed inhibitory mechanisms which move him to control or limit the size and complexity of his social and natural settings so they will be consistent with the scale of his hunter-gatherer past, the past within which much of his adaptive constitution was forged. Control of personal or private property, for example, is minimal for the hunter-gatherer, for there is little to control; there is little surplus wealth. Likewise, abusive and arbitrary use of political power is limited by the fact that humans live in small units; all know one another intimately; all share a sense of protective concern for all members of the band.

The problem of technology, then, is really grounded in man's paradoxical evolutionary development. He has the technical capacities—as well as an inclination to use them—to destroy the material and social conditions within which he can feel comfortable or, at least, adequate. Faced with increasing material wealth and social power made possible by the control of complex technology, he tends to create highly stratified societies, for which his hunter-gatherer past ill-equipped him. For, as Lenski notes, "if any single feature of the life of hunting and gathering societies has impressed itself upon observers, it is the relative equality of the members" (1966, p. 102).

Culture

With the exception of our concern for environment and technology, our distinctions between culture, social structure, and personality are much like those developed by Spiro. Spiro sees social systems (what we would call social structure) as "configurations of reciprocal roles which are shared by members of a group in virtue of their inheritance from a prior generation" (1972, p. 588). He states that there are three bases for such social systems or structures: genetic inheritance (as in the case of social insects); roles acquired through social learning (as in the case of some mammals, including primates); and roles inherited not through social learning, but which are symbolically prescribed. This latter potential is almost exclusive to man.

I would now argue . . . that culture consists, among other things, of the norms which govern social relationships; that these norms are to be distinguished analytically from that system of social relationships which may be termed the social system of a society; and that both are to be distinguished from personality, by which I understand the motivational system (including internalized norms) that characterize individuals. (p. 589)

Very generally, culture would be defined as implicit or explicit rules which channel behavior. In their most obvious form, they appear as prescriptions or proscriptions. They are, however, surrounded by belief systems or ideology which rationalize and set the rules in broader context—value statements, facts, generalizations, law, systematic social theory, philosophy, symbols, myths, history, folktales, as well as methods for validating and knowing.

If we construe culture as largely language or concept-bound, then human limits on culture are set by the way man uses language, symbols, and concepts. There is evidence that he has a universal grammar (Chomsky 1968). His nervous system is wired in a particular way which limits and determines his logical potential.

He tends toward a dichotomized construction of reality (George Kelly 1955), and perhaps even toward specific dichotomies such as good-bad, strong-weak, active-passive. He tends toward metaphor and analogy which links his experience with the natural phenomena around him (Jung 1968; Lévi-Strauss 1963). His thinking tends to function on a continuum from fluid imagery to sensory messages to very directed purposeful instrumental thinking (Jung).

The language characteristics seen as "human" vary considerably among individuals. There is, for example, a wide range of ability to think along the concrete-abstract dimension, or to create imagery in symbolic terms (e.g., poetry). Piaget (1955) has discovered a developmental sequence through which humans ordinarily pass in their ability to symbolize and "think about thinking." There are degrees to which individual humans internalize culture or rule-systems. For example, attitudes may be formed and shift because (1) one wishes to *comply* with a message source (presumably an authority), (2) one *identifies* with the message source, or (3) one has genuinely *internalized* the meaning and force of the message. Kohlberg and Mayer (1972) make a similar set of distinctions in their study of the way humans handle moral dilemma stories verbally or conceptually. Moral judgments may have a "preconventional basis" (the rightness of a position is justified on the basis of force, fear of punishment, etc.); a "conventional basis" (the rightness is justified on the basis of group consensus, opinion, or specific rules which maintain order within the group); or a "postconventional basis" (the rightness is justified on the basis of an abstract principle of justice such as utilitarianism). The extent to which culture is conscious or unconscious is, of course, a central concern of depth psychologists. Conflicts between culture and personal drives are presumably often handled by unconscious coping and defense mechanisms such as denial, repression, overcompensation, and the like.

Universal ideological dimensions of culture have been schematized by Florence Kluckhohn (1961), and are shown in table 4.2. Human cultures can also be described in terms of more abstract qualities: for example, *comprehensiveness* (extent to which potential or real social behavior patterns are covered by rules, values, or ideology); *level of specificity* (how detailed and delineated are the rules); and *level of integration* (extent to which rules in various behavioral domains such as work, love, religion, and play, are interrelated).

Judgments about the quality of life which various societies encourage, allow, or prevent are often difficult if not impossible to make within the framework of culture as a single dimension of a society. In general, such judgments apply to sociocultural or culture-and-personality relationships. One might, however, hazard the following speculations.

Table 4.2
Dimensions of Culture

Orientation	Postulated range of variations					
	Evil		Mixture of good and evil		Good	
	Mutable	Immutable	Neutral Mutable	Immutable	Mutable	Immutable
Human nature						
Man-nature	Subjugation-to-nature		Harmony-with-nature		Mastery-over-nature	
Time	Past		Present		Future	
Activity	Being		Being-in-becoming		Doing	
Relational	Lineality		Collaterality		Individualism	

Notes:

(1) This table is based on the following assumptions:
  (a) There is an ordered variation in value-orientation systems;
  (b) There is a limited number of common human problems for which all peoples at times must find some solution;
  (c) All alternatives of all solutions are present in all societies at all times but are differentially preferred.

(2) Explanation of terms which are not self-evident:
  (a) Being orientation—preference for kind of activity which is a spontaneous expression of what is conceived to be "given" in the human personality;
  (b) Being-in-becoming orientation—emphasizes that kind of activity which has as its goal the development of all aspects of the self as an integrated whole;
  (c) Doing orientation—demand for the kind of activity which results in accomplishments that are measurable by standards conceived to be external to the acting individual;
  (d) Individualism—each individual's responsibility to the total society and his place in it are defined in terms of goals and roles which are structured as autonomous;
  (e) Collateral—primacy of the goals and welfare of the laterally extended group;
  (f) Lineal—group goals again have primacy; in addition, continuity through time and ordered positional succession within the group become crucial issues.

Source: Florence Kluckhohn and Fred Strodtbeck, *Variations in Value Orientations* (Westport, Conn.: Greenwood, 1973): p. 12.

1. Culture which seriously inhibits the normal functioning of basic human drives is destructive (e.g., rules preventing normal heterosexual relations until ten years after puberty, rules which prevent outgroup aggression).

2. Culture which greatly enhances the value of behavior which is difficult for large numbers of people to learn or perform is destructive (e.g., the rule that all humans should have control over reading and writing complex and abstract language; rules which press for transcendent levels of human consciousness).

3. Culture which legitimizes human exploitation is destructive (e.g., rules which allow or require some humans to live in poverty while others live in luxury).

Social Structure

A third analytic component or behavioral channel in a social system we would call *social structure*. Social structures can be construed in individual terms as roles or learned behavior patterns which occur predictably and regularly through time regardless of what individual plays them. Structure can be thought of more generally as sets of interrelated or reciprocal roles which together constitute *institutions*. The family might be seen as an institution in which various age and kinship roles are filled; a factory might be seen as an institution in which various authority-power and instrumental work roles are filled.

A continuing source of ambiguity is the extent to which we see institutions as universal, that is, occurring across different societies versus the extent to which we see them as the invention of a specific society or type of society. Families, villages, and cities are often seen as universals; schools, factories, and offices are often seen as society —or culture—specific. We make the distinction between general social forms and specific institutions. We maintain that social forms are universal types of collective behavior which man will generally create under certain specified circumstances. We would suggest the following, for example, as universal social forms:

Intense dyads (lovers, marriage partners, friends, parent-child)
Nuclear families
Sodalities (work groups, friendship groups)
"Bands," neighborhoods, villages

Corporate organizations (factories, businesses, offices, schools, etc.)

Preindustrial cities

"Modern" societies

Universal social forms which human societies create can be described along a number of dimensions, for example, complexity, basis of cohesion or integration, degree of integration or cohesion, the looseness or tightness of behavior patterns, or the harshness or leniency of sanctions used to enforce prescribed patterns. In general, more complex social forms use a greater variety of methods of integration or cohesion. We would consider the following mechanisms as representing man's more important integrative capacities:

Biosocial bonding (heterosexual bonding, cooperative work bonding, nurturance-dependency bonding)

Dominance hierarchies

Division of labor

Cultural codes or formal political structures legitimizing and rationalizing dominance hierarchies

Negotiated contracts

The concept of tight versus loose social structures seems to us especially important because of its relationship to more primitive societies characterized by tribal or band relationships and more modern societies characterized by corporate organizations. It is not necessarily the case that communal or tribal relationships are loose or tight, but rather that they can be, while corporate organizations always tend toward highly bureaucratic structured relationships.

Looseness or tightness of social structures may be characterized as: (1) the extent to which roles or role relationships within a social system are clear and explicit; (2) the extent to which roles are closely related to or locked into a set of reciprocal relationships; (3) the extent to which there are limited categories of people who can play roles (e.g., is the biological father the only person who can play a child's father-role, or can the role easily be played by uncles, older siblings, etc.); (4) the extent to which there is behavioral variation or flexibility within a role; (5) the extent to which there are harsh or lenient sanctions (and forgiveness) for deviation from role expectations.

The general issue of tight and loose social structures was examined in an essay by Embree (1969, pp. 3-15) in which he compared

Japanese and Thai village life. The essay sparked considerable controversy because of the seeming contradiction between social structure
as a categorical characteristic of a social system and the implication
that "tight" equalled "more" and "loose" equalled "less." If social
systems have, by definition, social structures, you cannot have more
or less of a social structure—you simply have different types of structures.

Putting this somewhat academic argument aside, we would
maintain that the tight-loose distinction makes a good deal of sense,
as suggested by our defining characteristics given above. Piker (1969,
pp. 61-76), for example, states that role demands for Thai villagers
are loose for a number of reasons:

1. Civil servants are given much paid leave (job truancy is legitimated);

2. It is difficult to offend someone beyond forgiveness;

3. There are few stable expectations about lifestyles others are
to maintain over the long run (except for ritualized politeness in
face-to-face settings);

4. There is relatively open social mobility.

Piker then concludes:

... these findings suggest two conclusions with respect to the correspondence
between personality and the social system in rural Thai society: if such correspondence does in fact obtain, it consists largely, first, of the adequacy of the
sum total of institutions for the expression of those diverse personality traits
that are widespread in the population and, second, of the accessibility of these
institutions to the bearers of diverse personality traits. (p. 74)

Phillips made a related comment on Thai personality:

... cooperative, mutually expectable interaction as we know it in the West does
not "simply take place" in Bang Chan. Rather, there is always the intervening
factor of whether individuals want it to take place. . . . It is the individual that is
primary, not the social relationship. The assumption is: "If he did not do it, he
must have had his own good reason." (1965, p. 60)

Both writers seem to suggest considerably looser role demands on the
individual personality than in highly organized modern societies.
Schooling in modern societies, for example, makes uniform demands
on very diverse personalities, especially for younger children.

While the social structure of societies or groups can be described along such dimensions as degree of integration, basis of integration, or looseness or tightness of structure, statuses or roles themselves can be described along another set of meaningful dimensions first developed by Parsons.

[Parsons] uses a set of 5 "pattern variables" to distinguish the aspects of any social relationship. According to Parsons, each time we act, and in each role in which we act, we are, in effect, emphasizing one or another of the 5 basic divisions. If a role is *specific*, our relationship is limited to one particular narrowly defined exchange; if it is *diffuse*, our involvement will extend over a wide variety of problems or relationships. We stress either *affectivity* (that is, feeling, emotion, and gratification), or *affective neutrality*, which means we place more emphasis on instrumental or moral considerations. We manifest *particularism* when we give special consideration to people because of their relationship to us, whereas if we evidence *universalism*, we treat more or less alike all who come before us in a given status-position. If my treatment of you is mainly on the basis of what you are in yourself, in contrast to what you do or have done, I stress *quality* over *performance* (ascribed status vs. achieved status). When my concern is mainly to advance the goals of the group, I display a *collectivity-orientation*, whereas if I am most concerned to advance my own interests through our relationship, I stress *self-orientation*. Described in these terms, the relations of husband and wife, and indeed all nuclear family relations, tend to be diffuse, affective, and particularistic, and reflect stress on quality and collectivity-orientation. The relationship between a clerk and a customer would be at the opposite pole on each dimension. (Inkeles 1964, p. 74)

As Inkeles suggests, Parsons' pattern variables are obviously derived from an intuitive sense that so-called primary groups (groups with sustained face-to-face relationships) are somehow fundamentally different from secondary groups.

With this level of analytic differentiation, we might speculate about what characteristics of social structure tend toward higher quality of life and which tend to diminish the quality of life in human societies. One might ask the following questions:

1. To what extent is the availability of primordial social forms such as the nuclear family, the extended family, sodalities, and small communities or neighborhoods a prerequisite for emotional health, security, and adequate societal integration?

2. To what extent can humans function with reasonable equan-

imity or without great stress in social forms which require competing types of social integration, for example, in neighborhoods integrated by sexual, kinship, and sentiment bonding and at the same time in corporate organizations (stores, offices, factories, schools) where integration is maintained through cultural codes, centralized control of sanctions, and negotiated contracts?

3. To what extent can humans function with equanimity or without great stress in a variety of social forms which are either highly integrated (as a religious commune) or highly fragmented (as suburban life in modern society)?

4. To what extent are societies or social forms characterized as having tight or loose or moderate social structures conducive to high or low human stress?

5. To what extent does role diffuseness or specificity or the looseness or tightness of roles lead to higher or lower stress?

6. To what extent do institutions having social forms which mix primary and secondary characteristics (e.g., schools and small family businesses) generate greater or lesser stress compared with institutions which have pure forms (e.g., family, or large corporate business)?

Personality

Personality refers to underlying motivational structures or overt behavior patterns which characterize individual humans. The forces which shape personality and affect individual behavior are multiple: human constitution (via inheritance, imprinting, or early biosocial learning); socialization (learned orientations toward basic human functions such as work, love and attachment, play, dream and fantasy); the interaction between constitution and socialization, especially during critical developmental periods in the human career; and finally the press of sociocultural systems (institutions, roles, etc.) within which the individual always functions.

A central tension in any human society is the fact that culturally defined or general rules, ideology, and roles must be channeled through diverse human beings. Wallace has described this tension by suggesting that there are two ways of looking at culture and society: one as the "replication of uniformity," and another as "the organization of diversity." From the point of view of the "replication of uniformity":

the society may be regarded as culturally homogeneous and the individuals will be expected to share a uniform nuclear character. If a near-perfect correspondence between culture and individual nuclear character is assumed, the structural relation between the two becomes nonproblematical, and the interest of processual research lies rather in the mechanisms of socialization by which each generation becomes, culturally and characterologically, a replica of its predecessors. (1970, pp. 22-23)

From the point of view of "the organization of diversity":

Culture . . . becomes not so much a superorganic entity, but policy, tacitly and gradually concocted by groups of people for the furtherance of their interests, and contract, established by practice, between and among individuals to organize their strivings into mutually facilitating equivalence structures. (p. 24)

We are here focusing on human diversity as the central problem of personality, that is, we need to categorize the major sources of variation through which different aspects of human nature are channeled. We would suggest two significant categories of variation: (1) the salience and complexity with which different levels (in the Freudian sense) of personality are expressed; and (2) the differences in common human characteristics such as age, sex, temperament, talent, etc. Regarding the first type of variation one can imagine that human personality is constructed as a set of layers:

Cultural values and rules, which rationalize role behavior

↑

Learned social roles through which underlying personality type is expressed

↑

Patterned constitutional tendencies interacting with environment (e.g., oral or anal personalities)

↑

Universal human strivings (e.g., love, work, meaning)

↑

Undifferentiated libidinal energy

Given this model, one can imagine basic human strivings as more or less crudely or directly expressed, or as more or less refined by socialized roles or cultural values.

One can speculate that there are archetypal social callings which, when matched with archetypal personality types, require less role behavior and are a more direct expression of underlying impulses.

The clown or buffoon, the reflective teacher, the priest or shaman, the doctor or healer—all may be an expression of such role archetypes. When the bland unquestioning personality type, for example, takes on the work of reflective teacher, we would guess that the behavior is much more an expression of a highly socialized role than the underlying need to probe the meaning of his social or natural world.

Personalities vary in their degree of socialization potential; some are relatively easily socialized; some are socialized with great difficulty. Relating the concept of socialization potential to quality of life, one might argue that a higher quality of life is possible in a society in which humans who socialize with great difficulty can select themselves into roles which are reasonably consistent with their underlying constitutional tendencies; or conversely, a society in which those humans who socialize easily are not required to creatively fashion innovative roles. If normal human variation yields more clowns, buffoons, or comedians, for example, than can be accommodated in a society (especially where there is the technology of mass media), and comedians are then forced to become bank clerks or shoe salesmen (more exacting and highly socialized roles), presumably there is considerable human stress. Or conversely, if society demands a great many questioning, interesting, and charismatic teachers who cannot be found, their places must be filled by over-socialized bank clerks.

The second category of human variation includes such characteristics as age, sex, temperament, talents, etc. We might suggest the following as examples.

1. *Energy level*
As Robert White states:

When one assists at the birth of a litter of puppies it is impossible not to see differences among the new arrivals with respect to activity and vigor. The mother dog notices the differences and may even callously push aside a puppy that does not meet her minimum standards of responsiveness. . . . It is hard . . . to think of high vitality and zest as traits that could be wholly learned if they were not built into the organism in the first place. Some babies do not display these qualities and develop in a consistently quieter and less colorful way. (1966, pp. 236-37)

2. *Sensory-conceptual modes of relating to the environment*
There is some systematic evidence and a good deal of intuitive

evidence that different humans relate to the environment through emphasis on different sensory processes. Three strong candidates for "relational modes" are *kinesthetic-motor, sensory,* and *conceptual-verbal.* These terms might be defined by considering very talented people who express themselves through each mode. Professional athletes and dancers have a dominant kinesthetic-motor way of relating. Painters and film-makers have extraordinary sensory sensibilities. Scientists and academics relate in a more conceptual-verbal mode. Obviously any individual is a mix of these (and other) modes of relating, all of which are, to a considerable extent, subject to learning.

3. *Interpersonal tendencies*

It is possible to make a case for extroversion-introversion as a dominant dimension along which individuals relate to one another.

4. *Physique and temperament*

William Sheldon has probably done the most systematic study on the relationship between physique or body type and temperament. White summarizes Sheldon's work as follows:

Sheldon reached the conclusion . . . that temperament could be described as having three main components. The first, which he called *visceratonia,* was represented by a cluster of traits such as relaxation, love of comfort, amiability, and a need for affection and approval of others. The second component, named *somatotonia,* was characterized by vigorous assertiveness, a love of action, and a dominating but somewhat insensitive attitude toward other people. The third component, *cerebrotonia,* had as its chief traits a tense vigilance, sensitiveness, a tendency for action to be inhibited, and a certain ineptitude in social situations. All three components are present in everyone, but in different relative strengths. . . .

Sheldon seemed to give his components of temperament a more clearly constitutional cast when he developed a systematic scheme for the measurement of physique, and related visceratonia to a soft rounded physique, somatotonia to a solid muscular one, and cerebrotonia to a slender, lightly built frame. (1966, pp. 231-32)

5. *Male-femaleness*

While there is considerable controversy over the extent to which personality differences between sexes and the masculinity-femininity dimension within each sex is biologically or socioculturally based, substantial differences seem universal. Males, for example, seem more object- and task-oriented, more aggressive, and have more focused sexual interests. Females appear more people-oriented, have stronger interpersonal needs, seem less openly aggressive, and have more diffusely expressed sexuality.

6. *The human career cycle*

While it is obvious that infants, children, and old people have specific, constitutionally-based developmental resources and needs, there is little systematic information on differences among other adults at different points in the human career. Erikson (1964) has suggested that developmental crises occur throughout life, and that each crisis requires a new integration with previous developmental problems. We would speculate that the orientation of American society (and of modern societies more generally) is toward construing all adult humans as equal and interchangeable—hence we become somewhat insensitive to age differences in our public discourse. There is, of course, a tremendous cosmetic industry which attempts to make plausible the illusion that everyone is the same age—through wigs, hair coloring, face lifting, cosmetics, and the like.

We would argue that the essential criterion for quality of life for personality is the extent to which an authentic self can be constructed and expressed (at whatever age). The primary problem for the realization of such authentic personalities is the tendency of culture to construct a range of worthy types of people which is more limited than the normal range of differences which commonly occur within the species. Social roles, moreover, tend to be ordered on a hierarchy of privilege or prestige such that some individuals are constantly tempted to "not be themselves" in order to gain prestige or avoid discrimination (e.g., the friendly generous teacher who is told to be tough with rowdy students). In this sense the potential for authentic personalities within a society is very much dependent on the range of roles within the social structure, the privileges associated with these roles, and the definition of these roles by the culture.

Interaction Among Personality, Culture, and Social Structure

Disciplinarians in the various social sciences constantly war over the relative importance of various subsystems of human society. Psychologists tend to stress the significance of individual learning, especially early childhood experience. Anthropologists stress the impact of common culture, often assuming a level of cultural uniformity that defies common-sense experience. Sociologists and social anthropologists stress the importance of institutions and roles, construing the significance of personality simply as a constellation of internalized others; or they assume that different personality types cancel each other out, and thus account for no great impact on a society.

This kind of analytic fragmentation leads toward several kinds of social mischief. First, it leads individual social scientists or "schools" of social science to grossly oversell the level of reliability with which any particular analytic orientation or theory can make a useful contribution to theories of social amelioration. Behavioristic psychology (Skinner) and more recently developmental psychology (Kohlberg) are examples.

Second, disciplinary blinders often prevent social scientists from developing more complex theories which would square better with the realities of common-sense human experience. A case in point where disciplinary blinders have been somewhat removed is Fromm's theory of social character. Fromm (1970) suggests that there are relationships between personal constitution, early socialization experience, and sociocultural press. The socialization requirements which would allow an individual to achieve authentic love and productive work, for example, may be very different for the tender-minded, sensitive person than for the aggressive, task-oriented person. And more importantly, sociocultural constraints in the larger society may prevent one or the other type from achieving an authentic self because of the press it makes on the primary group environment. Social stratification which places different values on people at different levels of society (on their work, their lifestyles, their values, their speech, etc.) may in fact be a way of sorting out people according to their constitutional abilities to adapt to the dominant cultural values and structural constraints in the society. It may then be more realistic to talk about *modal adaptations* to a given sociocultural system than to talk about modal personalities.

Conclusion

We have taken the general position that human nature is channelled through four societal subsystems—environment and technology, culture, social structure, and personality—and that each component or subsystem has natural limits and tendencies which bear on the quality of life in society. Describing or developing these components is a way of elaborating our position regarding the more general limits placed on man by the direction of his own evolution. Regarding technology, for example, man can respect or ignore his own evolutionary connectedness with his natural environment, but if he ignores it, there is a cost in quality of life. Regarding culture, man has the capacity to create, understand, and maintain certain limited kinds of rules, and quality of life is improved if the rules are consistent with such basic needs as personal security and support. (The cultural rule in this society that all worthy people must have gainful employment, for example, is probably destructive of quality of life.) Regarding social structure, man has the capacity to create certain limited types of social forms which provide stable social roles. When certain primordial forms are destroyed, such as the extended family or neighborhood, he becomes anxious and insecure. In terms of personality, broad natural diversity requires a breadth and looseness of culture and social form.

Our central point is that the concept of channels suggests that under certain conditions human behavior and institutions flow in some directions more easily than others. The irony of the human condition is that despite his reflective nature, man often creates destructive environments, cultures, social structures, and personalities, and thus directs his nature away from its more obvious channels. And it is for this reason we find the concept of quality of life an issue at all.

References

Banfield, Edward C. *The Moral Basis of a Backward Society.* New York: The Free Press, 1958.

Chomsky, Noam. *Language and Mind.* New York: Harcourt, Brace & World, 1968.

Embree, John F. "Thailand—A Loosely Structured Social System." *Loosely Structured Social Systems* (Cultural Report Series no. 17), edited by Hans-Dieter Evers. New Haven, Conn.: Yale University Southeast Asia Studies, 1969.

Erikson, Erik H. *Childhood and Society.* New York: Norton, 1964.

Fromm, Erich, and Maccoby, Michael. *Social Character in a Mexican Village.* Englewood Cliffs, N.J.: Prentice-Hall, 1970.

Goodman, Percival, and Goodman, Paul. *Communitas: Means of Livelihood and Ways of Life.* New York: Random House, 1960.

Inkeles, Alex. *What Is Sociology?* Englewood Cliffs, N.J.: Prentice-Hall, 1964.

Jung, Carl G. *Man and His Symbols.* New York: Dell, 1968.

Kelly, George A. *The Psychology of Personal Constructs*. New York: Norton, 1955.

Kluckhohn, Florence, and Strodtbeck, Fred. *Variations in Value Orientations*. Westport, Conn.: Greenwood, 1973.

Kohlberg, Lawrence, and Mayer, Rochelle. "Development as the Aim of Education." *Harvard Educational Review* 42, no. 4 (November 1972): 449-96.

Lenski, Gerhard E. *Power and Privilege*. New York: McGraw-Hill, 1966.

Lévi-Strauss, Claude. *Structural Anthropology*. New York: Basic Books, 1963.

Mumford, Lewis. *Technics and Civilization*. New York: Harcourt, Brace & World, 1963.

Parsons, Talcott. *The System of Modern Societies*. Englewood Cliffs, N.J.: Prentice-Hall, 1971.

Phillips, Herbert P. *Thai Peasant Personality*. Berkeley: University of California Press, 1965.

Piaget, Jean. *Language and Thought of the Child*. New York: New American Library, 1955.

Piker, Steven. " 'Loose Structure' and the Analysis of Thai Social Organization." *Loosely Structured Social Systems* (Cultural Report Series no. 17), edited by Hans-Dieter Evers. New Haven, Conn.: Yale University Southeast Asia Studies, 1969.

Slater, Philip E. *The Pursuit of Loneliness*. Boston: Beacon Press, 1970.

Spiro, Melford. "An Overview and Suggested Reorientation." *Psychological Anthropology*, edited by Francis L. K. Hsu. Cambridge, Mass.: Schenkman, 1972.

Wallace, Anthony F. C. *Culture and Personality* (2nd ed.). New York: Random House, 1970.

White, Robert W. *Lives in Progress*. New York: Holt, Rinehart & Winston, 1966.

5

The Functional Requirements of Human Society

We have attempted to derive criteria for quality of life by looking at underlying qualities of human nature directly or by looking at characteristics of channels through which human nature is expressed in society, such as environment-technology, personality, social structure, and culture. Another way of deriving quality-of-life criteria is by looking at the functional requirements of man or society or man-in-society. Maslow, for example, has developed what he calls a hierarchy of human needs (see figure 5.1).

The functionalists in sociology and anthropology have attempted to develop a similar list of requirements for society. (One thinks especially of Parsons and Malinowski.) More recently Aberle et al. (1950, pp. 100-11) developed a statement of what they call the "functional prerequisites of a society." These functional prerequisites include:

Figure 5.1
Abraham Maslow's Hierarchy of Needs

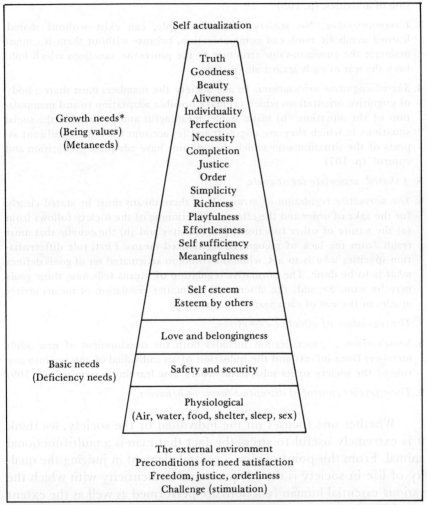

Self actualization

Growth needs*
(Being values)
(Metaneeds)

Truth
Goodness
Beauty
Aliveness
Individuality
Perfection
Necessity
Completion
Justice
Order
Simplicity
Richness
Playfulness
Effortlessness
Self sufficiency
Meaningfulness

Self esteem
Esteem by others

Love and belongingness

Basic needs
(Deficiency needs)

Safety and security

Physiological
(Air, water, food, shelter, sleep, sex)

The external environment
Preconditions for need satisfaction
Freedom, justice, orderliness
Challenge (stimulation)

*Growth needs are all of equal importance (not hierarchical)

Source: Frank G. Goble, *The Third Force* (New York: Grossman Publishers, 1970): p. 50.
Copyright 1970 by Thomas Jefferson Research Center.

1. *Provision for adequate relationship to the environment and for sexual recruitment*. . . . providing for basic physiological needs of enough adult members to insure reproduction and to man the essential status positions. (p. 104)

2. *Role differentiation and role assignment*. . . . the systematic and stable division of activities. (p. 105)

3. *Communication.* No society, however simple, can exist without shared, learned symbolic modes of communication, because without them it cannot maintain the common-value structure or the protective sanctions which hold back the war of each against all. (p. 106)

4. *Shared cognitive orientations.* In any society the members must share a body of cognitive orientations which (a) make possible adaptation to and manipulation of the situation; (b) make stable, meaningful and predictable the social situations in which they are engaged; and (c) account for those significant aspects of the situation over which they do not have adequate predication and control. (p. 107)

5. *A shared, articulate set of goals.*

6. *The normative regulation of means.* That these means must be stated clearly for the sake of order and the effective functioning of the society follows from (a) the nature of other functional prerequisites and (b) the *anomie* that must result from the lack of recognized legitimized means. First, role differentiation specifies *who* is to act, while the common articulated set of goals defines *what* is to be done. The normative regulation of means tells *how* those goals may be won. Second, the absence of normative regulation of means invites apathy or the war of each against all. (p. 108)

7. *The regulation of affective expression.*

8. *Socialization.* . . . socialization includes both the development of new adult members from infants and the induction of an individual of any age into any role of the society or its subsystems where new learning is required. (p. 109)

9. *The effective control of disruptive forms of behavior.*

Whether one focuses on the individual or the society, we think it is extremely useful to stress the fact that man is a multifunctional animal. From this point of view a central element in judging the quality of life in society is the adequacy and authenticity with which the various essential human functions are performed as well as the extent to which they are carried on in some reasonably balanced and integrated relationship to each other.

Specifically, our list of functions includes the following:

1. Attachment, love, bonding;
2. Adaptation, work, coping;

3. Renewal, play, sleep, relaxation, fantasy, dreaming;

4. Planning, deciding, conflict resolution;

5. Celebration or acting out of universal events in the human condition, story telling, drama, sports, dance;

6. Creation of myth and meaning: placing man in relationship to past and future events or human and cosmic events.

We are not concerned here with an elegant scheme or a carefully developed rationale to justify our particular functional categories— any such selection and categorization of "basic human functions" is somewhat arbitrary. We are concerned that one look at the requirements of society as a whole, as several interrelated functions. As O'Dea states:

... functional theory sees society as an ongoing equilibrium of social institutions which pattern human activity in terms of shared norms, held to be legitimate and binding by the human participants themselves. This complex of institutions, which as a whole constitute the *social system*, is such that each part (each institutionalized element) is interdependent with all the other parts and that changes in any part affect the others, and the condition of the system as a whole. (1966, p. 2)

This "unity-equilibrium" viewpoint in functional theory bears directly on the problem of inventing or maintaining constructive culture. It assumes that there is a limited fund of human energy to be expended; energy not spent in the fulfillment of one function will presumably be expended on another. The critical point, however, is that functional theory assumes that a set of problems are continuously present and must be solved or at least handled simultaneously, and that when some problems are not adequately resolved, energy will be diverted to the unsolved problems. If inadequate resolutions persist, compensatory mechanisms come into play, comparable on the societal level to adjustive or defensive mechanisms hypothesized by psychoanalytic theory for individual personality. And like Freudian defense mechanisms, societal compensatory mechanisms do not really solve problems; they simply expend human energy, often in a dysfunctional way, so that one has the illusion of successful coping. At a personal level, for example, the anal-compulsive individual may reduce anxiety by constantly washing his hands, but the underlying problem (for example, guilt over unconscious strivings toward sex or autonomy) is never touched. Likewise, at the societal level if there is no adequate meaning system or symbolic ritual to explain or work through inevitable conditions of human pain (e.g., personal loss of a friend, climatic catastrophes, sickness and death), unrelieved emotional pain or anxiety may be suppressed by compulsive work. The work will drain off energy, but the nagging concern over the meaning of the human suffering will continue in a potentially destructive way. For as work itself loses meaning, it may take the threat of survival itself (through fabricated fears of internal subversion or external conquest) to keep the system going. From this point of view war may be construed as a compensatory mechanism integrating work, celebration, myth-making, and the rechanneling of sexual energy through aggression, which temporarily staves off the more profound long-term problem of a meaningful life in a less crisis-ridden society. But like washing one's hands, war "solves" the problem of a meaningful life for relatively brief periods of time (unless, of course, it is institutionalized).

In a sense the distinction between functional solutions and dysfunctional compensatory mechanisms is arbitrary. Functional solutions apply to constructive cultural elements or social institutions which allow humans to cope without inordinate stress; dysfunctional compensatory mechanisms apply to cultural elements which make it possible for humans to live under unnecessarily high stress. In general we assume as a practical matter that it is possible to distinguish whether the quality of life is enhanced or diminished by alternative functional institutions. Below we attempt to suggest various analytic distinctions as a way of clarifying this assumption.

Criteria for Successful Functional Solutions

1. *Attachment, love, bonding*

The quality of human attachments is, of course, a very large subject in religion, philosophy, psychology, etc. While we might discuss human attachments within the framework of a multitude of theories, we shall simply suggest Fromm's analysis as one insightful way to think about human relating. Fromm (1970) distinguishes among the following kinds of interpersonal relatedness:

1. *Symbiotic relatedness:* In the symbiotic relatedness the person is related to others but loses or never attains his independence; he avoids the danger of

aloneness by becoming part of another person, either by being "swallowed" by that person or by "swallowing" him. The former is the root of what is clinically described as *masochism*. Masochism is the attempt to get rid of one's individual self, to escape from freedom, and to look for security by attaching oneself to another person. . . . The impulse to swallow others is the active form of symbiotic relatedness and is sadism. It is the attempt to dominate others, and is rooted in and compensates for deep—and often unconscious— feelings of impotence and powerlessness. (pp. 73-74)

2. *Withdrawal-destructiveness:* The feeling of individual powerlessness can be overcome by withdrawal from others who are experienced as threats. . . . Its emotional equivalent is the feeling of indifference toward others, often accompanied by a compensatory feeling of self-inflation. Withdrawal and in- difference can, but need not, be conscious. . . . in our culture they are mostly covered by a superficial kind of interest and sociability. . . . Destructiveness is the perversion of the drive to live; it is the energy of *unlived life* transformed into energy for the destruction of life. (p. 74)

3. *Narcissism:* In this form of relatedness (or unrelatedness) only that which re- fers to one's ego, i.e., body, sensations, feelings, thoughts, is experienced as fully real, hence important. The reality outside, while perceived, has no weight, no importance, because one is not related to it. . . . the world outside is perceived without depth or intensity. (p. 75)

4. *Love* is the productive form of relatedness to others and to oneself. It implies responsibility, care, respect, and knowledge, and the wish for the other person to grow and develop. It is the expression of intimacy between two human beings under the condition of preservation of each other's integrity. (p. 76)

Although it is clear that of Fromm's four types of relatedness, love is the "good" one, the successful one, it should be understood that an individual is not a caricature of one form of relatedness, but rather there are blends of the various components within the person- ality. Our own guess is that within limits humans might bond nor- mally by any of the mechanisms listed.

   2. Adaptation, work, coping

   To describe work in terms of quality of life is a more frag- mented task than to describe human attachment. A variety of cri- teria, however, come to mind.

   a. *Adequacy* for meeting the burden of survival and the basic economic needs of a society. It should be understood that adequacy is construed more in absolute than in relative terms. From our point of view it means meeting the basic biological needs of the society as well as biosocial functional needs (e.g., celebration, play). There is, of course, a delicate line between an absolute definition of adequacy and a relative definition. Many of the activities of civilization, such as building pyramids, museums, universities, etc. allow humans to do productive meaningful work. Whether or not the absence of these institutions would make a society's work functionally inadequate, however, is highly doubtful. We would describe a society that is required to practice infanticide, or to abandon old people, or where there is highly competitive intraspecific behavior in obtaining food and shelter, as inadequate in absolute terms. Societies with high death rates from starvation, malnutrition, and exposure are at the extreme of negative adaptation.

b. *Efficiency,* or the relationship between energy expended and the production of goods and services the society presumably needs. A low-energy—high-production economy would be considered efficient. (One might make distinctions between expenditure of human energy versus the expenditure of mechanical energy or the energy of domestic animals, and suggest that conserving human energy is more efficient.) The distinction between adequacy and efficiency is obvious: one might have an affluent economy which is either efficient or wasteful.

c. *Authenticity,* or the extent to which one can justify a specific kind of work or adaptation as genuinely related to the needs of human survival. While one can make delicate distinctions in the gray area between the necessities and the luxuries of a society, it is less difficult to make the case at the extremes. In American society, for example, farming is probably more authentic work than is embalming; preparing food is probably more authentic than making television commercials.

d. *Nondestructive or nonexploitative work.* Work can be destructive ecologically, that is, destructive to the natural environment required for the long-term survival of the species and the planet. Work can also be destructive in human terms, either physically (breathing coal dust in a mine), or emotionally (doing monotonous work on an assembly line). Work might be healthy for the individuals participating in it, but destructive for other people (building high-rise "projects" in the ghettos or building barracks to house soldiers training for war).

Another criterion applied to the quality of work might be the extent to which work done by one group is productive at the expense of other groups or individuals. An extreme example would be poor Haitians selling blood to help affluent Americans regain their health.

e. *Fair distribution of meaningful work,* or the extent to which monotonous, physically dangerous, or repetitive work is carried out by one group of people, while others do more meaningful work.

f. *Meritocratic dependency.* Some members of a society are more competent to carry out certain tasks than others. In general, however, elites emerge which combine the resources of political leadership, intellectual creativity, and inclination to act on the world. It is relatively easy for a society to build stable socioeconomic strata in which groups on the lower end of the scale depend for direction and the definition of work on those on the upper end of the scale. Our hypothesis is that stratified meritocratic societies generate dependency, poverty, and survival anxiety in the lower strata as well as insensitivity, sadism, and guilt in the upper strata.

g. *Flexibility to meet changing conditions,* or the extent to which adaptive institutions can change as human needs or natural conditions change: for example, to what extent can a modern society deal with the need to reduce energy use?

Before we proceed to our four other functions, it should be stated that the first two (often referred to as love and work) have the most fundamental place in any scheme of human needs or societal functions. The problem of healthy human attachments, while it can be construed as a separate functional issue, permeates all other functions. One cannot talk about work or play or celebration without some sense that they are affected by the various qualities of human relatedness. We would argue, moreover, along with Fromm, that while man has no specific set of instincts which guide his work and personal relationships, his common biological equipment and biosocial history (e.g., long period of dependency) create a limited set of alternative modes of relating to people and to the world. Thus, while man is not an instinctual animal with a universal set of behavior patterns, he is also not a plastic animal. His behavior tends to fall into major slots and can be understood (though poorly predicted and changed with difficulty) in these terms. The significance of this point is its relationship to criteria for the quality of life. We assume that there are a limited number of models through which man comes to relate himself to people or to work; and that some modes or qualities are healthier than others.

Fromm (1970), in his theoretical formulation of this issue, for example, describes a number of streams into which love or work orientations flow. According to Fromm there are behavioral complexes which develop as individual members of a society cope with the problem of establishing stable modes of human attachment (socialization) and work (assimilation). These complexes he calls "social character" and are defined as the "relatively permanent form in which human energy is structuralized in the process of assimilation and socialization" (p. 11). A gross distinction is made between productive and nonproductive characters, loving and nonloving characters. More specific distinctions are then made among various character types or orientations in which qualities of love and work come together. Those orientations which have the greatest pathological potential consist of:

> Receptive orientation: feels the source of all good (affection, love, knowledge, material goods) can only be acquired by having it given—in exchange for being "good," or "ill," or "in need."

> Exploitative orientation: does not produce anything for himself; it must be obtained by taking it from other people, either by force or cunning.

> Hoarding orientation: has little faith in anything new he might get from the outside world; security is based on hoarding and saving.

> Marketing orientation: has little faith that he can produce anything of value; but he can "sell himself" as in a monetary transaction.

The productive or healthy orientation is difficult for Fromm to describe. In general, it is a fundamental attitude, a mode of relatedness in which the person feels himself to be an actor, an agent in which he can exercise power in a constructive way. Nor is the power used exploitatively. "The productive person gives birth to his own faculties and gives life to persons and to things" (1970, p. 72).

While the nonproductive orientations tend toward pathological or neurotic forms of attachment and work, this is not necessarily so. We see these various character orientations as common channels or archetypal modes of relating to one's material and personal surroundings. As Fromm further states (although this is somewhat contradictory to his major premise regarding pathological relating):

There is no person whose orientation is entirely productive, and no one who is completely lacking in productiveness. But the respective weight of the productive and nonproductive orientations in each person's character structure varies and determines the *quality* of the nonproductive orientations. In the foregoing description of the nonproductive orientations it was assumed that they were *dominant* in a character structure. We must now supplement the earlier description by considering the qualities of the nonproductive orientations in a character structure in which the *productive* orientation is *dominant.* Here the nonproductive orientations do not have the negative meaning they have when they are dominant but have a different and constructive quality. In fact, the nonproductive orientations, as they have been described, may be considered as distortions of orientations which in themselves are a normal and necessary part of living. Every human being, in order to survive, must be able to *accept* things from others, to *take* things, to *save* and to *exchange.* He must also be able to *accept authority,* to *guide others,* to be *alone,* and to *assert* himself. Only if his way of acquiring things and relating himself to others is essentially nonproductive does the ability to accept, to take, to save, or to exchange turn into the craving to receive, to exploit, to hoard, or to market as the dominant ways of acquisition. The nonproductive forms of social relatedness in a predominantly productive person—loyalty, authority, fairness, assertiveness—turn into submission, domination, withdrawal, destructiveness in a predominantly nonproductive person. Any of the nonproductive orientations has, therefore, a positive and a negative aspect, according to the degree of productiveness in the total character structure. The following list of the positive and negative aspects of various orientations may serve as an illustration for this principle. (1970, pp. 78-80)

Fromm then suggests negative and positive characteristics of personality which might be associated with three of his major character orientations.

Exploitative Orientation (Taking)

Positive aspect	*Negative aspect*
active	exploitative
able to take initiative	aggressive
able to make claims	egocentric
proud	conceited
impulsive	rash
self-confident	arrogant
captivating	seducing

Hoarding Orientation (Preserving)

Positive aspect	*Negative aspect*
practical	unimaginative
economical	stingy

Positive aspect	*Negative aspect*
careful	suspicious
reserved	cold
patient	lethargic
cautious	anxious
steadfast, tenacious	stubborn
imperturbable	indolent
composed under stress	inert
orderly	pedantic
methodical	obsessional
loyal	possessive

Receptive Orientation (Accepting)

Positive aspect	*Negative aspect*
accepting	passive, without initiative
responsive	opinionless, characterless
devoted	submissive
modest	without pride
charming	parasitical
adaptable	unprincipled
socially adjusted	servile, without self-confidence
idealistic	unrealistic
sensitive	cowardly
polite	spineless
optimistic	wishful
trusting	gullible
tender	sentimental

The most interesting aspect of Fromm's theory from the quality-of-life perspective is its affirmation of the fact of human diversity
at a very basic level of personality. One must take this fact into account in looking at the interface between personality, culture, and
social structure. That is to say, there must be available respected and
worthy roles supported by positive cultural rules and values which
allow the full range of social character to express itself in the society.
While no one is so naive as to suggest that all statuses in any society
are likely to end up equally valued—all human societies tend toward
dominance and leadership hierarchies and humans seem anxious
without them—one can argue (1) that all statuses should be seen as

having essential worth, and (2) that no one will be forced to occupy statuses and play roles which substantially violate their authentic sense of self. From this point of view the marketing orientation might be viewed as either sick or well. A healthy marketing orientation would allow a temperamentally outgoing gregarious individual to spend time "making himself liked" because that is his own authentic way of relating to people. The person with a pathological marketing orientation—perhaps under the stress of competition and job success—might lose any sense of authentic self in the process of selling himself.

3. *Renewal, play, sleep, relaxation, fantasy, dreaming*

The human organism is biologically constructed so that it must pass through cycles of physical stress and emotional anxiety on the one hand and relaxation, renewal, and sleep on the other. Although in Western societies we see the work-rest cycle in terms of a means-ends relationship, with a little reflection it becomes somewhat difficult to distinguish the means from the end. One can imagine work as a nagging distraction from play-fantasy-sleep; or one can imagine rest as the necessary pause that refreshes so that one can get back to work. Few would question the fact that play and human renewal are necessary functions of society; controversy arises over its purposes and relative place among other functions. Some possible criteria are:

a. *Authenticity*. Modes of renewal must relate to the developmental needs of individuals: babies, children, adolescents, adults, and old people have different renewal modes and needs. Contrived or managed renewal, such as Esalen type experiences, may be more work than play, and in this sense nonauthentic. Highly controlled sports like basketball or football, involving adolescent boys, may be experienced more as work than renewal, and therefore may provide less play-fantasy-dreaming than classroom activities.

b. *Fantasy-participation balance*. Renewal carried out totally by active physical or social play or totally by fantasy-dreaming would seem inadequate. The working person in a modern society whose only source of renewal is silently sharing television fantasies, as well as inventing fantasies of his own through his autistic processes, is probably missing something.

c. *Diversity*. Renewal should be diverse enough to meet the needs of different kinds of people (e.g., verbal play, physical play, artistic activity).

4. *Planning, deciding, conflict resolution*

To some extent society is the spontaneous playing out of complex behavior patterns, some of which are fully learned and some of which are improvised. Many activities are not spontaneous, but are carefully directed and managed. Human management requires planning and decision making, and one can search for quality-of-life criteria which apply to decision making.

a. *Requirement that decisions be just.* A criterion for justice might be some reasonable balance between utilitarianism (greatest good for the greatest number) and respect for the dignity and worth of the individual.

b. *Consensuality.* A second criterion might be the extent to which members of a society feel they have some say in how decisions are made, what decisions are made, and how they are implemented.

c. *Legitimation.* This is the acceptance by members of the society that decisions are binding on them without force or coercion.

d. *Efficiency.* This is the relationship between the amount of energy spent making decisions and the quality of the decisions (in such terms as utilitarianism or justice).

5. *Celebration or acting out of universal events in the human condition, story telling, drama, sports, dance*

Celebration is similar to renewal, but its purpose is more integrative, that is, directed toward personal expression and binding of groups, tribes, or societies to provide security against individual frailty by dealing successfully with anxieties and limitations. The celebration of birth, harvest, death (rebirth), marriage, or community is on the whole positive, although man has invented pathological celebrations to serve short-run goals (e.g., witch trials and burnings, mass meetings in Nazi Germany). Quality-of-life criteria for human celebration are similar to those for human renewal.

a. *Authenticity.* Are there genuinely shared joys, anxieties, and hardships? Is there genuine fellowship?

b. *Transcendence of man's anthropocentric bias.* There are universal elements in the human condition and universal elements in nature which bind man-in-society to the planet. Transcendent celebrations recognize not only human life but life more generally; the biological unity of many forms of life and nonlife; man's evolutionary past, bound to other forms of life in a common history (e.g., man has salt in his veins because he rose from the sea).

c. *Diversity*. Can the diversity of humans in a society (old-young, weak-strong, men-women, conceptual-sensuous-kinesthetic, etc.) find authentic meaning in a common celebration?

6. *Creation of myth and meaning: placing man in relationship to past and future events or human and cosmic events*

As O'Dea says, "Culture is the creation by man of a world of adjustment and meaning, in the context of which human life can be significantly lived" (1966, p. 3). Both because it is instrumentally useful (symbols and concepts are tools) and because man has a drive for a sense of purpose, societies create constellations and systems of meaning which surround their lives. The loss of meaning leads to suicide.

While secular thinkers are prone to separate empirical knowledge from religion, both spheres are included in our term "belief system." We would argue that modern religion has become trivialized precisely because it is separated from the common concerns and everyday facts of life encompassed by instrumental (useful) "true" knowledge.

Functionalists such as O'Dea state explicitly that the purpose of religion is to deal with man's need to transcend common human experience. The need for transcendence, according to O'Dea, is rooted in man's frailty—his sense of uncertainty, powerlessness, and scarcity, and the consequent frustration at not being able to control these conditions. Our own view is that man's drive for meaning is rooted in the nature of the organism itself—man inherently has the capacity and the need to create and communicate meaning. Most forms of life exist in conditions of uncertainty, powerlessness, and scarcity, but few if any have a meaning system in the human sense. Man is driven not only to ask the ultimate "why" of the human condition, but also to ask the why of day-to-day events—why did his friend let him down? why did he injure himself or become ill? Man's life is enclosed within a web of meaning. From our point of view it is somewhat misguided to separate out the more ultimate questions as sacred and call the day-to-day questions secular, especially since the domains of reality shift about within these two categories. (The nation-state or the Communist Party may replace the Roman Catholic Church as a sacred domain.)

O'Dea argues that a major social and cultural development of the last several centuries has been the secularization of culture.

We have seen that in primitive and traditional societies religion is a pervasive matter, and that religious beliefs and rites play an important part in the activities of various kinds of groups, from the family to occupational groups. We have seen that in such societies religion tends to provide the over-all point of view—the ideational system or complex of thought-ways—in whose context human experience in general is understood. (p. 81)

On the other hand, in modern societies this world view has become fragmented and emptied of strong emotional response, in short, secularized.

Secularization may be said to consist fundamentally of two related transformations in human thinking. There is first the *"desacralization"* of the attitude toward persons and things—the withdrawal of the kind of emotional involvement which is to be found in the religious response, in the response to the sacred. Secondly, there is the *rationalization of thought*—the withholding of emotional participation in thinking about the world. Rationalization implies both a cognitive attitude relatively free of emotion, and the use of logic rather than an emotional symbolism to organize thought. (p. 81)

One could describe a sacred meaning system for contemporary man, including a sacred attitude toward such ideas as technology and purposeful progress, and such artifacts as automobiles and electrical appliances. Moreover, it is doubtful that medieval monks and priests behaved with stronger feelings about their day-to-day religious beliefs than do their modern counterparts (e.g., psychiatrists, physicians, engineers, and television celebrities).

Our point is that man has probably changed as a species very little over the past centuries. What we call sacred today seems archaic only because we need sufficient historical distance to understand what has contemporary spiritual significance. We are embedded in sacred meanings in contemporary times precisely because man needs that level or intensity of experience.

Given these general remarks we would suggest the following as quality-of-life criteria for a human meaning system.

a. *Authenticity.* To what extent does our world view authentically describe the human condition on the planet? One might look, for example, at the contrast between Social Darwinism and Quakerism in terms of the problem of human aggression. Social Darwinism sees man as an aggressive, competitive, predatory animal and celebrates the fittest who survive. Quakerism sees man as a friendly, cooperative animal and celebrates his ability to solve problems of human conflict through peaceful negotiation. At least superficially, both would seem inadequate.

b. *Range of abstraction.* To what extent do beliefs deal with human meaning at various levels of abstraction and concreteness so all members of a society can share in the meaning? One might take as an example of this issue the problem of man coming to terms with the origin of life and the origin of his own species. The most authentic meaning system currently available is derived from theories of biological evolution and organic chemistry, both of which are abstract and complex. So most humans live with an archaic belief system (Genesis, or a similar myth), because no religio-scientific thinker has bothered to translate organic chemistry or evolution into sufficiently simple and concrete symbols or meanings so that common people can share in the more authentic system.

c. *Comprehensiveness.* To what extent are there domains of human life which are avoided or omitted from a meaning system? For contemporary man in modern societies the meaning of death, for example, is quite obscure. Given our dominant orientation toward technology and science it is somewhat disconcerting that we have so little to say about human death. It is interesting that technology-science does have an elaborate meaning system for human health and illness, including countless artifacts and symbols. Perhaps we assume that keeping people healthy will, in the long run, make them immortal.

d. *Level of integration.* It is probably safe to assume that a meaning system which can relate various domains of human action, at least in some loose way, is going to be more adequate than one which deals with the human career as a set of fragments. Puritanism, for example, suggests relationships among human attachment, work, and celebration. Modern Freudian meaning systems, including the Frommian analysis in this paper, attempt to relate love and work.

One can generate quality-of-life criteria by looking separately at individual functional requirements (as we have), by looking at relationships *among* various functional requirements, and finally by consideration of the requirements as a whole. In the last category, one might say that any society or subsociety with a relatively balanced expression of basic human functions might have a higher quality of life than one which has focused most of its energies on one or two functions. One might consider the decision-making executive, the playboy, or the compulsive worker as exhibiting pathological life-styles on a *prima facia* basis. One can also look at the whole set of functional requirements in terms of the extent to which various functions are integrated within common activities. Slaughtering an animal might, for example, be seen as a religious act (as celebration imbued with meaning), as an act of human sharing (bonding), and as adaptation or work. Our suspicion is that highly integrated societies tend to be oppressive because their structures must be so tight and controlled; that poorly integrated or fragmented societies tend toward insecurity and stress because any single function seems in itself marginally significant and therefore dispensible.

Analytic Systems and the Integrity of Human Community

However one looks at human community or society, we assume that quality of life is derived in some final sense by intuitive, albeit careful, sustained reflective thinking. In the last analysis, man's capacity for human society is a product of a long and poorly understood evolutionary process, while man's conception of his own condition is based on one small evolutionary product, the human mind. In the words of Hallowell:

Society, culture, and personality may, of course, be conceptually differentiated for specialized types of analysis and study. On the other hand, it is being more clearly recognized than heretofore that society, culture, and personality cannot be postulated as completely independent variables. Man as an organic species, evolved from a primate ancestry, constitutes our basic frame of reference, and we find ourselves confronted, as observers, with the complexities of the human situation that have resulted from this process. Here I wish to consider man as the dynamic center of characteristic modes and processes of adjustment that are central to a human existence, in order to emphasize the integral reality of society, culture, and personality structure as human phenomena. It is this integral reality that constitutes the human situation as our unique subject matter. Our abstractions and constructs, which may be ordered in different ways and for different purposes and which may vary in their heuristic value, are derived from observations of the same integral order of phenomena. (1953, p. 600)

It is to this "integral reality" we must always return for the validation of whatever judgments we make about the sanity, stress, and quality of life in human societies.

Conclusion

We have presented two schema by which one might describe human communities. It is our hope that through such analyses one might systematically generate a more complex and holistic set of criteria by which to judge quality of life. One might look, for example, at the interaction between channels and functions as suggested by the following matrix:

Functions	Channels			
	Social structure	Culture	Person-ality	Environment-technology
Work				
Renewal				
Attachment				
Meaning				
Celebration				
Decision making				
Conflict resolution				

Looking across line one of this matrix, one can ask:

1. Within what social forms or institutions is work carried out? in families? sodalities? corporate organizations?

2. What is the culture (rules, ideology) of work within these institutions?

3. What types of personalities are best adapted or least well adapted for the kinds of work carried on in the society? How is human diversity handled within work settings? Are workers of different types and statuses segregated (as in a modern corporation)? Do they work and relate together (as in a kibbutz)?

4. What are the environmental conditions within which work is carried out (e.g., household industry, factories)?

One might also look at relationships within and among channels or functions. Regarding channels, for example, one might ask to what extent the various channels mutually support and reinforce or contradict one another. A society which carries on human interaction in relatively intimate social forms (e.g., household industry) yet whose culture stresses impersonalness or distance might well create dissonance and stress. A society, like our own, which functions within three major social forms—intimate dyads, nuclear families, and impersonal corporate work settings—presumably must create somewhat contradictory sets of cultural rules. The central myth of the intimate dyad, for example, is that fulfillment comes from finding the perfect love; fulfillment in the corporate setting comes from work success.

One might look at the extent to which a society is functionally integrated; that is, the extent to which several functions are carried on in common settings, or the extent to which several functions are at least culturally (ideologically) related. Puritanism, for example, developed a meaning system which related work (successful work was considered evidence of grace), celebration (church-related activities), and decision making (elders in the church were seen as wise decision makers). In the Bruderhof described by Zablocki (1971) virtually all human functions are tied together around a common meaning system, a common culture in an isolated and intimate setting. Modern societies are comparatively highly fragmented. Celebrations, for example, are carried on quite independently and focus on a wide variety of human meanings: football games celebrate violence, manliness, competition, and discipline; rock concerts celebrate hedonistic release; quiz shows and shopping malls celebrate material success and consumerism; school ceremonials celebrate the value of difficult and often meaningless work.

While we feel that our analytic schema of channels and functions have considerable heuristic value in generating hypotheses about quality of life, we have a continuing concern about the relationship between quality of life and the potentials, constraints, and contradictions in the human condition based on the evolutionary nature of the species. The most focused statement of this concern might be the extent to which any human society incorporates in its functions and channels some expression of the human potential along the primal-modern continuum. (See tables 5.1 and 5.2 for a summary comparison.)

From an evolutionary point of view, we have assumed that man's more primal capacities and characteristics continue to make substantial demands on individuals and societies which, if ignored, lead to dysfunctional stresses and personal alienation. The central

Table 5.1

Modern-Primitive Aspects of Human Nature Channels

	Primitive	Modern
Culture	Religious or magical bonds with nature	Scientific tentative view of reality
	Concrete operations: words inextricably linked with objects	Formal operations: ideas and words separated from concrete objects and phenomenon
	Cyclical nonprogressive view of the human condition	Progressive ameliorative view of the human condition
	Conventional morality; grounded in sensitivity to immediate interpersonal realities	Principled morality
	Dreams and fantasies taken as serious reality	Universal knowledge
Personality	Use of "primitive" defense mechanisms, e.g., denial, repression, displacement	Rational, purposeful, directed behavior
	Concrete operations	Formal operations
	Tendency toward stable traditions, faith in tradition	Tolerance for ambiguity; nonauthoritarian
	No highly developed skills or talents	Use of higher coping mechanisms; intellectualization and rationalization
	Acceptance of various kinds of incompetent people as well as "natural" callings	Specialized knowledge and skills
		General civic competence
Social structure	Social forms emphasize extended primary group life: bands, villages, neighborhoods, guilds, etc.	Two major social forms: specialized corporations based on contracts and instrumental efficiency, and nuclear family to prepare for a future life
	Roles emphasize primary form of human integration: kinship, friendship, visible division of labor, visible charismatic leadership	Schooling used as a transitional social form to separate young people from the family for life in the corporation
		Impersonal objective criteria used for selection of people into roles
Environment-technology	Labor intensive economy	Capital intensive economy
	Use of beasts of burden	Omnipresence of human artifacts
	Visibility of man's dependence on nature	Disappearance of unmodified natural objects
	Visibility of ecological chains	High use of nonhuman energy

Table 5.2
Modern-Primitive Aspects of Human Functions

Primitive	Modern
Work	**Work**
Visible relationship between work and requirements for survival	Relationship between tasks performed and requirements for survival often remains opaque
Nonuniformity of products; personal relationships between people and products	Products of work are uniform and replaceable
Less fragmentation of work roles	Highly developed division of labor and work roles
Visible relationship between division of labor and efficiency; various parts of a task are visible to all	Relationship between individual task and other tasks required to complete a whole task is often opaque
Tasks tend to be associated with the personalities of people, rather than being seen as abstract jobs	Jobs have abstract requirements separated from the personalities of individual workers
Contribution of various members of society cannot be reduced to common denominator—money	Value or contribution of individual members of society can be reduced to a common denominator and expressed quantitatively through money
Work performed with simple tools owned or controlled by worker	Work performed with complex expensive tools owned by impersonal corporate groups
Attachment	**Attachment**
Primary bonds are at band or extended kinship level rather than in nuclear family or to produce corporate work	Primary bonds are within transitory nuclear family or in job roles
Long-term bonds, often for life	Geographic mobility leads to short-term bonds
Tendency toward more diffuse bonds; less intensive, more extensive	Tendency toward small number of intense relationships
Age, sex, and kinship relationships tend to permeate relationships rather than job roles or specialized interests	Tendency toward relationships based on common interest, common jobs
	Age, sex, and kinship minimized as bases for relationships
Renewal	**Renewal**
Spontaneous social relating; fantasy, gossip, small talk	Organized play; continuing concern with self-improvement or performing recreation
No sharp line between reality, fantasy, and dreaming	Fantasy and dreaming demarcated and labeled

Celebration

General participation, often with specialized parts based on age, sex, and kinship relationships	Participation by professional performers based on special talent, competence, and training; large group of nonperformers act as audience and share experience vicariously
Often linked to natural cycles: human life cycle, daily or seasonal cycles	Often not linked to natural cycles; performances based on utilitarian criteria such as size of audience and availability of talent
Accompanied by music, dance, bodily movement	Performers active; audience passive
Related to religious or magical meaning	Tendency to celebrate quality of performance rather than religious or magical significance of the celebration
Embedded in tradition; tendency toward repetitiveness	Innovation and novelty valued
	Because performances are novel and follow a literate script, they must be highly managed and practiced
	Impersonal relationship between performers and audience

Creation of meaning

Embedded in natural environment	Tendency toward description of man-made environment
Slowly evolving	Rapidly changing
Nonrelativistic; words and symbols intrinsically linked with the reality they describe	Relativistic; words and symbols seen as abstractions to be manipulated and played with
Meaning in the environment to be discovered and used by man	Meaning only partly in the environment; meaning partly related to man's sensing equipment and nervous system

Decision making and conflict resolution

Authority based on tradition, often linked with age and sex	Authority based on meritocratic requirements of instrumental accomplishment
Strong press for consensus of small face-to-face groups	Acceptance of authoritarian hierarchy based on impersonal contracts
Sanctioning of emotional outbursts and personal conflict and violence	Strong sanctions against personal emotional outbursts; support of impersonal managed violence and destruction of people

challenge for creating positive culture in modern society is inventing social institutions in which primal and modern elements of human evolution are allowed expression in nondestructive or noncompetitive ways; or in which the modern and primal are integrated within a common setting.

References

Aberle, David F., Cohen, A., Levy, M., and Sutton, F. "The Functional Prerequisites of a Society." *Ethics* 60 (1950): 100-11.

Fromm, Erich, and Maccoby, Michael. *Social Character in a Mexican Village.* Englewood Cliffs, N.J.: 1970.

Goble, Frank G. *The Third Force.* New York: Grossman, 1970.

Hallowell, A. Irving. "Culture, Personality, and Society." *Anthropology Today,* edited by A. L. Kroeber. Chicago: University of Chicago Press, 1953.

O'Dea, Thomas F. *The Sociology of Religion.* Englewood Cliffs, N.J.: Prentice-Hall, 1966.

Parsons, Talcott. *The System of Modern Societies.* Englewood Cliffs, N.J.: Prentice-Hall, 1971.

Zablocki, Benjamin. *The Joyful Community.* New York: Penguin, 1971.

PART III

Selected Applications of the Concept of Quality of Life

6

Social Forms

Chapters 6, 7, and 8 are initial attempts to elaborate points made in Parts I and II. This chapter deals with two questions: (1) To what extent is the relatively primitive social form, the human band or village, functionally necessary for the security and quality of life of a substantial proportion of the human species? (2) To what extent is this relatively primitive social form consistent or compatible with more complex forms such as the preindustrial city, the modern city, or the modern corporation?

Chapter 7 deals with the problem of human diversity. It assumes that humans vary substantially in talent, temperament, and social character; and further, that attempts at equalization through differential socialization or education may be misguided or destructive. (This is not to be construed as support for any principle of differential privilege based on talent, temperament, or social character.) Given the fact of human diversity, the question is: How does one take this condition into account in the creation of positive (or destructive) cultures?

Chapter 8 deals with the problem of social change. The major thrust is to reorient our thinking about social change away from managed systems toward the concept of the spontaneous and organic development of social inventions and the conditions which cause a society to incorporate or reject such inventions.

In all three chapters there are extensive quotations and heavy reliance on existing scholarship. This suggests that our approach or theoretical frame may not be new or startling; it is, in fact, latent in much social science scholarship which may have gained little sustained recognition because it is set in an unpopular or indistinct framework or social theory.

The Development of Social Forms

With our limited knowledge of the conditions of natural selection which gradually shaped man's biosocial makeup, it is difficult to map out or reconstruct the complex stages of human social development. Attempting to imagine even the earliest steps is, however, instructive. The following excerpt from Service is illustrative:

Early human social structure in its simplest outlines was probably that of a pre-human primate group altered and subdivided in ways directly related to reciprocal, virilocal marriage modes. We cannot know, nor even make a guess, about the size of the proto-human hordes or troops. It is reasonable, however, to assume that they included several females and their offspring and more than one male simply because all primate groups which forage in ecological circumstances similar to those of the Australopithecenes are of that sort. Those modern primates whose adaptation most resembles the proto-human kind are the baboons, and they have been observed in troops ranging in size from 13 to 185 animals. . . . But all we need posit here is that a number of adults were present. . . .

The human nuclear family, we may judge, was formed when the total group created the reciprocal marriage rule, making such marriages not occasional (as they must have been for simple short-term individually expedient purposes), but regular between themselves and one or more other groups. The family then crystalized as a relatively stable heterosexual pairing of adults in some consistent association with each other and their offspring.

Another way to say this is that the original primate dyad of mother-offspring, a biological pairing, becomes linked with another, the adult male-female, or conjugal, dyad. It is this latter, of course, which is the most cultural, thus variable in human society, and which therefore should be the focus of investigation in comparative studies of family organization. Many sociologists and anthropologists regard the family as having come into existence *in order* to rear children (because families *do* rear children), and define marriage as a means of legitimatizing the offspring (which it does). Here is another instance of the very different interpretations that come from evolutionary theory as opposed to functionalist theory. In the view taken here, marriage originally had to do with children only incidentally, however important the "incident" might have been to the children.

This is to say, also, that the social position "father" and its status and role are also secondary. "Husband" must be prior, not only in the temporal sense, but also in that if the most significant early social rule is marriage, "husbandness" and "wifeness" are the first results of it. The father-child dyad is then seen to result from husbandness, that is from the husband's role as provider and protector in the division of labor imposed on the conjugal dyad.

The total exogamous group now became a part-society, inasmuch as some of its former members—its married females—were living in the other group or groups and forms of friendship, alliance, and cooperation now existed among these groups. Within the exogamous groups a nucleus of cooperating males ("brothers") hunted and defended the camp. This, in a sense, was the horizontal solidary unit. The nuclear families formed the vertical solidary units—vertical because each conjugal unit normally begets offspring so that in time this organization bridges two generations and, with luck, three. (1962, pp. 50-52)

From Service's analysis it seems clear that as new capacities for social bonding evolved in the human nervous system potentialities are created for both variety and complexity in social forms, for example, traveling in social troops or bands and developing semipermanent husband-wife relationships and institutionalized relationships among exogamous bands. A key issue is whether these potentialities are expressed as a limited set of archetypal forms which fulfill basic needs in the species, or whether man can live and function comfortably in any of a great variety of organizational forms, depending on the specific historical or environmental circumstances in which a particular society finds itself.

Despite constant claims made by philosophers and social scientists about the plastic and flexible nature of man, one is struck by the common presence in human societies over the past 10,000 years of a particular constellation of human social arrangements: the nuclear family unit embedded within extended kinship groups related to a small community or village, which itself is linked to or set within the preindustrial city. It is in fact estimated that half the human population still lives in small communities or villages. It is only

within the past 200 years that the highly specialized corporate organization linked with expanding technology has become strong
enough to threaten, envelop, dominate, and often destroy these
earlier forms. It is precisely this possibility that makes the question
we are posing so pressing. Does man need the intimacy, sharing, and
support of the family, the clan, the peer sodality, the small community, or the stable traditions of a preindustrial city as bases for his
emotional security? Or can he sustain himself as a relatively transient
individual or dyad relating directly only to other individuals and
dyads or to individuals and groups within relatively impersonal corporate settings?

We believe there is substantial biosocial press toward cultural
expression of human bonding capacities exercised within relatively
supportive familial and communal forms; and that when the society
does not allow for such expression in the interest of more efficient
corporate economic or political institutions, it undergoes stress
which must be handled by compensatory institutions, for example,
schools which carry out prolonged coercive modes of socialization.
We assume that the level of security created and maintained within
nuclear families, extended kinship relationships, and small communities of men is not an acquired need learned from scratch; it is a
universal, biologically-based human potential pressing to be realized.

Accepting this general position, however, does not answer the
question: What are the basic "natural" forms of human association
toward which societies evolve? Service develops the case for the evolutionary order of some relatively primitive social forms: the band,
the tribe, and the chiefdom. When one looks beyond Service's analysis at more complex social forms, two theoretical works stand out:
Redfield's conceptualization of the small community and Sjoberg's
work on the preindustrial city. Redfield clearly sees the small community as a generic form of social organization:

The small community has been the very predominant form of human living
throughout the history of mankind. The city is a few thousand years old, and
while isolated homesteads appeared in early times, it was probably not until the
settlement of the New World that they made their first appearance on a large
scale. To Tocqueville, the village or township was the only association ". . . so
perfectly natural that wherever a number of men are collected it seems to constitute itself." One estimate is that today three-quarters of the human race still live
in villages; and to these villages are to be added the relatively very few who still
live in nomadic bands or other unstable small settlements. (1960, pp. 3-4)

Sjoberg makes a similar statement based on his analysis of the preindustrial city.

Our principal hypothesis is that in their structure, or form, preindustrial cities—whether in medieval Europe, traditional China, India, or elsewhere—resemble one another closely and in turn differ markedly from modern industrial-urban centers. . . . preindustrial cities everywhere display strikingly similar social and ecological structures, not necessarily in specific cultural content, but certainly in basic form. (1960, pp. 4-5)

If one assumes that there are a limited number of archetypal social forms which occur in human societies, one can then look for the degree of human stress based on the adequacy with which available forms fulfill human needs. For example, is stress increased or decreased as a result of abolishing the nuclear family, or reducing its influence? Or one might look at the extent to which available social forms are compatible or incompatible with one another. For example, stress might be caused when humans are committed early in life to styles of relating characteristic of extended families and small communities, yet drawn later to spend much of their lives within intimate dyads and relatively impersonal corporate organizations. Perhaps the most obvious hypothesis regarding the compatibility of various social forms is to imagine that simpler ones (dyads, nuclear families) based on more primitive elements of social integration (affective bonding, visible shared tasks and ritual) are compatibly nested within the more complex forms (villages, cities, corporate organizations), which themselves are built on "higher" elements of integration (highly specialized occupations, formal contracts defining work and consumer relationships, a formal legal system for the resolution of disputes, and legitimated use of physical coercion to maintain order).

As Hillery states:

Communal organizations exist on levels. Families . . . coalesce to form neighborhoods which coalesce to form villages or cities, which coalesce to form regions, culture areas, or nations. This finding means that communities quite often are contained within communities. But it also means that one must be careful to distinguish the level of inclusiveness. (1968, p. 9)

This hypothesis has a number of difficulties. First, it implies that the primal social unit for humans is the family. As Service indicated, evolutionary evidence suggests that the band is the earliest social unit. This suggests that humans generally live most comfortably within bands in villages or small communities, and that the capacity for male-female bonding can be expressed in a variety of familial forms. Second, the building block theory of human social forms suggests that there is organic growth toward increased complexity (from families to communities to cities, etc.), which implies compatibility among the forms. On the surface, at least, the compatibility assumption is simply not borne out. Small communities, for example, are generally torn with tensions among their constituent family units. These tensions are often handled by elaborate customs regulating the exchange of gifts, shared work responsibilities, shared kinship (e.g., uncles being considered fathers). In fact, what Banfield (1958) calls "amoral familism," the inordinate concern of families with their own private self-interest, would seem to be a major force keeping peasant communities from improving their material quality of life.

Third, stress may be caused by the difficulty with which many humans make transitions from one social form to another. The most stark transition may be the shift from the familial setting to the corporate organization. Often in the corporate setting primary group behavior is frowned upon or suppressed (informal talk, laughing, singing, humming, whistling, etc.). While there is little doubt that humans can be taught very young to distinguish between these two settings and exhibit appropriate behavior (one simply has to visit first-graders in traditional schools), we suspect that such behavior is exacted at considerable emotional cost.

In summary, our analysis of archetypal social forms leads to a number of quality-of-life issues:

1. How well can humans tolerate stress caused by confusion in moving between primary and secondary social forms, for example, living part of one's life in a "family" or "neighborhood" and part of one's life in a corporate organization?

2. To what extent can humans modulate their behavior to deal with mixed primary-secondary forms, for example, teachers and children dealing with schools both as corporate organizations (which emphasize functional efficiency) and as an extension of the family (which emphasizes growth, social relatedness, and personal concern)?

3. To what extent can humans tolerate a society in which primary communal social forms are distorted, threatened, or all but replaced by corporate forms? (See Nisbet 1953.)

Many of these questions deal with an indistinct qualitative difference between "communal" versus "secondary" forms of human association. The definition of community is, in fact, one of the stickiest issues in sociology and anthropology. Hillery struggles with this question in a comparative study of folk villages, cities, and total custodial institutions. He asks: If one induces criteria with which to compare these forms by looking at a series of instances of each, can all three be appropriately considered "community," or will all three be qualitatively different? He concludes:

folk villages and cities are connected by continua, and total institutions differ qualitatively from both folk villages and cities. Thus, total institutions systematically lack certain things that are found universally in vills (both folk villages and cities) and visa versa. Vills have families and are based on cooperation, localization being functional for these two things. Total institutions lack these foci. On the other hand, total institutions have the staff-inmate split, dominance of staff over inmates, and a primacy of orientation to specific goals. Vills lack these foci. Consequently, we argue that each type of vill is distinguished from total institutions by means of discrete and qualitative differences. (1958, p. 143)

Hillery sees the village and city (or a constructed type called the "vill") built around kinship groups and cooperation, with no focused or shared instrumental goals, as differentiated in some fundamental way from the total institution (a variant of the corporate organization). He deals only tangentially, however, with the issue of "mixed forms" and the relative compatibility of primary and secondary forms, a problem which is central in the thinking of Sjoberg and Redfield and Singer. Sjoberg is alarmed at American and Western European efforts to modernize or industrialize cities and their surrounding environs, a process which seems at first glance to be unequivocally beneficial to all. His study reveals compatibility between communal village life and the cosmopolitan urban life when each exists within the preindustrial city (as Hillery maintains), but radical and incompatible differences between village or communal structures and culture and those which characterize the modern industrial city. Sjoberg's thesis is excerpted below:

Cities of this type have been with us, present evidence indicates, since the fourth millennium B.C., when they first began their development in the Mesopotamian riverine area. Before long, in response to the growing technology and a variety of political forces, city life proliferated over a broader area. To an astonishing degree, preindustrial cities throughout history have prospered or floundered, as the case may be, in accordance with the shifting tides of social power.

In terms of their population these cities are the industrial city's poor relations, few ranging over 100,000 and many containing less than 10,000 or even 5,000 inhabitants. Their rate of population growth, moreover, has been slow and variable as well, in accordance with the waxing and waning of the supportive political structure. Yet throughout the shifting fortunes of empire, and the concomitant oscillation in population growth and decline, certain persistent structural characteristics signalize preindustrial cities everywhere.

As to spatial arrangements, the city's center is the hub of governmental and religious activity more than of commercial ventures. It is, besides, the prime focus of elite residence, while the lower class and outcaste groups are scattered centrifugally toward the city's periphery. Added to the strong ecological differentiation in terms of social class, occupational and ethnic distinctions are solemnly proclaimed in the land use patterns. It is usual for each occupational group to live and work in a particular street or quarter, one that generally bears the name of the trade in question. Ethnic groups are almost always isolated from the rest of the city, forming, so to speak, little worlds unto themselves. Yet, apart from the considerable ecological differentiation according to socio-economic criteria, a minimum of specialization exists in land use. Frequently a site serves multiple purposes—e.g., it may be devoted concurrently to religious, educational, and business activities; and residential and occupational facilities are apt to be contiguous.

As to class, one is born into a particular stratum and usually must live out his life in accordance with the rights and duties of his position. Few aspects of daily activity escape the pervasive influence of class. A small urbanized, privileged group commands the local community and the society and is nourished by the lower class and an outcaste group; this last, by performing functions considered defiling and beyond the bounds of respectability, is ostracized by both the lower and upper strata. Social mobility in the city, at least as viewed over several generations, seems, relative to the industrial norms, inconsequential. The small upper class, immediately identifiable by its dress, speech, and personal mannerisms, controls the key organizational units of government, religion, and education in the city and society. Distinctive familial arrangements and clear avoidance of economic activity mark the elite as well. Of course, as earlier emphasized, there are contrary forces at work that disturb these neat arrangements.

The preindustrial urbanite functions within a family system and subordinates himself to it. One consequence is that, typically, marriages are arranged by families, not by individuals. The large extended family, with numerous relatives residing in a single "household"—i.e., one that is a functioning social unit—is the ideal toward which all urbanites strive, though a sizeable, closely knit family is generally attainable only by the upper class. Economic circumstances prevent the urban poor and the peasantry alike from maintaining large households; for them the famille souche is more normal. . . .

The family is the key socialization agency in the community and serves, for the women and children, and men to a lesser degree, as the focus of leisure-time activity. But more than this, given the low level of social mobility, a man's family is the chief determinant of his future career, be this in the top-most levels of the governmental, educational, or religious bureaucracies or, in the case of the commoners, in the lower-status jobs. Personnel are recruited according to kinship or personalistic criteria far more than on objective, universalistic grounds.

Economic activity is poorly developed in the preindustrial city, for manual labor, or indeed any that requires one to mingle with the humbler folk, is depreciated and eschewed by the elite. Except for a few large-scale merchants, who may succeed in buying their way into the elite, persons engaged in economic activity are either of the lower class (artisans, laborers, and some shopkeepers) or outcastes (some businessmen, and those who carry out the especially degrading and arduous tasks in the city).

Within the economic realm the key unit is the guild, typically community-bound. Through the guilds, handicraftsmen, merchants, and groups offering a variety of services attempt to minimize competition and determine standards and prices in their particular spheres of activity. Customarily also, each guild controls the recruitment, based mainly on kinship or other particularistic ties, and the training of personnel for its specific occupation and seeks to prevent outsiders from invading its hallowed domain. . . .

Turning from the economy to the political structure, we find members of the upper class in command of the key governmental positions. The political apparatus, moreover, is highly centralized, the provincial and local administrators being accountable to the leaders in the societal capital. The sovereign exercises autocratic power, although this is mitigated by certain contrary forces that act to limit the degree of absolutism in the political realm.

The sovereign, and the societal leaders in general, along with the bureaucracies they control, base their authority upon appeals to tradition and to absolutes. The political bureaucracy, and the educational and religious systems as well, are characterized by rigid hierarchical arrangements; notwithstanding, the lines of authority in decision-making are most imprecise. The result is that decisions are arrived at not according to impersonal rules but rather with reference to the "persons" involved. Bureaucratic personnel are selected mainly on the individualistic grounds—i.e., according to whether they have the correct community, kinship, and friendship ties. Clientele are served on a similar basis, which means that the elite determine policy to their own advantage. These patterns, combined with the lack of a fixed salary system, are conducive to graft and, from the point of view of industrial-urban systems, marked inefficiency. Nevertheless, as we have sought to show, this bureaucracy can, from the perspective of the preindustrial system, be considered quite rational in its operation. . . .

Relative to the industrial-urban community, communication in the feudal city is achieved primarily by word-of-mouth, specialized functionaries serving to disseminate news orally at key gathering points in the city. Members of the literate elite, however, communicate with one another to a degree through writing. And the formal educational system depends upon the written word, the means by which the ideal norms are standardized over time and space.

Only the elite, however, have access to formal education. And the educational and religious organizations, with few exceptions, are interdigitated. The curriculum in the schools, whether elementary or advanced, is overwhelmingly devoted to predication of the society's traditional religious-philosophical concepts. The schools are geared not to remaking the system but to perpetuating the old. Modern science, wherein abstract thought is coherent with practical knowledge and through which man seeks to manipulate the natural order, is practically non-existent in the non-industrial city. The emphasis is upon ethical and religious matters as one is concerned with adjusting to, not overcoming, the order of things. In contrast, industrial man is bent upon revising nature for his own purposes. . . .

The End Product

Aside from its distinctive ecological features, as contrasted with the non-industrial-urban forms, the industrial city-type displays a fluid class system, status being based primarily upon achievement rather than ascription. In part this latter reflects the requirement that occupational posts be filled more according to universalistic than to particularistic criteria. Sociologists who perceive the industrial city's class system as rigid and well defined undoubtedly gain this impression from their penchant for contrasting reality with the ideal of absolute fluidity which, after all, given the contradictory demands of the industrial-urban order, is quite utopian.

The industrial city is also characterized by a loosely organized familial unit, primarily conjugal in form, with comparatively few superordinate-subordinate relationships with respect to age and sex. A family system of this nature, permitting and encouraging the exercise of individual choice in the realms of marriage and occupation, is compatible with the high degree of social and spatial mobility encountered in the industrial order.

The economy is mass-production oriented. And it is dominated by large-scale enterprises whose networks of relationships, extending across cities and societies, link the ever-expanding numbers of highly educated, specialized experts who are steeped in the scientific tradition that lies at the vortex of the industrial system. . . .

In the realm of government we find a rather loosely defined power structure, reflecting the fluid class system. Social power in the industrial city is translated into authority chiefly through appeal to the governed and appeal to experts; reliance upon traditions and absolutes is deemphasized. . . .

Anent the religious sphere in industrial centers, its norms are generally permissive. Actors play divergent, and often contradictory roles, and the new technology ensures a continuous cycle of change, all of which requires flexibility in the norms. Though elements of the traditional religion remain strong in some industrial cities, "secular religions" like science and nationalism are looming more significant.

Mass education, where selection tends to be according to ability, is interlinked with the fluid class and family systems; it is a must if the industrial city is to prosper. At the same time, only a highly industrialized system can educate all of its members. Education in the industrial city is geared primarily to emphasizing experimentation and change, negation, and man's ability to manipulate and revise the natural order. Not only has the availability of formal education reached monumental proportions, but knowledge is becoming ever more widely diffused through mass communication media. . . .

A cataloging of the internal contradictions in industrial cities, to say nothing of the opposition between "external" and "internal" demands upon the industrial-urban order viewed as a whole, requires another treatise. (1960, pp. 323-42)

While Sjoberg draws contrasts between the preindustrial city and the modern industrial city, Redfield and Singer (1954) are more explicit about a dynamic movement of social forms associated with folk societies through preindustrial cities ("primary urbanization") to industrial cities ("secondary urbanization"). Their position is summarized in the following excerpt:

In the primary phase a pre-civilized folk society is transformed by urbanization into a peasant society and correlated urban center. It is primary in the sense that the peoples making up the pre-civilized folk more or less share a common culture which remains the matrix too for the peasant and urban cultures which develop from it in the course of urbanization. Such a development, occurring slowly in communities not radically disturbed, tends to produce a "sacred culture" which is gradually transmuted by the literati of the cities into a "Great Tradition." Primary urbanization thus takes place almost entirely within the framework of a core culture that develops, as the local cultures become urbanized and transformed, into an indigenous civilization. This core culture dominates the civilization despite occasional intrusions of foreign peoples and cultures. When the encounter with other peoples and civilizations is too rapid and intense an indigenous civilization may be destroyed by de-urbanization or be variously mixed with other civilizations. . . .

This leads to the secondary pattern of urbanization: the case in which a folk society, pre-civilized, peasant or partly urbanized, is further urbanized by contact with peoples of widely different cultures from that of its own members. This comes about through expansion of a local culture, now partly urbanized, to regions inhabited by peoples of different cultures, or by the invasion of a culture-civilization by alien colonists or conquerors. This secondary pattern produces not only a new form of urban life in some part in conflict with local folk cultures, but also new social types in both city and country. In the city appear "marginal" and "cosmopolitan" men and an "intelligentsia"; in the country various types of marginal folk: enclaved-, minority-, imperialized-, transplanted-, remade-, quasi-folk, etc., depending on the kind of relation to the urban center. . . .

The most important cultural consequence of primary urbanization is the transformation of the Little Tradition into a Great Tradition. Embodied in "sacred books" or "classics," sanctified by a cult, expressed in monuments, sculpture, painting and architecture, served by the other arts and sciences, the Great

Tradition becomes the core of culture of an indigenous civilization and a source, consciously examined, for defining its moral, legal, esthetic and other cultural norms. A Great Tradition describes a way of life and as such is a vehicle and standard for those who share it to identify with one another as members of a common civilization. In terms of social structure, a significant event is the appearance of a literati, those who represent the Great Tradition. The new forms of thought that now appear and extend themselves include reflective and systematic thought; the definition of fixed idea-systems (theologies, legal codes); the development of esoteric or otherwise generally inaccessible intellectual products carried forward, now in part separate from the tradition of the folk; and the creation of intellectual and esthetic forms that are both traditional and original (cities of the Italian Renaissance; development of "rococo"; Maya sculpture in the later cities).

In government and administration the orthogenesis of urban civilization is represented in chiefs, rulers and laws that express and are closely controlled by the norms of the local culture. . . .

In short, the trend of primary organization is to coordinate political, economic, educational, intellectual and esthetic activity to the norms provided by the Great Traditions.

The general consequence of secondary urbanization is the weakening or suppression of the local and traditional cultures by states of mind that are incongruent with those local cultures. Among these are to be recognized:

1. The rise of a consensus appropriate to the technical order: i.e., based on self-interest and pecuniary calculation, or on recognition of obedience to common impersonal controls, characteristically supported by sanctions of force. (This in contrast to a consensus based on common religious and non-expediential moral norms.) There is also an autonomous development of norms and standards for the arts, crafts and sciences.

2. The appearance of new sentiments of common cause attached to groups drawn from culturally heterogeneous backgrounds. In the city proletariats are formed and class or ethnic consciousness is developed, and also new professional and territorial groups. The city is the place where ecumenical religious reform is preached (though it is not originated there). It is the place where nationalism flourishes. On the side of social structure, the city is the place where new and larger groups are formed that are bound by few and powerful common interests and sentiments in place of the complexly interrelated roles and statuses that characterize the groups of local, long-established culture. Among social types that appear in this aspect of the cultural process in the city are the reformer, the agitator, the nativistic or nationalistic leader, the tyrant and his assassin, the missionary and the imported school teacher.

3. The instability of viewpoint as to the future, and emphasis on prospective rather than retrospective view of man in the universe. In cities of predominantly orthogenetic influence, people look to a future that will repeat the past (either by continuing it or by bringing it around again to its place in the cycle). In cities of predominantly heterogenetic cultural influence there is a disposition to see the future as different from the past. It is this aspect of the city that gives rise to

reform movements, forward-looking myths, and planning, revolutionary or melioristic. The forward-looking may be optimistic and radically reformist; it may be pessimistic, escapist, defeatist or apocalyptic. In the city there are Utopias and counter-Utopias. In so far as these new states of mind are secular, worldly, they stimulate new political and social aspirations and give rise to policy. (p. 53)

As suggested by the Redfield and Singer analysis, the process of secondary organization is guided by the logic of the technical order —finding the most efficient *means* of meeting man's needs (adventure, shelter, love, transportation, physical health, etc.)—rather than the logic of any substantive integrated ideology which speaks to the ultimate concerns of human life. The technical order is liberating; it ignores the constraints of traditional culture as well as human nature. It envisions the human environment as a gigantic cafeteria which can meet the plurality of human wants in a plurality of ways. While the ends are plural, the means seem monolithic. The most efficient means by which to meet any or all human needs turns out to be highly structured, rationally ordered, efficiently managed corporate organizations. So while some primary social forms remain, perhaps temporarily, such as husband-wife dyads and small nuclear families, life increasingly revolves around work, consumption, and leisure which are all carried on within the framework of efficient organizational settings. The efforts required to live (preparation of food, maintenance of shelter, heat, moving about from place to place, child care, education) are reduced through rational, organized, and specialized work. Each individual works at a single, highly-specialized task of his own, and engages in consumption and leisure through packaged products created by the specialized work of others (purchasing products, listening to records, watching television, etc.). Even the artifacts and services required for a "real time" contemporary event like a football game or skiing are created through the highly structured organizational behavior of consumers and workers.

Conclusion

It is in the transformation of the orthogenetic city, representing a Great Tradition, to heterogenetic urban life, representing the technical order, that we see the sharpest break with man's evolutionary past. We know that the human species over a period of thousands of years developed both the capacity and need to maintain stable primary group life cemented or integrated through geographic limits, kinship statuses, sentiment, visible cooperation, and interdependence, embodied to some extent in an intimately shared set of cultural rules and rituals. And yet some men have the political and intellectual talent to create at an accelerating rate societies based almost solely on impersonal contractural relationships coercively enforced, which constantly shift and change in the interest of building a technically more efficient economic and political system.

Whatever the selective press that created the family-band structure, one must assume that prehumans or human types who were not genetically capable of functioning within these primary group structures selectively died out. Now we are increasingly requiring that man give up participation in these more primitive structures and find his central meaning in the more complex structures of corporate organizations and rapidly changing antitraditional urban-suburban centers. These more complex social forms, moreover, require new modes of integration: willingness to obey impersonal objective rules (punching time clocks, stopping at traffic lights); willingness to obey authorities, although the basis of their authority is not always understood (doing what the boss, the policeman, the teacher, the politician, the expert order); and, finally, willingness to concur in a complex view of how rules and authority combine to create a more efficient economic system.

We would now ask: by what evolutionary process can one imagine that those humans who require continuous support from primary groups and who cannot function or who function only marginally within impersonal corporate organizations will be selectively eliminated from the species? The evidence is that these people are not eliminated: they continue to live, but under substantial stress both within and without. And as Jules Henry (1959) suggests, those humans are selected for survival not because they find pleasure in the dominant social forms of modern society, but because they can withstand the emotional and physical stress required of such institutions. This is the irony of belonging to the human species.

Favored human types in modern society (conceptually talented, politically aggressive, interpersonally manipulative) undergo the least coercive and intensive socialization; they function with the least stress, the most joy. Less favored human types—interpersonally sensitive people, intellectually dull people, impulsive people, lazy people, the physically or mentally handicapped—are perceived as deviants and put out of circulation for treatment or rehabilitation. The vast majority of the population, we would argue, fall somewhere in between and are socialized at tremendous economic and psychic cost to substitute highly ordered work, consumption, and recreation for more normal primitive forms of work and social intercourse.

References

Banfield, Edward C. *The Moral Basis of a Backward Society.* New York: The Free Press, 1958.

Henry, Jules. "Culture, Personality, and Evolution." *American Anthropologist* 61, no. 2 (April 1959): 221-26.

Hillery, George A., Jr. *Communal Organizations.* Chicago: University of Chicago Press, 1968.

Nisbet, Robert A. *The Quest for Community.* New York: Oxford University Press, 1953.

Redfield, Robert. *The Little Community and Peasant Society and Culture.* Chicago: University of Chicago Press, 1960.

Redfield, Robert, and Singer, Milton B. "The Cultural Role of Cities." *Economic Development and Social Change* (vol. 3). Chicago: University of Chicago Press, 1954.

Service, Elman R. *Primitive Social Organization.* New York: Random House, 1962.

Sjoberg, Gideon. *The Preindustrial City.* New York: The Free Press, 1960.

7

Human Diversity

Cultural Uniformity and Human Diversity

There are two kinds of Utopians: those who would create perfect social arrangements where various fallible humans of different types and qualities will somehow live in harmony; and those who seek to perfect people, who can live happy lives under almost any conditions.* The modern educator, as well as others in the helping professions, is clearly committed to the latter position. This explains in part the educator's long-term infatuation with psychology as the favored academic base from which to launch solutions to perennial problems of schooling. (See Kohlberg and Mayer (1972) for a description of three different psychological camps and their

---

*There are, of course, Utopians and social interventionists who would manipulate both dimensions—people and social arrangements.

various approaches to educational reform.) Like medicine, education is very much wedded to the procedure of running tests on individuals, diagnosing their sicknesses, shortcomings, and weaknesses, prescribing treatments, and waiting somewhat impatiently for the cure. The underlying assumption is that within some relatively narrow range of ability on a large number of various human talents, people should all be pretty much the same. They should all have similar competencies to work, to love, to create, to think, to moralize, and to arrive at some final state or process of self-actualization. While token concern may be given to something called individual differences, it is usually related more to the rate at which the individual grows toward perfection than the notion that people might actually end up at different places. One rarely finds schools offering students of different sexes, ages, and abilities genuinely different options of equal prestige.

Quite apart from the ethical justification for training humans to be the same, there is the feasibility question. Is it possible? For a long time American anthropologists who presumably would know about the plasticity or flexibility of human behavior have been echoing the egalitarian credo of the psychologists. Human behavior (or personality), they have been saying, is largely a function of training, socialization, enculturation. In Benedict's terms:

The vast majority of the individuals in any group are shaped to the fashion of that culture. In other words, most individuals are plastic to the moulding force of the society into which they are born. . . . The deviants, whatever the type of behavior the culture has institutionalized, will remain few in number, and there seems no more difficulty in moulding the vast malleable majority to the "normality" of what we consider an aberrant trait, such as delusions of reference, than to the normality of such accepted behavior patterns of acquisitiveness. . . the majority of mankind quite readily take any shape that is presented to them. (1934, pp. 74-75)

Even after such expert advice, one continues to be struck by the stubborn diversity that persists in the species despite the most systematic and rigid efforts at schooling in modern progressive societies. It would seem time for a realistic theory of human personality and culture. We are presenting here a view of the functioning of human society which stresses the fact of human differences as well as cultural similarities. From this point of view the wonder of any social system is not how individuals are processed so that they all turn out the same (how they become Hopi, Balinese, or Americans); rather it is how the immense differences in humans along such dimensions as age, sex, temperament, and talent are somehow orchestrated into reasonably constructive roles within common social settings.

Wallace (1970) distinguished between these two aspects of society in his explanation of culture, denoting the socialization position as "the replication of uniformity" as opposed to "the organization of diversity." He sees both as culture-building processes.

For the sake of convenience in discourse [members of a society] may even be considered to have learned the "same things" in the "same cultural environment." Under such circumstances, the society may be regarded as culturally homogeneous and the individuals will be expected to share a uniform nuclear character. . . . it is sometimes more interesting to consider the actual diversity of habits, of motives, of personalities, of customs that do, in fact, coexist within the boundaries of any culturally organized society. When the fact of diversity is emphasized, the obvious question must immediately be asked: how do such various individuals organize themselves culturally into orderly, expanding, changing societies? When the process of socialization is examined closely, it becomes apparent that, within the limits of practical human control and observation, it is not a perfectly reliable mechanism for replication. And culture, far from being, with the exception of recent Western civilization, a slowly changing, sluggish, conservative beast, appears to be a turbulent species, constantly oscillating between the ecstasies of revitalization and agonies of decline. Culture shifts in policy from generation to generation with kaleidoscopic variety and is characterized internally not by uniformity, but by diversity of both individuals and groups, many of whom are in continuous and overt conflict in one subsystem and in active cooperation in another. Culture, as seen from this viewpoint, becomes not so much a superorganic entity, but policy, tacitly and gradually concocted by groups of people for the furtherance of their interests, and contract, established by practice, between and among individuals to organize their strivings into mutually facilitating equivalence structures. Nor can the phenomenological world of an individual, or of a people, be assumed to be understood by the anthropologist, once he can predict the movements of their bodies; rather, he must recognize the possibility of a radical diversity of mazeways that have their orderly relationship guaranteed not by the sharing of uniformity, but by their capacities for mutual prediction.

From this organization-of-diversity viewpoint grows a (as in the "replication of uniformity") different sense of tragedy. The unwanted inevitability is not sin, nor conflict, but loneliness: the only partly bridgeable chasms of mutual ignorance between whole peoples and the failures of understanding between individuals. A modicum of this loneliness would appear to be as irreducible in interpersonal relations (including the relation of the anthropologist to his subjects) as is the complementarity of perceptions in physical observation. . . .

One of the most hoary assumptions of the uniformitarian viewpoint is the belief that a society will fall apart and its members scatter if they are not threaded like beads on a string of common motives. Numerous sources may be quoted that attest to the "common thread" belief. Thus Aberle, Cohen, Davis, Levy, and Sutton in an essay on the functional prerequisites of a human society, include as prerequisites a "shared, articulated set of goals." Erich Fromm asserts that a nuclear character structure must be shared by "most members of the same culture" in order for the culture to continue; socialization must make people "want to act as they have to act." Emile Durkheim's thesis that society depends for integration upon the "common sentiments" of its members is a similar view. John Honigmann expresses the position in the plaintive assertion, "In any community, there must be some congruence between what different people do, believe, and feel, otherwise social order would be impossible." Margaret Mead has carried the argument to the point where cultural heterogeneity is conceived as almost ipso facto pathogenic:

> in a heterogeneous culture, individual life experiences differ so markedly from one another that almost every individual may find the existing cultural forms of expression inadequate to express his peculiar bent, and so be driven into more and more special forms of psychosomatic expression.

Social philosophers, less humane than the scientists quoted above, but equally disturbed by the problems of their societies, at times have found the "common motive" theme a congenial one and have used the threat of social disintegration and individual degeneration to justify draconian measures for the standardization of sentiments.

It is, however, impossible to demonstrate empirically that any social system is operated by individuals all driven by the same motives; indeed, the data of personality-and-culture studies, as well as clinical observation, show conclusively that a sharing of motives is not necessary to a sharing of institutions. (Wallace 1970, pp. 23-25)

Americans seem to have particular difficulty handling such a dual theory of culture, perhaps because the concept of diversity is so often translated as inequality. In our common sense experience, moreover, the major elements of diversity—age, sex, and stable qualities of talent and temperament—all seem more or less out of one's control. The notion that one's abilities, or level of motivation, or even general behavior patterns may emanate from or be partly determined by the genetic roots of one's nature is a direct assault on a central myth of the culture: Horatio Alger. One can do anything, become anything, be anything provided he tries hard enough; and if he fails, it must be his fault.

The virulence of this myth is, we feel, one of the most destructive elements in our own and perhaps most modern societies. We assume that an adequate meaning system for constructive culture building must posit a balance between the two human tendencies. There must be sufficient cultural uniformity and continuity to provide a reasonably predictable sense of social environment; yet cultural rules must allow for the positive use of human diversity always present in the species. As Wallace notes, the press toward uniformity leads to a sense of oppression (compensated for by the constant celebration of "freedom"); the press toward individual diversity leads to a sense of isolation and loneliness (compensated for by the search for "perfect love" and "community").

We feel that there is a relationship between the presence of supportive "neighborhood" or "village" groups in a society and the possibility of adequate balance between uniformity and diversity. Perhaps most humans must be sufficiently embedded in primordial group life in order to transcend the fear of social exclusion and risk inherent in expressing individuality. This is another area in which some American social scientists have inadequately conceptualized a critical human paradox. Because *some* humans have particular intellectual and emotional characteristics which allow them to internalize for life the sense of trust and autonomy provided in early childhood experience, it is assumed that *all* humans have this capacity. The sophisticated social scientist likes to contrast the highly conformist and static village man with the autonomous free modern man whose decisions are based on internal controls. Thomas and Znanieckie, for example, see the Polish peasant as submerged in culture.

It is clear that an individual dominated by [primary group] attitudes . . . can develop the very kind of character which society requires. His personality will be relatively stabilized at an early period . . . his character will be relatively simple, because primarily constituted by attitudes on the ground of which he can get response and recognition of many members of the group . . . it will present few, if any, important conflicts, for conflicts appear when the individual has many incompatible interests, whereas here all interests are subordinated to the social interest; finally, it will be positively appreciated by the whole group, since all the members of the latter possess and want to possess in a large measure similar tendencies. (1960, p. 425)

This view of primitive or peasant society is in sharp contrast to observations of other anthropologists. Goldenweiser observed as long ago as 1936:

Anthropologists are no longer surprised when new evidence is brought forth of the existence of full-fledged individuality among primitives. In the heyday of folk theory it was glibly assumed that the primitive individual was literally submerged, that no room was left for personality or self-expression in a society ridden by tradition, dominated by established habits and dogmas, shot through with inflexible patterns. No one any longer believes this. We know now that the very uniformity of primitive patterns should not be taken literally. After all, variation is not completely spirited away; in art, craft, storytelling, dancing, social behavior, there is difference between performance and performance, difference in skill, in details of form, in facility of execution. So also in religion, as Radin and others have pointed out, some lead, others follow, some originate, others imitate, some throw themselves body and soul into supernatural participation, others offer little more than lip service to the divine. Again, the prevalence of hard and fast matrimonial regulations does not preclude occasional deviations, including elopements with a "wrong" mate, or even, in some few instances, suicides over romantic frustrations.

We learn from Malinowski that the Melanesian standards of beauty differ materially from our own, but also that, within these culturally conditioned limits, individual taste will have its sway. So also with crime; it may remain true that among primitives practice agrees with legal or customary regulation a little more closely than it does with us, but this does not preclude breaches of customs and taboos, secular or sacred. In brief, cultural uniformity as a feature of primitiveness must be accepted in a relative, not an absolute, sense. . . . Anthropological field records agree in representing primitives as leading a lusty, animated, exciting existence. (p. 99)

Goldenweiser's point is certainly born out by anthropologists such as Radin (1971) and Matthiessen (1962). The more general point is that the balance between diversity and conformity can be effected in two ways. One is to provide group support for being natural or being oneself and to remove threats of ostracism and exclusion for deviant behavior, such as the threat that one may lose one's job or be put in a mental hospital for hearing voices. The second is to provide childhood experiences which will permanently fix or internalize the personal sense of self. It seems clear that the latter approach is effective with only limited proportions of the population, and that both conditions must prevail in a healthy society.

Diversity and the Process of Social Selection

The fact of human diversity and its necessary expression in any healthy society is really only an indirect assault on the Horatio Alger myth. By assuming that people are different but equal one can accept diversity and equality as potentially compatible social facts. Or one can assume that all people begin life with substantially the same human potentialities (or that they should begin life thus), and account for differences in human behavior on the basis of differential learning or differential opportunity to learn. The first assumption conjures up the image of the symphony orchestra, where the sounds of all instruments are equally important and equally beautiful—the differences are only a matter of taste, not value. In the latter assumption, everyone has a similar potential for perfection; invidious differentiation occurs on the basis of unequal chances for human growth and development. (See, for example, Bloom 1964; White 1975.)

One can make the case that both assumptions are not only gross distortions of reality, but also serve to perpetuate exploitation of the weak by the strong. We would argue that human as well as non-human primate communities generally require more from the strong and the competent. What is borne equally is not the burden of coping and enhancing the life of community, but rather that burden in relationship to the adaptive gifts and talents the individual has to offer. The American ethos, which maintains that all people are endowed equally, may give the less gifted a greater measure of dignity, but in the process strips the more gifted of an opportunity to exercise their fair share of responsibility for the health and well-being of the whole group.

What is needed is a more adequate and realistic statement of the roots of human personality, which places less stress on learning, socialization, and enculturation and greater stress on the organic relationships between learning and other factors affecting human behavior, such as development and genetic talent. The particular circumstances that go into the making of individual human types is a poorly understood admixture of plural forces: human nature, personal constitution and temperament, social learning, immediate social press, etc.

Some behavior seems so essentially human that one might reasonably attribute the pattern as well as the motivation to underlying species characteristics. Male adolescents roaming about in small competitive groups, jockeying for status, releasing physical aggression (often in the form of antisocial behavior), jabbering stories (some true, some fantasied) about feats of physical strength or sexual prowess: this kind of behavior would seem very primate. The tendency of some humans to think about or try to make sense of the surrounding world is probably a result of idiosyncratic thought within the framework of cultural rules (including language). Much behavior is governed by cultural rules learned through a variety of poorly understood processes, such as social imitation, operant conditioning, and problem solving. These behavior patterns—species, personal, cultural—are channeled through the particular biological equipment of the individual organism. For example, the degree of complexity with which one construes experience depends on the level of one's capacity to see the commonplace world in finely differentiated and abstract terms; the available energy and coordination of the human body conditions how one approaches physical tasks; and so on.

The problem of building positive culture, then, is not simply educating or socializing the individual as humanely as possible to fit available social positions; it is an interactive process of inventing or adapting social positions which relate in some constructive way to the quantity and variety of human types that occur in nature. In exploring quality-of-life questions about a particular society from this point of view one might ask: To what extent are there noxious roles or positions (whether rewarded or disadvantaged) which tend to violate underlying human tendencies (e.g., doing sustained monotonous physical labor, or being pressed to compete and achieve at a peak level of competence in order to be included in any work group)? How many human types must simply be maintained (if not discarded) because there are no useful positions for them to fill (e.g., the unreliable or lazy, the mentally dull, the immature)? Or how much social press via socialization or schooling, special rewards and sanctions, anxiety-producing myths and fantasies, or direct coercion is required to fill and keep filled undesirable social positions?

There is substantial evidence documenting stress associated with dehumanizing positions in modern job- or class-oriented societies. (See Whyte 1956; Lane 1962; Presthus 1962; Terkel 1974.) There has been less effort to explore the availability or lack of availability of diverse social positions to accommodate various human types or to show the particular stress caused by inconsistencies between human temperament and social positions. This kind of research is illustrated in the work of Presthus, who studied differential adaptation to corporate organizations. He distinguished among the upward-mobile, the ambivalent, and the indifferent. The distinction between the upward-mobile and the ambivalent is especially interesting since presumably both have the motivation and special talent to succeed in leadership roles. The upward-mobile is characterized in such terms as "power-oriented," "fear of failure," "exceptional need for control over the environment," "physically large or exceptionally forceful," "ability to dignify commonplace observations," "idealizes action and knows that it requires oversimplification," "capacity for impersonal thinking," and "self-discipline." The ambivalent is described as "typically an introvert, with intense intellectual interests and limited interpersonal facility," "intellectual interests are narrow and deep, accuracy and persistence are highly developed." As the two types are described, it appears that the upward-mobile is better adapted to organization life than the ambivalent, the result being that the ambivalent spends a great deal of time in destructive anxiety over problems that are unresolvable.

While the upward-mobile is sustained by status rewards and great expectations, and the indifferent accommodates by limiting his aspirations, the ambivalent is chronically disturbed. While the upward-mobile anxiety seems to reflect mainly a *fear* of *failure*, the latter's fear mirrors *ethical conflict*, arising, for example, from bureaucratic claims for exploitative roles. Although incapable of playing the roles required for success, he badly needs success to validate his intense need for recognition. (1962, pp. 281-82)

Research based on comprehensive theories relating human diversity to role demands and selective rewards of society is almost nonexistent. A notable exception is the theoretical work of Fromm (1955), most recently applied in *Social Character in a Mexican Village* (Fromm and Maccoby 1970). The basic ingredients in Fromm's analysis include the individual's constitution or basic personality resources, the particular mode by which the individual comes to relate himself to the political-economic world (assimilation), and the particular mode by which the individual comes to relate himself to other people within the early family experience as well as later in life (socialization). All of these result in the formation of various types of social character.

Regarding the basic structure of personality, Fromm states:

By constitution (or endowment) we mean more than just temperament in the classic sense. Rather, we refer to the basic structure of personality. Relationships in the family either help bring out this structure to its best fruition, or they tend to distort it. Just as a pear seed cannot produce an apple tree, but only better or worse pear trees, depending on the conditions of the soil and climate, so a child can only develop his given potential structure in the most harmonious vital form or in a negative form. For instance, a highly sensitive and unaggressive child may become, under favorable influences, an introspective, artistic and spiritual-minded person. Under the influence of cold and authoritarian parents, the same child is likely to become intimidated, frightened, and resentful, with the result that he wastes most of his energy by not being able to *be* what he *potentially is*. This holds true especially when parents try to force on the child a pattern of personality which is socially desirable or preferable to them but which clashes with the constitutionally given personality. The growing child may *act* in terms of the superimposed personality, but he will not be in touch with the deepest sources of his original self. To be sure, one can condition a child by rewards and punishments, by manipulating his anxiety, to become what he is not, but the result will be inner conflict, waste of energy, lack of joy, in many cases neurosis, and sometimes psychosis.

All these considerations are based on the assumption that maximal well-being is attained only if the person becomes what he potentially is, if he develops his self, his center, hence an authentic sense of identity. (1970, p. 20)

A central criterion for quality of life is the extent to which the natural variation in human constitution along such dimensions as activity level, primary mode of relating to sensory information (e.g., conceptual-symbolic, kinesthetic, visual-oral), talents, introversion-extroversion, etc., can be expressed through available social positions to create authentic personalities. Fromm hypothesizes that the processes of assimilation and socialization through which variations in human constitution are channeled form semipermanent character types, which are the human substitute for instinct in other animals. Fromm argues that not only are there broad classes of human adaptation (character types), but also character structure common to groups and classes within a given society. As examples, he contrasts the middle class of nineteenth century capitalist Europe with the upper class of the same era. The middle class had a strong hoarding orientation (it valued economy, punctuality, and orderliness), while the upper class was profligate in both business and sex.

The fundamental thesis presented by Fromm and Maccoby (with which we concur) is that there is a tendency in both modern and modernizing societies for humans to sort themselves into exploiters and exploited as well as to create adaptations which are intrinsically stressful. These stresses, moreover, are commonly resolved in socially dysfunctional ways, such as alcoholism, mental illness, and criminality, which often result in internment in custodial institutions.

We would argue that there is a relationship between the availability of both primordial and modern social forms, within which man lives, and his ability to create a sufficient range of positive roles to accommodate the normal range of human diversity. Within folk communities as well as peasant village-preindustrial city complexes the principal elements of integration and cohesion are still personal bonding through kinship relationships, sodalities, shared work and celebration, and a shared sacred cosmology. Within these social forms a broad range of human variation is acceptable for two reasons: (1) people are forced to confront human heterogeneity and hence come to accept and deal with human differences (there is less segregation of children, old people, mental incompetents, etc. than in modern society); and (2) there is sustained social bonding with kin and peers, since there is little geographic mobility. Diverse people belong somewhere because they share common territory, a common history, a common visible economic relatedness, and a common world view.

The corporate organization is characterized by an overriding concern for the specialized instrumental value of a person in doing a job competently and efficiently. In corporate life humans are, in fact, rewarded for their ability to exploit others. The basis of social integration shifts from personal bonding to impersonal compliance to contractural rules supported by economic and political sanctions, such as loss of one's livelihood and freedom.

The challenge of a positive culture lies in its utilization of diverse humans to perform necessary social functions without stressful socialization or coercion to effect compliance. When culture is so created to systematically discriminate for and against certain human types, along a relatively narrow set of human competencies, it tends to trap itself into invidious stratification and segregation. Fromm and Maccoby's study of a Mexican village illustrate both the process and the result:

While these findings have in general confirmed the theory of social character, our study has led to new insights into the dynamics of social change. First of all it shows that character is one of the elements which contribute to increasing the gap between poorer and richer villagers: this occurs in two ways.
1. The landholder with a productive-hoarding character becomes richer, while the alcoholic landless peasant—and even some alcoholic landholders—with

an unproductive-receptive character, fall to the bottom of the economic pyramid.

2. Usually people marry a partner with a similar character structure: as a result, children of productive, and in general richer, couples in turn tend to be productive, while the opposite holds true for the children of unproductive, and in general poorer, couples. Thus both the elite and the poorest classes perpetuate themselves and move further apart in terms of both character and material resources.

Second, our study shows that the new economic opportunities tend to attract individuals with a character structure which in the past was a deviant type with a limited social function. These are the villagers with a productive-exploitative character. To be sure, in the past there were also villagers who made use of others or tried to introduce new services. But they were looked upon with suspicion, or were disliked, and furthermore their social role and their economic activities were strictly limited within the precapitalistic agrarian society. Today the capitalistic economy opens up much greater possibilities for such men by allowing them to own capital goods and to use the facilities of the modern economy. More important than this is the fact of their growing prestige. Instead of being suspected or disliked, they become the models, not primarily so because of what they do for the village, but because the movies, television, radio, and other forms of mass communication make them so. The adventurous, individualistic entrepreneur has become a symbol of progress, of the better and glamorous life which the villager sees only on the screen. But the entrepreneurs are by no means only symbols. They take the lead in promoting those changes in village life and its institutions which destroy traditional culture and replace it by the modern principle of rational purposefulness. (p. 231)

Fromm and Maccoby then extrapolate from this study of Mexican peasants a more general theory of social change and social stratification.

What we have just described leads to an hypothesis about the role of character in the process of social change. This hypothesis is an answer to the question of *how* social change is possible if we do not think only in terms of machines, techniques of production, political institutions, and scientific discoveries, but also in terms of human beings who have to function under these conditions.

We believe that a central principle in the process of social change is what might be called "social selection."

What is the nature of social selection? In a relatively stable society (or class) with its typical social character, there will always be deviant characters who are unsuccessful or even misfits under the traditional conditions. However, in the process of socioeconomic change, new economic trends develop for which the traditional character is not well adapted, while a certain heretofore deviant character type can make optimal use of the new conditions. As a result, the "ex-deviants" become the most successful individuals and the leaders of their society or class. They acquire the power to change laws, educational systems, and institutions in a way that facilitates the development of the new trends and influences the character formation of succeeding generations. Thus the character structure is the selective factor which leads to the successful adaptation of one part of the population and the social failure and weakening of another. The "superior" sector will have the advantage of greater wealth, better health, and better education, while for the "defeated" sector the opposite will be true. The stability of such characterological classes will, of course, be all the greater the longer the period of social stability. But however long it is, historical evidence shows that deviant and secondary trait personalities never fully disappear and hence that social changes always find the individuals and groups which can serve as the core for a new social character.

Our description so far does not do full justice to the complexity of the process of social selection. It would seem to be sufficient in the case where a small group becomes dictator over the whole population, imposing new laws and institutions: after one or two generations, new men whose characters have been molded by these new arrangements would have emerged. However, this case is purely hypothetical. In reality, even a gifted dictatorial elite could not remain in power for any length of time without a social and psychological basis in a considerable part of the population. What happens in fact is that the ex-deviants succeed in polarizing the whole society and attracting within a short time, if not the majority, at least a critical mass of the population; in this way their dominant position becomes increasingly a popular one.

In order to understand this process fully one must consider the fact that aside from the extreme deviants who form a small minority, there are much larger minorities whose social character is different from that of the majority, but not enough so to make them unable to function in their society. They may be said to have "secondary character traits" which are latent as long as the social structure remains unchanged, but which become activated when new socio-economic conditions attract and mobilize them. A simple example of this difference is a primitive agricultural society dedicated to a peaceful and cooperative mode of life. The few individuals whose character is dominantly destructive and suspicious are likely to be failures in this society, because they are totally unable to function under the given conditions. Many others with secondary destructive tendencies, that is to say, with a greater admixture of hostile traits than the majority—but not intense enough to prevent them from functioning—will tend to encounter more difficulties in adaptation to socio-economic conditions and be less successful than the majority. Let us assume, however, that through changes in the external conditions the peaceful cooperative system was no longer able to function. The tribe might be then forced to organize itself for warfare against other invading tribes, or the scarcity of land may have led to competition and hostility among the members of the society. In such a case the former deviants might become the new leaders, the minority with the secondary traits might become their most successful followers, while those whose character was most like the former social character might eventually play the role of the former deviants and become a minority representing a secondary trait.

While this example was constructed in order to illustrate the process of social selection in its simplest form, there are plenty of specific empirical examples which, although more complex, show the same process. An example is the new merchant class that developed in Europe and North America from the 17th and 18th century onward. This class was characterized by the hoarding-productive attitude. It was adapted to the need for capital accumulation (rather than consumption), personal industriousness, sobriety, the obsessional drive for work, and the absence of compassion. Only those who shared all, or at least some elements of this "obsessional-hoarding-productive" character syndrome could become successful under the new conditions of developing capitalism. The same social character would not have been adaptive for the medieval artisan whose character grew out of the precapitalistic mode of production in which not saving and obsessional work, but a tendency to enjoy life, including work, was outstanding. With the new economic opportunities, the many whose character had a more or less strong admixture of obsessional hoarding traits became the successful group, because their character fit the new circumstances. That this process of adaptation was mediated by Protestant ideology is by now widely recognized. Luther, the key figure in effecting the transition from Catholic to Protestant ideology, can be characterized as representing the radically deviant character: obsessional, hoarding (anal), father centered, unloving, and isolated. While medieval in his views he stamped Protestant thought with his personality, and thus indirectly became a pioneer for the emergence of the new hoarding character.

In the same way that the deviant character and the "secondary character trait minority" rose to the dominant position, those who most fully represented the traditional social character became less successful under the new social conditions, and the purest types of the old dominant character became the new deviants. The same process of social selection can be found in the change that occurred from the 19th-century, independent small-businessman to the managerial entrepreneur in today's large advanced technological organization. The successful new managerial type is not hoarding and authoritarian, rather he tends to be flexible, team oriented, detached, treating life in the spirit of a highly competitive game, and ready to switch his full loyalty to any organization (team) he works for. Those men who were most successful in business a hundred years ago would probably not be successful today, and vice versa. (pp. 232-34)

Diversity and Social Class

Fromm and Maccoby argue that selection into social positions having more or less power, privilege, or status both within the simpler village context as well as in modern societies is at least partly a function of the diverse social character types represented in the species. The quality of social character itself is determined by a number of complex factors, including genetic constitutional forces and early kinship and primary group relationships, which in turn are influenced by the socioeconomic press of the outside society.

While Fromm and Maccoby assume the family as the basic primary social form, one might well begin with the band (as does Service 1962) and look at the family as a secondary element of social organization in man's evolution. While familial bonds evolve from basic biological factors (childbirth and mating), tribal bonds are clearly multifunctional. They include work relationships, the celebration of common meanings, especially those related to the regulation of such basic human problems as sex, aggression, economic survival, etc. One might speculate that man's capacity for spontaneous cooperative culture building requires the constructive resolution of the band-family connection. And where this is lost there is released a new human potential for both alienation and individuation. One might assume that the destruction of tribalism (small quasi-self-sufficient communities integrated on the basis of kinship, visible division of labor, and the obvious value placed on the usefulness of all) is a necessary precondition of the modern social class system. A familial (as opposed to a tribal) society allows work to be a separate function, differentiated from the quality of human attachments, celebration, and meaning. For the family is clearly so small that it requires almost all members of the household to venture forth and relate to a larger society (in a village or city) at least in a work role.

For the individual this brings about the crisis of secondary socialization: learning the culture appropriate for the "outside," especially those standards that differ essentially from the culture of the "inside"—in this case inside the family. In the secondary socialization process the key issue is how one comes to view the outside world, including the underlying motives for conforming to the requirements of a secondary culture. Does one see the world outside the family as one would see the world outside the band (or tribe)? In other words, does the world appear to be populated by inferior, marginally human creatures who threaten one's existence by contamination, or by superhumans (gods) who threaten one's existence by enslavement? Or does one see the outside through the eyes of the modern liberal democrat, as made up of benign and helpful institutions (economic, governmental, etc.) in which one can successfully participate as an autonomous individual?

In fact, the individual in the familial setting might view the problem of secondary socialization in one of three ways: (1) the family becomes the suspicious protector against the hostile outside world, with the proviso that it is too weak to protect any member in any ultimate sense (e.g., from school, trouble with the law, jail, unemployment, etc.); (2) the family is viewed as a somewhat protected hothouse with a special nutrient environment to prepare the young for the larger society; (3) the boundary of family is diminished so that fundamental bonds of marriage and kinship are considerably attenuated, the distinction between one's mate and one's neighbor's mate is small; the distinction between one's own children and one's neighbor's children is small.

One is struck by the correlation between these three views of the problem of secondary socialization and the social class structure in the United States. If one looks at Gans' (1962) summary of differences in family structure and social ideology across social classes one finds the following distinctions:

1. In the lower class or "under-class," economic press is so great that human survival itself is at stake. There is a high degree of self-interest, except for the primary mother-child bond which is still maintained. The concept of stable organized work seems remote, since it is unavailable. The family is under attack, on the verge of disintegration, or has already fallen apart.

2. In the "working class," the family has a dominant role; major life satisfaction is gained through social life with relatives. The larger society (through such institutions as school, police, landlords, merchants) is viewed with fear and suspicion. Stable work is sought as a means of survival, not as intrinsically meaningful.

3. In the middle class the family is also central and dominant, but is seen as a vehicle for striving and mobility into higher strata of society. Work is seen as a series of stepping stones to improve family life and the mobility aspirations for children. It may or may not be intrinsically satisfying.

4. In the upper-middle classes, especially the professional classes, work and education are seen as integral to meaningful personal development and a fully actualized self. The family is construed as only one, albeit the first, context within which this development can occur.

In simplest terms, the relationship between primary-secondary group relationships and social class can be defined along three dimensions:

1. The centrality and meaningfulness of a cohesive, socially stimulating, and supportive primary social unit—the family;

2. The centrality and meaningfulness of work and preparation for work (e.g., schooling);

3. The nature of one's relationship with secondary groups (whether one views them as distant and alien or proximate and supportive).

American social scientists commonly interpret these various social class world views (and related behavior) as reflecting relatively superficial learning, which can quickly be changed with exposure to alternative world views. Teachers, psychologists, guidance counselors, ministers, and other professional helpers are constantly vexed at the stability and intransigence of what appear to be wrong ways of looking at things, for example, the world view of the working class. Our interpretation is that they are based on fundamental differences in human social character resulting from complex interactions among human constitution, socialization, and the press of social institutions. From this point of view social class differences (in behavior and world outlook) are likely to persist despite deliberate efforts to eradicate them through education or modest political-economic reforms. In a modern society productive-exploitative personalities, for example, are likely to end up higher on the scale of privilege, power, or contribution to society than are receptive personalities.

This analysis leads to a number of conclusions regarding dysfunctional stresses inherent in the modern social class system. First the Horatio Alger myth leads people to seriously underestimate the depth and persistence of normal human differences that inevitably occur. W. H. Sheldon's (1940) work on the relationship between physique and temperament is commonly referred to, but little work has been done to follow out its implications in social systems. As the individual in modern society is forced to confront his own personal limits, he either refuses to accept them (and often seeks remedial help), or he considers himself a failure. Second, the stress caused by the awareness of human differences is exacerbated by the high stakes: the real consequences of not succeeding in monolithic upper-middle-class terms. One does, in fact, end up doing grubby work for relatively small material rewards the rest of one's life. The specter of failure looms before the upper and lower classes alike. Keniston's (1965) bright and sensitive "uncommitted" youth were unable to come to terms with temperamental qualities which might prevent them from succeeding, such as lack of competitiveness and aggressiveness. Having arrived at elite status at age twenty, they were skeptical of the price they might have to pay to maintain that status for life. (Schooling in modern society is designed to implant permanent failure anxiety in all who take it seriously—even those who succeed in school.)

When the Horatio Alger myth was undermined by radical social class research in the 1940's and 1950's (see, for example, Hollingshead 1949), the first impulse was to assume that if social strata could be fully ventilated by something called equal opportunity everyone would succeed or at least everyone who deserves success would succeed. Equal opportunity has usually been translated to mean schooling and education. Jencks et al. (1972) have now brought this assumption into serious question, although child development scholars and behavioral engineers continue to press the issue. (See White 1975.)

Our interpretation and diagnosis of problems associated with social class inequities and oppression in modern and developing societies are quite different. We would begin with the assumption that human diversity must have been functional in the long-term evolutionary development of the species and therefore highly resistant to elimination, except by natural or systematic genetic selection. On the basis of this assumption, one can envision two types of society (assuming that the underlying impulse of human social systems is toward a balance among power, justice, and compassion). The first is a social class system based on utilitarian and meritocratic criteria with external political controls required to maintain a decent floor under those members of society considered marginally useful or useless and without social merit. In such a system, the elite who have the conceptual capacity to understand and regulate the corporate and technical system (e.g., lawyers, engineers, businessmen), as well as the tough-mindedness to manage and manipulate other individuals or groups, are likely to succeed. Individuals with less adaptive temperamental tendencies (for example, those who view the world at a low level of abstraction in highly personalistic terms or who have difficulty with a disciplined lifestyle or highly directed thinking) are unlikely to succeed.

The essential problems of this arrangement are three: (1) the centralized hierarchy within which success is defined in any given pursuit makes everyone anxious about the limited access to success (e.g., musicians and baseball players either succeed big or quit); (2) this leads to a very limited number of humans who can engage in pursuits that qualify as meaningful and worthy; (3) finally, a large number of people come to be seen as economically dependent on others (the unemployed, children, old people, alcoholics, etc.) and an even larger number are anxious lest they become defective and consequently dependent (they *might* lose their jobs; they will become old; their quirks or deviances *might* be discovered and they would be disgraced or discredited). The dependent are, of course, cared for with colonial concern (e.g., by teachers and social workers), with fascist brutality (as in prisons), or with indifference or benign neglect (as in slums and homes for the aged).

The second kind of society would consist of relatively small, semiautonomous, and heterogeneous groups within which no one can long be excluded from visible contact with his fellow men. Differences in talent and privilege or moral character or sense of responsibility are present and immediate. This was, of course, the great experiment in pluralistic democracy envisioned by Jefferson.

Dewey, in discussing Jefferson, makes the point clearly:

... in his theoretical writings chief importance is attached to local self-governing units on something like the New England town-meeting plan. His project for general political organization on the basis of small units, small enough so that all its members could have direct communication with one another and take care of all community affairs was never acted upon. It never received much attention in the press of immediate practical problems.

But without forcing the significance of this plan, one may find in it an indication of one of the most serious of present problems regarding democracy. I spoke earlier of the way in which individuals at present find themselves in the grip of immense forces whose workings and consequences they have no power of affecting. The situation calls emphatic attention to the need for face-to-face associations, whose interactions with one another may offset if not control the dread impersonality of the sweep of present forces. There is a difference between a society, in the sense of an association, and a community. Electrons, atoms and molecules are in association with one another. Nothing exists in isolation anywhere throughout nature. Natural associations are conditions for the existence of a community, but a community adds the function of communication in which emotions and ideas are shared as well as joint undertakings engaged in. Economic forces have immensely widened the scope of associational activities. But it has done so largely at the expense of the intimacy and directness of communal group interests and activities. . . .

I venture to quote words written some years ago: "Evils which are uncritically and indiscriminately laid at the door of industrialism and democracy might, with greater intelligence, be referred to the dislocation and unsettlement of local communities. Vital and thorough attachments are bred only in the intimacy of an intercourse which is of necessity restricted in range. . . . Is it possible to restore the reality of the less communal organizations and to penetrate and saturate their members with a sense of local community life? . . . Democracy must begin at home, and its home is the neighborly community." (1939, pp. 159-60)

The concept of the "neighborly community" assumes that issues of conflict and interdependence which inevitably surround the fact of diversity are mediated within the framework of unconditional acceptance of all members of the community. Segregation of different human types, whether on the basis of merit or personal defect, is not seen as an appropriate mechanism by which to deal with human differences. The core of the premise of community is that *all* humans in community, in some sense, need each other.

The utilitarian begins with the premise that the functional requirements of community or society are central along with the corollary that deviant or "defective" humans (those who have no obvious talent to perform functions) must be cared for or be corrected. The communitarian begins with the premise that all humans are needed (as, indeed, in most societies of primitive man they probably were). Culture evolves to create roles which meet both communal and personal needs. Two examples illustrate the difference in points of view. Small children are seen by the utilitarian simply as potential adults to be supported until they can pull their own weight. Within organic communities small children simply "are." In an abstract sense they obviously are useful: they cement a variety of human relationships, they allow strong adults to express deep nurturing tendencies, and they stimulate spontaneous generosity. There is no need to ask, as modern societies often do: What do we do with the children and adolescents until they are self-directed, productive, and self-sufficient?

The aged are seen by the utilitarian as the most serious of problems. They are unproductive and useless, yet the archetypal fear of deliberate human extermination will not allow them to be killed.

Like children, they are increasingly segregated with a specialized industry to care for them. For communitarian societies, especially nonliterate societies, the aged are often the repository of sacred myths and ceremonials. They share a kind of magical history with children, and lead celebrations which only they can fully understand. Whether the aged are "useful" in any ultimate sense is an unasked question because the concern of friends and kin give them intrinsic value.

Conclusion

As modern men we are prone to look on human diversity much as the farmer looks on a crop. Every effort is made to grow a product (say apples) of uniformly high quality. Apples which fall below this quality are not rejected; they are simply sold for a lesser price. But each apple is judged on its own: for size, taste, color, surface quality, and texture. Small apples are less desirable than large apples; sour apples are less desirable than sweet apples; scabby apples are less desirable than unblemished apples. We do the best we can with diversity (we can make cider out of soft or bruised apples), but there is little question about what our standards of uniform quality are. And it is on the basis of these standards that the apples are judged, graded, and valued.

But organic interdependent systems function on the basis of a very different logic. The system is seen as a single whole, and the parts, while they may be rated as having different relative importance for maintaining the system, are seen as essential. From an organic point of view, one does not see apples apart from the tree, or the tree apart from the soil or the rain or the sunshine. So from the point of view of the organization of diversity, one can view different kinds of humans as different parts of the whole called community. From this viewpoint one sees natural coalitions: old people and small children; mothers and babies; risk-prone male adolescents and male adults. And there are relationships among the coalitions, such as emotionally and physically mature males watching over mothers and babies. It is unthinkable to imagine that one would want all individuals in such a community to meet uniform standards of size, intelligence, age, temperament, etc. The community simply would not work; it would die.

From the organic view of community, one accepts some premises that are fundamentally different from those of the apple grower. For example, if the farmer cannot make a profit, he will let apples of poor quality rot on the trees, whereas the communitarian accepts the premise that everyone is needed and unconditionally valued. He also accepts the premise that human types complement one another—jokesters lighten the burden of the competent taskmaster; mothers nurture children and children give intrinsic meaning to the lives of mothers. (The farmer sees small apples only as a preliminary stage to large apples.) He further accepts the range of differences inherent in the species. The aging cannot be kept young, so the aged must have unique value in their own right. Women must bear children, so the experience of bearing children must give women unique value. And so on. (The farmer trims his trees, and fertilizes his ground, and thins his crop so that all apples will look as much alike as possible.)

But more than the ethical principles underlying the organic position are involved in our argument. One can make the organic argument for the complex modern society, which in fact uses a wide variety of people. Our position involves an assumption that the value of all, the interdependence of all, the value of diversity *must be continuously experienced* by all. The organic position states that we are equally worthy because we are all needed; and we are all needed precisely because we are different.

References

Benedict, Ruth. "Anthropology and the Abnormal." *The Journal of General Psychology* 10, no. 1 (January 1934): 59-80.

Bloom, Benjamin S. *Stability and Change in Human Characteristics.* New York: John Wiley & Sons, 1964.

Dewey, John. *Freedom and Culture.* New York: Capricorn Books, 1939.

Fromm, Erich. *The Sane Society.* New York: Holt, Rinehart, & Winston, 1955.

Fromm, Erich, and Maccoby, Michael. *Social Character in a Mexican Village.* Englewood Cliffs, N.J.: Prentice-Hall, 1970.

Gans, Herbert. *The Urban Villagers.* New York: The Free Press, 1962.

Goldenweiser, Alexander A. "Loose Ends of Theory on the Individual, Pattern, and Involution in Primitive Society." *Essays in Anthropology,* edited by R. H. Lowie. Berkeley: University of California Press, 1936.

Hollingshead, A. *Elmstown's Youth.* New York: John Wiley & Sons, 1949.

Jencks, Christopher; Smith, Marshall; Acland, Henry; Bane, Mary Jo; Gintis,

Herbert; Heyns, Barbara; and Michelson, Stephen. *Inequality: A Reassessment of the Effect of Family and Schooling in America.* New York: Basic Books, 1972.

Keniston, Kenneth. *The Uncommitted.* New York: Harcourt, Brace & World, 1965.

Kohlberg, Lawrence, and Mayer, Rochelle. "Development as the Aim of Education." *Harvard Educational Review* 42, no. 4 (November 1972): 449-96.

Lane, Robert. *Political Ideology.* New York: The Free Press, 1962.

Matthiessen, Peter. *Under the Mountain Wall.* New York: Ballantine Books, 1962.

Presthus, Robert. *The Organizational Society.* New York: Alfred A. Knopf, 1962.

Radin, Paul. *The World of Primitive Man.* New York: E. P. Dutton, 1971.

Service, Elman R. *Primitive Social Organization.* New York: Random House, 1962.

Sheldon, William H. *The Varieties of Human Physique.* New York: Harper & Bros., 1940.

Terkel, Studs. *Working.* New York: Pantheon Books, 1974.

Thomas, William, and Znanieckie, Florian. "Three Types of Personality." *Images of Man,* edited by C. Wright Mills. New York: George Braziller, 1960.

Wallace, Anthony F. C. *Culture and Personality.* New York: Random House, 1970.

White, Burton. *The First Three Years of Life.* Englewood Cliffs, N.J.: Prentice-Hall, 1975.

Whyte, William H. *The Organization Man.* Garden City, N.Y.: Doubleday, 1956.

8

Social Change

In the distinction we make between utilitarianism and the evolutionist point of view, it is obvious that the contemporary world is
increasingly populated with modern societies dominated by utilitarian men. While we talk much about the value of balanced societies—
balanced between primordial and modern social structures (e.g.,
neighborhoods and corporations) and balanced between primordial
and modern cultures (e.g., animistic-religious belief systems and science)—it is clear that in no sense are we living in balanced societies
today. One might, in fact, infer a heavy-handed utopianism in our
thinking and ask: Isn't the notion of inventing a "balanced community" based on scientific, technological-utilitarian thinking? Isn't
there a contradiction between the conservative posture underlying
the idea of evolutionist balance and the assumption that we ought to
plan societies so that they are more in harmony with man's underlying nature? The key to whether we are involved in a contradiction,

we think, is how one construes the idea of "planning." Pretending to plan total systems on a global, national, or metropolitan scale is the essence of the technical order; planning small innovations to improve one's own life, or the lives of one's kin and neighbors, is as old as the race. Not only is the distinction a matter of scale, it is also a matter of how one sees the failure, or unforeseen consequences, of planning. The utilitarian sees unforeseen consequences as grounds for remediation in "the plan." This usually means that the planner needs more information, more resources, and more power over the resources he already has (i.e., material goods and people). The evolutionist reacts very differently. He sees the success or failure of planned innovation as based on gradual, often unconscious, selection or rejection of such innovations. That is, artifacts, technics, expressive arts, and words and symbols are constantly invented within all societies. These inventions are somewhat analogous to mutant genes in biological evolution. Some are rejected because they are seemingly not adaptive or indeed they may be positively harmful; others are rejected because they are inconsistent with existing sociocultural patterns—although they may, in fact, support a higher quality of life.

Within recent times, for example, cultural inventions such as the automobile, professional spectator sports, and public schools have "taken," that is, have become integrated into American societies. But strewn along the way are other elements which have failed: close ethnic neighborhoods; the three- or four-day work week; the use of mass transit for moving people between suburb and city; various forms of communal living.

From the evolutionary point of view, culture shifts and changes almost as mysteriously as the species. The reason that some mutations "take" and become self-generating while others languish or are sloughed off is often apparent only years later. Moreover, some mutations which seem adaptive in the short run (and hence become institutionalized) may later lead to destructive consequences (e.g., the automobile, the superhighway, and the sense of rootless mobility that has accompanied these inventions).

In any event it is by no means obvious that we can evaluate with much accuracy which innovations will be adaptive in the long run: which will improve the quality of life and which will be destructive. The underlying selective mechanisms are presumably related to the constraints and complexities within man's natural potentialities.

The Development of Technology

What is qualitatively different for man within the past 5,000 years (since advanced horticultural and agrarian societies), and especially within the past 200 years, is the massive development of technology coupled with centralized elites which have the organization and power to manipulate it. A new dynamic comes into play, and complex systems of social stratification are formed. It is no longer simply a matter of creative individuals "inventing" cultural elements to be accepted or rejected by the group; it is a matter of which groups within larger and more complex societies have the leisure to invent and the power to manipulate and control that which is invented. Much energy is used, for example, simply controlling the antagonisms which develop between creative elites, conservative elites (i.e., those who run complex political and legal systems), and the common folk. The power of both scientific and political elites to impose large-scale, long-term, almost irreversible changes in the lives of the common people is tremendously magnified. Examples are abundant: requiring members of tribal societies to work, pay taxes, and become a stable labor force; substitution of a money economy for direct exchange of goods and services; large-scale military adventures in the interests of imperial or national pride; placement of children in the custody of professional educators; use of the factory system to take people away from households and communities. Moreover, as man becomes a sufficiently abundant species, "inventions" developed within a society are only one source of change. He comes into contact not only with new inventions from the outside, but whole new cultures. At this point we see the rise of complex civilizations, and the institutionalization of social class systems, including slavery and war. And most important, we see the inevitability of the growth, decline, and disintegration of civilizations. While the seeds of this disintegration are mysterious, our hypothesis is that complex, highly stratified civilizations have built within them the seeds of destructive alienation, especially for elite groups. This alienation is defined—as we pointed out earlier—as disconnectedness of man from the primordial roots of his evolutionary past. He substitutes science and technology for religion and magic and loses touch with his nonrational capacities; he substitutes complex social organizations and bureaucracies for primary communities; he substitutes highly specialized labor for meaningful work visibly related to survival; he substitutes spectaculars (chariot races and the Super Bowl) and spectatorship for participatory ritual and celebration; he substitutes centralized government for consensual decision making. Our assumption is that complex civilizations eventually spawn such sick elites that they come down of their own weight. What is left is the village life—the infrastructure within which the common people lived all along. (In our own contemporary situation, we may well go through periods of greater violence and disorder than in the decline of earlier civilizations, partly because we have destroyed so much of that infrastructure.)

Although it would appear that, in the long run, there is much evidence to support a cyclical rather than a progressive view of human history, the myth of progress and positive social and cultural evolution dies hard. For the modern order persistently assumes that man can consciously and deliberately plan not only positive societal mutations (technics, beliefs, institutional change, and the like), but that he can foresee, plan for, execute, and control large-scale social institutions. Accompanying the rapid technological accomplishments of Europe and North America over the past 200 years have come ideologies which suggest there are massive world-wide changes with predictable consequences that man can, in fact, initiate and manage. Marxist socialism and Parsonian sociology are illustrative.

The question we would raise here is the extent to which power and control exercised by modern man is fact or illusion. There is little doubt that the technical order does affect the material conditions which surround humans in modern societies in a profound way. One can plan and create factories, cars, buildings, even cities. Planning, managing, and controlling human stress is another matter—it is less tangible, less visible, but fully as real (e.g., anxiety over personal failure; guilt over the existence of dehumanizing institutions such as prisons, slums, old age homes, and assembly lines; physical and emotional degeneration caused by passive reception of the world rather than action on it). We question the assumption that large-scale planning, management, and control over the external, visible world (men working together in highly structured settings), where everything seems to be going peacefully and smoothly, is correlated with underlying conditions of human happiness and human stress. Perhaps the most apt metaphor is the zoo. If the animals are housed and fed and given exercise room, it is assumed that they are content. However, animals in zoos often display visible discontent under these circumstances. Man has a complex set of psychosocial symbolic defense mechanisms which often mask discontent and stress: frustrated fantasies; denial and repression; scapegoating; displaced aggression often directed inward.

For the truly committed modern man, however, Freudian assumptions about civilization and its inevitable discontents, or the evolutionist's assumptions about man's need for primordial social environments, are romantic projections of those who are stuck in a bygone era. For him it follows quite naturally that when more efficient social forms evolve to better fulfill man's more obvious functional needs, these forms will become dominant because of their inherent superiority. This is, in fact, his rationalization for destroying primitive or underdeveloped societies on a world-wide scale—societies based on extended kinship groups and village life—in order to provide a life centered around the transitory nuclear family and the stable but relatively impersonal corporate organization (factories, offices, schools, department stores, etc.). With his mind uncluttered and unfettered by such obsolete commitments as kinship ties, permanent friendships, religious prohibitions, or communal traditions, modern man can relate himself to the technical order in whatever way his own talents are best expressed. In this way, each individual will be fulfilled, and the system will be efficient.

There is little doubt that the world may be currently characterized as in the process of rapid self-generating change. It is doubtful, however, that the stress caused by personal and social dysfunctions hinted at by modernists as a transitional condition of the species are any more temporary than the modern order itself. We are convinced that many of the stresses in modern life are inherent in the ideology and social structures of this type of society. For although systems analysts and planner-managers can and do effect massive changes in the social and physical environment through centralized power exercised by hierarchically organized bureaucratic institutions, the best-intentioned inventions have often enough reaped negative results (e.g., superhighways and massive public housing projects in the center of the American city; the creation of reformatories and correctional institutions for the treatment and rehabilitation of antisocial deviants; large-scale military forces to maintain peaceful relationships among nation-states; the use of machines housed in large factories to reduce the monotony and drudgery of social labor).

From our point of view, managed social change in large-scale rationalized societies is generally precarious and often destructive for a number of reasons. First, it grossly underestimates the complexity, fragility, and necessity of the simplest and most basic social forms— dyads, families, sodalities, and neighborhoods—and the limiting conditions which allow these forms to be maintained with any degree of stability and continuity. Second, the managers of change underestimate how profoundly their own formulation of culture differs from the majority of humans around them. Robin Horton (1967) develops this point by setting forth fundamental ideological differences which characterize what he calls the "open predicament" and the "closed predicament" which correspond to what is commonly called a traditional versus a scientific view of reality. Included in this set of ideological differences are dichotomies such as:

Magical versus non-magical attitude toward words;

Ideas-bound-to-occasions versus ideas-bound-to-ideas;

Protective versus destructive attitude toward established theory (or meaning systems);

Protective versus destructive attitude toward one's category-system (i.e., hypothesis testing);

A slowed-up cyclical versus a speeded-up linear sense of time.

Horton then goes on to raise two questions: How easy is it for humans to move from the traditional to the open ideological frame, and how universally shared is the "open predicament" in well-established modern societies? In his words:

. . . the transition seems inevitably to be painful, violent, and partial.

Why should the transition be so painful? Well, a theme of this paper has been the way in which a developing awareness of alternative world views erodes attitudes which attach an absolute validity to the established outlook. But this is a process that works over time—indeed over generations. Throughout the process there are bound to be many people on whom the confrontation has not yet worked its magic. These people still retain the old sense of the absolute validity of their belief-systems, with all the attendant anxieties about threats to them. For these people, the confrontation is still a threat of chaos of the most horrific kind—a threat which demands the most drastic measures. They respond in one of two ways: either by trying to blot out those responsible for the confrontation, often down to the last unborn child; or by trying to convert them to their own beliefs through fanatical missionary activity.

Again, as I said earlier, the moving, shifting thought-world produced by the open predicament creates its own sense of insecurity. Many people find this shifting world intolerable. Some adjust to their fears by developing an inordinant faith in progress toward a future in which "the Truth" will be finally known. But others long nostalgically for the fixed, unquestionable beliefs of the closed culture. They call for authoritarian establishment and control of dogma, and for persecution of those who have managed to be at ease in a world of ever shifting ideas. Clearly, the "open" predicament is a precarious, fragile thing.

In modern western Europe and America, it is true, the "open" predicament seems to have escaped from this precariousness through public acknowledgement of the practical utility of the sciences. It has achieved a secure foothold in the culture because its results maximize values shared by "closed-" and "open-" minded alike. Even here, however, the "open" predicament has nothing like a universal sway. On the contrary, it is almost a minority phenomenon. Outside the various academic disciplines in which it has been institutionalized, its hold is pitifully less than those who describe Western culture as "science-oriented" often like to think.

The layman's ground for accepting the models propounded by the scientist is often no different from the young African villager's ground for accepting the models propounded by one of his elders. In both cases the propounders are deferred to as the accredited agents of tradition. As for the rules which guide scientists themselves in the acceptance or rejection of models, these seldom become part of the intellectual equipment of members of the wider population. For all the apparent up-to-dateness of the content of his world-view, the modern Western layman is rarely more "open" or scientific in his outlook than is the traditional African villager. (1967, pp. 185-86)

Conclusion

This analysis is, of course, an extension of Gouldner's (1970) and Habermas' (1970) positions presented in chapter 2. It emphasizes, however, the fact that members of modern societies in different social strata occupy very different positions regarding a sense of control over the effects of rapid social change. This fact is strikingly supported by Gans' (1962) characterizations of the various world views of social classes. While we generally support the premise that modern man brings about change on such a large scale that no one can really predict positive or negative effects, it is important to understand possible bases for the tenacity with which the myth of planned change is held.

Our belief is that elites in modern society have enough power (over other people and the material conditions around them) to make the managed society seem plausible. They embrace the "open predicament" and generate inventions for a rapidly changing society in which one can live comfortably only if he will scrap his closed, tradition-bound orientation and accept the ambiguity and tentativeness of the open predicament. Those who do not must struggle to maintain a life surrounded by the remnants of traditions spawned in transitory families, social clubs, neighborhoods, television reruns, and the like; or worse, they must be treated or institutionalized for incompetency.

Perhaps the most unfortunate consequence of the illusion of large-scale managed change is the extent to which the planner-managers exercise an exploitative posture toward the common people, and the extent to which the common people become increasingly passive and dependent on elites to resolve the most elementary problems of social living—anxiously wondering how to pass through adolescence, how to relate sexually, how to rear their children, how to obtain safe food, shelter, security, and work, as well as how to evaluate meaningful news and entertainment.

In the midst of the ideological stress described by Horton and the exploitative-dependency relationships nourished by the rapid change, the complexity, and centralized control required in the technological order, modern societies seem to live from one anxious crisis to another. The common people patiently wait for someone to come up with the right answer for each accelerating problem. For all have come to believe that life is a straight, albeit somewhat rough, path to paradise rather than a circle of events punctuating a human career that goes to infinity. After a half-million years, we might know better.

References

Gans, Herbert. *The Urban Villagers.* New York: The Free Press, 1962.

Gouldner, Alvin. *The Coming Crisis of Western Sociology.* New York: Basic Books, 1970.

Habermas, Jurgen. *Toward a Rational Society: Student Protest, Science, and Politics.* Trans. Jeremy Shapiro. Boston: Beacon Press, 1970.

Horton, Robin. "African Traditional Thought and Western Science, Part I." *Africa* 37, no. 1 (January 1967): 50-71.

Horton, Robin. "African Traditional Thought and Western Science, Part II." *Africa* 37, no. 2 (April 1967). 155-87.

PART IV

Quality of Life and Education in Communitarian Settings

Introduction

The first major thesis of this book is that there are two systems of thought, two basically different kinds of culture within which humans live. One is a managed system. It is the social analogue to modern technology. It assumes that one decides what one's objectives are, the processes required to attain these objectives, the materials and resources necessary to carry out these processes, and the nature of the organization required to process the materials and resources. When all this is ascertained (generally called planning), one undertakes to build, rebuild, or alter some particular facet of one's life. As this is done, one notes mistakes, feeds back this information into the system, and gradually hones down new "tools" for successfully approaching such social activities as childrearing, education, therapy, conflict resolution, etc. Within this system, ultimate or long-run purposes are of less concern than the means by which they are attained. Eventually, human purposes are characterized in terms of

179

material acquisitions and status-defining activities. The problem is only how to allow the maximum number of people to attain the maximum number of diverse ends. This system of thought we have characterized as "modern," based on what Redfield has called a technical order.

The second major system is based on an established or traditional social order, the underlying premises of which are essentially unquestioned. Change does occur, but slowly and unconsciously. The traditional system stands on an underlying moral order in which a common lifestyle dictates priorities and limits for a substantial part of one's life. Diverse roles are built into the system because of the inevitable differences among humans, but the roles interlock in a common lifestyle.

A second major thesis is that the destruction of traditional systems of thought and culture and their replacement with modern ones create tremendous stress for most humans. Our assumption is that reasonably stable culture is a requirement for personal and societal sanity. In this sense "utopian" thinking, embracing the idea that one can plan and create increasingly perfect social arrangements, is generally difficult and threatening.

We are, however, now in the position of watching the destruction of almost every traditional society on the planet, often with little regret, since the concept itself is often associated with physical poverty and suffering. And, at the same time, humankind has very little idea about how to set in motion *the process by which new traditions might be created.* We seem to move with increasing speed from one "tradition" to another, each grounded in different principles, each coming into question, and each becoming undefined or rejected in its turn. Most recently basic concepts of the modern democratic state, which were embraced in the first half of this century, are now under question. Perhaps the most fundamental of these concepts is the notion that an enlightened intelligentsia, guided by principles of professional and technical expertise as well as long-range self-interest, if given sufficient economic resources and political power, could solve the persisting problems of the planet. The problem of war would be solved by world government; the problem of poverty would be solved by increased capital and productivity; the problem of inequality would be solved by education; and so on. Many of us are now much more pessimistic about these solutions.

World government would require a world police force, and we have difficulty creating and maintaining responsible police forces for local governments. Raising the standard of living of the world to the level of developed nations might well exhaust the resources of the planet (to say nothing about the fact that "poverty" is always relative; so as long as there is inequality there is poverty). And so it goes.

Many of us are coming to a new awareness of the limits within which the human species must assess itself. These limits run all the way from a respect for underlying biological rhythms to the need for traditional networks of social ritual and social support to maintain one's sense of personal meaning and well-being. So it turns out that our most fundamental thesis is to point up a paradox: man must figure out how to "plan" or "manage" a society which respects the basic limits of his own bio-social heritage, one limit being the need for a sense of small community and cultural tradition.

At the very least we believe that modern societies have to be constructed on two levels: the world system or macro-level and the small community or micro-level. The macro-level must operate within the framework of two moralities: utilitarianism *and* the respect for the rights of a plurality of decentralized microsocieties. Broad problems of technology, pollution, world order, and the regulation of the use of natural resources certainly must be treated at the national and transnational level; but a great many social welfare issues might well be treated more humanely and responsibly at the microcommunity level. This applies particularly to areas of social life such as childrearing, education, and the productive relationship between those who can and cannot cope with the pressures of the macrosociety, that is, those who work regularly at jobs and those who are treated as dependent people (children, the aged, the neurotic and psychotic, the chronically unemployed, etc.). And while we have a good deal of experience with a wide variety of problems on the macro-level, we know very little about how to create or maintain or sustain microsocieties.

It is important to emphasize again the distinction between different levels of "community," which are really aspects of the contractual network of the macrosociety, and what we are calling microcommunity. Thus the idea of "local education" has little to do with microcommunity. Although public schools are usually administered locally within guidelines set up by state and national organizations (including, now, the federal courts), children attend "local schools" only in a very limited sense of the word. Rather, they walk to the street corner or to the end of a driveway, are picked up by large yellow buses, transported several miles away to a factory- or office-like building, and treated either as dependent people needing custodial care or as raw material to be processed. The fact that the local political jurisdiction (a town or city or school district) manages this process does not make it any more a function of microcommunity than if it were managed at a state or national level. Towns, cities, and other local political jurisdictions are little more than convenient administrative units for the macrosociety; very few are what one would call microcommunity.

This leads to perhaps the most problematic aspect of this book: we advocate a two-level society in which we cope with some problems through a modern system (including systematic planning and administration of resources, technology, and humans), and other problems within the framework of microcommunity (which has more of the aspects of small traditional societies). Where, then, are examples of microcommunity that might help us work through and construct this more personal social form? Postindustrial societies abound in both positive and negative efforts to deal with social problems through planning, and administration through specialized professions. But where are examples of constructive microcommunities dealing with these problems?

Part IV is an effort to present this question in a concrete way. Our selections are from a variety of sources and represent communities engaged in a broad range of problems. It is hoped that the reader will understand these selections in a number of ways. First, they provide evidence that the model of social amelioration carried out through a two-level society is not totally hypothetical. Modern societies do provide examples of viable microcommunity. Second, one can develop relationships between the theoretical schema and issues of quality of life presented in Parts II and III, and the case examples presented here in Part IV. We would certainly not argue that microcommunity by its very nature provides a high quality of life. Our position is that community is a necessary, but not sufficient, condition for dealing with certain basic human needs. The point is to learn to discriminate between those aspects of community which engender positive cultural elements and those which engender negative elements. Nor would we encourage the reader to think in categorical good and bad terms: "Community A has a higher quality of life than Community B because . . ." Rather, the point of much of the theoretical work in the earlier part of the book is to encourage a more differentiated view of community comparison. Better, for example, to ask about the efficiency and authenticity of work in the kibbutz as compared to a modern Japanese ethnic community than to state broadly that one kind of microcommunity in some general sense is better than another. In this connection one might refer to the matrix on page 123 to analyze comparative community issues.

Finally, we would hope that the broad view of quality of life presented here (it is often construed in straight economic or educational terms) would open a new field of social and educational research. Rather than seeing societies such as kibbutzim or ethnic neighborhoods as interesting sociological or anthropological contexts, they might better be understood within the framework of an alternative social policy for improving the quality of people's lives. Rather than seeing microcommunity as an anomaly of the past, especially as social scientists have written about primitive peoples and ethnic neighborhoods, it might be seen as a rich context within which to carry on many societal functions we now consider the exclusive realm of helping professionals.

9

Kibbutz: A Modern Secular Community

Although Spiro's classic work, Kibbutz: Venture in Utopia, *is almost twenty years old, much of his description applies to the modern kibbutz. (We would note that we are as interested in historical examples of community as we are in contemporary ones.) It is, perhaps, useful to present a few preliminary remarks about the general nature of kibbutzim—Spiro's description is focused on the one community he studied intensively—as well as point out some of the more important relationships between education and community as they apply to a highly integrated society such as the kibbutz.*

The kibbutz is perhaps the most successful intentional communal experiment in modern times. Because these communities were developed in a foreign country and a great deal of research and writ-

This introduction is based on Joseph Blasi, "An Introduction to the Kibbutz" (Cambridge, Mass.: Harvard University, unpublished manuscript, 1975).

ten material about them is in Hebrew, the movement has still to be given the global importance it deserves. The first kibbutz was really a rural commune founded in 1909. As the movement expanded and the communes began to resemble communities, the word "kibbutz" was invented to denote a larger community group. Today there are some 240 kibbutzim with a total population of about 94,000 people (about 30,000 men, 30,000 women, and 30,000 children), or approximately 3.3 percent of the total Israeli population. The population of an individual kibbutz varies from 50 to 2,000, although the size of most settled communities is between 500 and 700 people.

The kibbutz is the small community alternative for people who live in modern Israel and is an accepted part of Israeli society. (One must therefore question the common assumption that such cooperative movements can exist only if they are isolated or cut off from the larger society.) Most Israelis have visited a kibbutz or have relatives who live in one. Telephone operators do not hesitate or draw a deep breath when one asks for the number of "Kibbutz such-and-such"—as often occurs if one calls directory assistance in some mid-western state to ask for the number of "Order of the Universe Commune."

Kibbutzim are responsible for 33 percent of Israeli agricultural production and 11 percent of industrial production. Their members take an active part in the life of government, industry (in their own factories), and educational institutions. Nevertheless, kibbutzim are unified into federations that fend for their cooperative existence in the capitalist-oriented economy of Israel.

A unique aspect of the kibbutz is the relationship between education and community that this type of society permits. Learning (or education more broadly) is not seen as a narrow, specialized function separated from the life of the community. The process of schooling is not burdened with providing individual solutions to such basic problems as finding worthwhile work, economic opportunities, and justice. Thus, the "life is collapsing around you and so try to figure it out in school" phenomenon found in many American schools is not the way the kibbutz operates. The close relationship between life and learning must be compared with the paradox in modern suburban life: the more humane and supportive the school becomes in terms of cooperative and generous relationships with other people, the more unrealistic is the picture of the essentially competitive character of economic relationships in the larger society. Kibbutz education leads children into the community through communal work. As soon as they are able, children within their own peer setting begin to help clean the house and do chores. Older children begin with a short period of work each day. High school students have regular work responsibilities from two to three hours daily. Children in the early years spend much time touring the farm and learning about the different branches. Throughout the process of growing up, economic rewards and opportunities are held equal in the context of the collective society. Children are encouraged to learn and expand their lives through organized group activity and individual development of special interests and skills, but not through rewards for competitive behavior or learning. In the later years of grade school and high school, children are encouraged to make group decisions and group plans, preparing them for political participation in the community. Spiro notes that this "lesson" not only extends to planning trips and activities, but to the discipline of the group itself.

The project method attempts to apply the values of participation and the totality of the kibbutz learning environment to formal instruction. In elementary and high school the underlying pedagogical assumption is that children are born with the instinct for meaningful contact with the environment, and that certain kinds of teaching can enhance or destroy the child's desire to learn. It is generally agreed that the project method is impressively applied in kibbutz elementary schools. For example, fourth graders learn about their own kibbutz and in the process study its history, the ancestry of the people who built it, its geography, and its economic base. The kibbutzim have constructed materials and outlines of many such projects for use with their youngsters connected to questions children ask at different points in their development. While teachers are trained to teach definite skills (e.g., reading and writing), they are also attuned to the developmental exigencies of each stage of childhood. On the whole, the first six years of schooling is a total cultural learning environment intertwined with community life, its cultural milieu, and the children's inquisitive concern about their existence. This kind of education, with the close integration between experiences in school and in the larger community, is possible, of course, only when there is genuine microcommunity.

The Kibbutz as a Communal Society

The People and their Setting

The population of Kiryat Yedidim numbers approximately five hundred persons and comprises three generations. There are approximately 250 adult members of the kibbutz, most of whom migrated to Palestine from Europe, more specifically, from Eastern Europe. This immigration, however, did not occur at one time, so that the adults can be stratified into age groups, depending upon their year of immigration and their eventual arrival in the kibbutz. The remaining chaverim [members] are native-born Israelis who came to the kibbutz from the cities or who were born in Kiryat Yedidim and joined it as adults.

These age groups represent an informal age grading system and, indeed, they are referred to as *shichvot*, or "layers," by the kibbutz. The oldest layer consists of the founders of Kiryat Yedidim, about eighty strong, who are roughly fifty years old. In most respects this is the most important layer in the kibbutz. The latter's social structure was designed to implement its values; the leadership within the kibbutz, both formal and informal, stems primarily from its ranks; kibbutz representation in the national kibbutz movement, in the labor movement, and in national politics is comprised primarily of members of this layer; and the intellectuals of Kiryat Yedidim are, in the main, members of this group.

Reprinted from Melford Spiro, *Kibbutz: Venture in Utopia* (New York: Schocken, 1971). Copyright Harvard University Press.

The second layer also consists of immigrants from Eastern Europe who joined Kiryat Yedidim from ten to twenty years after its founding. All had been trained in The Movement and, therefore, had acquired the values of the kibbutz and had received extensive preparation for kibbutz living before their arrival. This is the largest layer, numerically speaking, consisting of about 120 chaverim. Although some of its members are highly cultured, this is the least intellectual layer in Kiryat Yedidim and it has the least amount of formal education. Many of the officials of Kiryat Yedidim, committee chairmen, and economic foremen come from its ranks. At the same time much of the pressure for innovation—that is, for retreat from the original values of the kibbutz—is exerted by members of this layer.

The third layer, comprising individuals in their late twenties, consists of about forty chaverim who, for the most part, are either sabras* or European immigrants who arrived in Israel at a very young age. A small number of this group consists of children of Kiryat Yedidim who are now members of the kibbutz. The great majority, however, consists of former members of The Movement in Tel Aviv and other cities in Israel, who were invited to join Kiryat Yedidim (about ten years before the inception of this study) so as to provide the kibbutz youth with a larger peer group. This is the group from which the kibbutz youth has chosen its marriage partners. This layer, and particularly those of its members who were trained in The Movement in Tel Aviv, is highly gifted intellectually; in it are to be found at least one composer, painter, dancer, dramatist, actor, and ideologue. It is beginning to assume greater and greater responsibility in the economy and is becoming more articulate in the various councils of the kibbutz. Moreover, much of the pressure against innovation and the insistence that the kibbutz remain faithful to its original values arises from within its membership.

The youngest layer consists of about twenty chaverim in their early twenties, who are recent graduates of the high school. About half of them are children of Kiryat Yedidim, the other half consisting of city children who studied in the kibbutz high school and who, upon graduation, chose to become members of the kibbutz. More

---

*A sabra is, in current Israeli usage, any native-born Jewish Israeli. In general the term will be used in this monograph to refer to those individuals, children or adults, born in Kiryat Yedidim.

than half of this layer are still serving in the army, however, and return to Kiryat Yedidim on Saturdays or holidays. This group occupies important economic positions and some of its members have even been elected as foremen of their economic branch. It is still a highly inarticulate layer, however, seldom expressing its opinions in kibbutz councils.

In addition to the chaverim and their children, who also number somewhat more than 250, there are other groups living in the village. These include the parents of some of the chaverim, who were brought to Israel by the kibbutz from their European homes, and two youth groups sent by the Jewish Agency to study and work in the kibbutz. One of these groups is composed of immigrant children and the other of urban children from economically depressed families. At the time of the writer's visit, there was also an Army group stationed at Kiryat Yedidim (both males and females in Israel may serve part of their term of compulsory military service by working in agricultural settlements). We shall not be concerned with the latter four groups.

The physical environment in which the chaverim live is quite different today from the swampland first inhabited by the founders of the kibbutz. At the foot of a mountain range famous in Biblical history, Kiryat Yedidim is now part of a fertile valley. On the other side of the mountain lies an enemy country, and the night guard patrols with a loaded rifle.

The climate alternates between the hot, dry heat of summer and the cold rain of winter. The burning heat of the summer day makes labor between the hours of noon and 2:00 p.m. prohibitive, and a *siesta* is generally taken at that time. Even the morning hours are intensely hot at the peak of the summer, so that during the grape harvest, for example, the workers rise at the first hint of daylight— 3:00 or 4:00 a.m.—to pick grapes until 10:00 a.m., at which time the harvest ceases lest the heat of the sun ruin the grapes in the harvesters' baskets. During this season, the earth is parched, gardens are shriveled, and the mountain looms a dead brown, bereft of shrub or flower. The winters, on the other hand, are marked by steady rains and cold winds, although snow is a rarity to be regarded with wonder by the children. The rooms, which remain damp throughout this winter season, and the clothes, which never seem quite dry, are probably responsible for much of the "rheumatism" which afflicts many of the vattikim. The general unpleasantness of winter is exacerbated by the morass of mud, making walking a clumsy effort, and necessitating the constant wearing of knee-length boots.

The short spring and fall seasons, however, are welcomed by the chaverim as times of great beauty. The weather is mild, and—in spring—the emergence of a mountain in bloom and of gardens riotous with color creates a perceptible change in the general temper of the people.

The kibbutz and the land it works cover an area of approximately 11,000 *dunam.** Like the typical European agricultural village, the village proper is situated in a hub, as it were, from which radiate the various fields and orchards. Those members who work in the remote fields leave the village in the morning and return in the evening, although many whose work is closer to the village return at noon for their noonday meal.

The houses are laid out in parallel rows on either side of the communal dining hall, which is the physical and social center of the kibbutz. Surrounding the dining room is a large landscaped lawn, which serves to set it apart from other structures and to emphasize its centrality. The houses themselves are built in the form of ranch-house apartments with, as a rule, four individual living units in each apartment. Each unit consists of one room and, in some cases, a small porch which serves in summer as a second room. Generally, each apartment is separated from the others, as well as from the network of sidewalks traversing the village, by large lawns surrounded by high shrubs. Much attention is devoted to the care of these lawns, and almost every chaver has a flower garden, which he tenderly nurses in the evenings after work. Because of the individual's pride in his garden, and because there is at least one full time gardener in the kibbutz and one on the high school campus, Kiryat Yedidim has the reputation of being one of the loveliest villages in Israel.

Not all dwellings follow the pattern above, however; as Kiryat Yedidim has undergone considerable expansion, its architecture has changed. The growing wealth of the kibbutz has permitted each successive housing project to be better than its predecessor. The vattikim lived in tents when they first settled on the land, and some of the younger chaverim, who have only recently graduated from high

---

*A dunam is approximately one-fourth of an acre.

school, do so today. The first permanent housing to be constructed consisted of wooden houses, which are still in use today, and are inhabited generally by the young married couples. The next construction period witnessed the erection of brick houses, stuccoed on the outside, with a small porchway at the entrance. All entrances faced in the same direction, as is the case with the wooden houses, providing a minimum of privacy. In the next period, the buildings were constructed so that half the entrances faced in one direction, and half the other—thus affording greater privacy—and each unit was provided with a sitting porch with an overhanging roof. The last building project, in process of completion during the writer's study, was luxury housing by kibbutz standards. The units comprise a room and a half, a large porch, and private bathroom.

Each room is inhabited by one couple, and serves as a combination bedroom-living room—the minimum housing required, since cooking is done in the communal kitchen, meals are eaten in the communal dining room, and children sleep in the children's dormitories. Communal toilets and showers, separate for men and women, take the place of private bathrooms.

The typical room is simply, but attractively, furnished with products made in the kibbutz. Basic furnishings comprise a bed, writing table, combination clothes closet and chest, chairs, bookcases, and lamps. Bedspreads and rugs, of subdued colors and simple, skillful designs, are woven in the kibbutz and are reminiscent of the more subdued Mexican products. In addition, each room may have a radio, supplied either by the individual or the kibbutz, books acquired by the individual, and one or more good prints, either borrowed from the kibbutz or acquired by the individual. Thus, each room is provided with approximately the same furnishings, but each couple uses its own ingenuity and skill in arranging the colors and furnishings, so that rooms express the inhabitants' individuality.

In addition, the village includes a laundry, sewing room, clothing storehouse, kosher kitchen and dining room for the elderly parents of the chaverim, dispensary, office, store, library, reading room, and the children's dormitories and school. In construction during the author's stay was a *bet tarbut* (literally, "culture house"), which was to house the library and to provide an auditorium for concerts, lectures, and plays. On the periphery of the dwelling area are the sheds and barns for cattle, horses, sheep, and goats; chicken coops; garage;

tractor sheds; warehouse; produce storeroom; packing plant; and carpentry shop. Separated from the village by the main highway is the high school, with its classrooms, dormitories, and dining room. . . .

Economy

Extending out from the living quarters of the village is the kibbutz farm, in all its diversity. When it was founded, Kiryat Yedidim received from the Jewish National Fund 100 dunam of land per couple, making a total of approximately 800 dunam. Today it is working 11,000 dunam, though not all of it is in the immediate area of the kibbutz proper. Unlike some kibbutzim, Kiryat Yedidim has resisted the introduction of industry, so that its sole source of income is agricultural, with the exception of the small amount it receives from the wages of those few chaverim who work outside the kibbutz in non-agricultural jobs. For the most part, however, even these jobs are undertaken, not for their income-value, but for the contributions they make to the kibbutz agricultural economy. Hence, these men work in an olive press, a bus line, a trucking line, or a garage—all regional cooperatives which serve to promote the agricultural interests of the kibbutz. . . .

Since the economy of Kiryat Yedidim is socialist, its accounting system demands a brief explanation. It is based on the man-day income (*yom avodah*) of each economic branch—that is, the total income of a branch, divided by its total number of workers. In Kiryat Yedidim, about two-thirds of the labor is performed by chaverim and the remaining third by temporary workers (youth groups, Army, etc.). Labor is divided into two categories for accounting purposes: productive labor (*avodah productivit*), that is, labor which produces a profit, or which increases the capital investment of the kibbutz; and nonproductive labor (*avodah lo machnisa*, literally, labor which does not produce an income). . . .

Since about 50 percent of the total manpower of the kibbutz is involved in "nonproductive" work, the half which is engaged in productive work must produce enough to provide for the entire kibbutz. It costs an average of 90 *grush* (nine-tenths of a lira) to maintain a member for one day (*yom kiyyum*); the average man-day productivity (*yom avodah*) of each member, including those engaged in non-productive as well as productive labor, is about two lira. Hence, the

productivity of the average member is more than twice his maintenance cost.* This difference, however, does not represent profit. Kiryat Yedidim has many expenses in addition to those entailed by the
maintenance of its members. It owns only about 20 percent of its
capital investment; the remainder represents borrowed money and a
large mortgage. The interest rates on its loans and mortgage are high,
and they consume much of its income. Nevertheless, the kibbutz is a
going concern, economically speaking.

We may now turn to the division of labor in the kibbutz. With
some few exceptions, the branch in which a person works is determined by his desires and skills. Since the profit motive is absent, and
since, theoretically, all manual work enjoys equal prestige, a person's
choice is determined primarily by the intrinsic satisfactions he ob-
tains from his job. Ideally, the kibbutz attempts to satisfy the desire
of the chaver, on the simple grounds that an unhappy worker is an
unhappy kibbutz member. If a person not only has a strong desire to
work in a certain branch, but also shows some skill in this work, it is
most probable that he will be assigned as a permanent worker to the
branch of his choice, and the work-assignment chairmen automatically assign him to that branch when they plan the daily work list.
On rare occasions, however, when a particular branch is in desperate
need of men for a special task, and there is a draft of personnel from
other branches, he may be transferred for a few days. . . .

Kiryat Yedidim has always been suspicious of formal authority,
and it has been as reluctant to introduce formal leadership patterns
into its economic system as it has been to introduce such patterns
into any other aspect of its social structure. Nevertheless, as the
economy increased in complexity, patterns of authority also gradually increased, so that today Kiryat Yedidim has a relatively complex
system of committees, officials, and foremen who are charged with
the determination and execution of its economic policies. At first it
was assumed that any chaver could, with proper experience, occupy
a managerial position. Hence it was believed that all offices would
rotate among the entire membership, and that this restriction on the
tenure of office, in addition to the restriction on the rewards of

---

Yom kiyyum is computed by dividing the total maintenance cost by the
number of chaverim, just as *yom avodah* is computed by dividing the total productivity by the number of members.

office, would preclude the rise of bureaucratic power. It was discovered through experience, however, that this assumption was untenable, and that if the kibbutz were to achieve and to retain its economic solvency, it could not afford to permit any but the most skilled and the most efficient to assume positions of responsibility. Hence, though the important offices do rotate, so that no individual holds a job for more than two or three consecutive years, they rotate within a small group of twelve to fifteen men whose abilities are recognized by the others. . . .

Authority and Social Control

In order to understand the dynamics of social control in Kiryat Yedidim, which has few patterns of *formal* authority, it is necessary to grasp an essential psychological feature of this community. Kiryat Yedidim is not like an ordinary Western village whose inhabitants may be united by the sheer fact of physical proximity. Nor are the chaverim united by bonds of kinship, so characteristic of the folk society. Nevertheless, the kibbutz is a *gemeinschaft*, not only because of its small size and the opportunity this affords for the frequency and intimacy of interaction. It is a *gemeinschaft*, rather, because it functions *as if* it were united by bonds of kinship, *as if* it were a lineage or a large extended family. In their own eyes, as well as in the eyes of the outside observer, the chaverim constitute a family, psychologically speaking, bound by ties of common residence, common experiences, a common past and a common fate, and mutual aid—all the ties which bind a family—as well as a common ideology.* The kibbutz, like the shtetl, presents a "picture (which) is less of the family as a segment of the community than of the community as an extension of the family" (Joffe 1949, p. 239).

Since the chaverim view each other as psychological kin, conformity to group mores—even mores as exacting as those found in Kiryat Yedidim—poses no special problems. The chaverim, like the

---

*This familial aspect of the kibbutz is manifested on the biological level, as well. In all instances, children who have been born and reared in Kiryat Yedidim have obtained their mates from outside the kibbutz. This voluntary exogamy is entirely explicable by the statements of the sabras that endogamous marriages are viewed by them as incestuous.

members of any family, take it for granted that he who is sick shall
be given the best care; that the individual's needs, not his contribution to the economic welfare, determine what he shall receive; that a
person's superior economic position does not entitle him to better
food, or finer clothes, or a nicer room. The discussion of kibbutz
authority and social control must be perceived, therefore, within this
sociopsychological context.

The sovereign body of Kiryat Yedidim is the town meeting
(*sichah kellalit*), which includes every chaver of the kibbutz. As the
ultimate authority on all intra-kibbutz matters, the town meeting is
very jealous of its powers. The chaverim still retain much of the distrust of authority that characterized their youth movement days, and
they are reluctant to delegate authority. Most important decisions,
and sometimes those less important, are made in the town meeting.
The annual budget, a new building program, the expansion of an agricultural branch, the election of officers and committees, all are
debated in the town meeting. The stand to be taken on a political
issue, the amount of activity to be devoted to a political campaign,
the decision to admit an American anthropologist to the kibbutz to
do research, the problem of the intellectual level of the children, the
complaint of the women concerning kitchen facilities—these and
countless other problems, large and small, are the domain of the
town meeting.

Town meetings are regularly held twice a week. There are at
least three reasons for the frequency of such meetings. In their opposition to bureaucracy, the chaverim are reluctant to entrust decisions
to executive responsibility, and in their desire to remain a "pure
democracy" they have not created a representative legislative body.
Hence, most matters which in other societies would be delegated to
administrative officials, or which would come within the jurisdiction
of the legislative body, remain the responsibility of the entire community. Secondly, since the kibbutz is similar in many respects to a
large family, many decisions that in most societies are made within
the family are made in Kiryat Yedidim by the town meeting. Should
a student be sent to study in the city? Should a disturbed child be
sent to a psychiatrist? These, and similar "familial" questions, must
be decided by the entire community. Finally, the kibbutz is a religio-
political community, and many problems which are not viewed as
subjects for community discussion in other societies are frequently

part of the agenda of the town meeting. The problem of the women in the community, the participation of the younger people in community life, the meaning of a recent political event for the future of the kibbutz, the proper role of the Arabs in the national life of Israel —all are subjects for town meeting.

Underlying all these town meetings is the implicit belief that proper decisions—proper, in the sense of just and efficient—can be made only after intensive group discussion. These are often heated and long, and many meetings do not adjourn until after midnight. Even after the formal adjournment, groups of chaverim may remain in the dining room to continue the discussions informally.

Informal discussions are as important, as heated, and even more frequent than are the formal ones. In the fields, in the dining room, in the showers, there is constant discussion—a current book, American politics, a bill in the Israeli Parliament (*Knesset*), the desire of a couple to leave the kibbutz, an art exhibit, the prospects of a good crop, the advantages of a new tractor, a recent lecture on existentialism—these and countless others are debated interminably. Long in advance of town meetings, most people have made up their minds on issues to be presented; on the basis of these informal discussions, lines are drawn and partisans are prepared with arguments. And long after the meetings have been held, the discussions continue unabated. . . .

The expansion of the kibbutz made it impossible to operate with any degree of efficiency on the basis of a town meeting alone, and it became necessary to institute a system of formal leadership and authority, comprising "offices" and committees. When they found it necessary, however, to institute this system of formal leadership, they attempted to preclude the possibility of any one individual assuming too much power by restricting the tenure of office to a few years. This was accomplished by instituting a system of office rotation, and by the restriction of the "rewards" of office, so that no one could, or would, remain in office beyond his allotted time. . . .

The fact is, that the rewards of authority are not commensurate with the responsibilities entailed. There is no financial remuneration; there is little formal prestige; and there is not a great deal of power attached to these positions. In addition, many of these jobs are extremely time-consuming and, in many cases, persons who hold them are not relieved of other responsibilities—so that most of the work must be done in the evenings, after they have already devoted a full day to their regular jobs. This means not only that they are tired, but also that they seldom get to be with their families, a serious misfortune to the average chaver. Hence the kibbutz cartoon depicts a candidate for office in the city running after people asking them to vote for him, in contrast with the "candidate" in the kibbutz, shown fleeing his fellow-members, begging them *not* to vote for him. . . .

For those to whom these original motives are no longer as compelling as they formerly had been, there are public forms of social control, both informal and formal. The most effective informal technique of social control in any *gemeinschaft* is public opinion. In the kibbutz, public opinion is of even greater importance because of the almost complete absence of privacy to be found in this society. The simple fact of communal living itself places a premium on privacy. It is rare that one has the opportunity to be alone during the day—one works in a work gang, eats in a communal dining room, showers in a public shower, etc. It is even difficult to find privacy in one's room. During the summer months, the windows are open, and one can never escape the noises from outside the room. In the winter months, children must be entertained inside, rather than on the lawn, as is customary in the summer, making privacy impossible. Even after the children leave, it is difficult to find complete privacy in only one room with a spouse always present.

Evenings yield little more privacy than days. The average chaver participates in some group activity almost every evening. The intensive kibbutz schedule includes holidays, celebrations, committee meetings, classes, lectures, movies, and the bi-weekly town meeting. "Our lives," say the chaverim in a tone of both pride and complaint, "are too full." It is little wonder that a chavera who was studying English in her spare time complained that she had only one free evening a week in which to study. Hence, the sheer frequency of interaction, brought into being by the nature of communal living, as well as by the intensive kibbutz schedule, keeps one constantly exposed to the public eye.

Communication, moreover, is rapid in a small society, so that few activities can long remain concealed. As in any small society, activities are reported and conversations are repeated, so that secrecy is all but impossible. Moreover, with some few exceptions, the chaverim are exceptionally straightforward in their relations with their fellows. Just as they do not attempt to conceal their own thoughts or behavior—because of the futility of attempting such concealment—so they do not attempt to conceal their opinions of their fellows. It is expected that people will treat others with candor, and with little evasion or circumlocution. Indeed, the chaver who does not employ such candor is not trusted. One person, for example, has been given positions of responsibility in the kibbutz because of his exceptional talents. Nevertheless, the chaverim generally dislike him because he is not *yashar*, literally, straightforward. Should a chaver violate the group norms, it would not only be known in a short time, but he would be openly criticized for his behavior. Such group censure, informal though it is, is highly effective in a small community, and would render his existence in the kibbutz untenable. It is not surprising, then, to be told that: "Everyone is concerned about public opinion. Here you can't escape it. Everyone in the kibbutz knows about everyone else. Sometimes it is too much so."

But public opinion operates in semiformal and formal ways, as well as on an informal basis. Two semiformal techniques employed during this study may be reported here; one dealt with a relatively unimportant problem, the other with two serious problems. One of the vexing problems that confronts the kibbutz is the general reluctance on the part of chaverim to accept a work assignment in the dairy. Attempts had been made to induce certain of the young men to accept such an assignment, but these attempts had met with failure. At no time, however, were these young men publicly censured for their refusal. Another grave problem for the kibbutz is the slow but steady increase in private property. The acquiring of a small refrigerator by one couple aroused much private comment, but there was no official reaction. Although the kibbutz views this situation with grave concern, it has not yet devised any formal techniques for coping with it. Both these problems, however, were prominent in two skits that were presented as part of the celebrations of the Jewish festivals of *Purim* and *Succot*. In the Purim skit, there was a pointedly witty scene devoted to the unnamed, but easily identifiable, young men who refused to accept an assignment in the dairy. And in the Succot skit, there was a prominent reference to the "refrigerator." The author does not know the reaction of the couple who owned the refrigerator, but the reaction to the "dairy" skit was immediate. The following day when the author was working in the fields with one of the young men, the latter spontaneously referred to the skit and voluntarily admitted that he had been seriously affected by it.

Another problem, not so serious, but one which demanded immediate attention, was handled in still another way. Kiryat Yedidim celebrates the festival of Passover with an annual public *Seder*, or Passover ceremony, to which friends and relatives outside the kibbutz are invited. Its choir usually plays a prominent part in this celebration, but it had not been diligent in rehearsal attendance this year, and there was a strong possibility that it would not be prepared by Passover eve. Three days before the celebration, a notice signed by the Holiday Committee appeared on the bulletin board. The notice stated that only three days remained till Passover, and the choir was not yet prepared because its members had not attended rehearsals. If the choir did not meet the following three nights for rehearsals, the Holiday Committee would recommend to the Secretariat that the festival be cancelled. Beneath this announcement appeared the names of the choir members, and the sections in which they sang. The notice had its desired effect. Rehearsals were held with full attendance each night, and the choir sang at the Seder.

When the pressure of public opinion, exerted in informal and in semiformal ways, is not effective, the kibbutz has recourse to more formal procedures. These procedures are resorted to when a serious breach of kibbutz norms has occurred—such as a refusal to abide by an official decision of the kibbutz, or a violation of some part of its moral code. The first procedure is to bring the person's dereliction to the official attention of the kibbutz at a town meeting. This is a powerful sanction, and the very threat to use it is usually efficacious in this community where people are so sensitive to public opinion. A young man, for example, who had been asked by The Federation to accept the leadership of its national Youth Movement, refused to comply with the request. The Secretariat informed him that they would bring the matter before a town meeting, whereupon he agreed to accept the invitation.

On the other hand, when the mere threat to bring the matter to the attention of the town meeting is not sufficient to change the person's behavior, it then becomes necessary to carry out the threat. A woman who was working in the dairy, for example, was assigned by the Work Committee to the kitchen detail, as her turn in the rotation system had come up. She refused, and her case was brought before the town meeting. The entire meeting was devoted to this problem, but before it could be resolved, other and more pressing business occupied the agenda at succeeding meetings, and the author does not know the outcome. In another case, a person who had access to the kibbutz "store" was accused by another member of utilizing some of the goods for his private use. This charge evoked a heated debate, and the Secretariat appointed a committee to investigate the charge. After completing its investigation, the committee reported that the accused was innocent of the charge, although they did note some irregularities in his behavior. The town meeting which was called to hear the evidence was stormy and did not adjourn until 2:00 in the morning. The accused was finally exonerated.

The ultimate sanction that Kiryat Yedidim has at its disposal is expulsion. If a member is brought before the town meeting and is found guilty of a crime, or if a member refuses to acquiesce in a kibbutz decision, it may vote to expel him. Some time before our arrival in Kiryat Yedidim, a man had been accused of stealing, had been found guilty at a town meeting, and was expelled from the kibbutz. His family, of course, were not expelled and they chose to remain.*

During the writer's stay in the kibbutz, a couple asked for leave of absence, and a town meeting refused to grant it. The couple announced their intention to take a leave, whether it was granted or not. This deliberate challenge could not be ignored, and they were threatened with expulsion. They persisted in their plans, and were expelled.

This ultimate sanction of expulsion, however, is seldom employed. The chaver who would be so offensive as to merit expulsion is a person who is discontent with kibbutz life and who would probably leave eventually anyway. . . .

Reference

Joffe, Natalie F. "The Dynamics of Benefice among East European Jews." *Social Forces* 27 (1949): 238-47.

---

*About six months later, this man wrote the kibbutz that he viewed it as his home, that he could not live happily anywhere else, and that it was his intention to return. He did so, and there has been no attempt to force him to leave, particularly since the evidence had not been conclusive.

To the author's knowledge, this is the only incident of stealing on the part of a kibbutz member. In a village where doors were never locked, stealing was unknown until the arrival of the "oriental" youth groups.

The Kibbutz as a Learning Environment

The Kibbutz Educational Program

What is it about the kibbutz educational system that accounts for its generally positive results in building community and creating healthy individuals? We would like to single out two aspects of learning in the kibbutz which may account for this:

1. The wider meaning of learning within a society like the kibbutz; and
2. The structure of "schooling" and childrearing.

By developing these aspects we hope to illustrate the unique stand the kibbutz takes on creating a common ideology for the members of its society.

The Wider Meaning of Learning in Kibbutz Society. The economic sphere in the kibbutz is not neatly divided from the sphere of social relations. Fellowship and cooperation mutually support each other. One does not make money with one crowd, make friends with another, and make decisions with still another. The communal nature of kibbutz society means that most of its members are constantly interacting around the multiplicity of functions in the society. These interactions in the communal economy, in the political arena, in the family, and in the cultural life have resulted in many clear behavioral characteristics of kibbutz members. Because as a society the kibbutz is a deliberate attempt to structure experience so that *relatively*

Reprinted by permission from Joseph R. Blasi, "An Introduction to the Kibbutz" (Cambridge, Mass.: Harvard University, unpublished manuscript, 1975).

permanent changes in behavior occur, it is a learning society. This is actually the definition of learning. In fact, the whole community can be considered a "school of living," centering on the norms discussed above: the balancing of individual and community commitments, work, economic cooperation, political participation, ideology, and national service. One can say that life in the kibbutz prepares the person as much for the school as vice versa.

The community itself creates the appropriate conditions which instruct members in how to succeed in community. Neither does learning stop and "real life" begin after high school in the kibbutz. Real life is comprehensible and intelligible within the framework of what schoolchildren are taught. The half-hour story which a kibbutz kindergarten teacher reads to the children about economic cooperation is consistent with the economic cooperation the child may experience each day. The parent's rewarding of a child for sharing toys is consistent with the cooperative behavior of the children's play group which is rewarded by the teacher-member. The knowledge that each Saturday night one's parents go to the general assembly meeting is consistent with the emphasis the children's nurse puts on group consultation before decisions. The separation between education and life is, in fact, an artificial one. The kibbutz avoids this separation and thus constitutes a total learning environment where school and living broach a common set of real issues. Although it is true that adult life is not the life of a child and learning is not just living, the fact remains that children can participate in community activities and, perhaps more importantly, the meaning of adult work and life is transparent and visible to children. This presumes that they are developing, and have special needs, and require a certain amount of reserved attention and guidance. The free school or extreme de-schooling approach is not accepted by the kibbutz, which organizes itself quite seriously for the special developmental exigencies of children. A review of the structure of the educational program will illustrate this.

Structure of the Children's Society Educational Program. Education in the kibbutz is social change. The community formed its early educational system out of a desire to create a "new person" who would accept the values of a just society. Several historical studies by Viteles (1966) outline the source materials for this original conception of education by the early kibbutz members. In the beginning, Degana Aleph (the first kibbutz) established collective child-rearing and education as a utilitarian necessity so that more members, especially women, could work. Only in the 1920's, around the time of the arrival of Russian immigrants to Israel, did more ideological kibbutz members begin to root the communal learning system in a radically new social ideology. One can examine the fascinating documents from the meetings and councils that bore this unique system in the late 1920's, along with recent statements of kibbutz educational ideology. In the past, however, a common mistake has been to over-idealize education in the kibbutz by describing it in ideological terms. While the excellent description of collective education given by Rabin and Hazan (1973) presents a detailed summary of principles, it is difficult to visualize the day-to-day complexities of educating a whole society's children. Spiro's classic empirical work, *The Children of The Kibbutz* (1958), provides a realistic day-to-day picture of kibbutz education and childrearing and an assessment of the "psychological price" it, like any socialization system, exacts from its products.

The structure of child care and learning in the kibbutz has three goals: to shape development, providing resources and conditions for the kind of development the kibbutz considers important; to watch development, providing special guidance and care in attending to children's needs; and to adapt development to kibbutz society and cultural goals. These goals will be discussed in connection with the structure of the general educational program, and then more specifically in connection with the kibbutz high school.

In shaping development the kibbutz provides the best possible resources. Child-care nurses and teachers are trained in specially designed programs at the three branches of Seminar Ha Kibbutzim coordinated by Oranim, the Pedagogical Center for the Kibbutzim. The kibbutzim have created an alternative child development research and education complex to foster the values they consider important and integrate progressive knowledge and research on childrens' lives with their own culture. Each individual kibbutz gives priority to the children's budget and provides them with high quality housing, food, medical care, supervision, and play and study facilities. These conditions are under fairly constant scrutiny not only by the community as a whole but especially by the various branches of the Education Committee. Each kibbutz has infants' houses for children from birth to one and one-half years with four to six children to a room, cared for by a nurse (*metapelet*). Children from one and one-half to four years live in the toddlers' house. These more spacious quarters provide toys, a play area, and other amenities geared to their physical development and potentialities. The group formed in the babies' house will continue as a unit until the beginning of high school. At the age of three or four, several groups of children are combined to form a kindergarten group of fifteen to eighteen children who live in their own house made up of bedrooms, a playroom, a dining room, and an outdoor playground with suitable equipment. In the later childhood years, from approximately eight to twelve, the junior children's community is formed. It consists of four educational groups (third to sixth grade) of fifteen to twenty children, providing a wider choice of companions for play. Each group has a full-time educator and child-care nurse (responsible for guidance in the children's home, personal care, and training). On the whole the young child's society is made up of fifty to sixty children. From approximately the age of thirteen on the children move to the youth society of the high school, made up of about 150-200 children. Each group continues to live and learn together but all the groups cooperate in social and cultural activities. Usually, the high school is done cooperatively with other kibbutzim and, thus, may be located at another kibbutz. This distance gives the group the opportunity to remain in the kibbutz movement yet outside their own kibbutz with a larger and more diverse group of persons (usually including eighteen to twenty-five children from cities and villages not kibbutzim). It also discourages, as Rabin and Hazan (1973) note, "premature imitation of adult life and safeguards the value of studies and youthful activity."

The high school community is actually a "little kibbutz" with its own common dining room, meeting rooms, work branches, and committees. The children live with one or more roommates in dorm rooms usually scattered in one-story structures around the community dining room and study halls. The youth society has shops, hobby rooms, and music rooms for common use. The older high school students have rooms at their home kibbutz where they live during the summer and on vacations, and which they use as their "base" when they return home each afternoon to work in their community.

The integration of learning with the community does not mean that the community is not finely attuned to the developmental exigencies of each child or age group. Nurses are specially trained in baby care and mother-infant relations. During the first six weeks after birth the kibbutz mother spends full time with the child, for the kibbutz recognizes that the link between mother and child is the basis for future development. The mothers breast-feed the children together in a relaxed atmosphere in the babies' house. The mother gradually during the first year begins to resume the normal work schedule (six hours for women, eight for men), especially after weaning around the fifth month. The nurse does not act as the child's mother, neither does she attempt to form a highly intimate bond with each child. Today, she is considered a child-care professional who assists the mother, attempts to supervise, understand, watch over, and provide special assistance to the early development of the children. To answer charges that kibbutz children suffered from emotional difficulties because of this pattern of childrearing, several researchers discovered that kibbutz children did not suffer from maternal deprivation. Rabin (1958), Neubaurer (1965), and Spiro (1958) agree concerning the children's emotional and physical health.

In the toddlers' house, ideally the nurse who began working with the children's group continues to be their nurse. Working with a small group, she can give extensive individual attention and guidance to each child, creating a direct, loving relationship. The children from babyhood have an increased awareness of each other and it is the special attention and guidance the nurse gives to the forming of this awareness and these relationships that makes her guidance so valuable. She is responsible for much of the training given to the children (toilet training, eating, dressing) and she organizes activities which include walks, play, and work in the garden. When the children are three, several nurses begin to collaborate in merging their groups in preparation for kindergarten.

The kibbutz views the nurse as supporting the parental relationship rather than confusing the children or depriving them. As Rabin and Hazan (1973, p. 25) point out, "One individual cannot possibly fulfill all these needs (of the child) adequately as every mother who has raised a child in the kibbutz will confirm. Greater success is assured when the mother and the permanent metapelet work together to create an environment that will afford the infant many forms of contact." A tenet of the child-care program is to provide support for parents so that their relationship with their children does not compete with the demands of a busy life, but occurs in relaxed, pleasurable encounters when the parents can give children great attention. One must admit that the disintegration of American family life, the economic and time pressures, and the fragmentation of the whole society often create many strains and tensions between children and their parents. The kibbutz hopes that by relieving some of this tension, better mental health for children and better family life is possible. The parents visit the kindergarten at different times during the day or sometimes the children visit their parents at work. Parents observe their children in the group and spend much time sharing reactions with the kindergarten educator and the nurse. They participate in special events, such as presentations of the group's art, and help prepare for holidays and other occasions. In addition, the education committee, the federation's visiting educational personnel, and the staff of the three kibbutz child guidance clinics provide assistance in individual and group therapy and diagnosis of children and parents.

Throughout the early life of the child the educators are concerned with providing ample opportunities to develop abilities that have significance at that stage. Thus, a concern for providing ample affection and physical care is significant with infants; directing the instinctual drives into positive activities is significant in the toddler stage; and providing a variety of activities, educational resources, and changes to create new and different relationships is significant throughout the elementary years.

After the elementary years the emphasis is on the formation of the peer group. Children spend most of their time in the company of other children who begin increasingly to care for each other's development with the guidance of the nurse and the educator. The group is encouraged to set positive goals and experiment with leadership patterns that emerge in a variety of different settings requiring different abilities. For example, some group activities are: preparation of plays, investigation of the farm, sports, camping trips, and gardening. At this stage the parents and educators encourage the children in creating their own society. Group meetings are held and a farm committee is elected to supervise work. The children also have a library committee and a community newspaper. Rabin and Hazan (1973) summarize the developmental priorities of this stage of the educational program:

Kibbutz society is based on the free education of the individuals living within it. The children's community therefore is not another means of imposing correct behavior on the children; rather, it is a sphere in which they learn correct social behavior in the course of experiences while at the same time satisfying their need for play, work, and enjoyment. It is not an organizational framework, but one of essence, in which the child molds his or her personality and learns to impose limitations on himself or herself and to respect the rights of others. Above all, the children's community assures the children a happy childhood. (p. 60)

The High School and Youth Society

Let us now consider how the young adult's development is guided in the kibbutz high school. The emphasis on the group's importance in affecting the development of its members continues. This results in complaints that the low prestige or status of an adolescent within the group is a disadvantage of this approach. Adolescents in Kibbutz Vatik mentioned that there were clearly a few members in each group who felt they did not fit in, had low status, and to an extent were hurt because of this. It has not been determined, however, if this problem is more extreme in the kibbutz than in adolescent society generally.

Another younger adolescent of Vatik criticizes the group about a different issue, lack of diversity:

When one lives all one's life with the same people, and for seventeen or twenty or how many years you have seen that person, learning their strengths or weaknesses, their characteristics in a very basic way as a result of living so closely, one develops a rude or vulgar attitude. People have had it with one another. In this closed society, people stop caring, stop paying attention to one another. It is as if they figure that it would not make any difference to them if they acquired different habits of relating. You do not change your society, it is not like changing air (when you breathe), it is human. This is a problem here that people are bored and have had enough of each other. I think it is that way in every kibbutz.

While it is not the author's experience that this is a widespread phenomenon, this adolescent's opinion points to the strain on high school society in the kibbutz. Childhood is over. Adult life is creeping up and this fellowship-oriented collective society does not seem to have removed the pains, the angry and sweeping evaluations, and the bitter social accounting of adolescence.

High school in the kibbutz is mainly a social experience. As mentioned, the youth society is even more like a mini-kibbutz than the little children's farm. It has its own organization, cultural activities, dining room, and newspaper. The youth society does not control its own budget, security, or curriculum. Their planning of social and cultural activities and work is done through a general assembly meeting with the advice of adult representatives.

Each group has a full-time advisor, counselor, and educational coordinator. The educator tries to direct the development of the group by intervening with various individuals, conducting weekly group discussions on personal and organizational problems, and mediating individual-group conflicts. The educator has a difficult job and is very carefully chosen by the educational committee and the parents. As a member of the same community and not a paid outsider, he or she is open to constant criticism and feedback without the ability to expell, punish, fail, or otherwise manipulate the children. The group's nurse provides for the living quarters of the adolescents and cooperates with the educator and the parents in figuring out what is happening to the group. Kibbutz adolescents generally exhibit a high degree of tension toward the adult society as they wonder about, criticize, observe, and approach it. Our interviews at Vatik show widespread criticism of the kibbutz community and an active consideration of its pros and cons. Probably because they are not forced or brainwashed into membership, kibbutz adolescents are in a frustrating position. Developmentally, they need to question their society, but for the long term many of them will stay in the kibbutz. The three and one-half years in the army and a year or two travelling abroad, plus the usual university study, give ample time for the balancing of accounts and the decision about membership.

There are several problems with high school education in the kibbutz which stem both from the fact that it is a kibbutz and the fact that adolescent years are difficult and problem-laden. Because the high school is in the kibbutz it is not really *only* a high school. Kibbutz educators and the children themselves admit that the main events during this period are social and developmental, that is, people are interacting, changing, and growing. Intellectual learning is only possible through intellectual interest and motivation. Grades, expulsion, and family pressure ("You can't have spending money unless you get A's") are nonexistent. Spiro (1958) reported that classes were often disruptive, while the teachers are unwilling or unable to use personal authority to bring order. Youngsters at Vatik reported that each teacher had a different method of evaluation and that his or her ability to interest them and relate to them was a central dynamic in determining the nature of a particular class.

Let us consider three special problems in the high school: authority, ideology, and outside educational norms. Regarding authority, Spiro (1958) noted that the issue of alternative schools was in fact a central one for kibbutz teachers, students, and parents. Should the teachers exercise their authority to achieve educational goals or should they appeal to conscience and the responsibility of the group? While Zvi Lavi, a former director for the Educational Department in the Shomer Hatsair Federation of Kibbutzim, recognizes several prominent free school experiments as influential in kibbutz educational practice (see Rabin and Hazan 1973) the kibbutz is clearly not using an approach which favors basically spontaneous learning in a variety of unstructured situations. There is an organized educational program and students are expected to participate in it, but because it is an organic part of the children's society it does not have the quality of being an authoritative place where one fails or succeeds, as does the high school in modern society. Rather, learning is a function of the person's interests and motivation, the goals set with the educator and teachers, and the ability of the educational staff to be responsive to the student's needs. Lacking legal and educational enforcement structures (no police, no expulsion, no marks, no ability to ruin the future work career), the kibbutz high school cannot force its member-students to participate more than they are actually desirous of participating. Thus, "educational performance" is not a closely measured statistic. Success depends more on life experience, personal goals, and development. Many a "poor high school student" has, with the development of subsequent career goals, become quite creative. The success correlation between high school and later life is not a forced issue.

Another problem with high school education intrinsic to the kibbutz is ideological education. At the time of Spiro's study in 1951-52, membership in the kibbutz political movement and weekly ideological meetings was compulsory. Adults were determined to teach the younger members about socialism and kibbutz ideology. In recent years, this has all changed. Ideological education includes an emphasis on Zionism and on the structure and history of the kibbutz, but no attempt is made to recreate the young and vibrant Movement that the original kibbutz founders tried to pass on to their children. Some senior members deeply resent the Movement's passing, but it was the result óf a lack of interest on the part of young kibbutz members based on their radically different formative experiences. Spiro spoke of this situation:

The Movement in the Mosad is not successful. The students seem to be apathetic to its program and display only a perfunctory interest in its meetings. The Organizer attributes its lack of success to the absence in the mosad of the usual motivations for participation in youth movements—cameraderie, group belongingness, social activities, the opportunity to meet people of the opposite sex— since these needs are already filled by other aspects of mosad life. It has been his experience that a successful youth movement is based on rebellion against parents and the latter's way of life; and in the kibbutz the Movement is supported by the parents. (1958, p. 303)

When we interviewed high school students in Vatik many of them, as their parents had predicted, evaluated the kibbutz in emotional and personal, rather than ideological, terms. "It is my home," "all my friends are here," "I like the actual environment of the village," and "Kibbutz life is less pressuring, more cooperative" were common responses. The educators, however, feel that it is "impossible to maintain attachment to the kibbutz solely on the basis of such motives; it must also stem from ideological firmness" (Rabin and Hazan 1973, p. 110). The problem and challenge to kibbutz education now is to understand the present disposition of the young people, and to figure out how early learning experiences can encourage a common identification among them with criteria important to the kibbutz. Because the kibbutz is dynamic and changing, its members must be continually "learning what they believe in."

A third problem with the kibbutz high school is that, more than the other sectors of the educational program, it is affected by educational norms of the outside world and the surrounding society. Recently, for example, the project method, which saw learning experiences and material growing from the child outward to the school, has been modified. The kibbutz decided it was necessary to have subjects and stress skills in a more programmed way; math, language arts, crafts, and physical training were taken out of the project method. The Israeli Ministry of Education also made various demands for the standardization of the kibbutz curriculum with national norms and, in fact, connected the kibbutz's ability to receive municipal education aid on this process. Demands for standard facilities, class size, etc. was one of the factors that led to the joining of the high schools of many kibbutzim—in order to be able to deal financially with the demands—and the consequent disappearance of the community high school of each kibbutz. The school began to have subjects, time periods, pre-set goals, and increased specialization on the part of the teachers, although grades have not been formally introduced in spite of the fact that some students and parents favor their introduction. The desire on the part of youngsters to go to the university has meant that they must pass the national matriculation exam, a rigid requirement for university admission. This was long fought by the kibbutzim and eventually they gave in to the government.

These developments have raised cries that high school education in the kibbutz is losing its unique and original qualities. After the war of 1972, when high school students ran many communities while their fathers went to the army, some students questioned the need for high school since they proved they were able to take responsibility in the kibbutz. While it is generally agreed that in the university the kibbutz students work hard and achieve as well as or better than others, this is not connected with the formal aspects of the high school program but with their unique socialization and motivation. Although the kibbutz high schools have been accused of becoming increasingly prestructured, the issue is complex. The organic fit between "school" and community necessarily reduces the degree to which the kibbutz high school can become bureaucratized.

It is difficult to put these problems in perspective. Adolescence is always a time of questioning and disorganization, and perhaps no suitable structure can be grown to contain it. In the end, kibbutz adolescents do develop considerably through their high school experiences, which virtually eliminate much of the stress found in modern urban high schools.

Results of the Kibbutz Educational Program

Existing research shows that the kibbutz educational program achieves many of its broad cultural goals. Kibbutz education is one of the most studied parts of the kibbutz community. Recently, kibbutz members and educators have focused their concern on the plight of the second generation in the kibbutz. These are the sons and daughters of those who were born into the community. Their attitude toward the kibbutz and their position in the community represent a crucial test of the notion that education and community can be combined. Even if integrating community and education is a persuasive alternative ideology, a central question is: can this be practically worked out in a large number of communities? One of the main criteria for the success of the kibbutz way of life is its ability to socialize its second generation and, as Joseph Shepher (1971) has pointed out, "the ability of the second generation to enjoy kibbutz life and find roles and satisfactions in it." Little precise data exist concerning this success, which must be assessed and put in perspective before education in the kibbutz can be evaluated. Rosner (1976) studied the status of the several thousand members of the second generation of the Kibbutz Artzi Federation, which was founded after World War I. This Federation includes some seventy-three kibbutzim, including Vatik. Of the 2,904 second generation members born in the communities, 16.1 percent left for other kibbutzim, mostly because of marriage, and 70.5 percent remained in their own kibbutz. This is a very high percentage and there is no reason to believe it is different for the other Federations. It is generally accepted that the rate of departure has increased since 1967; according to recent research 30 percent of the second generation of the same Federation leave their communities. But, as Shepher (1971) has pointed out, the success of kibbutz socialization is impressive when we consider how unsuccessful many utopian communities have been in achieving continuity. When put in the context of the emigration that occurs in modern industrial or rural communities, the figure is even more impressive.

In addition to a fairly successful second generation, there are other indications that kibbutz childhood is healthy. Rabin and Hazan (1973) found that kibbutz children somewhat lagged behind non-kibbutz children in intellectual and ego development in the first two or three years of life. This was attributed to some frustration because of the temporary withdrawal of the mother at this time. Nevertheless, his research clearly established that these difficulties disappeared after the first few years, so that kibbutz children at ten are as well or better developed intellectually as non-kibbutz children. They showed greater emotional maturity, less sibling rivalry, less selfishness, and somewhat more anxiety and hostility towards their parents than non-kibbutz children. Seventeen-year-old kibbutz children functioned intellectually somewhat better and were as emotionally adjusted as their non-kibbutz counterparts. They had less conflict problems and hostility towards their parents. Rabin found kibbutz young men to be strong in ego, less aggressive, less rebellious towards society, and less oriented to defense mechanisms than their non-kibbutz counterparts. He discounted previous hypotheses (see Spiro 1958) that maternal deprivation produced social immaturity or that kibbutz adolescents were more hostile than non-kibbutz children. He also concluded that the children did not develop homogeneous personalities, and in fact exhibited a wide variety of personality traits.

Kaffman (1965 and 1972), who directs the child guidance clinic for the kibbutzim, found in two studies that kibbutz children were less prey to mental disturbance. He also notes that out of 3,000 emotionally disturbed kibbutz children which his clinic treated not one case of early childhood psychosis was found. This was attributed to the unique aspects of the educational and childrearing program in the kibbutz. He also found that kibbutz children had fewer mental problems than non-kibbutz children. Other researchers have taken these hopeful facts further. Kohen-Raz's (1972) book outlines how emotionally disturbed children are introduced from the outside into the kibbutz program and are greatly helped. Saar (1975) and Posnik (1975) have made two excellent proposals to effect a change in Israeli education using the kibbutz. Attempting to pin down the possible reasons for the greater mental health and ability of kibbutz children, Kohlberg (1971) and Reimer (1972) found that kibbutz children had higher stages of moral development and were more finely attuned to and responsive to justice than lower- and middle-class Israeli children, American working- and middle-class children, and children of several other countries. If kibbutz education and life has, indeed, such positive effects, these effects have deep significance. Drug abuse and juvenile crime are so rare as to be almost nonexistent. Yet, Spiro (1958), Bettelheim (1969), and others generally agree that the kibbutz has not created the "new person." The utopian dream of unbridled, unbothered, and fully dedicated human beings has not come true, if it is even desirable. Nevertheless, in certain critical areas the kibbutz has proved that childhood and society are deeply related, and that many positive experiences can be encouraged and negative outcomes eliminated by kibbutz child development.

References

Bettelheim, Bruno. *The Children of the Dream*. New York: Macmillan, 1969.

Kaffman, M. "A Comparison of Psychopathology: Israeli Children from Kibbutz and from Urban Surroundings." *American Journal of Orthopsychiatry* 35, no. 3 (1965): 509-20.

Kaffman, M. "Characteristics of the Emotional Pathology of the Kibbutz Child." *American Journal of Orthopsychiatry* 42, no. 4 (1972): 692-709.

Kohen-Raz, Revven. *From Chaos to Reality: Experiences in the Re-education of Emotionally Disturbed Immigrant Youth in Kibbutzim*. New York: Gordon & Breach, 1972.

Kohlberg, Lawrence. "Cognitive-Developmental Theory and the Practice of Collective Education." *Group Care: An Israeli Approach*, edited by Martin Wolins and M. Gottesman. New York: Gordon & Breach, 1971.

Neubauer, P. B., ed. *Children in Collectives; Child Rearing Aims and Practices in the Kibbutz*. Springfield, Ill.: C. C Thomas, 1965.

Posnik, Geri. *The Kibbutz and Israeli Society: A Proposal to Israeli Education*. Cambridge, Mass.: Harvard University, unpublished manuscript, 1975.

Rabin, A. I. "Infants and Children Under Conditions of 'Intermittent' Mothering in the Kibbutz." *American Journal of Orthopsychiatry* 28 (1958): 577-84.

Rabin, A. I., and Hazan, Bertha. *Collective Education in the Kibbutz*. New York: Springer, 1973.

Reimer, Joseph B. *The Development of Moral Character in the Kibbutzim with a Special Focus on Adolescents*. Cambridge, Mass.: Harvard University, unpublished manuscript, 1972.

Rosner, Menachem. Personal communication from Ephraim Rosen, director, social department, Kibbutz Artzi, Federation Tel Aviv. This research was completed under the direction of Menachem Rosner, Center for Social Research on the Kibbutz, Givat Chaviva, Israel, 1976.

Saar, Shalom. *A Study of the Educational Systems of Urban Schools and the Kibbutz in Israel*. Cambridge, Mass.: Harvard University, unpublished manuscript, 1975.

Shepher, Joseph. "Mate-Selection Among Second Generation Kibbutz Adolescents and Adults." *Archives of Sexual Behavior* 1, no. 4 (1971).

Spiro, Melford. *The Children of the Kibbutz*. Cambridge, Mass.: Harvard University Press, 1958.

Viteles, Harry. *A History of the Co-operative Movement in Israel* (7 vols.). Bridgeport, Conn.: Hartmore, 1966.

10

The Hutterites: A Modern Religious Community

In many respects the Hutterite communities are not unlike kib-butzim. They operate within the framework of a number of radical communitarian practices: much of the eating, laundry, and service elements of the group are done communally; they are economically self-sufficient; all members share equally in the work and economic rewards; childrearing and education are largely communal functions and prepare children for life in the community rather than for social or economic mobility in the larger society. The Hutterites are funda-mentally different, however, in their strong religious orientation. The kibbutz was founded and is to some extent maintained on the basis of two ideological threads: the pioneering thrust of Zionism, which assumed a common struggle to settle on and sink roots into the Jew-ish homeland; and the feeling that bourgeois life had become cor-rupted with materialism and a superficial or artificial sense of work, which had to be replaced by a simpler lifestyle and a more direct

relationship with the land. The fact that Israel is a modern capitalist state with material goals sometimes creates considerable ideological discomfort for those committed to the kibbutzim. The Hutterites have no such concrete image as a nation-state or territorial homeland to mediate the relationship between community and their broader ideological vision. Entry into the ideological vision is not based on an ascribed condition, such as being Jewish, but rather on a transcendent religious state of mind and behavior. This state is linked to the belief that absolute authority resides in an omnipotent God:

At all times the individual must be submissive to the will of God that is explicitly manifested in the believing community. Self-surrender and not self-development is the divine order. Since man is endowed with both a carnal and a spiritual nature, he can overcome his carnal tendency only by submission to the community and with the help of his brothers. (Hostetler and Enders 1967, p. 15)

This sense of ideological transcendence has several important implications which do not apply to the kibbutzim. First, it means that the test of membership is not simply one of prior religious or cultural membership (e.g., being Jewish and behaving as a good communitarian). One must embrace a religio-cosmic perspective and manifest the behavior implied by that perspective. Whereas kibbutz members work out of an individualistic-communitarian balance or dialectic, the Hutterites assume that individualism (in the sense of ego) and feelings of self-importance or personal autonomy are evil; they bar one from an accurate perception of ultimate reality. Egotistical expression must be substantially suppressed (or annihilated) as a condition of membership in the community. Second, while public opinion and the tight structure of the simple communitarian lifestyle are perhaps the strongest forces in controlling behavior (as in the kibbutz), the formal systems of governance are quite different. The ultimate basis of authority in the kibbutz is the town meeting. The Hutterite colonies are organized as a bureaucratic hierarchy, with the head preacher in the position of greatest authority. While there may be a correlation between status and decision-making power, this relationship is informal in the kibbutz—there is, in fact, strong pressure for all to participate in the decision-making process. The Hutterites, on the other hand, engage in mutual judgment of each other's attitudes and behavior, and those with higher formal status have a

*responsibility to keep other members ideologically "on the track."
Third, while both the kibbutzim and the Hutterite colonies have
been successful economically, kibbutzim have been much more concerned with increasing the standard of living of the whole community and sharing in the drive for economic development characteristic
of Israel generally. The kibbutz creates a balance between the prag-
matics of the immediate work-a-day world and the ideological concern to achieve a decent socialist community. The Hutterites, on the
other hand, require each individual to see life as a whole, as a unity
of thought, attitudes, behavior, and transcendent perceptions; work
is significant only within the framework of this unifying vision.*

*Finally, the two kinds of communities come out of two very
different religio-cultural traditions. The kibbutz has links with Juda-
ism, with its rational communitarian press toward dealing with problems and conflicts as they exist in the here and now. The Hutterites
have links with the perfectionist other-worldly tradition of Christianity—assuming that through the process of sacrifice one can find an
ultimate guiding vision of the good life. But perhaps the more interesting observation is that basic solutions to basic problems in everyday life are strikingly similar, for example, the balance between
maintaining the nuclear family on the one hand and communal
service institutions on the other (eating, laundry, child-care, education, etc.). From the point of view of quality of life, one must question the extent to which the more tolerant ideological atmosphere of
the kibbutz affects the meaning of the individual member's life. Is it
better for each member to accept the communitarian social structure
as the only given, and beyond that search for personal meaning (as in
the kikbutz); or is it better to have available an all-pervasive meaning
system which one must accept or reject?*

All Things Common

The people described in this chapter are attempting to establish a colony of heaven. They do not have illusory ideas that their colony is perfect, but they have acquired some utopian-like characteristics in their social patterns: economy of human effort, elimination of extremely poor or wealthy members, a system of distribution that minimizes privileged position, motivation without the incentive of private gain, and a high degree of security for the individual. All of these characteristics are contained in a communal society without the use of a police force and with an ideology that reasonably satisfies both spiritual and material needs.

By living on large acreages of communally owned land, the Hutterites maintain a degree of geographic isolation. Their German dialect and distinctive dress reinforce social isolation from their neighbors. The Hutterites think of themselves as a people who honor God properly by living communally. Honoring God, they say, requires communal living, devout pacifism, and proper observance of religious practices. They regard as inevitable the atrocities they have suffered throughout their history, as well as the misunderstandings with the outside world in modern times. To the Hutterites, suffering is a necessity for which they must be morally prepared at all times. During four centuries, the group has demonstrated a remarkable

Reprinted by permission from John A. Hostetler and Gertrude Enders Huntington, *The Hutterites in North America* (New York: Holt, Rinehart, & Winston, 1967).

ability to adapt to changing political, social, and technological environments. The Hutterites are the largest family-type communal group in the Western world. The society is noted for successful large-scale farming, large families, and effective training of the young. These distinguishing features are inseparable from their religion. All Hutterites inhabit the United States and Canada and none have survived in the countries of their origin, namely, Austrian Tyrol and Moravia. In 1965 the population numbered about 16,500 persons in 170 colonies. . . .

In the Hutterite view, the individual will must be broken. This is achieved early, primarily during the kindergarten age, and is reinforced continually until death. In place of self-fulfillment there must be self-denial. The individual must be humble and submissive. After approximately twenty years of intensive indoctrination, the individual is expected to accept voluntarily the teachings of the colony. When he is able to express the remorse, abasement, and loathing associated with his sinful self, he will receive baptism. Individual identity must be fused with the community. Just as a grain of wheat loses its identity in the making of a loaf of bread (Rideman 1950, p. 86), so the individual must lose his identity in one corporate body. "God worketh only in surrendered men."

Self-surrender, not self-development, is the Hutterite goal. The communal will, not the individual will, becomes important. The good of the majority governs the stages of life from birth to death. Since human nature is sinful from birth, Hutterites value education as a means for "planting" in children "the knowledge and the fear of God" not for self-improvement. The consequences of original sin are moderated by intensive teaching from an early age. "We should let the Heavenly Gardener implant such fruit that will bear everlasting life. The child's will should not be fulfilled, but the Father's will. Our will should be locked in His will."

Although the individual is "grafted into the divine character or nature" (Rideman 1950, p. 18), he is never free from temptation of his carnal nature. His security in the divine order depends not on his verbal affirmation or the rite of baptism, but on his "proven works" or daily behavior. Behaviorally this means adherence to the rules of the church community. The individual may not conform to his own interpretation of the "word" or his own notion of obedience. Since "God worketh in surrendered men," the individual must submit to the will of the community because community is the will of God. . . .

During his life span the Hutterite has the opportunity to change his destiny by giving up his individual will for the welfare of the community. This change in destiny requires a lifetime of submission to communal living in order to achieve the hope of eternal life after death. Death is managed in such a way that it becomes not a dreadful experience devoid of purpose, but the final triumphant step in restoration to a divine order.

The Hutterite world view includes the following:

1. Absolute authority resides in a single supernatural being, an omnipotent God, who created the universe and placed everything in a divine order and hierarchy. All events are ordered of God and nothing happens without the knowledge of God.

2. Through transgression of the divine order and the disobedience of man toward God, all nature became perverse. In its fallen or carnal state human nature desires self-recognition, self-ownership, and bodily (carnal) pleasure. Human nature is helpless and can never completely overcome the carnal tendency, and only by believing the word of God, by repentance, by receiving the grace of Christ, and through continual submission of the self to the will of God in communal living can the individual attain eternal life after death.

3. The carnal nature and the spiritual nature are inevitably antagonistic to each other and constitute two separate kingdoms. The fallen or carnal nature is displeasing to God; the spiritual nature permits an individual to be restored to the divine order where he will voluntarily share his life and his possessions.

4. The spiritual kingdom is ruled by the spirit of Christ and is known by the complete obedience experienced in sharing all material goods. Only in a divinely created fellowship, separated from the world, can men succeed in living communally, and only in this way can God be properly honored, worshipped, and obeyed.

5. At all times the individual must be submissive to the will of God that is explicitly manifested in the believing community. Self-surrender and not self-development is the divine order. Since man is endowed with both a carnal and a spiritual nature, he can overcome his carnal tendency only by submission to the community and with the help of his brothers.

6. All persons are born in sin and with a tendency toward evil and self-pleasure. This tendency can be modified by teaching young children the divine discipline. Children must be taught to be obedient to the "law" of their elders and superiors until they accept the mature discipline of the believing community.

Spatial Patterns

Dariushof is a colony located on the northern edge of the Great Plains about one hundred miles from a large trading center and ten miles from a small town which is their post office. The colony is sufficiently near to its parental colony (fifteen miles) so that work and services can be exchanged, but not near enough so that young people can walk between colonies. The colony buildings (numbering about fifty) are reached by a gravel road and cannot be seen from the public road nearby. This colony owns 6,000 acres and leases 3,000 additional acres, which is about the average for lands owned or leased by other colonies in the area.

Although there is no Hutterite style of architecture, there is a characteristic colony layout. The center of the colony is the kitchen complex and the long houses or living houses, with their associated sheds and the kindergarten. The long houses run due north and south, for as a preacher put it, "they are squared with the compass. You don't walk crooked to the earth, you walk straight; that is how our buildings should be, straight with the compass and not askew." Typically each long house has four apartments, each with a separate entrance. A normal sized apartment has three rooms. There is an entrance room containing a table, straight chairs, a wash basin, a cupboard for a few dishes, and the stairway entrance to the attic; off either side of the entrance room is a bedroom with two double beds, one or two day beds, and a crib. The second story of the house is one long unpartitioned attic in which the families store their out-of-season clothing and tools. Usually, there is no basement. The many other buildings in a colony are laid out parallel or at right angles to the long houses.

All the people over six years of age meet in the kitchen three times a day to eat their meals. Here the women work preparing food for the colony, launder their family's clothes, and the colonists come to bathe or shower. Outside the kitchen is the bell that signals mealtime, announces that the women must come to work, or that calls for help should there be a fire.

Ideally the color of the buildings reflects the use of the building or the attitude of the people toward the building. In one colony the kitchen, the long houses, and the kindergarten are all painted white with blue trim. The small buildings near the long houses that are primarily for colony use, such as the bee house, the shoe shop, and the small traditional goose houses, are also painted white with blue. In contrast, those buildings used primarily for economic activity that brings in money from the outside economy are painted, in this particular colony, a bright red. They include the machine shop, the pump house, the root cellar, and various barns. An exception is the public school house, which in *Dariushof* is stucco instead of wood, is painted yellow, is oriented to face the state road rather than the colony, and from which the sign giving its former name and school district has never been removed. Although physically within the colony, the members have emotionally placed it outside.

The spatial orientation of the buildings and the unified color scheme reflect Hutterite thinking: everything is classified; each part of the universe has its correct place, which in turn determines its correct function and proper use. "By their fruits ye shall know them" is interpreted to mean that one's appearance reflects one's attitude or the strength of one's belief. Or, more succinctly, as one strict minister said when discussing the dress of the women of his colony, "I don't care how frilly and frothy their underwear is, it's what shows that counts." What shows classifies the woman, just as it classifies the building. Her dress indicates that she is: (1) an adult woman, (2) a Christian, (3) a Hutterite, and (4) that she knows her position relative to men. It also shows whether she is dressed for work, for evening church, or for Sunday.

Hutterites consider life in this world to be transient, temporary, and of no consequence where it is lived, for they are always "in strange lands under Jews and Gentiles." In these strange lands they create their own physical environment which is remarkably uniform. The colony is the concrete expression of the Hutterite belief system and the social environment in which the beliefs are transmitted to the children. What gives a Hutterite identity is not the place he has lived, nor having lived in one or many places, but rather that in spite of geographic moves the pattern of his life has always been the same, even to the floor plan of his house and the position of his home relative to that of his neighbors. A specific place is not important—specific orientation is of utmost importance.

Time Patterns

Hutterite theology teaches that there is a right order for every activity. Consequently, time functions to organize Hutterite activities and social relationships. The daily schedule involving all the members of the colony is severely patterned. The weekly schedule builds up to a climax in the Sunday complex, preparing for Sunday. The liturgical calendar is integrated with the change of seasons and the agricultural cycle. Most women's work is organized by a time schedule, and their family work follows daily, weekly, and seasonal patterns. Their colony work is of two types: general food preparation and cleaning that is performed by the women working together in a group and the rotating colony jobs for which one or two women assume responsibility for one week at a time.

Within this small face-to-face society, time spent on earth functions as an impartial means for establishing order in social relationships. The individuals are ranked by age and sex; age determines both the group to which an individual belongs and, generally, his place within the group. The stages of life do not correspond simply to biological phases but represent social functions.

Age Sets. Age sets are as follows:

House children: birth to two years. The small child who is still fed at home is referred to as a house child.

Kindergarteners: three to five years. The child in this age set attends the *Klein-Schul* or kindergarten. Some colonies will admit the child to kindergarten at the age of two and one-half years.

School children: six to fourteen years. These children attend the *Gross-Schul* or German school, and they also attend the public or English school from the time they are approximately six until the day before they are fifteen. At age fifteen the child enters the adult dining room.

Young people: age fifteen to baptism. This age sometimes has been called "the in-between years," or "the foolish years." Foolish does not imply any juvenile delinquency, but that the person is immature and sometimes wavering in his loyalties. Boys of this age are given the most challenging physical labor; girls do most of the colony painting.

Baptism (about age twenty) to marriage: Baptism signifies membership in the colony and is usually followed rather closely by marriage.

Marriage and adulthood: Following marriage the adult man is eligible for leadership positions, such as German teacher, chickenman, or blacksmith. After he has proved himself in these categories he becomes eligible for an executive position by being elected to the council.

Aged: The older men gradually retire from their leadership positions but remain advisers and interpreters of tradition. The older women admonish the young people, distribute the colony allotments to individual families, and help care for the babies.

Although the age sets are distinct in the life cycle, one concept may overlap several stages. For example, a child is considered a baby until he hits back, until the next one is born, until he enters kindergarten, and until he enters German school. A person becomes an adult through a series of stages: when he begins eating with the adults at fifteen, when he is baptized, when he is married, when he grows a beard, and when his first child is born. . . .

Religious man in traditional and preliterate cultures has conceived of two classes of time—the sacred and the secular—and the Hutterites participate in both of these realms. Sacred time is related to the beliefs about creation and is nonflowing, that is, it is eternal, and pertains to God who is believed to be without beginning or end. It also is characteristic of the word of God, for God's words always remain an inseparable part of him and therefore are eternal. The Hutterite soul has a beginning but no end.

Secular time is the measure of events that take place on earth, which have both a beginning and an end. It applies to all material objects, including the human body.

Intermediate between sacred and secular time are history and dreams. For the Hutterites, history is important as a dimension of the presence of God in the world. They are not interested in history in terms of dates on a secular time scale but as steps in the development of the church of God. Therefore, historical events that are unrelated to their own outlook on life are of little meaning to them and even their own history is remembered as it strengthens their faith rather than as a dated sequence of events. This means that there is some fusion of the beginning of Christianity (the historical period of Christ's birth and the writing of the Bible) with the beginning of the Hutterites (during the persecutions of the sixteenth and seventeenth centuries and the writing of the Hutterite sermons). Miracles of the sixteenth century may be mixed with those of the nineteenth, for the worldly date is unimportant compared with the fact that God "broke into history." History is a dimension of secular time that is recalled primarily because it illustrates eternity. Dreams are also intermediate between secular and sacred time. Unlike activities in secular time that should pass quickly and that one does not wish to extend, a Hutterite may report that he did not want to "leave that dream." Occasionally dreams may be equated with visions and then, too, they are outside the secular time scale.

Almost every evening, between the end of the day's work and the evening meal, secular time on the colony is interrupted by sacred time. The total community of school children and adults gathers together for the evening church service. Here they symbolically return to the time of their origin. The daily renewal of motivation through ritual participation is of utmost importance. For the Hutterite it is the sacred time which makes secular time meaningful. As the preacher slowly reads the sermons, unhurriedly recites the prayers, and the congregation sings the long, slow hymns, time is suspended: There is no rush to complete this task for the members are participating in a nonsecular time dimension. God's time is eternal, nonflowing, sacred.

In the daily round of meals and work the Hutterites are keenly aware of the passage of time. The day is broken into small units of time that form a tight, although not rigid, schedule. This severe patterning means that the individual members of the colony have little free choice and few decisions to make with regard to time. Just as material objects are not owned by a Hutterite, he also has little concept of private time. Time is not something that can be reserved for private use; it is not equated with money. The time that is needed for the completion of an operation, for example, the building of a feed shed, is considered, but not the time given by the various contributing individuals. However, the speed with which an individual works gives him status. A woman will always know how long it took her to make an article of clothing, and both adults and children set up tasks in such a way that the speed with which they are finished is obvious. There is little savoring of the moment, for the attitude toward almost everything in this early life is to get it over with. This applies to meals, to work, even to life itself, which is believed to be short, transitory, and of real significance only as it relates to eternal time.

Daily Schedule. The daily schedule involves all members of the colony, and the patterns of all individuals mesh in such a way that the colony runs smoothly and efficiently. The basic schedule varies with the time of year; it is modified in accord with the weather on a given day and is adjusted slightly to accommodate special tasks or an emergency. Thus in winter when the daylight hours are few and there is less agricultural work, the rising bell rings later (at 7:00 a.m. instead of 6:15 a.m.) and supper is earlier (at 6:15 p.m. instead of 7:00 p.m. If it rains during haying season, the rising bell may ring at 7:00 a.m. instead of 6:15 a.m. because the hay is too wet to cut. When the men are busy haying, food is sent out to the fields to them and they are fed supper when they return for the night, which may be as late as 10:00 p.m. If the women are not finished with their colony work, supper may be served late for all the adults in order that the task may be completed before the meal. When colony work is pressing, the evening church service is omitted.

Each age set has its own daily schedule. Most adults are up an hour or more before the rising bell. The time of rising is determined by their special work assignments and the age and number of their children. The woman who is baking mixes the bun dough at 3:30 a.m., the cowman starts milking at 4:30 a.m., the mother of a young baby nurses him at 5:00. At 6:15 the rising bell rings, and at 6:30 the bell for adult breakfast is sounded. At 6:45 the school children eat breakfast, and the three- to six-year-olds go to the kindergarten for their breakfast. After eating, the school girls clean the dining room and kitchen. Before the children's breakfast the women clean the adult dining room, wash the dishes, and gather food to carry back to the house children whom they feed in the apartments. The men do their chores, and the unassigned men and boys assemble informally to learn their job assignments for the morning. The work bell for the women rings any time between 7:15 and 8:50, depending on the amount of colony work. About 9:00 a.m. the adults and any children working with them pause at their places of work for a snack of a cool drink or coffee with buns. At 10:00 a.m. the bell rings to announce dinner for the kindergarten children and the house children. Dinner is brought to the kindergarten, and the three- to six-year-olds are fed by the kindergarten mother who then puts them to sleep. Mothers carry food home for their house children, feed them, and put them to bed. At 11:00 the bell rings for the school children's dinner. At 11:30 the warning bell rings to remind the men to get ready for dinner. At 11:45 the dinner bell rings, and all the adults eat their main meal, seated at their assigned places, the men on one side of the room, the women on the other, arranged around the tables according to age. Afterward the women wash the dinner dishes, the adults rest, and then have a light snack. After the snack the men return to work, and some time between 1:30 and 2:30 the work bell rings signaling the women's return to the kitchen for colony work. At 3:00 p.m. the kindergarten children are fed a snack, recite their prayers and go home about 3:30. At 5:00 the mothers carry food back to the apartments and feed their house children and kindergarten children. At 6:00 the bell rings for the school children's supper. At 6:30 the school children and all the adults assemble for the daily church service. The adults eat at 7:00. After the meal area is cleaned up and the men have finished the evening chores, the members of the colony are free to talk, visit, or work on individual projects until it is time to give the children a snack, supervise their prayers, and put them to bed. It is a schedule that keeps everyone busy, but unhurried. Time seems to pass quickly, partly because the day is divided into such small blocks of time.

The colony bell is rung to announce rising time and most of the meals; it is rung to call the women to work or to announce a wedding shivaree; its ring summons the members to help put out a fire or cope with an emergency. The bell pertains to worldly events that involve large segments of the colony. Unimportant details like snacks are not signaled by the bell, nor does the bell ring for a meal that is served directly after a church service, for the colony is already together and it would be superfluous to ring it. The bell is never used to call the members to church as is the custom among "worldly" people. If there is a question about whether there will be a church service, children are sent around to inform the families. When the minister starts to the service, the others follow. Church services are of a different order of importance from regular temporal activities; this supremely important gathering of the entire community is never announced by the bell.

Weekly Schedule and Sunday Complex. The weekly pattern of activity builds to a climax in preparation for Sunday. The men are caught up in the Sunday complex only on Friday and Saturday, but the women's work and the food served follows a traditional weekly schedule. On Monday the women do the family washing at the community wash house at a time assigned to them. They wash in rotation, beginning with the oldest woman and ending with the youngest, moving up one turn each week. Ideally a woman does all the washing for her family and finishes the ironing and the mending on Monday. This is possible if she is fortunate enough to wash early that week and if there is no colony work in the afternoon. A colony may mildly boast that everyone is finished washing before 10:30 Monday morning. In some colonies the women try to polish their floors every day, but if they are unable to do this, they always polish them on Tuesdays and Fridays. During the summer the school girls pick peas for the kitchen on Tuesday morning. On Wednesday, Thursday, and Friday the women hoe the garden and pick vegetables. Women with small children wash again on Thursday. Friday is a major cleaning day. The kitchen and dining room cement floors are scrubbed with hot water and soap by all the women. The women clean their own apartments and wax and polish their floors. The cook, the baker, and the milking woman clean their respective work areas because women's work assignments change on Sunday night and they want to leave their places of work clean. One of the work teams makes noodles. Saturday morning all the women roll buns, and the unmarried girls scrub the school house so it will be ready for the Sunday church services. On Saturday afternoon everyone bathes, hair is combed, and beards are trimmed. Everything and everyone must be clean for Sunday. . . .

The meals have a pattern that varies somewhat with the season and varies considerably from one colony to another. The sweetened orange pekoe tea that is served at Saturday supper is called "Saturday tea" to distinguish it from the medicinal or herbal teas that are drunk in the homes. A person with stomach trouble may regularly skip a certain meal because he knows that the food to be served does not agree with him. Sunday dinner consists of noodle soup and roast duck or, if there is no duck, chicken or goose.

Sunday begins with the Saturday evening church service. Among the *Dariusleut* the women and girls wear special Saturday afternoon dresses to this service and to supper. Saturday evening everyone sings hymns informally and visits, discussing religion and retelling Hutterite history. People try to go to bed early on Saturday night so they will not be tired for Sunday. Sunday morning the waking bell rings late at 7:30. The women wear nice dresses to Sunday breakfast, the school children wear clean clothes to breakfast, and the kindergarteners, because they do not attend church, wear regular clothes. The kindergarten children are often cared for during this time by one of the school children so that the kindergarten teacher will be free to attend church. After breakfast the women and girls change into "Bible clothes," and at 9:00 go to the service wearing dresses that are worn only for church. The sermons delivered were written during periods of persecution when the Hutterites were becoming a distinct people; they are not spontaneous or intellectual lectures on contemporary concerns. Even the rhythm of the preacher's voice differs from ordinary speech during this period of suspended temporality. The function of the sermons is not only to interpret the meaning of Biblical passages, but to guide the Hutterites through the present, secular, "evil times."

When church is over at approximately 10:30, the women and girls change into Sunday afternoon dresses and proceed immediately to Sunday dinner. After dinner the adults take a long Sunday afternoon rest. At 1:30 p.m. the unbaptized members of the colony assemble with the German teacher for Sunday school. Here they demonstrate how well they have listened to the morning sermon and recite the hymn verses they have had to memorize during the week. Families are together Sunday afternoon; there is some visiting within the colony, and if another colony is within easy traveling distance, there will often be an exchange of visits, with the visitors attending Sunday evening church (4:30) and supper (5:15) at the host colony. Weekdays are fairly uniform, but Sunday is a very different day. The leisurely Sunday schedule functions to distinguish this holy day from work days. In a Hutterite colony Sunday is long; the church service is long, the rest period is long, and there is almost no work done. Each person is reminded that God's time is measured by eternity, in strong contrast with the swift flow of hours during the busy work week.

Colonies vary in the strictness with which they observe Sunday. Some allow absolutely no unnecessary work, although none are puritanical in their definition of necessary. Other colonies are quite relaxed about observing Sunday and permit clothes to be washed, garden produce to be picked, and ducks to be plucked on Sunday afternoon. When the weather is unseasonable for harvesting during the week, a colony may decide to work in the fields on Sunday. The rule of no Sunday work that is so pervasive in many denominations in America can be adjusted by the Hutterites through a community decision made in the interests of the total colony. Since goods and time all belong to God, no individual is benefiting from Sunday work and God is still being honored.

Liturgical Calendar. The liturgical calendar punctuates the year and divides it into definable seasons. It begins with Advent (the preparation for the coming Christ) and ends with Pentecost (the establishment of the Christian Church) (Friedmann 1965, p. 158). During the long and uneventful winter events are placed by relating them to the liturgical calendar; during the busy agricultural season events are usually related to the major agricultural activity. Pigs are butchered "between Three Kings Day and Easter," but the baker makes Tuesday treats "from before seeding till after harvest." The liturgical cycle and the agricultural cycle are interrelated. In addition to the universal Christian holidays of Christmas and Easter there are special services that are performed at the correct time for the specific colony. The harvest sermon is read the Sunday after the harvest is gathered. Specific sermons are read to meet colony needs, such as discipline or comfort for the sick; otherwise Hutterite preachers follow a traditional yearly pattern in selecting the sermon to be read aloud on a specific Sunday. Each of the two preachers keeps a record of the date and text of all sermons delivered, who read them, and the hymns that were sung. The liturgical pattern specifies the celebration of important Christian holidays, but it is sufficiently flexible to allow incorporation of sermons that celebrate significant colony events.

Authority Patterns

All authority both inside and outside the church is believed to originate with the supernatural. Governmental authority is believed to have been ordained by God in his wrath to take vengeance on evil and to discipline the godless. Within the church there is order without physical coercion; baptized members are believed to have received the supernatural gift of the Holy Spirit through obedience and submission, and they have more power and responsibility than those who have not been baptized.

Bureaucratic Organization. All the baptized members of the colony make up the *Gemein* or church. The group, not individuals, has the power to exclude and to accept members. Women participate in the church service by being present and by joining in the prayers and hymns and by formally greeting newly baptized members, but they "have no voice" in church and therefore do not participate in formulating colony policy nor are they eligible for church leadership positions. Only baptized men are eligible for the departmental positions such as cattleman, pigman, shop mechanic, shoemaker, and only they may vote to elect members to these positions and to decide the economic, social, and religious life of the colony. . . .

The bureaucratic organization of the colony can be described briefly as follows:

1. *The colony.* The colony is a domestic group consisting typically of all persons of Hutterite parentage or persuasion residing on the premises. It is the biologic, economic, ceremonial, and self-sustaining unit within which the needs of its members are met through the activities of communal living.

2. *The church,* or *Gemein.* The church consists of all the baptized men and women. They celebrate communion as an exclusive unit and welcome back into their midst repentant members. Only baptized men may vote in formal decisions. They vote on major colony policies and determine who will hold positions of leadership.

3. *The council.* The council consists of five to seven men selected by the *Gemein* to serve an executive function. The first minister, the assistant minister, the householder, and the field manager are always on the council. Sometimes one individual will hold two of these offices or there may be no assistant minister. Except in a small colony these positions are usually represented by four different men. Generally one or two other department heads or older men also serve on the council. They sit in order of rank, facing the men of the congregation. They make practical day-to-day decisions, grant permission for travel, judge minor disagreements, and help the colony to run efficiently by making many semiroutine decisions.

4. *The informal subcouncil.* This group is so informal that it is questionable whether or not it should be listed separately. However,

the first minister (sometimes the assistant preacher), the house-holder, and the field manager generally meet after breakfast each day to lay out the day's work and assign men to the various jobs.

5. *The householder.* The householder is in a peculiar position for, under the direction of the council and the *Gemein* and with the help of the department managers, he is responsible for the economic prosperity of the colony. In the economic sphere he represents the colony to the outside world.

6. *The head preacher.* The head preacher is responsible for all aspects of community life, both economic and, to a greater extent, moral. He must "shepherd his flock" and "keep his hive in order." He is directed in this all-inclusive role by his own colony *Gemein* and by the preachers of his *Leut* who ordained him to his position and have the power to remove him should they see fit. He represents the colony in all its aspects to the outside world and interprets the world to the colonists.

Male and Female Subcultures. Within the Hutterite colony two subcultures exist, that of the men and that of the women. Women are believed to be inferior to men intellectually and physically and to need direction, protection, guidance, and consideration. For while it is believed that man was molded in God's likeness, reflecting something of God's glory, woman was taken from man and has weakness, humility, and submission. "Women just *are* inferior." At the time of marriage the husband does not leave his colony; his bride is usually from another colony and must move into his and adjust to new people and a new life. The women do not formally participate in colony decisions nor do they select their own leaders. The man's work is assigned by the colony and is virtually unaffected by obligations to his family, except that married men do not work on the night shift during harvest and are expected to help their wives with rotating colony work if that work is heavy.

Although women do not participate in formal colony decisions as a group, they are relatively free to intervene when they or their families are affected. Women may never defend their position on the basis of being an individual, but must appeal to the welfare of the group. Such patterns of behavior can be observed with respect to the socialization of children. Hutterite youngsters who are punished by the German school teacher (always a male) seek and receive comfort from their mothers. When hurt physically, the children seek comfort from the father (the protector from the world and the environment). While the father tends to uphold the rules of the patriarchal system due to his own involvement in the structure, his wife may be more lenient in her attitude and more critical of the punishment. Wives feel less restrained in making complaints, while husbands will try to avoid confrontation with the colony power structure. A husband would rather suffer unjustly than complain openly. A wife has little to lose by complaining, but she may be frustrated because her husband will not give her the support she wants. She often projects her annoyance and mildly dislikes men as a group. Women, as a group, support each other against masculine influence, and even a dominant female will receive the support of the weaker ones and vice versa. The cultures of men and women are different and at points are opposed. Psychologists have reported striking differences in the scores of Hutterite men and women on various personality tests (Kaplan and Plaut 1956, pp. 34-44).

The loyalties of the men are somewhat divided between their peer group (the colony power structure), their family of orientation, and their family of procreation. The women are primarily oriented toward their family of procreation and therefore are more difficult for the colony to manage and integrate—especially when this attitude is coupled with some antagonism toward the men. One preacher declared: "Our colony troubles would amount to very little if it were not for the women." Married women appear to have less identification with the colony than do the men. This is indicated by the fact that men (and boys) seldom complain about the hard work even when they are haying from 7:00 in the morning until 10:00 at night. But the women complain openly when they have too much colony work in one day. . . .

Economic Patterns

Although social patterns are believed to be divinely prescribed and must remain stable, economic and technological pursuits vary greatly in time and from colony to colony. The production patterns consist of rational and modern methods of large-scale agriculture, frequently on the more arid regions of the North American plains. A diversity of small grain, cattle, dairy, swine, and poultry enterprises are maintained by all colonies to provide cash income and to insure meat and produce for consumption. There is minimal conflict between the religious ideology and the dynamics required for collective utilization of agricultural resources. The constant need for capital expansion is intensified by the high rate of natural increase of the population.

Every person capable of working is expected to perform work assigned to him. Work patterns are clearly specified within age and sex groupings and by formal authority patterns that are firmly supported by informal associations in small groups. Men are more directly engaged in the income-producing phases of colony operations, while women are assigned to family, domestic, and food preparation tasks. There is over-all efficient use of labor groups in spite of certain inefficiencies resulting from strong authority patterns. Work is considered important, not in terms of individualistic concepts of time, money, or man hours, but as a means of communal living.

Branching (forming new colonies) is the institutionalized response to biological growth, and the need of the communal system to maintain a small, manageable, face-to-face domestic group. The new colony is usually formed from a single over-populated "mother" colony. Branching achieves a redistribution of authority, leadership roles, work patterns, economic resources, and balancing of kinship and family influences. Every colony requires dynamic adjustments to the changing needs from its beginning until it forms a new colony.

The consumption patterns of the society are predetermined by the world view forbidding private ownership of property, the rejection of personal pleasure as an end, and an attitude of frugality rather than spending. The conceptions of "need" and "equality" are culturally defined and socially sanctioned by both informal and formal consensus on an intercolony basis. Austerity and simplicity are consciously accepted by the individual as a necessary way of life in which the carnal desire must be subjugated to the spiritual nature. Although personal and family needs contrast sharply with the North American farm family in clothing, house furnishings, and appliances, the colony as a whole manifests the characteristics of modern, large-scale, capital-oriented agriculture.

The distribution patterns reflect colony conceptions of impartiality and equality in sharing. The amount and kind of goods, determined by the rules of the intercolony association, are distributed according to the age and sex of the individual and according to family size. Although the society is communal and modern in its technology and productive features, its adherence to religious authority prevents a distributive economy based on the maximization of individual wants. Hutterite society is not only communal in production, but also in its consumption and distribution phases. Food is consumed in a communal setting. Clothing and most needs of the individual are distributed through resident household units. Profits realized from the marketplace are held by the corporation for the welfare of the whole colony.

Conceptions of property are clearly shaped by communitarian values, and by the view that material things are unimportant in comparison to spiritual things. To the individual, property means the right to use but not to possess. The formal adult relation to property is one of stewardship but, on the informal level, tools and machines are frequently neglected. Children are not trusted with valued property, and the young adult must learn the appropriate restraints on property use not expected of him as a child. Patterns of reciprocity between individuals and families are made possible through small monthly allowances to individuals from the colony. Kinship is especially relevant in the exchange of gifts, favors, and work substitutions. The Hutterite view of property forbids merchandizing or profiteering from mere exchange of goods. Gift giving to outsiders in exchange for colony favors, for minor deprivations, and as a means of expressing appreciation is normative. . . .

Schoolchildren: Six to Fourteen Years

Significant aspects of the socialization of school-age children include the following:

1. Most of the children's day is spent under close supervision by someone in a position of authority—the German teacher, a parent, or a work supervisor. During each day, however, there are periods when the child is working with his brothers or sisters and when the child is unsupervised in his peer group.

2. The groups of brothers and sisters working together within the nuclear family develop patterns of interaction that will continue into adulthood when groups of brothers will be in leadership

positions in the colony and when, it is to be hoped, sisters will marry into the same colony where they can help one another.

3. Every day there are brief periods when the schoolchildren are completely free from authoritarian direction and can function as a self-contained peer group working out relationships that will last into adulthood. During the school years the children learn to function both within the sibling group and within the peer group. They learn how to adjust their dual membership as the two groups overlap, interact, and supplement one another. The two configurations persist, with traditional modification, until the peer group embraces the whole colony.

4. The school-age children are taught unquestioning obedience to Hutterite authority—their parents, teacher, the colony, to any Hutterite older than they, and to Hutterite traditions and teachings. If in the weakness of childhood they do not obey, they are taught to accept their punishment meekly.

5. They are not taught to discipline themselves, deciding what is right and following their own concept of truth; rather they are taught to do what they are told and that those in authority will watch over them, punish, and protect them.

6. The children do not develop a strong sense of guilt. Because it is natural for a child to sin and because the child is not responsible for his sin, it is not "his fault" that he misbehaves. His actions need to be directed through praise and punishment by those over him.

7. The schoolchildren master the basic ritual of Hutterite life. They abide by the rules because they are told to and they must be obedient. The children learn the verbal expression of the belief system. They must memorize the material, but it is not yet expected that they will really internalize the more difficult aspects of the beliefs.

8. The children learn to accept their proper position in the society. One German teacher begins each day's lesson with, "Dear children, content yourself gladly with a lowly place. . . . Do not interfere in things that are not your concern." The children learn to accept many frustrations passively. They learn to interpret teasing as attention, to enjoy hard physical labor, to begin to appreciate life uncluttered by material objects, and to accept the cleansing process of pain and punishment with a kind of pleasure.

During the height of the Hutterite development in Europe, the *Gross-Schul* was a boarding school and was responsible for the children twenty-four hours a day. Today all children sleep in their parents' apartments at night and a large part of the time that formerly was spent in German school is now spent attending English school. However, the children start German school before starting English school. Among the *Schmiedeleut* the children enter German school at five so they have at least one year in the German school before entering the English school. Among the *Lehrerleut* there is a subdivision of the German school called *Schulela*, which the children attend from their sixth birthday until they enter English school at about seven. There are regular class hours for the *Schulela* students that meet during English school sessions. All children are taught their German letters and read German before learning English. During the period that the children attend only German school, they eat in the children's dining room under the supervision of the German teacher, attend German school when it is in session, go to Sunday school, church, and the evening service. While the children are in English school the few younger ones help with the prekindergarten babies, or accompany their fathers around the colony. They may not go with their mothers when the women are doing colony work.

The schoolchild can contribute some labor to the smooth functioning of the colony and can help within the nuclear family. They work as babysitters for the house children and kindergarteners, ordering their young charges around and punishing disobedience. Schoolchildren are not greeted formally by Hutterite visitors nor are they introduced to adults. There are slight changes in dress when the child enters German school.

German school is taught by a married man who has been selected for his job by the *Gemein.* The position is equal in importance to any other department leadership position. Often the German teacher is on the colony council, although not invariably. It is considered an advantage for him to be on the front bench because then he can easily watch the children and note any misbehavior. The schoolchildren must sit very still and be absolutely quiet during church. If a child should fall asleep, he is not scolded, for he is still observing the ritual by being in church and being quiet. The German school mother is frequently the wife of the German school teacher (especially among the *Dariusleut*) or she may be an older woman who is appointed to the position by the council. She helps to supervise the children's meals, serves them, and teaches manners. She also teaches the girls how to clean the dining room, set the tables, wash, dry, and put away their dishes. She has no responsibility to teach any of the religious material nor does she give permission, assign jobs, and punish. She assists the German teacher and instructs the schoolgirls in their female work roles, teaching them the pattern of work rotation that will organize their colony work for the remainder of their lives.

German school is usually taught in the English schoolhouse. Every day the children assemble in the dining room for morning prayers and breakfast. From the moment they assemble until after supper in the evening, the children are either under the direction of the German teacher or are technically released by him to do specific work such as babysitting, helping with chores, or attending English school. During the English school year the children meet before and after English school from an hour to an hour and a half. They meet a half day on Saturday and all day during vacations or when the English teacher is sick. During this time they practice writing German script, read German, recite their memory verses from Hutterite hymns, the Book of Psalms, the New Testament, or a biblical history book. The German teacher admonishes them about their beliefs and even more about their behavior. Here rules are announced to the children, and those who have broken the rules are punished. For example, the teacher may announce that the children are not to touch the car of any English person who comes to the colony. If at a later time, any child is seen climbing on the car or playing inside it, he is reported to the German teacher who gives him the standard number of straps. This is usually three on the palm of the hand for the first offense or for a minor infringement. If a child lies about what he did he gets two more. If the offense merits greater punishment he is turned over the bench. During the long, cold winters the children wear so many layers of thick cotton flannel that when a switch is used it is more the disgrace than the physical discomfort that causes the pain.

In addition to teaching the schoolchildren to pray together, the German school teaches them to work together. Often the German teacher is the gardener or the husband of the gardener. This is a convenient arrangement, for the schoolchildren regularly help in the garden during the summer when they have no English school. The potatoes are often dug by the schoolchildren, and cucumbers and other vegetables are sorted for sale. When the children have worked especially hard or especially well, the whole group is rewarded. After they have spent the morning gathering potatoes, each child may be given a chocolate bar at dinner.

Except when they are babysitting, all the children's work is closely supervised, for children are not expected to be able to work on their own. Each girl has an assigned task in the dining room cleanup routine for one week at a time, but some jobs are more popular than others and the children race to get these. If the girl to whom the job has been assigned does not stand up for her right or enlist the help of the German school mother to defend her place, she will have to perform one of the less popular tasks. This rushing to grab a preferred job functions to hurry the girls from the table to work, for the easiest way to defend one's job is to get there first. Jockeying for a favored position is expected among the schoolchildren, but it would be beneath the dignity of anyone old enough to eat in the adult dining room.

When the German school is in formal session the teacher holds a willow switch or a leather strap in his hand throughout most of the period. This functions more as a symbol of authority than as a ready implement for discipline; as a sceptre rather than a whip. When, for example, the preacher took over the German school and called it into session outside of regular school hours, he picked up the willow and sat down at the front of the room. The children went quickly to their assigned places and sat expectantly waiting to be told what to do. It was not merely the presence of the preacher that elicited this reaction, for he had been in the room for several minutes talking to individual children and watching them play jacks and run around the school room before he decided to take over.

The naturalness of discipline in the German school is illustrated by the following incident. Children are not allowed to speak unnecessarily during meals. (One can realize the need for this rule watching two adults serve and control fifty-six school-age children who must pray, be served, eat, and pray again—all this within fifteen minutes.) During breakfast one day two of the little girls were whispering and giggling. As the German teacher walked past he switched the noisier child with his rod. Her skirt was hanging over the edge of the bench and instead of striking the child, he hit the bench, knocking his switch under the table. The girls quickly picked it up and sat on it, hiding it under their long skirts. For the rest of the meal the teacher was without his switch. This was considered a humorous incident by the teacher as well as all the children. A single switch or being flicked on the head in the dining room is primarily a means for directing the child's attention to his eating without having to speak to him, rather than a real punishment. The dining room is always to be quiet, except when the children are singing, and even the teacher and the German school mother do very little talking during the meal.

One of the functions of German school is to continue to teach the child to accept punishment without resistance and without anger. The German teacher uses traditional colony methods of punishment. An erring child is spoken to, is made to stand by his desk, must sit on the front bench, may have to kneel, may be sent to stand in the corner, or must come forward and receive three straps on his hand. All these punishments function primarily to remove the child from the group and shame him in front of his peers. Other punishment may be given in front of the group or after German school is dismissed, depending on the discretion of the teacher. For repeated offenses a child is first spanked with a switch and, if he persists, with a leather strap. If these methods do not work, he is placed with the youngest children in the German school until he is ashamed and claims by proper conduct his age-determined place in the hierarchy. Praise is used to encourage all the children, even the slowest.

Children's native abilities are taken into account and children who are slow learners are given less material to memorize. German school is "ungraded" in the modern sense, with the children progressing at their own speeds. There are no grades or formal levels, rather an accepted sequence of material to be learned. First they learn to recognize their German letters both in Gothic print and Gothic script; they learn to recognize numbers. Then they learn to write the letters and the numbers. Next they are taught to recognize common syllables; these elements they combine together to form words. After several months they are reading and writing the medieval German script. Throughout their school years they practice handwriting, memorize prayers, hymns, Bible stories, the catechism, and episodes of Hutterite history. The children also learn the directions of the compass, measurement equivalents, and how to write to ten thousand. The children are taught to work efficiently; they know what to do, how to do it, and when to do it, but they are never given an opportunity to ask if it should be done at all.

Within the system there is no room for doubt. The intellectual content of the German school curriculum is but a small part of the total learning that takes place in the school. The primary function of the German school is to teach the Hutterite children the ritual of life, which applies primarily to two different areas. The first is ritual that insures the smooth social functioning of the group in all the details of everyday interaction. The second class of ritual reduces the fear of death and physical injury. The children in the German school learn primarily the first type of ritual although the second is not neglected. Psychological studies of Hutterite adolescents show they are not frightened by threats to their bodily integrity although there are in fact many instances of physical injury (Hostetler 1965, p. 79). These are not anticipated nor do they serve as a source of worry.

One of the tasks of the German teacher is to teach his charges table manners. They learn to eat with a knife and fork in addition to a spoon, to serve themselves from the nearest quarter of the serving plate, the oldest taking the first helping. The table rules that the children memorize are very similar in form (rhymed couplets) and content to those widely circulated in Europe during the fifteenth and sixteenth centuries. These rules dictating how they are to behave at the table are memorized and recited in unison.

Within the larger context of ritual the children learn the verbal content of their religion. They will internalize the theological and moral content when they seek baptism. At this stage in the child's development he is taught to avoid punishment at the hands of supervising adults. Children memorize the material because they must be obedient; only when they grow older are they expected to understand the concepts they recite. This pattern of learning is consistent with that observed in other cultures having an oral tradition. Wisdom, which is preeminently social rather than technological, is first memorized then understood.

Schoolchildren learn a great deal about the authority structure of their society and how to live comfortably within it. They have internalized the Hutterite hierarchy that gives precedence to age, but they have also learned that the authority of each individual is limited. Therefore, the child knows when and whom he must obey and what orders can be safely ignored. If the children are disturbing the young pigs and an adult tells them to stop, they pay little attention other than to stay beyond reach of the reproving adult. If the pig boss tells the children to "get away," they leave.

The German teacher's role is defined by tradition; his work is watched over by the council members and noted by all the members of the church. Concerning his task, one German teacher wrote: "I feel that the greatest challenge in my work is to put a good religious foundation under the children so that they may become respectable and honorable members of the *Gemein.* I always like to think of them as young tender plants in the Garden of the Lord where the school teacher's duty is to trim, weed, and water as he finds it necessary. Of course I realize that neither the plant nor the waterer can achieve anything without the Lord's blessing.

The peer group, which functions beyond the supervision of the German teacher and the child's nuclear family, contributes to the socialization of the individual. Every day, while the adults are eating, the children of the colony who are younger than fifteen are left with no adult supervision. During these few minutes the children are virtually free to settle their own disputes and to apply peer group pressure on deviants.

Boys and girls are taught to play differently. When a group of girls played leapfrog ignoring their long skirts, the preacher picked up a switch and walked toward the scattering group admonishing firmly with "girls don't play that way." In some colonies the sisters in each family have an assigned play house. This may be the family's goose house, which the little girls use when there are no goslings in it, or it may be an extra shed or even an infrequently used room in one of the houses. Here they spend hours playing with each other and with the girls from other families. Usually each little girl brings a doll out from hiding under her skirt and plays house happily knowing that she will be undisturbed by the preacher who would throw the doll in the trash were she to flaunt it. Occasionally the girls will play that they are "English" women, wearing funny clothes, strutting about, and talking loudly. On the very rare occasions when one of the girl's brothers is allowed into the play house, the children may play "doctor," drawing realistic incisions complete with sutures on one another's arms. The oldest sister in each family keeps the key to the play house and children are free to exclude the children with whom they do not wish to play. Boys are customarily excluded; among the girls, the play groups constantly shift and there is almost always at least one girl who temporarily is being locked out of the favored play house. Sometimes the girls divide into cliques, each clique using one play house. The cliques, so separate in their play, quickly unite to confront the boys or an adult. Most of the girls' play is near the long houses and the center of the colony. In contrast, the boys range much further in their play. The boys are more individualistic and often will work or play alone. The girls demand detailed conformity within the clique or the dissenter is excluded. Only by adjusting completely to the group may a girl remain to play.

Much of the children's play is physically vigorous and often rough. They run and chase and climb. They fight hard, quickly, and quietly. They vie with one another, showing no physical fear jumping off high places or pushing one another in front of the tractor. Adults ignore the children's dangerous play; they are busy, and the children are the German teacher's responsibility. If an adult should not like the play, he might yell at the children, who would momentarily scatter. If he were really bothered he might tell the German teacher who, if in agreement, would make the children stop their play. Normally, however, no one notices how the children play if they are quiet. Schoolchildren play such games as "whistle when it hurts," in other words, games that are exercises in discomfort and endurance. The free play of schoolchildren reinforces community values: the children learn to ignore physical discomfort and fear of injury and to minimize the importance of the body; the changing play groups teach the unpleasantness of being excluded.

During the school years the children identify closely with their respective peer groups. When the group works hard or some of the members do especially well, everyone in the group is rewarded. When most of the group misbehave, everyone is scolded. The child learns not only that the behavior of the group directly affects the rewards and punishment he receives, but he also learns that peer-group solidarity can protect him from "outsiders" (adults) and from punishment. Transgression can go unnoticed if no one reports it. If no one will tattle on another, often the transgressor is protected; it generally requires too great an effort to punish every child. However, the schoolchild also learns that his own peer group can punish him even more severely than does adult authority. The rules of the colony can sometimes be circumvented, even more often the rules of the family can be ignored; but the child cannot ignore his own peers.

All assigned babysitters in the colony are schoolchildren between the ages of six and fourteen. Usually only girls are assigned to a specific family but, if needed, boys may be assigned; however, all boys babysit informally within their nuclear families. The primary functions of the babysitters are to keep their charges quiet and out of the adults' way and to protect them from serious injury. The sitters enjoy being able to boss their charges and to punish them, but they do not like the work involved. The babysitters are highly responsible in that while they are in charge, they never leave their charges unattended. When there is a conflict, the older child is supported against the younger. During the summer there is some exchange of babysitters among colonies. Older schoolgirls may be sent to help a sister or an aunt who has married into another colony. These girls help with the young children and with the family work and attend German school. Boys of this age do not perform comparable exchange work: it is not considered right for a young boy to be away from his father or his home colony. For a girl it does not matter, because she will probably leave her home colony when she is married.

A child is never punished by depriving him of food. When an English teacher kept a child in school during the dinner period, the German teacher went to the school house and got the child, firmly explaining to the English teacher that children, no matter how they have behaved, need to be fed. Work is never used as a punishment, for there is no colony work that is categorized as unpleasant and everyone must be willing to do his share of any type of work to which he is assigned. Privileges are not withheld from a naughty child; if the group goes on an excursion to help butcher sheep or brand cattle, he goes too. If it is his turn to visit another colony when the truck is going, he may go no matter how recently he has misbehaved. When a child is observed to be misbehaving, he is punished immediately; if misbehavior is reported to the German teacher or to his father, the child is punished at the first opportunity. If a child is strapped by his father, he is comforted by his mother the moment it is over; if his mother is not present, his father may comfort him after strapping him. It is believed that the punishment removed the misbehavior, and the child is fully accepted without having to atone further. When a child is punished in front of school-children with no parent present, he is not generally comforted, unless it is at the end of the session and he can return home. Occasionally if a parent is considered to be too lax with a child, the father may be asked by the colony to punish him at home, or to punish him in the presence of the council. There is a basis for this practice in the biblical story of Eli recounted in one of the Hutterite sermons on child training. If a father, especially one in a high-colony position, feels that his child is not being properly disciplined, he will take over the task. In one colony the English teacher was almost unable to manage one of the larger boys. She did not report this to the German teacher, but the boy's father learned of the problem. The next morning he came into the classroom with the child, sat on one of the church benches during the opening exercises and then asked the teacher, "Has John been misbehaving in school?" The teacher answered, "Yes." The father went to his son's desk, turned him over it, strapped him in front of the children, and then he walked out. Punishment is considered part of the pruning that is needed to shape the individual to fit into colony life.

Children are expected to misbehave when they are unwatched, for that is believed to be their nature. These same children are expected to grow into responsible colony members. Misbehavior during childhood does not endanger the child's future reputation nor foretell an unsuccessful adulthood. Throughout his life, the expectation is that the child will become a more responsible, highly socialized person. The school-age child must accept his place in the social structure of the colony, respecting those older than he and caring for those younger. It is not his responsibility to care for himself nor to discipline himself. The same child who is completely responsible in his assigned colony job may get into serious mischief during unsupervised play with his peers. Thus, if several children play with fire, accidentally setting the barn aflame, they are punished but not made to feel guilty, for lack of judgment and misbehavior are natural to children. It is not the responsibility of the individual but of the adults and of the system to protect the children from their natural instincts.

Childhood comes to an end with the fifteenth birthday. The young Hutterite leaves the children's dining room and is said to be *bei die Leut,* with the people. The *Mandle* (little man) has become a *Buah* (boy); the *Dindla* (little woman) has become a *Die-en* (girl).

Young People: Age Fifteen to Baptism

On the eve of his fifteenth birthday the child goes, alone, to the German teacher. For weeks he has been counting the days until his birthday with eager anticipation, but the last few days the child frequently becomes apprehensive about the impending change. Those older than he tease him, saying that the German teacher will give him a whipping he will never forget. The child does not really believe the teasing, but the change in life patterns is both enticing and frightening to him. The German teacher exhorts the child to be good, to work hard, to show good manners, and to do quickly and pleasantly everything that an older person asks him to do. On leaving the German school, the individual accepts the responsibility for saying his evening and morning prayers without supervision. The person is given a catechism and several Hutterite books for his personal use.

The child takes his place in the adult dining hall, for he is now "one of the people." The boy sits with the men, occupying the "lowest" position at the table. The girl sits with the women in a similar relationship. She must wait on the men, should they rap for anything during mealtime. The young person will do assigned colony work with adults of his own sex. He no longer does the work of children such as babysitting, gathering potatoes, or cleaning up the colony grounds. He no longer attends English school. He is greeted with a handshake by visiting Hutterites and is allowed into the fringe of adult social life. There is no ceremonial recognition of the person's new status, for such a recognition would give undue emphasis to the individual.

The young person is in a transitional stage from childhood to adulthood. The colony recognizes both aspects of his personality. Physically he is considered to be an adult who is capable of hard work and of working with adults. Religiously he is considered to be a child who must attend Sunday school and must memorize his weekly verses. Emotionally he vacillates, and this period is sometimes called "the in-between years" or "the foolish years," meaning that the loyalties of the individual have not completely crystallized. Some disregard of colony mores is expected during this period, but moodiness or poor work performance is not tolerated. A good young person is "always obedient and never talks back."

Soon after his birthday, but gradually and at the colony's convenience, he is given various gifts that reflect his change of status and are needed in his new role. Both boys and girls are given a locked wooden chest in which to keep their personal belongings. The boy is given cloth for good suits and shirts, the girl receives material for dresses. Boys are given work tools that they are responsible for keeping in good working condition: a spade, a pitchfork, a hammer, a saw, and in some colonies a spoon with the individual's name inscribed on it. The girls receive tools that they will care for and use for colony work: a scrub pail, a paint brush, a hoe, kitchen knives, a broom, knitting needles and in some colonies a rolling pin and, until recently, a spinning wheel.

For two years the young person is in an apprentice position. He is not given responsibility for an expensive machine nor for work that, if it should go wrong, would cause a great deal of inconvenience or much money lost. A boy is usually assigned the responsibility for a tractor at about the age of seventeen or eighteen. It is his to use for the colony, to care for and keep in good condition. Formerly boys of this age were given a team of horses to train for field work. At the age of seventeen, girls begin to take their turn baking and cooking for the colony, being responsible for all the food prepared or all the baking done during the week. The boys and girls of the in-between years constitute a mobile labor force that can be used throughout the colony as needed (in jobs suitable to their sex) and they also may be sent to other colonies to help during a time of need or stress. The boys in this group supply most of the hard labor and enjoy the opportunity to demonstrate their strength and stamina.

The young person is subject to the control and influence of the colony, his family, and his peer group. The influences of these three groups are less well integrated during the years preceding baptism than at any other period. Because the areas of control are more diversified, the young person has slightly more freedom. His work is under the control of the colony, although there may be some tendency to let the son work with the father and the girl work with her mother or with a sister. While working, the boy is under the direction of the departmental director who may send him off the colony on an errand. His religious development is under the direction of the

German teacher, who is in charge of Sunday school. In areas of moral and social behavior the young person is primarily the responsibility of the German teacher in some colonies, while in other colonies he is the responsibility of the preacher. Depending on the degree of infringement, the transgression may be handled by the German teacher, the preacher, or the council. Permission to leave the colony, other than to do an errand needed for work, is granted by the German teacher among the *Dariusleut* and the preacher among the *Lehrerleut.* It is not granted by the parent. The colony permits dating among the young people, although a specific family may forbid it. If a young person is dating someone of whom the colony disapproves, such as a first cousin or the English school teacher, the German teacher or the preacher speaks to him; if he is dating someone whom his family dislikes, it is a family responsibility and the colony is not involved. Both the colony and the family expect a certain amount of deviant behavior. Much of this takes place within the peer group who participate together in forbidden activities of singing English songs and playing mouth organs, but the peer group tolerates only certain approved activities. If an individual deviates too radically, he is excluded by his peers.

Within the family, the young person is no longer grouped with the schoolchildren. His parents take a greater interest in his wants and needs and identify somewhat more closely with him. The relationship is still completely hierarchical, but now that the child has become a person and the German teacher is no longer responsible for virtually all the child's waking hours, the parents concern themselves more with their child's free time. "A wise mother has always an odd job for the idle hands of her daughter." Parents have almost complete veto power over the marriage of their children, and they start early to express interest in this aspect of their children's lives. Among the *Dariusleut,* physical punishment is not used by the colony representative after a child is fifteen (for girls over twelve it is not used, other than straps on the hand), but it may be used by the parents; however, in practice this is not necessary. Among the *Lehrerleut* a disobedient daughter may be locked out of the apartment and forced to seek lodging with another family for the night. (The parents know that she will not leave the colony and that other families will give her shelter.) Mothers continue to teach their daughters homemaking skills and girls of this age often take over the family laundry and do much of the sewing.

The young people in the family support one another. The girls may sew for their brothers, making clothes for them that deviate slightly from the accepted pattern. An adult woman would not make a shirt with a forbidden pocket on it, but a young girl will make such a shirt for her brother (or boy friend) or will add a pocket to a shirt he already owns. A sister will iron her brother's clothes just the way he likes them. Boys have some opportunities to earn extra money that they may lend or give to their sisters or girl friend. Brothers in one family frequently will date sisters in another family. Brothers support one another, and sisters support one another during the period of dating and after they are married. It is common to find marriages where several brothers are married to women who are sisters. The cooperative patterns learned in the nuclear family influence the pattern of courtship. Colonies that frequently visit back and forth and exchange work and produce and from whom marriage partners are chosen are usually ones that are closely related by family ties.

Although the young person has left German school and English school, his education is continuing. The family continues to teach its sons and especially its daughters skills helpful for colony life. In the religious sphere the formal education of the individual continues, for the young people must attend Sunday school on Sunday afternoon. Sunday school functions to reinforce the sermon and to discipline the young people to listen to the sermon. Although all the German-school children also attend and participate in most of the program, the emphasis of the Sunday-school program is directed to the young people who have finished the colony German school but who have not yet been baptized. The colony punishes young people for moral or social transgression by admonishing them or by making the offender stand in Sunday school. If there has been a gross infringement, the offender may have to stand in the back during the evening service or, for a worse offense, he may have to stand in the back during the Sunday service. For a still worse offense, he may have to stand at the front of the church. This is considered too harsh a punishment for a girl to endure. The attitude toward the punishment is revealed by an older Hutterite who said, with intense emotion, "He needs to stand there like a 'dumb ox,' in front of everybody." The implication was that the erring one would really feel how stupid he had been. An offense for which a boy might have to stand in Sunday school would be having his hair cut too short or attending a movie. A boy might stand in church for sneaking off the colony and being arrested by the local police for drinking with minors. The Sunday-school program does not let the young people forget their spiritual status as children who must memorize and recite their lessons correctly at the bidding of their teacher. By physically grouping them with the young children and continuing their ritualistic participation with the schoolchildren for religious training, those who are not yet baptized are constantly reminded that they are not yet fully adult. Each week, in effect, they are told, "Although you may look like an adult and work like an adult, really, you are still a child." Sunday school is a place where behavior problems that may arise among the young people can be discussed. The push of society is toward adulthood, even while recognizing and tolerating the childish elements that still remain.

During the work day, both the boys and the girls work with and under the direction of older colony members, but they also work in peer groups: all the young men hay together, all the young girls paint together. Work and social life intermingle, for as they work together they talk together, especially when beyond the hearing of adults. It is considered a privilege to go to other colonies to work, because here too the young people work with their peers and establish new friendships. After supper the peer group expands to include both sexes and visitors of the same age group from other colonies. Frequently there is no one in his home colony whom a young person can date, because all those his own age are his first cousins; or if there are some to whom he is more distantly related, they may be "going with" someone else.

The intermingling of work, visiting, and dating is illustrated in the following account. On Friday afternoon a truck arrived from a colony in a neighboring province. The driver was a young unmarried man who was related to this colony by marriage and was known to be dating one of the girls in the host colony. She did not know in advance that he was coming nor did he know he would be chosen to drive the truck until he was told to get ready. With him, riding inside was an older woman who was the sister of one of the older men in the host colony. The woman had her youngest child with her, a boy of about nine. She had come to visit her brother. Eight girls came along in the back of the truck, because the host colony had a bumper crop of cucumbers.

The truck arrived too late that Friday to do any picking. Saturday morning the girls picked, but Saturday afternoon everyone needed to prepare for Sunday, so no more cucumbers were gathered. Sunday the young people were neither allowed to pick vegetables nor to travel; they stayed over Sunday. Early Monday morning they picked more cucumbers before the truck left. The visit enabled the girls to work and also to spend the entire week-end visiting. The girls of the host colony were with the visitors constantly, helping them pick, pack, and showing them around. Who was to stay with whom was easily decided, for each girl stayed with her closest relative. Early in the evening all the young people gathered together and sang western songs, usually ones with a plaintive tune and many verses telling some sad tale of worldly life; an orphan with no one to care for her, a mother whose only child is killed after her husband has deserted her, a dutiful son killed in a war. Later in the evening the young people separated into couples. The boys in the host colony decided who would date whom. The oldest boy has first choice and the others decide in order of age. If a boy has a girl friend at another colony, he will indicate that he does not want to date. If it is known that one couple is going together, this is, of course, accepted. If a visiting girl does not want to date, or does not want to date a specific person, she says "No." If boys and girls do not know one another, they tend to pair up by age. The younger boys at the host colony will be included in the group of young people but probably will not have a date, for the older boys will have claimed all the visiting girls.

Dating generally begins when the child becomes a young person. Occasionally and surreptitiously it may begin earlier in colonies where there are children more distantly related than first cousins. Some parents do not allow their daughters to date until they are seventeen or eighteen or even older. There is a considerable individual variation among the young people; some date whenever and whomever they may, others go only with one person for a long period of time. It is not unusual for courtship to last five or six years. Whether or not a young person is dating, he is included in the mixed peer group activity and remains absolutely loyal to the group.

The peer group is of supreme importance, for within it virtually all the young person's social life takes place and many of his working hours are spent with his same-sex peer group. The group demands absolute loyalty. Anyone who transgresses by not supporting the group or by talking about their activities or plans is completely ostracized. Good times are planned, such as picking and boiling corn in the kitchen to eat after dark, and the ostracized one does not hear about it until afterwards. In large colonies or among the young people of neighboring colonies, exclusive cliques may develop, but they present a united front to all those who are not in their age set. The adults conveniently "do not see" the mild transgressions, and the young people enjoy the thrill of semiforbidden behavior and of escape from adult surveillance.

The "foolish years" are a time for trying the boundaries. The young person will eventually grow to the point where he will reject the world and choose the colony way of life, but during this time there is some flirtation with the world, some learning about that which will be rejected. Most young people have photographs taken (no one should make a graven image), many have their own cameras. Some boys own small transistor radios on which they listen to western songs and from which they memorize the songs, some trap during the winter and sell the furs or moonlight to earn extra money, quite a few of the boys own wristwatches and occasionally boys smoke secretly. The girls have colored nail polish, and may use it to paint their toenails which are hidden under heavy black laced shoes. They have perfume, dime-store jewelry, and sometimes fancy underwear. The in-between years are a period of limited self-realization. In extreme cases a young man may leave the colony for a few weeks, several months, or even for a couple of years. He is a "tourist" in the outside world, he learns about it, earns some money, but always plans to return to the colony to marry and raise his family.

There is a tendency, more pronounced among the girls, to create a secret world. As long as the make-believe does not interfere with the young peoples' work and is not flaunted, adults tacitly accept it and, remembering their own youth, are tolerant. Sometimes the secret world is confined to a locked wooden chest; sometimes a corner of the attic is made into a personal microcosm. Here are stored bits of the temporal world, photographs, sheet music, suntan lotion, and souvenirs. These artifacts represent, however meagerly, what the individual has the freedom to pursue or the freedom to renounce. They represent the world outside the colony; they represent the self in its indulgent, vanity-pleasing aspects. As the individual matures and measures these trinkets and indulgences against the full life around him, and as he participates more completely in this very real and very busy life, he generally finds the satisfactions received from active participation in the colony far outweigh those of self-development. His self-image requires colony identification.

During much of this transitional period, the young person is measuring himself first as a member of his peer group and then as a colony member. He generally has a considerable interest in the outside world that eventually helps him to understand better what it means to be a Hutterite. His status within his nuclear family is quite high during this period, before he will begin a family of his own. During the last year or so of his status as a young person, he is expected to show by his works, in other words by his daily behavior, that he can adhere to the rules of the colony. When he has displayed by his actions, and knows with his heart and mind that he cannot continue as an irresponsible child, he willingly and humbly requests baptism that he may become a true member of the colony. The goal of the Hutterite system of childrearing has then been achieved.

Baptism

Hutterite ritual prepares the individual for two important rites of passage. The first is baptism, the second death. Baptism is essential for adult participation in the ritual of daily life; death leads the true Hutterite into life everlasting. There are close parallels between baptism and death. In order to be baptized, the "old man," the natural man, must die so the "spiritual man" may be born; the human body must die, in order that the spiritual man may be released into eternal life. Both rites of passage stress death as an essential step to life.

Every Hutterite has a birthright place in his colony that insures his constant care. Should he die during childhood before he reaches the age of discretion, he is assured a place in heaven. When the individual is able to differentiate between good and evil he becomes responsible for making the correct choice. He requests baptism and, after a period of instruction, is initiated into church membership. He retains this membership until death, unless some major transgression of the rules should cause the church to exclude him either temporarily or permanently.

Baptism is equated with submission to the church. The applicant must desire "to yield himself to God with all his heart and all

his soul and all his members . . . to live no more to himself" (Rideman 1950, p. 79). A present-day Hutterite bishop writes: "He who
will not be steadfast with the godly, to suffer the evil as well as the
good, and accept all as good, however the Lord may direct, let him
remain away. . . . We desire to persuade no man with smooth words.
It is not a matter of human compulsion or necessity, for God wants
voluntary service" (Hofer 1955, pp. 24-25). A seventeen-year-old
Hutterite girl said, "Before you ask to be baptized you know here
[pointing to her heart] and here [pointing to her head] that you
can't live any longer without it."

Since babyhood, the Hutterite has been socialized to believe
that the collective unit is more important than the separate individuals who make up the group. From the time he was seven weeks old
he has learned to fit into a group pattern, and he has been treated as
a member of a group rather than as an individual. He first identified
with his nuclear family, then with his peer group in school and, finally, with his postschool work group. With each successive stage of
development the number of people above him has decreased, and the
number below him has increased. He has been taught to serve and
obey those above him, and to care for and direct those below him.
Within his peer group there is some competition (primarily in work
performance), but there is strong support, especially in the face of
threat from the outside. Now, when he requests baptism, the whole
colony becomes, in effect, his peer group. From the time he has
known what a comb is used for, the Hutterite child has been taught
to obey. "When children from little up are used to obeying their
God-fearing parents," says a Hutterite sermon, "then they will have
formed a habit of obeying, and it will be a lot easier for them to
obey Jesus Christ."

Girls are about nineteen or twenty and boys between twenty
and twenty-six when baptized. One preacher explained that even the
state does not allow people under twenty-one to vote, and baptism,
being a much more important decision than voting, should not be
undertaken much before twenty-one and perhaps a little later.
Another preacher explained, "Christ was baptized at thirty years of
age and so if someone does not desire this until twenty-five or thirty
years of age we must be patient with such a person. Some people
don't seem to understand until they are quite old—but it's not right
to make God wait so long." The goal of childrearing among the

Hutterites is the individual's voluntary decision to submit himself to the *Gemein*. All the child's life has been, in effect, a preparation for this major rite of passage.

"He who is to be baptized must first request, ask for, and desire it," wrote Rideman in the sixteenth century. In all colonies the individual makes the request to be baptized in a highly stylized form and generally with the support of a peer group. The colony members decide months in advance, often a year or so in advance, that they will have baptism that particular year, and generally it is known by everyone in the colony who is going to request baptism and who will wait. There may be a question about one or two of the candidates, but these too are discussed so that by the time the young people are ready to submit formal application the colony is in agreement; quite often a young person is advised not to request baptism yet. The instruction period lasts six to eight weeks during which time the candidates are admonished as a group on Sunday afternoon for about two and a half to three hours. Baptism is held every year in *Schmiedehof,* but many colonies baptize only once every two to five years. If there is only one person who needs baptism he may be taken to a neighboring colony to join their group of applicants for instruction. Normally the baptismal service takes place on Palm Sunday, but also occasionally at Pentecost.

The Hutterites teach that right belief leads to right behavior. Thus it is not enough for the young Hutterite to profess his belief verbally; he must also show in his everyday actions the fruit of this belief. His behavior in all areas must be acceptable to the church community. There is a greater emphasis on correct acting than on correct thinking. The catechism asks, "What is the inner shame?" The reply is "When a man has sinful thoughts, which he should dispose of." It asks, "What is sin?" The answer is "The transgression of the law." Wrong thinking is bad, but wrong behavior is sin.

The whole colony cooperates in admonishing, punishing, and forgiving its members. During the period of instruction for baptism, the applicants are carefully watched, for they must demonstrate that they have really humbled themselves, are devoid of self-will, and are completely obedient to the community. In the course of instruction in one colony, the applicants formally request baptism thirty-six times. Each must know that he really desires and is ready to make the greatest commitment of his life.

The baptismal ceremony consists of two parts: Saturday afternoon the candidates are examined about their belief, and are asked as many as twenty-five questions. On Sunday afternoon the candidates are baptized. The preacher places his hands on each applicant, while his assistant pours a small quantity of pure water on the head of each. The preacher offers a prayer that they may be preserved in piety and faith until death.

One adolescent Hutterite girl explained, "When you are baptized then you are really old." The German school mother said of the changes baptism required, "Up until this time, his will was not renounced, now it is; and he's obligated to report anything he sees that is not correct in the colony. He must always speak to such a one before he reports. He has restricted himself." In other words, baptism signified the voluntary acceptance of responsibility for the actions of everyone in the colony. It signifies the internalization of Hutterite values.

After baptism, men are given voting privileges and are eligible for more responsible work assignments. There is no change in the work status of the girls. Both men and women who have been baptized may attend weddings and funerals in other colonies. It is customary for the newly baptized young people to travel to other colonies. Baptism is assumed to be the first step leading to marriage, for baptism must precede marriage as one's commitment to God takes precedence over one's commitment to one's spouse. Ideally the time between baptism and marriage is not long, especially for a young man. It is said that an unmarried man is like a garden that has no fence. "He needs a wife and family to protect him." Defection is less likely to occur after marriage. Often a young man is not baptized until he is contemplating marriage. A young girl who is seriously interested in a young man may be persuaded to wait to be baptized, and this often has the effect of postponing her marriage for several years.

The baptized but yet unmarried person is on the fringe of the young people's social life. He participates in the pattern of dating, but has little to do with the testing of the boundaries or the tasting of the world that is characteristic of this age. He has made his choice and has, to a considerable extent, lost interest in the material trinkets of a rejected way of life. He prefers to use his energies to help his colony succeed.

With baptism, the relationship between the parents and the child becomes closer. The child has become a member of the colony and his parents treat him as a colony member as well as an offspring. They, with the help of God and the colony, have accomplished their task of raising this child, "in the nurture and admonition of the Lord," and now that he has become a part of the *Gemein* they can enjoy him. The children have become the spiritual brothers and sisters of their parents and they can work together almost as peers and can identify more closely with one another. The child remains emotionally dependent on his parents, but there is no longer the sharp division between parent and child that existed earlier. Within the hierarchical power structure of the colony, the sons tend to cooperate closely with their father and with their biological brothers, and in a highly integrated colony, these patterns are extended to include all the baptized men of the colony. . . .

The Genius of the Culture

The culture demonstrates a unique social adaptation to a high rate of natural increase. The population characteristics of Hutterite society resemble that of a stable population model (Eaton and Mayer, 1954). The age-sex distribution within the group has remained fairly constant during its entire period in North America. The birth rate and death rates remain almost constant. The population remains overwhelmingly youthful, but not in the usual "primitive way" characterized by a high birth rate and a high infant death rate. The proportion of young children in the total population remains high due to a consistently high birth rate. Adults have about the normal life expectancy, but old people are a small minority because of the successive waves of new children. Thus, the fertility rate resembles that of underdeveloped countries, but the mortality pattern resembles that of industrialized countries. The high rate of natural increase requires appropriate social organization, flexibility, and expansion to meet these conditions.

The Hutterite society approximates the conditions required of any society to maintain a continuous high rate of population growth. These conditions include: (1) a stable society which is highly structured, (2) resources and factors favorable to expansion, and (3) a value system prescribing a high fertility rate (Lorimer 1954). The high fertility rate creates social problems which can be solved only through access to sufficient resources; in this case the acquisition of land and the accumulation of capital. Capital is accumulated by work and modes of behavior that are severely patterned. The values support a high fertility pattern and at the same time engender motivations that include sufficient spiritual and material rewards.

Typically most sects and subcultures are forced to change their social structure as the population expands. With the coming of industrialization and Western influence, many aboriginal bands of people in North America simply fled or disintegrated because they were unwilling to adapt their economy to the requirements of agriculture and a sedentary life. The Hutterites have not only fully accepted mechanized agriculture, but have adapted to a high rate of population increase by their institution of branching, which allows new units of the society to develop. The most significant social unit, the colony, is firmly controlled in size and location in a manner that prevents urbanism and merchandising. Each colony is a primary social unit consisting of several nuclear families in a face-to-face group.

Hutterite society exhibits a remarkably stable pattern of communal living. Of all communal groups in the United States, the Hutterites are the largest, have the longest history, and are the most successful in maintaining communal life. There have been many attempts at communal living in the United States. Most of these have been short lived. Of 130 communal type settlements, ninety-one lasted less than a decade, fifty-nine less than five years, fifty only two years, and thirty-two only one year (Deets 1939, p. 22). Four endured for a century or more and are now extinct. They were the Amana Society, the Ephrata Cloister, the Shakers, and Old Economy. The Doukhobors, who organized in Russia in the eighteenth century, settled in western Canada in 1879 and are still living in several cooperative communities. When the Hutterites came to the United States in 1874, there were eight different communal societies in seventy-two separate colonies. During the ensuing years, all eight societies have declined or completely vanished as social systems while the Hutterites have grown from three to over 170 colonies.

The explanation of the stable social pattern is multifaceted. The goal of the society to live communally is achieved through a combination of factors. The most pervasive of these are acceptance of supernatural authority, a dualistic view of nature sanctioning separation from the world with a tendency toward isolation, limited addition of new members other than offspring, and a willingness to die or be killed rather than change their basic beliefs and social institutions. Supernatural authority is incarnated in the colony authority pattern. The belief that divine order governs material and social relationships is learned in infancy, perpetuated throughout life, and acknowledged on the death bed of the aged. The ordered universe is conceived as hierarchical, with one part always submissive to the other. The lower obeys and serves the higher. The central beliefs are unusually explicit about goals, subgoals, and norms of practice, and have a high degree of internal consistency. There is no speculation about theology, and logical thought and reasoned solutions are applied mainly to the economic activities of making a living. The basic ideology is supported by appropriate ritual, constant teaching, highly patterned social relationships, and clear delineation between power that may be democratically managed by man and power that is exercised only by God. The central beliefs appear to be sufficiently comprehensive to satisfy individual inquisitiveness within the scope of the colony environment.

The dualistic view of human nature, spiritual and carnal, is pervasive in the social organization and becomes the reasoned basis for separation from the world. The activities of the colony, the training of the young, and the management of specific problems are approached by the predetermined spiritual, rather than carnal, assumptions. The deification of social unity on a subverbal level and the submission of the self to the will of God tends to minimize arguments and speculations of a theological nature. Geographic isolation as well as symbolic isolation through language and dress are manifestations of the central belief in separation from the world. Isolation effectively minimizes the problems of communal living as the Hutterites practice it.

The small number of nonethnic converts to the colonies is conducive to a stable social pattern. The practice of sending out missionaries to preach and make converts outside of the community in their early period of history has been discontinued entirely. This practice eliminates the problems of assimilating large numbers of outsiders.

As the Hutterite movement became institutionalized and strongly patterned, the group relied on its own offspring for new members. In its charismatic or prophetic stage the movement attracted converts, but during the seventeenth century the group tended toward institutionalization.

Hutterite child rearing and socialization practices are phenomenally successful in preparing the individual for communal life. The individual is taught to be obedient, submissive, and dependent upon human support and contact. Socialization is consistent and continuous in all age groups. From early childhood to adulthood there is no relaxation of indoctrination within clearly defined age and sex groupings. Every individual is subservient to the colony at every stage of his life. The goals for each stage of socialization are attainable by virtually all Hutterites. Individuals are well trained to meet clearly defined roles, and each is rewarded by the smooth execution of his work and by the awareness that his contribution is needed by the colony. A certain amount of deviance of an acceptable type is permitted within each age set and relieves the system of stifling rigidity.

Socialization is achieved in a supernaturally based authority system. All elements of knowledge, motivation, and activity are directly related to a single source of authority and are subordinated to it. No segment of knowledge remains unrelated to the dominant source of authority nor is any permitted to develop aside from it. The scope of socialization includes a conception of time that is temporal as well as eternal and involves the active participation of the individual in both. Ritualization of temporal and sacred activity is well proportioned. The individual is socialized within a spatial relationship that includes all of the social institutions, activities, and resources he will need as an individual. Interaction with and dependency upon outsiders is minimized.

In infancy the child learns to enjoy people and to respond positively to many persons. After age three he is weaned away from his nuclear family and learns to accept authority in virtually any form. He learns that aloneness is associated with unpleasant experiences and that being with others is rewarded with pleasant experiences. During the school years he is further weaned from his family, learns more about authority, and acquires a verbal knowledge of his religion. He acquires the ability to relate positively to his peer group and to respond to its demands. As a small child his universe is unpredictable, but as he matures in his peer group and takes part in colony life his universe becomes highly predictable. He learns to minimize self-assertion and self-confidence and to establish dependence on the group. As a member of a categorically defined age set the young child learns explicitly when and whom to obey. School-age children receive limited companionship and little indulgence from their parents; they learn how their peer group protects and punishes them; they learn to accept frustrations passively, and to enjoy hard physical labor. When the child becomes an adult, he is rewarded with responsibility, privileges, and greater recognition and acceptance by his nuclear family. After becoming a full member of the colony through baptism, the self-image expands to include the whole colony with which he identifies.

The expectations for the individual within the social structure are clearly defined by the ideology and are reinforced by the social patterns. Each individual knows what is expected of him; he wants to follow these expectations and, in most instances, is able to do so. He identifies ideologically and emotionally with the colony system. There is a strong aversion to the ways of the *Draussiger,* the outsider, who is a child of the world. The Hutterite looks at himself as belonging, not to a world created by Newton, Beethoven, Sartre, or Einstein, but to the model described in the Bible. The colony is for him, as for certain other ascetic Christian groups, a paradise surrounded by vast numbers of unconverted human beings whose destiny is determined by God and whom he will not judge.

The ascetic demand of the society does not ask the individual to mortify the basic human drives, but to subject them to a community of love that is both human and divine. Sex is managed in such a way that it is not a threat to the reproductive patterns, as with some communal Christian groups. In its socially sanctioned place, the practice of sex is distinguished from the "lust of the eye," which is illegitimate desire. Sex is limited to married pairs, and there is no evidence of any tendency toward celibacy or continence after marriage. Families are generally happy and supportive of the colony's superior power position. As an individual, a Hutterite may demonstrate what appears to the outside as egocentrism or pride. But to the Hutterite who knows that his system is right, he is not expressing personal pride but simply a state of mind that has no doubts. The emotional

identification with the colony is evidenced by the number who return after "trying the world" and the relatively few who permanently desert the colony.

The Hutterite appraisal of human nature is functional in the
communal system. In some respects it is dynamic. A child's nature is
regarded as carnal (selfish) and must be supplanted by the spiritual
(selfless) nature. The spiritual nature is expressed within a social hierarchy that is based on moral obligations among the members. The
Hutterites regard the child's personality as intrinsically good only as
he (behaviorally) gives up his individual will and conforms voluntarily to the will of the colony. The consequences of this appraisal of
human nature for delinquent individuals is somewhat opposed to
that of contemporary society in North America. When a Hutterite
youth transgresses the rules, he will be punished, but not because he
was bad. Since the society knows everyone is bad from the start, it is
required that the wrongdoer suffer the consequences of his behavior.
The society expects that the badness will, with maturity, be supplanted by responsibility. The adolescent who occasionally transgresses the rules can still see himself as being on the road toward
goodness. Hutterite society makes it a point to forgive when true
signs of betterment are observed. These manifestations are encouraged and rewarded. When the individual becomes a full member, he is
obligated to teach and uphold the morality of his society.

In North American society, by contrast, the child is thought of
as good, primarily needing a chance for self-development and self-
realization. When the child transgresses the rules of the society, he is
disappointing. The adolescent who comes into conflict with the law
tends to be labelled as bad and this will stand against his reputation
in the future. Transgression has a certain irreversible and unredemp-
tive direction, and the road to goodness becomes almost exclusively
the task of the individual himself. The Hutterite practice tends
toward the acceptance of deviancy within manageable proportions,
frequently within a small peer group. The Hutterite position is simply that the individual is not perfect and cannot attain perfection
without the aid of his brothers. The net effect is a view of the individual that leads toward rehabilitation with a minimum of condemnation. The Hutterite individual knows why he is alive, how he
should live, and subjectively he feels able to meet the standards of
behavior.

Innovation without acculturation: innovation is selective, managed, and tends to be consistent from the viewpoint of the dominant goal of communal living. Innovation does not alter the internal hierarchy and social structure. As in all societies, culture change among Hutterites is selective and proceeds according to a pattern that is more or less consistent with their world view. Innovations are evaluated with reference to the basic objectives of communal living. Hutterite society is unlike the ideal, typical folk society in several important respects. The ideology of intentional communal living contrasts sharply with the nonliterate style of primitives. Their rational-bureaucratic approach to economic and technological aspects of living contrasts sharply with the tradition-directed type of society. Their native ability to adapt to change is important to their survival in the modern world. The past migrations of the group with their strong preference for living in countries and in regions geographically isolated from large urban centers have minimized many of the complex problems brought about by change. When the external pressures became too great in the past, the group has moved to other lands.

Innovations in the colonies are carefully considered and evaluated on the basis of their possible effect on communal living. Informal talk always precedes any formal discussion of change. Modernity is not necessarily stereotyped as being evil or worldly. Most leaders fail to acknowledge any conflict between religious beliefs and technological change. "Nothing is too modern if it is profitable for the colony." The dominant criterion for introducing change is whether the innovation supports the welfare of the colony. A firm boundary is drawn between changes that involve the economic well-being of the whole colony and changes that are primarily for personal comfort and convenience. "We do not believe in making everything nice for the flesh," they say. Installing showers (in addition to tubs that they already had) in the central laundary required more time and discussion in one colony than buying a new combine. Changes are considered safe when they are anchored on spiritual rather than carnal grounds. Innovations in the outside world, by contrast, are believed to be made on the basis of satisfying the carnal nature of man. Changes are spaced, as too many changes at one time are not considered good for the colony. Even more important for survival than "controlled acculturation" (Eaton 1952) is the necessity that all members share alike in any changes permitted. In this way the relative status of any one individual to others has not changed at all. No person is made richer or poorer or more powerful over others. The preacher is still the spiritual leader, the younger are still subordinate to the older, and women are still subject to rule by men. The use of trucks, tractors, mechanized poultry and livestock raising in the colony, and the introduction of sewing machines and electric irons have not changed the social relationships. The Hutterites adjust to a changing technology, but they would rather die than change their basic social patterns, which they believe to be ordered by supernatural authority.

Hutterites maximize the power of informal, primary group consensus. The daily, constant association between leaders and followers, among persons of all ages, tends toward solidarity and an intimate knowledge of the values and opinions held by other persons. Normative practices tend to develop and determine the issues that will be discussed formally. Nothing is discussed formally that is not already a problem or an issue of concern to the group. When there is pressure for change on the part of the foreman and managers, the leaders are able to assess it informally, and after there is widespread informal agreement, the colony formally votes on on issue. Decisions are made on the basis of a majority vote. The acceptance of innovations by consensus before there is widespread breaking of the rules and before pressures become unmanageable has the effect of maintaining members' respect for the authority system. The emphasis on group welfare and de-emphasis on individual rights and convictions minimizes the friction often associated with innovation in sectarian societies.

On the formal level, individual colonies may allow only those changes that are in keeping with the preacher assembly. A given colony is not autonomous but is subject to the discipline (*Gemeinde-ordnungen*) of the preacher assembly. These rules perpetuate uniformity among colonies, and slow down the rate of innovation. The balance in decision making between any given colony and its preacher assembly appears to have great advantages in terms of satisfying human needs. When one or more colonies deviate from a formal disciplinary rule, the preacher assembly will place the issue on their agenda. The violation may be discussed and the rule that was violated may be reaffirmed by majority vote; it may be modified, or a vote may be postponed to allow time for further informal consensus. Issues of special concern to the preacher assembly result in a formal statement, which is circulated and read to all colonies by their preacher. The colonies in turn vote whether to accept the ruling. Thus, while the Hutterites give their complete loyalty to a theocratic rule, the rules that govern behavior are democratically managed. The reasons for changes are neither individual wants nor expediency, but are based entirely on the welfare of the colony.

Cleavages that normally develop between competing families or individuals for acquiring property in North American society have no formal basis for existence in Hutterite society. Consequently, material innovations are managed so as not to be disruptive. Family units are not competing against each other for wealth. When a colony is prosperous, the family units benefit equally, and none are symbolically excluded. Wealth, property, and knowledge are denied as a means of social distinction. The competition that is often very marked between colonies is integrative rather than disruptive to any given colony. Any impression, however, that the colonies express no anxiety about the effects of change would be misleading. The contacts engendered by commerce and trade with the large urban centers near their colonies have undesirable consequences for them.

Through its many self-sustaining colony units, Hutterite society is sufficiently patterned to integrate the meaning of economic values with spiritual values. Each colony is a believing community, a community of worship, and a community of work. The absolutism of their ideology has made it necessary for them to migrate to various countries where they have tended to live in isolation from their neighbors. The ideology has not forced the members to isolate themselves from biologic, economic, and technological solutions to living. The group has retained vital links between the generations. Hutterite society is a school, and the school is a society. In shaping patterns within the culture, the group has managed the problem of fragmentation, of individualistic and dictatorial leaders, defection, and senile decay. The bond of community is defined in such a way as to include the physical and emotional components of human need. The deep feelings for the correctness of their way of life was expressed by a thoughtful Hutterite who said: "If there will ever be a perfect culture it may not be exactly like Hutterites—but it will be similar."

References

Deets, Lee Emerson. *The Hutterites: A Study in Social Cohesion.* Gettysburg, Pa.: Times and News Publishing, 1939.

Eaton, Joseph W. "Controlled Acculturation." *American Sociological Review* (June 1952): 331-40.

Eaton, Joseph W., and Mayer, Albert J. *Man's Capacity to Reproduce: The Demography of a Unique Population.* New York: The Free Press, 1954.

Friedmann, Robert. *Die Schriften der Huterischen Täufergemeinschaften.* Wein, Germany: Hermann Böhlaus Nachf, 1965.

Hofer, Peter. *The Hutterian Brethren and Their Beliefs.* Starbuck, Manitoba: The Hutterian Brethren of Manitoba, 1955.

Hostetler, John A. *Education and Marginality in the Communal Society of the Hutterites.* University Park, Pa.: Pennsylvania State University, 1965.

Kaplan, Bert, and Plaut, Thomas F. A. *Personality in a Communal Society.* Lawrence, Kan.: University of Kansas Publications, 1956.

Lorimer, Frank, et al. *Culture and Human Fertility.* Paris, UNESCO, 1954.

Rideman, Peter. *Account of Our Religion, Doctrine and Faith.* Trans. K. E. Hasenberg from the German edition of 1565. Bungay, England: Hodder and Stroughton, 1950.

11

Learning and Therapeutic Communities

This selection is taken from Commitment and Community, *in which Kanter explores processes by which individuals become committed to intentional communities. In her words:*

Commitment mechanisms are specific ways of ordering and defining the existence of a group. Every aspect of group life has implications for commitment, including property, work, boundaries, recruitment, intimate relationships, group contact, leadership, and ideology. These pieces of social organization can be arranged so as to promote collective unity, provide a sense of belonging and meaning, or they can have no value for commitment. The strength of the group and the commitment of its members will be a function of the specific ways the group is put together. Abstract ideals of brotherhood and harmony, of love and union, must be translated into concrete social practices (1972, p. 75)

Basic commitment mechanisms include:
Sacrifice: *This may include abstinence from various kinds of food (e.g., coffee, meat) and sex, and the austerity associated with giving up certain material comforts or luxuries.*

Investment: *This can mean giving up money or property to the community or committing time and energy to the community (e.g., working in the community for a long period as an apprentice before being admitted to membership).*

Renunciation: *This generally means giving up old contacts with the past, controlling continued contact with the outside world, encouraging isolation, and controlling levels of intimacy within mating dyads and nuclear families.*

Communion: *This refers to specific devices to encourage the sharing of common experiences, such as encouraging entry to the community of people with common backgrounds, sharing property and work, sharing basic elements of a common life (eating, group meetings, ritual), and sharing the experience of persecution from the outside which often attends the creation of intentional communities.*

Mortification: *In Kanter's words, "mortification processes provide a new set of criteria for evaluating the self; they reduce all people to a common denominator and transmit the message that the self is adequate, whole, and fulfilled only when it lives up to the model offered by the community" (p. 103). Perhaps the most powerful mechanism to achieve mortification is confession and mutual criticism. Outward, more symbolic mechanisms are common dress and common housing facilities.*

Transcendence: *This means that the individual comes to feel that his particular life is part of an all-embracing world view or cosmos. Kanter suggests that charismatic people have the capacity to give significance and distinction to what would otherwise seem small and petty. Thus, strong personalities bring this quality to community, which may later be institutionalized as religion, ritual, or ideology, and later still as tradition.*

While the focus of Kanter's book is on the social processes which encourage commitment to community, the book includes discussion of a number of intentional communities, their problems, and the quality of lives within them. The selection included here discusses a number of settings we would call "therapeutic communities," which she calls "communes with missions." These include Cumbres, a retreat community (in which Kanter herself participated) and Synanon. From our point of view Synanon is an important cultural development for at least two reasons: it has continued to flourish; and it is based on the systematic use of the mutual criticism group as a means of cohesion, conflict resolution, and decision making. This suggests that it is replicable.

While Kanter's account is somewhat hypercritical, it is essentially accurate and provocative. The core issue we see coming out of the Synanon experience is the extent to which the mutual criticism group can be a dynamic substitute for a substantive tradition. The mechanism is dynamic in the sense that it allows for the continued reassessment of the balance between egotism and mortification, rather than surrender of ego to a common cultural identity (as in Bruderhof). It is, in a sense, a culture or tradition of process with the substance constantly being reassessed and shifting. In terms of our earlier discussion of the effort to build a new synthesis between modern and primal modes of culture, Synanon appears to be successful. As compared to the kibbutz, for example, there is a less stable routine, more openness in one's work schedule, and less emphasis on the nuclear family. And the stresses caused by this flexibility are handled by the mutual confession group which the kibbutz does not have.

They Also Serve: Communes with Missions

Another kind of communal group has grown up today which deals with the social environment in a very different way from retreat communes. The orientation of this group of communes is toward service to a special population; they have a mission. Since it is impossible to separate completely from contemporary American society, these groups define themselves instead as "serving" the society. Where the retreat communes seek withdrawal from the society, these communes seek engagement and involvement, often settling in cities. Where retreat communes fail to erect effective boundaries that permit them to cohere and endure as groups, these communes produce strong boundaries and strong commitment. Where the retreat communes minimize the collective, these groups maximize it. Where the retreat communes dissolve easily, many of these communities have already demonstrated their longevity. Where the retreat communes can be accused of fostering anarchy, these groups are sometimes attacked for too much order, too much organization, and for stifling the individual through a strong group.

Service communes define themselves as "helpers" to the society. They choose a constituency, then concentrate their energies on reforming it. Their interactions with this constituency renew the sense of mission and zeal that binds the commune. The service adaptation makes it possible for a community to interact with the envi-

Reprinted by permission from Rosabeth Moss Kanter, *Commitment and Community* (Cambridge, Mass.: Harvard University Press, 1972).

ronment not out of weakness but out of strength, for the commune has something valuable to offer society. It is not dependent on the environment, but rather it develops an exchange relationship. All types of tools and techniques and behaviors from the society can be incorporated instead of rejected by the commune, since they are used against the current established order of the society in some way, in order to change it. This adaptation represents a kind of co-optation of elements from a threatening, intrusive environment. Philip Selznick (1966, p. 13) defined co-optation as the incorporation of potentially threatening elements into a system's leadership structure, but the concept is also applicable here. Defining the group's mission as one of service also promotes a certain elitism or sense of superiority, which enhances ingroup feeling and reduces external threats; occupying the "helper" role places the helper in a dominant position with respect to the helped. Even when the service is performed with humility, it still promotes a sense of moral superiority. Even when outsiders refuse to accept the service or persecute the helpers, this adaptation builds cohesiveness within the commune. Doing a service for society also permits the commune to seek support on the outside without creating undue dependency, as by acquiring financial aid through charitable contributions or purchase of the group's product, or securing legal and emotional support from outsiders who respect the group's mission.

Service communes, therefore, tend to be stronger than retreat communes. Many have lasted over ten years. The service chosen varies. Koinonia, an interracial community, was founded in 1942 on a farm near Americus, Georgia, by Clarence Jordan, a theologian-farmer. Its purpose was to bear witness for Christian ideals of community and sharing and to assist local farmers by introducing scientific farming methods. Its goals were the extension of Christianity, an end to segregation, and rural development. Its constituency was the rural poor. Although it encountered hostility from the immediate area, in the form of shootings, beatings, bombings, burnings, and an economic boycott, Koinonia received financial and moral support from friends throughout the world. The commune still exists today, having reorganized in 1968. It has several businesses, from pecans to records. Reba Place Fellowship, another service commune, grew out of a gathering at Goshen College Biblical Seminary in Indiana. The group moved to Evanston, Illinois, in 1957, with the aim of providing an alternative to the corporate structure of established churches and of performing services for the city, such as day care. In 1969 it numbered thirty-six adults and over fifty-five children. The orthodox missionary activity of other religious communes, such as the Brotherhood of the Spirit, can also be interpreted as "service," in the sense of helping those who are unenlightened to see the light.

Growth and Learning Communities

The vast majority of service communes are engaged in education or re-education. The connections between community and learning have always been strong. Institutions such as Oberlin and Antioch, for instance, were involved with utopian communities in the last century. Today this combination is increasingly important. Many communes have either organized as free schools or contain free schools in their midst. Many learning communities include those that have grown out of the contemporary human potential movement and spiritual revival. Of over one hundred "growth centers" or human relations centers that have formed in the last decade, some are decidedly communal in form and spirit, from the modified Zen monasteries in Hawaii, California, and Vermont, to Lama in New Mexico and Cumbres in New Hampshire. In many cities macrobiotic houses teach the Zen macrobiotic life style and diet. There are also communities centered around caring for the mentally handicapped, such as Camp Hill Village, or rehabilitating drug addicts, like Synanon and numerous urban houses.

Such communities not only offer a mission around which to organize but also have found a way to legitimize the drift and mobility characteristic of the commune movement today. They tend to be composed of two sets of people—a core group that makes a permanent commitment and takes responsibility for the commune's learning functions, and a transient group with a more limited involvement and an expectation that they will move in and out of the group. At Lama the core group remains at the commune through the rugged New Mexican winter, while transients tend to come in April and leave in October.

To be organized as a school, therapeutic center, or learning community also makes it possible for the group both to generate and elaborate its own ideology and to ensure that members know these beliefs deeply and intimately. On a visit to four New Mexican communes, I was struck by how completely each of them built its community around four very different sets of ideas, growing out of the centrality of the group's educational mission. At Cedar Grove, a Ba'hai religious group with a newly organized free school, the school was the center and focus of life. Schoolrooms doubled as central dining and living rooms, their blackboards filled with diagrams of the Tree of Life, spiritual and practical messages, and quotations from scriptures. Thus, learning occurred while eating as well as in formal classes. The philosophy of the group infused its daily life in a way reminiscent of the Shakers. For instance, they compiled a household book of domestic guides from religious texts as varied as the Koran, the Bhagavad-Gita, and the Torah, and a message on the board extolled the "joy of sweeping."

Similarly, at Synergia Ranch, a joint venture including ecological experiments, a theater workshop, and craft enterprises, the scientific and ecological focus informed daily life. Written on the wall in the dining room were eight "laws of the universe," from $E=mc^2$ to $PV=NRT$. At Lama the focus was Eastern spiritualism; and at the fourth group, personal growth and humanistic psychology formed the basis for an alternative school. All of these groups had constituted themselves as schools or laboratories dedicated to their particular mission. This plan provided both a focus for daily life and a basis for internal order that made the groups viable. Cedar Grove, for example, is already over twelve years old; Synergia is four.

One of the strongest—and most controversial—of the communities in this group is Synanon, which sees itself as a "social movement of immense significance." Founded in 1958 by Charles Dederich, a former alcoholic with a $33 unemployment check, Synanon by 1968 had over twelve hundred resident members, urban communities from California to New York to Puerto Rico, and over $6,000,000 in property. Beginning as a kind of group therapy for drug addicts, it evolved into an intentional community that runs its own schools and businesses, including gas stations and an imprint advertising firm. It is now consciously utopian in its concept of the "Synanon lifestyle," a style that the community thinks may gradually sweep the world. The children especially hold this view. In 1968 a nine-year-old Synanon boy wrote: "I think sometimes the whole world is going to be Synanon . . . If the whole world does become Synanon, and that might happen someday, not so many people would be getting killed and they wouldn't be having so many fights because they get their [bad feelings] out in a stew or a game . . . and there wouldn't be any separation of the whites and the Negroes . . . and the whole world would be happy." Synanon is one kind of therapeutic community offering to enhance human potential, and in the process, build a better society.

In contrast to retreat communes, service communes develop strong boundaries. Their boundaries are more affirmative than negative, more exclusive than inclusive, and more strict than permissive. Such boundary conditions derive from the existence of a strong central purpose, giving focus and meaning to the group, and providing it the means to distinguish clearly between desired and undesired members, or desired and undesired behavior. Its mission enables the group to set criteria for making choices, based on whatever will further the mission, and justifies its becoming a closed society. The boundary conditions of service communes, therefore, foster the development of commitment mechanisms that produce strong, coherent communities.

Defining the Boundaries: Affirmation. Service communes define themselves by their values, and by what positive steps they take to implement those values. They tend to have elaborate belief systems and integrating ideologies and to insist that all members share them. They are clear about who they are and what they are doing.

The group has at its center a purpose, and it often has an individual representation of this center in the person of a charismatic leader. The charismatic leader symbolizes the values of the group, representing the state of perfection that will be attained when the group's service is completed. He is the ultimate "helper," aiding the other helpers in the group. By affirming and believing in his guidance, one also affirms the purposes of the group, which supersede individual whims and fancies.

Cumbres, a New Hampshire growth community, illustrates how such affirmative boundaries help generate commitment mechanisms. In 1969 Cesareo Palaez collected a group of former students and friends to form a community and staff a personal growth center. The purpose was to create an environment for enhancing human potential; community members would be growing and living a more spiritual life at the same time that they were communicating this spirit to paying guests. The name Cumbres is Spanish for "highest peak." This focus informed all aspects of daily life. Cumbres members participated in encounter groups, listened to lectures on psychology and religion, learned body awareness from visiting teachers, spent weekends on Zen meditation, and did the T'ai Chi Chuan (a Chinese moving meditation) every morning and evening. In Palaez's vision, even chores around the old New England inn housing the group were to play their part in the growth and development of members. When one of the young men working on the groups complained about the work, Palaez told him to read *Boyhood with Gurdjieff*, recounting an incident in which a boy had to mow the lawn for six months before the great spiritual master granted him an audience.

Palaez was a dramatic and forceful presence at Cumbres; he was everyone's teacher and guide. A former Cuban revolutionary, psychologist, and psychodramatist, he commanded great respect. When questioned by members about his dictates, he would often reply that he knew better than they what was good for them. Cumbres was built around affirmation of humanistic psychology and Eastern spiritualism, as chosen, interpreted, and preached by Palaez. Members unwilling to share this affirmation, primarily those near his own age (the mid-thirties) who were not willing to accord him the same reverence as the young, gradually left the community. The size of the group varied from twelve to twenty-five, with additional neighbors and guests swelling its ranks on weekends.

Because of the affirmative boundaries surrounding Cumbres, commitment mechanisms developed naturally. A sacrifice like giving up drugs was justified on spiritual grounds. As members were investing in something meaningful to them, they committed their resources and livelihood willingly. Cumbres' location seventy miles from Boston on ninety-five acres made the outside easier to renounce, and its isolation was reinforced by the monastic image that Palaez often advanced. A decision was made in the first summer not to open a branch in the city, for that would have detracted from the coherence of the community. Other kinds of renunciation flowed from the large number of activities at Cumbres and the energy required to sustain them. Though several couples shared their own houses, their time alone together was severely curtailed, and the emphasis on the free expression of affection extended relations beyond the couple to the whole group.

Communion was built in several ways. Chores were shared and rotated, and people often worked together as a group to complete a particular job. Undesirable as well as desirable work was shared, from running the office and stuffing envelopes to washing dishes. Meals were eaten in a central dining room in the inn, cooked and served by rotating crews. Members had several days a week for themselves, but during the rest of the week, every waking moment was infused with Cumbres—from T'ai Chi at 7 a.m. on the front lawn to evening coffee after group meetings at 10 or 11 p.m. On Zen meditation weekends, the Cumbres day started even earlier, at 5 a.m., to meditate before greeting the sunrise. The human potential movement and Eastern religions provided an abundance of rituals, symbols, and holy places, such as the daily T'ai Chi, exercises in which every group member was lifted and rocked, and blindfold walks by the stream in the woods. Special Cumbres celebrations were abundant. One weekend, members and guests participated in a pantomime circus; on another, some members erected a house of mystery and surprise, through which other members were led. Rituals to express appreciation of self and others were an important part of almost every group meeting at Cumbres, contributing to the love and warmth in the group.

Mortification and transcendence also flowed easily from Cumbres' sense that the community provided the path to growth. Encounter groups offered confession, criticism, and confrontation. Increased respect was given to those considered by Palaez to be ready to guide others in growth. Philosophies explaining the nature of human existence were read and discussed in seminars. Besides Palaez, others were considered as teachers. They did not constitute a hierarchy, since Palaez retained decision-making power, but they provided another set of examples and models to emulate. Master Liang taught T'ai Chi, Jan Kessler taught mime, and others came from Boston and New York to impart their wisdom. Palaez, however, remained the center, and he surrounded himself with much of the same mystery and awe characteristic of nineteenth century charismatic leaders. His insight was considered magical by members. His private quarters were almost sacred: he was not to be disturbed at Cumbres, and in Boston he maintained an apartment at a location unknown to most members and with an unlisted phone.

Cumbres had another problem, however, which plagues many service communes—financial constraints. The definition of many service communes as businesses or organizations as well as communal groups leads to tension. Cumbres was supported by fees paid by guests, but these alone were not sufficient to maintain the group. As a business, Cumbres had been heavily financed by backers. Like the nineteenth century groups, Cumbres had to weigh organizational against communal considerations. The decision not to move to Boston was made on communal grounds, to preserve the isolation enhancing group relations and learning, but it was a poor decision financially. As finances continued to decline, Cumbres became even more communal, the remaining members receiving greatly reduced support and sharing property. But in the end, financial pressures won out, the inn was sold to pay off investors, and Cumbres closed after two years. The example of Cumbres illustrates some of the limits as well as the strengths of service communes. Service communes may find it easy to establish affirmative boundaries around their purpose, but they are also subject to two kinds of tensions: the need to maintain simultaneously an organization and a community, and increased demoralization and disruption if the group's service does not attract the constituency to which it is oriented.

Across the Boundaries: Exclusion. Service communes are also exclusive in that they tend to have clearly defined membership and to know, at any given moment, specifically who belongs and who does not. They make positive choices as to membership. A person must be formally admitted by the group; he must be explicitly defined as being "in." Positive steps must also be taken to enter. Generally, the newcomer is a person being "helped," as part of the constituency that the group serves, and only gradually does he earn the right to become a "helper" himself, one of the core members of the group. Formal ceremonies and initiations may symbolize his admittance across the boundaries of the group; he may have to demonstrate his affirmation of the group through such acts as a financial contribution.

Service communes are exclusive with respect to permitting other movements across their boundaries as well. They do not admit visitors as freely as retreat communes, and when they do permit them, their activities are often monitored by group members. For example, visitors may be escorted through the community by an official spokesman for the group; they may be asked to pay fees. Many service communes have formal points of entry where visitors can legitimately gain access without disturbing the community's control over its boundaries. Reba Place, for instance, has a coffee house open once a week as a place for members and visitors to interact, a clever device which also ensures that visitors at least partially pay their way. Cedar Grove operates a small adobe cafe on the road through the community, run by a member and her daughter. Here visitors can purchase lunch, buy crafts made by the school children, and at the same time chat with community members. The cafe represents only a very small source of income, but it serves important boundary functions. Lama has open house on Sunday, when visitors can freely roam the groups, participate in activities such as Sufi dancing, collect Lama literature, and purchase such items as Tibetan prayer flags. At other times outsiders may be invited to attend special seminars, with the opportunity to camp on the hillsides for a contribution of a few dollars. Other communes permit entry through their store, such as the craft shop operated by Synergia to raise funds for its ecological work, or through programs of education or entertainment, such as Synergia's theatrical performances or the concerts by music groups in other communes.

Service communes often control information across their boundaries as part and parcel of their mission to serve. They incorporate new information from the outside that will further the group's ability to perform its service. Rather than finding the continual intrusion of communication from American society to be threatening, a service commune may consider it useful "data." Such groups also send out to the environment information that will meet the group's own purposes, by such means as pamphlets and speakers. Reba Place, for example, has a speaker service and several publications. In fact, one index of how serious-minded and organized a group is about its mission may be the amount of literature it produces. Service communes tend to generate reams of paper, especially when contrasted with retreat groups. These can include pamphlets telling "The Cedar Grove Story," "Why We Live in Community," or "How To Make a Contribution"; mimeographed handouts for members or guests on the latest philosophical input; books by the major philosopher, such as Clarence Jordan of Koinonia's "cotton patch" versions of the gospel; and even reprints of newspaper or magazine articles about the group. All of this indicates the community's intentionality and its eagerness to assert control over its relation with society.

Within the Boundaries: Strictness. Whereas retreat communes impose no limits, service communes that work effectively tend to impose many limits. The model of direction and discipline is an appropriate one. Service communes define behavior that is acceptable; they make coherent choices of lifestyle and expect them to be adopted; they do not shy away from making demands, developing organization, and creating rules—though not all the rules may be formalized. The group has work to be done. Whether decisions are participated in by a whole group or by single individuals acting for the group, it is important that decisions be made. Even helping individuals with their own growth is interpreted as requiring the imposition of limits, the acceptance of order from the group. The examples of Cumbres and Synanon illustrate this discipline and order in two very different settings.

Synanon: Can a Community Be Too Strong?

The boundary definitions of service communes permit the development of commitment mechanisms and in many cases produce highly committed members who are loyal, dedicated, obedient, and enthusiastic. Synanon represents an extreme case in this group, however, for its ex-addict members are so totally dedicated that critics have accused them of being "hooked on Synanon." But Synanon illustrates the ways in which the commitment mechanisms found in nineteenth century communes such as Oneida occur in modern dress. Synanon is also noteworthy for its extensive involvement with American society: not only has it helped many addicts who were not helped by traditional institutions (although many others abandoned the program before completing it), but its doors in several cities are open to its neighbors for recreation and entertainment, and it has accepted many recent nonaddict members who seek a communal lifestyle and like Synanon's way. Synanon, though strict, is completely voluntary, and its doors are always open for members to leave. Inside the community, however, is discipline and a sense of mission.

The contrast with Oneida is revealing. There are superficial differences, such as a shift of scene from the 1880's to the 1960's, and from upstate New York to California, and in place of a group of radical Christians there is a conglomerate of ex-drug addicts, former alcoholics, and once lonely people. But many of the processes are the same. There are businesses: Oneida manufactured animal traps and silverware; Synanon sells gas and advertising. There are feedback and encounter sessions: in Oneida, mutual criticism; in Synanon, "games" and "stews." There is music: hymns in Oneida; jazz in Synanon. There is a leader, thought by some to be godlike; John Humphrey Noyes in Oneida, Charles Dederich in Synanon. The language is different; instead of "saving souls," Synanon cures "hangups." Synanon is not called down by ministers for licentiousness but by city officials for zoning violations. The context is different, but many of the commitment mechanisms are the same.

Charles Dederich is the visionary behind Synanon. Many members look upon him as a kind of religious leader, if not a man of special inspiration, for he personifies many of the ideals of the community. One adherent stated that, "Chuck is my god, and Synanon is my religion." More modest worshipers claim that Dederich is not God but only Jesus. Others describe him as a "modern Socrates," engaged in a "total war against stupidity," of which "the present war against drug addiction is of course only one tiny segment" (Sagarin 1969).

Synanon's ideals are simple but have religious overtones. Every morning at community meetings the Synanon prayer is read:

Please let me first and always examine myself.
Let me be honest and truthful.
Let me seek and assume responsibility.
Let me have trust and faith in myself and my fellow man.
Let me love rather than be loved.
Let me give rather than receive.
Let me understand rather than be understood. (Yablonsky 1967)

Synanon abounds in rituals, special jargon, and symbols of the group's existence. These particularly involve its campaign against drugs, for newcomers must give up drugs immediately on entrance; the community also bans alcohol and recently waged a successful campaign against cigarette smoking. One Synanon celebration is the Big Copout, stemming from the night early in the group's history when the ex-addicts admitted ("copped") to taking an occasional fix, an incident that was responsible for eliminating the last vestige of drugs from Synanon. Celebration of this event has become a tradition, initiated by Dederich: "I got to musing on Synanon rituals . . .

like clean birthdays, Saturday night open houses, and the daily reading of the philosophy. And it occurred to me that we needed some kind of an annual Synanon celebration or taking of stock."

Synanon is communal not only in living arrangements but also in economy. New arrivals may pay an entrance fee, which is not refundable. No one in Synanon, at least in its early days, was paid, except for a few dollars a week of "walk-around money." Clothes and food are distributed equally, with meals eaten communally in large dining rooms, although older members have greater freedom and easier access to goods and services. Buildings and facilities such as cars are community-owned, but use of them is commensurate with members' responsibilities and group contribution. New ex-addict members enter at the bottom of the hierarchy; they contribute what resources they can and receive the lowest status chores to do, such as washing toilets and scrubbing floors, even if they had special skills or talents on the outside. For the first few months of their stay they may be prevented from seeing their outside families or leaving the house. Gradually, through participation in the community, they earn greater responsibility and can work their way up in the hierarchy, gaining even such major positions as director of a house, and they can again practice their special careers, such as art or music. Because Synanon's ideology specifies that "character is the only status"— character in the sense that Synanon defines it—as people show growth in commitment and contribution to the community, their status increases.

The "game" is Synanon's word for its own form of mutual criticism or encounter, in which members attack the imperfections of each other's behavior in a verbal and emotional battle, venting whatever hostile or negative feelings they wish. This is the core activity of the group, described as a combination of group therapy, evening entertainment, a law court, and a town meeting. In the game there is no status: leaders as well as newcomers are subject to attack and scrutiny and similarly have the chance to examine and question others, with everyone meeting on an equal footing—although experienced game players of course have the advantage.

Synanon views the world outside its boundaries as sick, as a breeding ground for stupidity. To critics who argue that Synanon members become addicted to Synanon instead of drugs, members offer replies such as the following: "If a man works in the coal mines and comes down with tuberculosis, you cure him by sending him out to breathe clean air. After he is cured, do you then send him back to the coal mines?"

At one of its branches, on an isolated hilltop in rural Tomales Bay, California, Synanon has created the Academy, a community of about fifty people who are in training to be Synanon's future utopians. Here, the well-known Synanon game has grown into a full-time, round-the-clock activity with shifting membership, called the "perpetual stew," or stew for short. Members' lives at Tomales Bay are planned entirely around participation in work activities and in the stew. The quality of life there was described in a letter written by a member to his father in the summer of 1968:

June 25, 1968

Dear Dad,

Let me tell you a little about my daily life and what is going on here in Tomales Bay. I get up at 7:00 each morning, and I work from 8 to 4. We are building a building here; I am on the "tactical" squad, which takes care of vehicles, buildings, etc. The other day my boss was teaching me how to weld; yesterday I was building (with someone who knows what he was doing) a walkway around a building. I shovel a lot, and by the end of the day I'm happy and tired.

From 4 to 5 p.m. I clean up, and from about 5 to 7:30 (dinner) I'll talk, read, walk around the property, listen to music, etc. After dinner a group of us usually get together and listen to tapes, discuss concepts, or just talk. If Chuck [Dederich] is around he is usually talking and we'll sit around with him. Last nite for example, one of the fellows gave a talk about basic training in the Marines. Tonight we're going to cut up an Emerson essay.

That's my day . . . 6 days a week. Once a week I spend 24 hours in the stew. It has been going now for about a month, and it will keep going until??

The stew occupies its own building—about 100 yards from the main building. There are about 20 comfortable chairs, inside a large room—with special chairs for Chuck and Betty (his wife) and Dan Garrett (Director of Legal Affairs and #2 man in the [Synanon] Foundation). They come in and out at all hours of the day and night and play the Synanon game. WOW! Do they!

Every two hours several people leave and enter the stew. So there is a constant flow of traffic. Tomorrow morning at 10 I will enter the stew and leave at 10 a.m. on Wednesday morning. Besides playing the game, we will listen to tapes and maybe have a discussion. Chuck and Dan might conduct some Foundation business. For example, Chuck frequently meets visiting "Big Shots" in the stew and concludes agreements with them about property, or buildings, right there!

The game-playing is very good and very honest! Lots of ridicule is employed and everyone is pretty hostile. Most of the time anybody who gets the game put on them gets completely smashed. Imagine this—the game gets on you, someone indicts you, you defend, dodge, slide, try to get the game off you.

In the usual 2-3 hr. game that might work! But two weeks ago the game was on me for three hours straight. You can't escape. Besides, you are tired—no sleep remember for 24 hrs. so your defenses aren't as good. SQUASH goes the image.

We got up here, we went into a "Cubic Day." A cubic day is the new Synanon life style. One type of cubic day is:

14 days "motion"
3 days pressure   28 days (one month)
11 days vacuum

Let me explain . . . picture a cube, now divide it in half, giving you two rooms. One "room" is the motion room. It consists of (lets say) 14 days. In these 14 days, people work 12 hours a day, very hard—they do the work of two people. The other room is also 14 days, three of those days are called pressure—you *stew*. Then you have vacuum—no work, no responsibilities—finally back into motion.

When we arrived, we went right into "motion." I was in motion for about two weeks. Then I went into the perpetual stew:

30 hours in a stew
6 hours break
20 hours in a stew
6 hours break
10 hours stew—60 hours of stewing, 72 hours total! WOW!

My sense of time was completely destroyed at times. I thought I had been in the room for years or five minutes. Through the window I could see the sun rising and falling, people yelling at each other. Chuck playing the game, he is the greatest, one of the most intelligent, funny, capable, manly, loving, human beings (the adjectives could go on and on forever).

After I got out of the stew (the game was on me twice, both times I was completely smashed) I went back to vacuum. Since then I've been in for a 24 hour bit, and working 8 hours a day.

Starting tomorrow we will all be going back into the cubic day life style. Every day two or four people will go into it. Everyone in this plant has a counterpart, someone who can capably do their job, so tomorrow two girls from the housekeeping staff will be going into a cube. Gradually the entire plant will move onto that life style.

Perhaps you are wondering what about the Academy? (the school at Tomales Bay)

Chuck says that education is a quality of the academy; classrooms, books, etc. have nothing to do with learning . . . they are tools used for a certain style of learning.

I am learning how to weld, how to work, how to listen, how to tell the whole truth, how to *trust*.

Chuck has told us that we won't be getting into books or ideas until we begin to trust each other, stop fighting and resisting, and have our contracts broken. Then we will proceed by massive dose. Using the stew setting, massive doses of information will be thrown at us. During vacuum we will read, talk, study.

Now our responsibility is to play the Synanon game, be honest, practice the Golden Rule. After the Fair (a money raising activity) is over we'll be moving full-bore on the building project. So far the foundations are down. The framework partially up, and a large steel roof erected. It's 120 feet by 120 feet! 2½ stories high . . .

Some interesting things, all the guys got ¼ inch haircuts a week ago. All of the Academy people are on a relationship/sex ban. We sleep in surplus army double bunks in the refinished attic of the main building.

Something else Synanon is going through . . . profound changes emanating from the Academy. Synanon I is changing into Synanon II.

The differences:

Synanon I	Synanon II
—Cures dope fiends but creates anxious little children	—Cures dope fiends and creates adults
—Games	—Stews
—Typical middle class life	—Cubic days
—Concentration on integration with responsible community and no use of drugs	—Concentration on producing people capable of living the Synanon philosophy
—Hospital or institution	—Social movement
—Cure	—Education

I don't know if that explains it, but there is a tremendous amount of pressure on everybody. Chuck wants to squeeze out all the "sickies" who are living at Synanon and no longer growing or contributing to the movement . . . He calls them retired dope fiends. Their symptoms (drug use, etc.) have been arrested, but they still are basically shit heads. They still lie, steal, cheat, etc. . . .

That's why we are up here (31 of us):

to protect us from the B.S. of retired dope fiends.

to educate us in Synanon II and the Synanon game.

to accelerate us, so we can help run the Foundation.

to experiment on us, so Chuck can create a college.

to rid us of our own corruption, after all, we are as dirty as everyone else.

to give us a full education, the best in the country, information as well as a setting in which to apply it.

to teach us some skills, e.g., welding.

There are more, I'm sure but that's enough. . .

Please run my story and Synanon's story to any of my old friends willing to listen!

Onward!!!!!!!

The commitment of Synanon's members has enabled the community to thrive and prosper to the extent that, as one member boasted, Synanon would like to see itself as "the oldest, richest and most successful commune in America." At various times in its history, Synanon has exemplified the use of a vast array of commitment-building processes. The most important sacrifice in Synanon (and its original *raison d'etre*) is complete abstinence from drugs and alcohol. Members, particularly in the early days, also lived an austere, nonindulgent, almost puritanical life. At Tomales Bay, they have constructed a whole village. Regardless of location, all Synanon members sacrifice their old careers, at least for a time. A musician may not be allowed to play his instrument or an artist to practice his art until he is considered completely integrated into the community. Investment is also a strong part of Synanon. Complete participation is necessary to reap any benefits of the commune. Members work on community economic enterprises and in turn derive their livelihood from Synanon. They contribute their money and property to the community, and the donation required for admission is not refundable. In many ways, members' futures become bound up with the success of the community.

Renunciation of the outside world is fostered, first, by Synanon's institutional completeness; it is a total community that offers everything within its own borders. If the nineteenth century communes could be considered villages, the new Tomales Bay facility may become a city. In addition, for the first months of their life in the community, members sometimes do not even step outside of Synanon. The outside world is condemned by Synanon, as are aspects of a member's previous life on the outside, particularly if he was an addict. Although Synanon tries to maintain good public relations, it is clear that the community considers its life style morally superior. Renunciation further occurs through the control Synanon maintains over movements across its boundaries, both of visitors coming in and members leaving. Special language, including the jargon of ex-addicts as well as new Synanon words and phrases ("stew," "cop out"), distinguish Synanon from the outside, as do special forms of dress sometimes adopted, such as the work overalls worn by all residents of Tomales Bay.

Renunciation of exclusive two-person intimacy is present to some extent, although Synanon also has many married couples. The community controls sexual relations through a highly puritanical attitude toward sex, particularly during members' early days, as well as by dormitory living that makes privacy difficult; many report that "courting" takes place on couches in the Synanon living rooms in full view of everyone. Occasional bans are placed on sex, such as the temporary celibacy rule at Tomales Bay; and the game serves to promote and enhance relations other than the couple. Renunciation of the family is fostered, first, by separation of new members from their biological families (a new person may not be allowed to communicate with his family for six months), and second, by communal dining and living. Even with separate apartments for families, meals are taken together in central facilities. In Tomales Bay and the Synanon school, children are raised communally, in their own quarters.

Communion, the strong group feeling that replaces renounced relationships, is strong at Synanon. Homogeneity is the first factor. Particularly in the early days, members had a common experience in the problem of addiction. Communal property and work arrangements also contribute to communion. The Synanon Foundation owns all property, supplying even the clothing. Jobs are rotated, with members moving from job to job and branch to branch, and there are also communal work efforts. Communal dwellings, ranging from large houses and apartment complexes to former hotels, as well as communal dining enhance group contact. There are regular group meetings, usually daily, from learning seminars to problem-solving meetings to games and "stews." There is much more group contact than privacy, and no matter is considered too private for group discussion in a game. Rituals are abundant, from the ritual functions of the game to the celebration of the Big Copout. Synanon has numerous symbols (one Synanon pamphlet is entirely devoted to translating the symbols), its own songs, music, and dances, and frequent concerts by its own jazz bands. It celebrates its own holidays and history. A sense of specialness and success pervade the group; any member will gladly tell any visitor how successful Synanon is. At the same time, the Synanon membership has shared in persecution and enmity from the outside, from Dederich's jailing in Santa Monica for a zoning violation to the arresting of two members for alleged parole violations, all in the early days.

Mortification is an important part of Synanon, justified as a tool in the program to tear down the dysfunctional character of the addict and rebuild a new identity. Confession, self-criticism, and frequently brutal mutual criticism are built into the games and stews that constitute Synanon's most routine and best-known activity. Members are differentiated on moral grounds and evaluated in terms of growth of character; rewards and punishments, such as the kinds of work a person is given, may flow from this evaluation. Rule breakers are publicly denounced and called to account in the game, and commitment is carefully examined. At one time, deviants were given haircuts as a visible sign of lost status. In keeping with the spiritual differentiation, old members become legendary figures, looked upon with awe by new people. De-differentiation of members also occurs, in two ways. First, a uniform lifestyle is provided for all members. Second, old identities and statuses are taken away. New members start at the bottom of the ladder, doing such unpleasant jobs as scrubbing toilets until they earn their way to better chores by demonstrating growth and commitment. Statuses that members bring in from the outside count for nothing in Synanon; everyone starts new at zero-years-old and celebrates Synanon birthdays.

Transcendence involves the person in a higher meaning system, and Synanon is strong here too. The community has a firm sense of purpose and has developed a coherent philosophy incorporating many well-known thinkers, from Lao-tze to Ralph Waldo Emerson to Buckminster Fuller. Pamphlets and philosophic guides carry the message. New members "convert" to this ideology in classes and seminars. Leadership similarly fosters transcendence in the strong, awe-engendering figure of Charles Dederich. His godlike status is enhanced by his distance from most members and his special privileges, such as an expensive car and comfortable upholstered armchairs for his table in the dining hall at Tomales Bay. Under Dederich, there is a hierarchy of legendary figures, Synanon's own stable of heroes, to administer the Synanon communities. Any member may aspire to be part of that hierarchy. Finally, Synanon involves large sets of highly specific behavioral and moral prescriptions for members.

Synanon, then, has strong commitment mechanisms which generate high commitment. In thirteen years it has grown from a dozen to over a thousand members, and many more have participated in Synanon and "graduated" from it during that time. It has become large and prosperous, advancing almost as far from the small retreat commune back on the farm as General Motors has from the neighborhood stable.

As it prospers, Synanon may also become subject to some of the influences pulling away from community that were faced by the successful nineteenth century utopian communities, including an increased emphasis on running an efficient organization. The growing development of its own internal businesses and a large bureaucracy may require organizational arrangements that will be detrimental to the communal structure. Some members have also expressed concern that the community may have difficulty surviving the eventual death of Dederich.

Its very strength raises many moral questions about Synanon. For one thing, it goes further than did almost any nineteenth century community in instituting the most restrictive as well as the most affirmative commitment mechanisms. Whereas no nineteenth century group had all of the commitment mechanisms proposed, Synanon makes use of every one and more, imposing controls on people that may go far beyond what is necessary to build commitment. Whereas too little commitment may generate stresses such as alienation or rootlessness, too much commitment may deny the volition of the person. And whereas people do indeed change dramatically in Synanon and eventually occupy responsible positions, the process of effecting that change may be more severe than necessary.

In its early days, Synanon was both radical and communal, but now it is so large and centrally organized that concepts like "total institution" may be more applicable than "commune" to describe the present community. The size and hierarchial power distribution of Synanon eliminate even the safety valve afforded to people in the more authoritarian nineteenth century groups, that is, the possibility of exerting influence through face-to-face interaction and by participating on committees making routine decisions. Synanon members reply to this criticism that the game represents such a safety valve, in that in the game hierarchy disappears, status dissolves, and any member can influence and talk back to even top leaders like Dederich. This answer makes sense up to a point, that point being that power still resides at the top, and the movements of individuals are still restricted. As a result, criticisms of Synanon have been just as strong as the commitment of its members. Whereas humanistic psychologist Abraham Maslow (1970) called Synanon a "eupsychia" or psychological utopia, Edgar Friedenberg (1965) referred to its operations as "brainwashing" and as undermining some of the most important processes of a free society. Chuck Dederich has himself been called a "megalomaniac" (Sagarin 1969). Synanon clearly arouses fierce objections as well as loyalty.

Retreat communes and service communes must be viewed as ideal types or extremes. Each of them may, in fact, draw on some aspects of the other, and they share the underlying idealizations of all communal life. Retreat communes, as ideal types, may go too far in imposing no order or limits, in building little commitment. Missionary communes such as Synanon, on the contrary, may go too far in imposing a tightly controlled order and in building more commitment than is possible for most people in this complex society. The examination of these two groups of communes illustrates an important paradox in social life: people often seek to create utopian communities in order to rid themselves of the authoritarian control of society and to gain a sense of mastery over their own destinies; but the survival of their utopian communities may depend on instituting their own authoritative system. Communes today struggle with this dilemma as they try to strike their own balance between freedom and control, mobility and permanence, variety and uniformity, inclusion and exclusion. These issues must to some extent affect all communes. Even the small urban "family" commune that sets out only to share a home may find that life together requires more commitment and more order than the limited involvement for which the group had bargained. It may even be impossible to derive the closeness and satisfaction of communal life without the limits.

References

Friedenberg, Edgar Z. "The Synanon Solution." *Nation* 200 (March 8, 1965): 256-61.

Maslow, Abraham. "Synanon and Eupsychia." *Journal of Humanistic Psychology* 7 (Spring 1970): 28-35.

Sagarin, Edward. *Odd Man In: Societies of Deviants in America.* New York: Watts, Franklin, 1969.

Selznick, Philip. *TVA and the Grass Roots.* New York: Harper & Row, 1966.

Yablonsky, Lewis. *Synanon: The Tunnel Back.* New York: Penguin, 1967.

12

Marathon House: A Therapeutic Community

Stephen Bookbinder's article bears explicitly on the distinction we make between the "corporate" and the "community" context. He describes in some detail the common life and ideology of a therapeutic community as well as the overall corporate structure which gives support and legitimation to the microcommunity. He then suggests a set of dilemmas or conflicts facing such a community, which must consider its residents as temporary communitarians being reeducated for life in the larger, corporate-oriented society. The actual focus of the article is on the writer's efforts to organize a "school" setting within the community. This effort was inevitably caught up in the conflicts between the two social forms. What about the role of the teacher? Is he a professional working for a corporation on a meritocratic basis or is he simply another member of the community with some additional skills? What about classrooms and schedules? Should they be organized for the convenience and efficient use of

time of the professional and the client, or should they be organically integrated into the life of the community? How should the student treat the teacher? Should the teacher command respect for his special basis of authority, or should he be judged and disciplined as another member of the community? Whether there are constructive compromises or syntheses between the two social forms and what demands such compromises make on individual personalities are suggested in the article.

Educational Goals and Schooling in a
Therapeutic Community

During the 1960's, social reform efforts sponsored by the Kennedy and Johnson administrations aimed to develop a wide variety of programs for the poor, the "disadvantaged," and the "deviant." These programs rested on a set of assumptions: (1) that social conditions created social problems which led to individual problems; (2) that individuals were to be isolated from the bad social environment and put into more benevolent settings; and (3) that recipients of social services should be directly involved in the planning and delivery of those services.

Among the programs embodying these assumptions was a new mode of service for drug addicts which became known as the self-help or therapeutic community. The first self-help community of this genre was founded by Chuck Dederich and was called Synanon. It involved addicts helping other addicts within a highly structured, one-context setting and thus represented a change from the "punishment or pity" approaches to drug addicts characteristic of most traditional, bureaucratic social service agencies. The quality of programs like Synanon and their specific approaches varied greatly, but they had a basic characteristic in common: they all sought to change individual behavior through communal living.

The general ethic of the War on Poverty meant that funds were available for this new approach. However, with the coming of the

Reprinted by permission from Stephen M. Bookbinder, *Harvard Educational Review* 45, no. 1 (February 1975): pp. 71-94.

1970's and the Nixon administration, federal spending for such social services was reduced and priorities and methods were shifted. No longer were the three assumptions of social service programs held to be valid—at least with respect to therapeutic communities—primarily because of the widespread belief that these programs had not produced the promised results. While addicts were cured of addiction in these programs, they did not seem able to reenter society or hold jobs in the conventional world of work. In short, the fact that many addicts remained in therapeutic communities to work as staff led to the allegation that self-help methods only prepared addicts for life in an artificial communal setting. (See, for example, Lennard and Allen 1974, pp. 212-13.) In addition, with the introduction of methadone and the growing interest in all forms of chemotherapy, the continued financing of therapeutic communities was jeopardized.

With the heyday of the 1960's clearly over, therapeutic communities increasingly were asked to prove their "success." Specifically, some argued that those members who continued to work for therapeutic communities were in some ways less "successful" than those who chose to reenter society. Critics did not question the ability of therapeutic communities to rid addicts of their drug habits; the definition of success was based on the ability of ex-addicts to function in the outside world. This notion of success was particularly problematic because it often compromised the values of the self-help community: the attitudes, goals and behaviors necessary to function in the larger society were often at odds with the ideology of these communities. This tension between society and the community can be termed the corporate-communal dilemma.*

Therapeutic communities are involved in attempting to reconcile two corporate and communal objectives:

1. To put former drug addicts efficiently and effectively through a program of rehabilitation that will meet the evaluative criteria of funding agencies—that is, to cure addicts of their drug dependence and return them to society as law abiding and productive citizens.

---

*"Corporate" will be used throughout the article to refer to those functions of the central office of Marathon House that deal with the larger society and as a synonym for the larger society.

2. To actualize a communal ideology based on concepts of reciprocity, honesty, consistency and affection that will help the individual to lead a responsible and fulfilling life.

The conflict between these two orientations as organizational modes ultimately can become a source of conflict for individual addicts. Ironically, this is in the nature of the rehabilitative process itself, which emphasizes behavior that is appropriate for a group rather than an individualistic lifestyle, but also has as its goal re-entry into a society where an individualistic lifestyle is valued and rewarded.

This article will focus on Marathon House which, as a corporation running therapeutic communities dependent on outside funding, characterizes the corporate-communal dilemma. These dual agendas are further manifested in the Marathon House staff organization, which is an alliance of "straight" professionals who are responsible for specialized tasks such as finance and grant management and former addicts who manage and supervise the delivery of services. Aware of the criticisms of self-help communities and pressed by the competition for funds, the Marathon House administration tried to ease the corporate-communal dilemma by introducing a school program into one House to prepare residents more fully for the transition back into society. Moreover, the school program was also seen as part of an expansion of services that would enrich the community. The first section of this article will examine the structure of Marathon House, its dual nature as a rehabilitative and a communal setting. The second section will focus on the introduction and operation of the educational program.

Structure and Operation of Marathon House

Marathon House, Inc., is a private, nonprofit, New England-based corporation operating therapeutic communities for drug rehabilitation. Incorporated in 1967, the organization was the result of a collaboration between social service professionals and former addicts who were graduates of Daytop Village, a therapeutic community founded after Synanon. (The term "graduate" here signifies individuals who have successfully completed a program of rehabilitation according to criteria set up by the community.) The first local Marathon House opened in Providence, Rhode Island, followed by five others in various places throughout New England. All of them were managed by former addicts. The executive director and several members of the central office staff in Providence were also former addicts, but the administration included a number of nonaddict, professional staff who were responsible for specialized corporate tasks needed to maintain the organization. The organization is therefore an alliance of people with different talents and experience which recognizes the credentials of those who were educated in the streets as well as those who were educated in more traditional environments.

Each of the six Marathon Houses has thirty to forty residents ranging in age from sixteen to thirty-five; there is a ratio of three men to each woman. Also residing in each House are four graduates of the program who serve as staff members.

Three-quarters of the individuals entering the Houses have criminal violations and have chosen the program as an alternative to jail. The remainder enter voluntarily, but in most cases they are people with serious drug problems who have been strongly influenced by friends or relatives to take this course of action. The admission process involves several letters or telephone calls and an interview in which the applicant must fully explain the reasons for wanting to enter the program. Since it is expected that the applicants are not entering the Houses solely on their own initiative, the lengthy procedure attempts to discover the applicant's potential for personal change and commitment to the communal life at Marathon House.

Applicants are accepted more often than not if there are available places in a House. The first stage of residency, aimed at the integration of the addict into Marathon House, lasts approximately one year. The resident's loyalty to the organization and its goals is expected to develop gradually. All members work, but the new resident in a House will be assigned a menial and often unpleasant job with little responsibility. The "older" residents and staff teach the newer members, through example, the important values of the House. One of these, showing "proper concern," means that individuals must learn not only to perform their tasks successfully, but also to take responsibility for monitoring the quality of performance of other residents' tasks. As the residents begin to learn this and other aspects of the communal ideology, they gradually are given more responsibility, and by the end of the first stage they have held several supervisory jobs. Despite the fact that the status system in Marathon

House is based on the criteria of length of residence and quality of work, there is a sense of what Wilmer and Lamb (1969, p. 65) call "coequality, sharing a sense of human dignity and worth."

The second stage, approximately six months long, directs residents toward eventual reentry into the larger society. For the first time, some residents may leave the House to work or study. However, residence in the House is still required, and the member's primary orientation and responsibility are still to the House community.

In the third stage, also six months long, the member moves out of the House, but still maintains close contact and involvement with the community. "Graduation" follows successful completion of stage three. Those who graduate continue to visit often and are regarded as siblings who have grown up and left the family.

The daily routine on weekdays begins at 7:00 a.m. After several morning chores are completed, a staff member or tenured resident conducts a meeting for all those who remain in the House during the day; work assignments, conduct, and the general attitude of the House are discussed. Residents talk about their individual attitudes during these meetings, often responding to specific personal criticism. If someone has lied, for example, an explanation of his or her behavior may be requested. Although work assignments are decided by the staff, residents who do not agree with their assignments can appeal to the staff, who must respond to the request. If, after the staff member has explained the reasons for the decision, the resident is still not satisfied, his or her only option is to "take the issue to a group."

The group meetings are encounter sessions on Tuesday and Thursday nights which are designed to mediate hostilities among residents and between residents and staff. Such hostilities often result from the self-centered behavior especially characteristic of addicts, the demands of the communal ideology, and the strains produced by House jobs, with their emphasis on both individual performance and responsibility for the performance of others. If an individual feels a problem with another resident or a staff member cannot be discussed and resolved in a reasonable way, he or she can drop a slip of paper with his or her name and the name of the offending person into a box for the staff, who will assign the pair to the same encounter group. At the meeting, the offended person has the right to be as verbally abusive as he or she wishes. Led by a staff member, the group then mediates the conflict and seeks a resolution. This is the only situation in which residents are encouraged to express aggression; any manifestation of overt hostility outside of a group context is reprimanded.

The goal for a resident is to go through the day with a positive attitude, showing proper concern for self and for other House residents. The structured situation theoretically facilitates the resident's gradual integration into the House. Slowly, by "acting as if," pretending to believe that the system of the House will help until it eventually does, the residents learn that they can trust a group of people. No one is expected to make an easy adjustment to such a heavily structured environment; each day is regarded as a new opportunity to live up to the code of behavior.

However, if one continually violates the rules, various sanctions are imposed by the staff and the residents; the more grave the offense, the more humiliating the sanction. It is important to note that the word "punishment" is carefully avoided and that all sanctions are referred to as "learning experiences." For a sanction to be imposed, the resident is first called before a number of House members, both "young" and "old," and told the offense. If the individual does not change after repeated warnings, he or she receives a sanction that reflects the gravity of the offense. Such decisions are made by the staff with the advice of other residents. Only physical violence or the use of drugs are grounds for immediate expulsion after a vote of the House membership.

Since the sanction is meant to teach, the resident will not be shunned after receiving the learning experience; on the contrary, it is the responsibility of all House members to talk to the individual about the offense, urging the offender to "clean it up and get rid of the label." Each person encourages the offender by relating personal experiences with sanctions, with the clear implication that no label in the community need be permanent. Ridiculing or "bad rapping" a person undergoing a learning experience is itself a serious offense because this would nullify the teaching purpose of the sanction. For example, as a newcomer to Marathon House, I saw a woman resident walking with a light bulb on a string around her neck because she repeatedly forgot to turn out lights in the House. When I made a joke about her necklace, the three or four people standing nearby fell silent; one of the group then politely explained why the teasing comment was inappropriate.

Despite the fact that interpersonal relations at Marathon House are structured so that residents gain confidence and self-awareness, the nature of those relationships is highly specific to communal life and can be at odds with what takes place in the larger society. Ironically, it is the very means of rehabilitation—living in a rich setting where problems that once led to drug dependence are dealt with in new ways—that can cause difficulties in the transition back to society. An examination of Marathon House, first as a program of rehabilitation for the larger society, then as an on-going community, will help put this dilemma into perspective.

Rehabilitation. As Sugarman (1970, p. 79) has noted, traditional attitudes regarding drug rehabilitation have supported approaches which either punish or pity addicts. Marathon House rejects these perspectives and presents a system of "reality therapy that includes unambiguous feedback on behavior and insistent demands for change." The attitude toward addiction is that the abuse of drugs is a futile attempt to deal with social and psychological problems. The object therefore is to enable individuals to understand why they used drugs and learn new ways of solving their problems. In theory, the immediate and continuous interactions among residents enable former addicts to face and manage problems in life and therefore to renounce drugs.

Rehabilitation is regarded as a process of learning to assume responsibility for one's actions. Thus individuals are started at stage one on a road of assuming greater and greater responsibility in the House and being held increasingly accountable for the consequences of their decisions. The assumption is that individuals really want to make responsible decisions, but at the same time they need to be pressured, sometimes harshly, to accept the consequences of such decisions and the views of others. The ideal in Marathon House is a person who is creative and decisive, but always acts with an acute awareness of others.

The goal of rehabilitation is not particularly unique to Marathon House; after all, other social service agencies dealing with addicts have as their goal ending drug dependence and uncovering the problems that led to addiction. Yet, generally, helping agencies and organizations are highly specialized and bureaucratized. "They offer an increasingly narrow range of help, so that each client must deal with several agencies and end up feeling that none of them understands him properly or sees him as a total person" (Sugarman 1974, p. 128). Marathon House, as a total context, regards rehabilitation as a process of treating a person "holistically, that is to deal with him from a sense of knowing all the problems and circumstances governing his life" (p. 138). For example, if a resident seeks counseling from another resident or staff member because he or she does not like a job, the counselor can evaluate the situation because he knows about the nature of the job and the person involved.

Moreover, many addicts entering social service agencies are all too willing to promise to change their lives and agree to the terms of the rehabilitation process. Faced with the immediacy of jail or the exigencies of a heavy addiction, this is understandable. However, drug addicts often identify themselves as "hustlers," people who have adapted and learned a complex set of mores that enable them to get what they want. They become experts in lying, manipulating people, and stealing. Frequently, residents make joking remarks and tell stories about how they conned psychologists and social service professionals in the past. In traditional agencies this behavior often is regarded as an impediment to rehabilitation, but in Marathon House it is considered an inevitable and expected part of the process. Since almost all of the residents and staff of Marathon House are former addicts themselves, and interactions take place in a total living environment, they are not easily fooled. As the House aphorism goes, "they know it all because they have done it all." "Getting away with things"—which is possible in a walk-in clinic or a social worker's office—cannot be carried off successfully for more than a short time in a one-context community.

More importantly, individuals are made to feel that the House staff are truly committed to them and can really understand them from the vantage of personal experience. Again, unlike workers in other social service agencies, the Marathon House staff are residents of their clients' community. They are involved in residents' lives because they eat, room, work, and relax with them. Gradually, new residents begin to feel they can make the changes demanded of them because they see that the people who are helping them have gone through the same process.

In these respects, Marathon House may seem to be a half-way

house. However, residents and staff strongly reject the labeling of Marathon House as a half-way program because of the implication that it is a short-term, custodial institution. They regard the House as a group of people to whom one makes a lasting commitment. In that sense, it is not a half-way point to anything, but rather an end in itself. Rehabilitation means changing one's life through changing one's goals, and it comes in the process of living in an honest and demanding small community. Thus, while the stated goal of Marathon House is rehabilitation for the society at large, the means to that end is a highly structured, one-context community where communal success is as highly valued as personal success; in fact, personal success is success in maintaining and strengthening the community.

Community. Marathon House is an intentional, ethical community, and Kanter's definition of an intentional community seems applicable:

it is identifiable as an entity, having both physical and social boundaries, for it has a physical location and a way of distinguishing between members and non-members. It intentionally implements a set of values, having been planned in order to bring about the attainment of certain ideals, and its operating decisions are made in terms of those values. Its primary end is an existence that matches the ideals. (1972, p. 2)

Kanter goes on to describe two concepts essential to communal living —sacrifice and investment:

Sacrifice involves the giving up of something considered valuable or pleasurable in order to belong to the organization . . . . Investment is a process whereby the individual gains a stake in the group and commits current and future profits to it so that he must continue to participate if he is going to realize those profits. (p. 72)

These processes are viewed as necessary to the development of commitment in the first year of residence in Marathon House. The organizers of Marathon House were well aware of the difficulties of creating a new lifestyle and the necessity of devising ways to bring about sacrifice and investment in the House. During the first year many of the residents' discussions revolve around whether they can do without the latest records, drugs, motorcycles and other things that made up their previous lifestyle. One of the most crucial activities sacrificed during the first year is the opportunity for sexual relations. There are a number of reasons for this moratorium. For one, men outnumber women three to one. For another, investment in a dyad at an early stage would compete with involvement in the community. But the moratorium on sexual relations also allows the residents to think through their past and prepare for more satisfying dyadic relationships. Gradually as individuals become trusted, they are allowed to begin to redevelop relationships. The House at all times keeps those close to the residents informed of their progress.

Group loyalties, group experiences, and communal solidarity are the focus of life at Marathon House. The longer one lives there, the more one is aware of what has been lost individually—privacy, material possessions, etc.—but also of what has been gained communally—the bond of a common daily experience, a common past and future. This is not unlike the kibbutz in Israel, where

... the ultimate criterion ... is whether it becomes a *chevra*—a group which is characterized by an intimacy of interaction and by mutual concern if not by love. [The desire for privacy] constitutes a threat to the group ... and either prevents the group from becoming a *chevra*, or symbolizes the fact that it is not a *chevra* for if it were, he would prefer to be with the group than to be alone. (Spiro 1963, pp. 30-31)

The sense of membership in a primary group is most important to the residents of Marathon House. Each person shares and works toward the same goals for himself and for his friends, and this sharing constitutes a common identity. Roles overlap in a manner not often possible in the outside world.

The Corporate-Communal Dilemma. Newmann and Oliver (1967, p. 66) argue that a sense of community "demands the ability to perceive (or at least unconsciously assume) relatedness among a variety of people, institutions, events and stages of life." This conception is the very strength of Marathon House, yet it is also the critical problem in a graduate's ability to reenter the larger society. It is difficult for members, who are accustomed to intimate and circumscribed communication, to relate to people and institutions outside the immediate environment of the House. This difficulty is the core of the individual's corporate-communal dilemma.

For example, a visitor might be surprised to see a person who is working very hard reprimanded for not taking an interest in his or her fellow workers. Most people in the corporate society value achievement of tasks much more than relationships between people. If a resident learns to expect personal involvement, he or she is preparing for what does not exist in most work settings. In this sense, then, reentry means readjusting to work attitudes (and attitudes in general) that were scorned in Marathon House—thinking and acting solely in terms of individualistic achievement.

The dilemma for Marathon House graduates can also be examined in terms of leisure time. Periods of free time in the House are oriented to the building of relationships; seldom would a person spend that time alone. When I first went to work at the House, it was pointed out to me that I often worked during the free-time periods, and that I should use that time to get to know people in informal and unstructured situations. The richness of interaction at these times is something fundamentally different from leisure in a society where informal group play and relaxation are not a daily part of most people's lives. Unfortunately, when residents reenter society, they often resort to the society's worst notions of play and relaxation, such as watching hours of television, because the options of communal play no longer exist. Also, because of the emphasis on group relationships, more fulfilling private pursuits like playing a musical instrument are seldom cultivated.

The House attempts to balance a need to be serious about the rehabilitative process with a desire to make the House an enjoyable place to live. Joking, singing, and just "fooling around" are very much a part of the relaxed atmosphere of Marathon House and connote the high level of camaraderie between people. Everyone is generally very affectionate in a nonsexual way, and it is not unusual to see people greet each other with a kiss or a hug. Humor in the form of skits or parodies is always a part of morning meetings or other activities, deliberately planned to give people an upbeat feeling, and there is the constant sound of music from a record player or a radio. Although there is a commitment to a daily schedule, this is not rigid and is broken frequently by spontaneous activities like a trip to the beach or to another Marathon House. Yet these qualities—singing, joking, displays of affection, and spontaneous breaks in the daily routine—are simply not a part of most people's work experiences in the general society. Most jobs involve a rigid schedule with only preplanned breaks. The atmosphere of most work settings is serious, and employers would regard singing, joking, and "fooling around" as impediments to productivity.

The dilemmas discussed above are not entirely apparent to first-stage residents who are almost totally involved in the House. During the second and third stages, however, residents begin to understand that once they enter society, they will not be able to work, play, and interrelate in the ways in which they have become accustomed. At first they are happy to be "on the outside" with increasing privileges to do as they wish, such as develop dyadic relationships, drink alcohol, have a car, go out whenever they wish, spend much more time alone or with people outside the House, and have considerable spending money.

But the outside world does not provide caring and direct feedback. Loss of this quality of life is often difficult for Marathon House residents. For example, instead of using prescribed ways for dealing with one's feelings, most people on the outside often deal with their feelings by some means of "escape." Perhaps they will "take it out on somebody else," use drugs or alcohol excessively, or just go off to feel sorry for themselves and sulk. These options do not exist in Marathon House, and it is not uncommon that as individuals begin to readjust to society during the second and third stages, while not returning to hard drugs, they may once again resort to destructive ways of dealing with their emotions.

It is clear in other ways that what the individual has learned in the House may not be appreciated by other people and institutions. One of the major goals of Marathon House is getting people to express themselves more effectively. Residents must attempt to talk to others about troubling problems. Yet residents have had reentry problems precisely because they become more honest and open. Stories abound in the House about the consequences of confronting a foreman about his shoddy practices, questioning a college instructor about his lack of concern for students, or being confronted by fellow workers for "goodie-goodie" or "eager beaver" attitudes.

For many of the reasons discussed above, second and third stagers were recognized as a special peer group with problems different from new residents. Second stagers started living together in one area of the House; third stagers often shared apartments. All came to regular encounter groups, but special groups were organized for "older" residents to deal with issues of reentry. They began to understand the ways in which American corporate society was different from an intentional community. They attempted to help one another by pointing out the ways in which they faced a common struggle—to make it on the outside. However, often in these special second- and third-stage groups, they found that their responses to reentry problems were very different. For example, in the area of dyadic relationships, getting intimately involved with a person outside the House was difficult for some because individuals found it so much easier to trust people inside the House. For others, dyadic relationships were easy because the experience of living communally had given them a new sense of confidence and enabled them to communicate more effectively. Sometimes this skill was used to manipulate people. To deal with these problems, second and third stagers and the staff constantly tried to evaluate each other, to strike an almost impossible balance between pushing some and restraining others.

It should come as no surprise, then, that many graduates of the House—45 percent in fact—when offered the opportunity to continue to work for Marathon House or another type of self-help community often preferred that job (Sugarman and Fisher 1973). The job offered a livable salary, good working conditions, and meaningful employment that is seldom possible for people lacking professional credentials. As noted previously, some critics of these communities deplored the fact that graduates stayed in the communities to work, arguing that this reflected their need to use the community as a permanent crutch. While there is considerable truth to this criticism, it ignores an essential and simple fact—graduates of Marathon House generally cannot find jobs elsewhere that are nearly so fulfilling.

Because of these issues, criticisms of therapeutic communities in general, and a feeling on the part of the Marathon House administration that the Houses could strengthen their services, a school program was introduced.

The School in Marathon House

Therapeutic communities have often been attacked for their lack of academic or vocational training programs and consequent inability to prepare ex-addicts to return to society. The corporate part of Marathon House, that is, the staff at the central office responsible for "selling" the therapeutic communities to society, was forced to deal with these criticisms and justify Marathon House as a mode of therapy deserving of funds. Believing that Marathon House offered more effective programs than other drug treatment methods, the corporation staff chose to broaden its appeal by adding a service aimed particularly at easing the transition to society. In 1971, a school was introduced into one Marathon House as an experimental program. If the program proved successful a school would be added to the other five Houses. The school was to have a dual function: to meet the corporate goals of preparing community members to return to school or jobs in the larger society; and to conform to and further the communal and interpersonal goals of the House. The introduction of the school with these different and sometimes contradictory goals raised the corporate-communal dilemma once again.

Teacher Selection. While the Marathon House administration was committed to introducing a school, there were no firm ideas about how the school would operate. This decision was to be left to the teacher in conjunction with the rest of the House. Thus, the first task was to hire a teacher.

The process of evaluating applicants and hiring a teacher involved the judgment of the entire House in cooperation with consultants from the central office. Although the central organization retained a highly qualified program director, it was felt that the input of those who were to be directly involved with the school was more crucial. Therefore each applicant resided in the House for two days in order to gain an understanding of the setting and to allow the House residents and staff to evaluate the applicant's ability to relate successfully to them. The residents and staff explained to the applicants that they were looking for a teacher who would believe in the validity of the Marathon House experience and would not be patronizing or show what the House termed the "liberal attitude."

The Role of the Teacher. The teacher was to be a professional whose role was circumscribed by the skills he or she would offer and by the fact that he or she had not undergone the rite of passage of living in the House for an extended period of time. Like everyone else, however, the teacher was expected to be involved in the broader educational and procedural goals of the community and was not simply to counsel or impart information. It was felt that the teacher could be effective only if he or she integrated the interpersonal goals and processes of the community into the operation of the school. The House staff hoped that the teacher would be, as they put it, gradually deprofessionalized by being a member of the community with responsibility not only to teach skills but also to become personally involved with all community members and activities.

The teacher's program responsibilities included three general areas: (1) academic skills development; (2) educational counseling for job training and college placement; and (3) enrichment activities. Academic skills development was to focus primarily on basic math and reading comprehension, particularly to prepare for the high school equivalency examination. Counseling meant helping residents locate job or college opportunities, investigating the details of admissions or placement, and assisting individuals to make their decisions. Enrichment meant providing the House with stimulating resources or opportunities ranging from creating a library to taking field trips. In this area, the teacher would especially try to respond to the students' expressed interests. For example, if a group of students wanted to study science fiction or learn to sculpt, it would be the teacher's responsibility to lead the class or find someone who could.

The Marathon House teacher needed to be a self-reliant individual because he or she could not expect to look to other staff members and residents for support and advice. In most school settings a teacher has other teachers, guidance counselors, or a vice principal available to help deal with problems, but at Marathon House the teacher was expected to make decisions in difficult situations and accept full responsibility for his or her actions. A number of applicants were considered in light of these criteria; I became the first teacher in the school at Marathon House.

The School. Classes generally met in two connected rooms set aside in a building very near to the House. I tried to make these rooms resource areas for personal or group enrichment. There were educational games, art materials such as a silk-screen press, science materials including microscopes and slides, and books ranging from novels to texts. Desks, chairs, and sofas were scattered in the style of open classrooms.

Most classes met regularly at specified times. A person at a very low skill level (third grade) could meet with me regularly in a tutorial situation. When there were about seven people at approximately the same reading and mathematics level, I could be much less directive because the students could help each other. I always tried to provide skill development classes which matched the academic levels of the students, but also offered many short courses, seminars, and experiences that bridged academic levels. Art classes or political discussions were designed to bring people together in this way.

When classes were not meeting, I was seeing individual residents, attempting to follow up on requests from students, finding materials for classes and seminars, or just "hanging around" trying to get to know people better.

Student Selection and Plan of Study. Anyone at Marathon House was eligible for the skills classes, counseling, or enrichment activities, but from the outset it was clear that not all residents would participate because they were at different levels of responsibility and development. A second-stage resident, for example, probably either was involved in a difficult training situation at the House or left the House daily to attend school or work. Consequently, those initially involved with the House school were first-year residents. As the school developed credibility, "older" members began to request services such as high school equivalency examination preparation.

An individual's decision to attend the school meant a commitment to complete whatever project he or she began to the satisfaction of all concerned. If a resident was known to be avoiding school because of fears of inadequacy, he or she would be strongly urged by the staff, other residents, and me to face the challenge and deal with those fears. In this situation, as in others in the House, the whole community provided support to the reluctant individuals, although fellow students supplied the most direct counseling. Schooling took place in the time reserved for work and had an analogous position to work in the House. There was no immediate financial reward for attending school, but as prestige was accorded to those who showed devotion to their work tasks, so, too, was prestige accorded to those who showed devotion to their school assignments. If a student chose not to go to class, he or she returned to work.

The determination of an individual's learning goals was viewed as a problem-solving process with no predetermined or universal patterns. I met with each resident, who expressed his or her educational goals, and together we evaluated the person's skills. The staff and I then made some recommendations and explained the basis for them. The individual thought about these recommendations and discussed them with House peers. Together, a decision was reached.

In one case a person lacked basic skills, but felt that he had the talent to be a musician. The staff, his peers, and I, however, felt that he should learn simple math and reading because these skills were necessary in the larger society. Moreover, we thought that the individual felt and would continue to feel inadequate about his lack of basic skills and that it would be therapeutic for him to make a sustained effort in this area. A compromise was reached: the individual went to classes for basic skills, and I arranged for him to have piano lessons. In the discussions there were generally several issues involved: Was the task possible? What were the sources of the individual's preferences? What were the crucial educational and rehabilitative needs of this individual?

Sometimes these sorts of conflicts never arose. Some students chose the single goal of a high school diploma and met to study material for the equivalency examination. In general, it was hoped that residents would see the classes as an opportunity to pursue a personal goal or for a group to study things unrelated to the House, such as poetry or painting. Initially, goals were set by consensus; later, goals were set on the basis of whether or not prior ones had been met. The student's responsibility was to invest himself or herself in a manageable set of tasks which made sense both personally and to the group. Of course, I was obliged to help the person fulfill these mutually determined goals. School and student, then, were theoretically interdependent: each student who fulfilled his or her plan made the school program a more credible and viable experience for everyone.

Relationship of House and School Processes and Goals. The school was set up in accord with the basic values of Marathon House —honesty, self-reliance, and mutual responsibility—and had the task of operating within this framework. In practice this meant that I was responsible for preparing my assignments and defending their validity just as the student had to complete his or her assignments or have a legitimate reason for not doing so. Students had to maintain a good attitude, work on their relationships with fellow students, and show proper concern for learning and for other school members. The exception to this would be special school meetings and encounter groups where discouragement and discontent could be expressed.

In the organizing stage of the school, neither I nor the students fully understood how the program would constantly meet the needs of diverse individuals. The students ranged in age from sixteen to thirty-five: some had five years of education, while others had completed high school and wanted to prepare for college. Therefore, conflicting interests often had to be negotiated. For example, if a group of students wanted to take a field trip or go to a play, they had to convince the other students and teacher of the merits of that activity in order to go. But learning also came about through the recognition that certain things were not possible. For example, a student could not change a reasonable commitment such as a contract between himself and the teacher to learn a specified amount of math by a certain time.

The school reinforced the more basic changes that Marathon House hoped residents would incorporate into their style of problem solving: to identify where the resident is, to "act as if," to progress at his or her own rate with support and guidance from the teacher and fellow students, and to discuss problems without self-indulgence. In this way the school attempted to help students deal with society by enabling them to feel intellectually confident and to gain the necessary skills and credentials.

The school also strengthened the basic interpersonal goals of the House because teacher and students were governed by the same code of behavior, and co-equality prevailed. Two examples illustrate what this meant in daily terms. In one instance I arrived late to class because of car failure. When I arrived, everyone was milling around the classroom. When I snapped at some students to sit down, I was politely informed by one student that I ought to leave class and calm down rather than "take out my feelings on them." All agreed, so I went to have coffee and calm down. At Marathon House, unlike traditional schools, students could be forthright about their reactions to a teacher's behavior.

The second example is more complex because there was not a clear violation of a norm. In this instance a student in a creative writing class "took the teacher to a group" because she felt I was excessively negative in my criticism of her poetry. I argued that I felt her poetry was good, but she argued that my long criticisms belied that. After a long discussion, it was decided that the criticism reflected the impersonal way I sometimes dealt with people and also that the student was hypersensitive to criticism. The group then worked out ways both the student and I could improve our relationship and general behavior. The same group evaluation, scrutiny, and conflict resolution processes which operated in the House also operated in the school.

In a similar way, the school incorporated the House ethic of mutual responsibility. Questions like, "What were you doing last night that kept you from doing your homework?" which in another context might be considered prying, were pro forma. Even if the question aroused hostility, it was part of showing proper concern and collectively arriving at a remedy for the situation. If a student was obviously lying about something, then in theory at least a peer was the first to question the individual. While there were problems in creating this mutual responsibility, they were accepted—as all problems are in the House—as an inevitable part of learning to trust one another and to live in a community.

The overall goal at Marathon House is that in the normal course of living in the House, residents will come to understand something about themselves, why they took drugs, and how to cope with an existence without drugs. The school had to deal with both a specific understanding of why addiction occurs as well as more academic skills like literacy or basic math. It was unique in that it encouraged Marathon House's communal goals, but it shared with other schools the role of socialization—preparing students for the corporate world.

The School and the Corporate-Communal Dilemma. Concerned about the insular nature of the House experience, both the House and the central office initially agreed that the primary focus of the school was to be on preparation for societal reentry. Instead of a first stager just going through a process of learning about his or her past and present behavior—"getting his head together"—each person would now begin early in that process to prepare academically and vocationally for the outside world. The first two responsibilities of the school were emphasized: each person should (1) be taught literacy skills and (2) be counseled about vocational or higher educational opportunities. Both of these tasks would help the students negotiate such systems as the Veterans Administration which might have intimidated them in the past. Since the House staff did not need academic credentials and disliked their role as job counselors (often because they acknowledged their inadequacy in this area), it became my job to argue that skills were necessary and, more generally, to explain how the society functioned. Moreover, since I was seen as an "educated person" who knew how to negotiate with bureaucracies, it was felt that I could be more effective at job counseling.

The school's additional responsibility of enriching House life was to be an effort to help people to develop leisure interests that would be transferable to society, such as photography or reading. In this sense it tried to bridge the corporate-communal dilemma by providing services which prepared people for reentry into the society while simultaneously enriching their lives in the community.

Although the school was intended to preserve the Marathon House community, it introduced potentially corrupting influences from the outside. Sometimes the introduction of outsiders was beneficial. For example, a trip to hear Jesse Jackson resulted in many subsequent discussions about issues not normally faced in the course of daily living in the House. In another instance a representative from a women's clinic came to the House to discuss personal health care and medical services. Many of the House women did not know such clinics existed and the visit provided a link to services in the outside world.

But along with the benefits, there were also risks. Residents and staff feared that short-term visitors might be unconsciously insulting. This was the case when one visitor remarked, "There are no bars on the windows and no lock-up and most of the people have prison sentences over their heads?" While such comments were abrasive, they made it clear to Marathon House residents what attitudes they could expect on the outside.

The idea of introducing a teacher from the outside presented similar risks to the residents. The members of the Marathon House community felt that it was inevitable that I as an educated, white, middle-class teacher would be patronizing or insulting in some fashion and might try to change their community in undesirable ways. However, this potential risk was largely averted; although I was an outsider at Marathon House, I had to conform to its rules. In practice this meant that problems were immediately pointed out and, if need be, I could be brought to a group. It was often made clear to me that I was coming into an on-going community. At one staff meeting I made a remark about the past lack of job counseling at Marathon House. I was quickly told that, to the contrary, a network of job opportunities had been developed and that other efforts had also been made to help residents going into their second stage at Marathon House. I was reminded that while job counseling and placement previously had been identified as a problem, considerable progress had been made in implementing solutions and, in fact, I had been brought in because they wanted someone with expertise to expend even more effort in this area.

The fact that I lived outside Marathon House was also perceived as a continuous risk to the Marathon House community. Since I lived in a college community where people allegedly smoked marijuana on the streets, could I really be trusted to honor the House commitment against drug use? Distrustful feelings often were expressed in half-joking questions about whether or not I had been "high" the previous night. At the same time, these questions revealed the residents' fears that they could not forego drugs on the outside. I often used the jokes and teasing to initiate discussions about the students' fears about leaving Marathon House.

I remained a quasi-member of the community nonetheless. Much of my life was spent outside the community. This was especially clear on Monday morning when I would return and hear the weekend news with the feeling that I had most likely missed important high and low points in Marathon House life. Yet my position as an insider-outsider made me a reference point to the general society and the source of a different and critical perspective.

The school program was intended to provide residents with a more comprehensive view of society. As has been mentioned earlier, Marathon House as a community is characterized by high social boundaries, and this tends to shelter the residents from social problems. This encapsulation is reflected in the fact that residents are faced with only the interpersonal aspects of larger social problems, aspects that they learn to manage; impersonal or institutional problems that in society are "unresolvable" are capable of resolution in Marathon House. The effort of the school to provide a more complex understanding of social problems as they are found outside of Marathon House, therefore, meant that explanations would often be in conflict with values and social analysis as practiced in Marathon House.

A typical issue of controversy was the significance of racism in the House. As enunciated by staff and residents, the ideology of the House is that racism is a serious problem in society, but can be successfully dealt with in the House because interpersonal relations are the focus; people are compelled to express their feelings and accept individuals for themselves. I tried to introduce the more complex aspects of racism in society as enunciated by social critics—aspects which often overrode the interpersonal dimension and thus contradicted the House ideology. Although the staff sharply disagreed with some of these materials, they were nonetheless aware that on the outside residents might encounter racism that could not be dealt with solely on interpersonal terms and that the educational material would be helpful to residents in facing society realistically. They were concerned only that I handle the issues in a "responsible" way. In this case, the responsible way meant that while I could present materials on race that were contrary to House ideology, I would have to make it clear that racism could still be dealt with in the House through successful interpersonal relations. The result was that because of the school, the issue of racism became increasingly complicated for the House as new interpretations were voiced.

It was the school's task to strike a balance between communal and societal demands so that the student could live in both worlds. The question of the transferability of what is learned in the school program highlights this dilemma. Some school skills clearly are transferable—for example, the high school diploma. The value of other school experiences is difficult to measure, but there were some individual problems in transferring from the school to learning environments outside of Marathon House. Several students had acquired reading and writing skills in the course of the school year but could not complete courses at local colleges. Those who did complete them complained of the lack of solid relationships with faculty or other students. Some students could not or would not make the jump into a societal learning situation that had no features of communal support or coequality. The very environment which enabled people to learn in Marathon House paradoxically raised their expectations of learning environments so that it was difficult for them to function outside.

The Evaluation of the School. The evaluation of the school program was an on-going process. From the outset the central office emphasized that the House staff and students should make an effort to participate in measuring the school's success. They felt that the evaluation should be a part of a continuous effort to make the school better and more responsive to the student's needs, rather than a one-shot judgment of whether or not the program had been successful after an extended period of time had elapsed. In practice this meant that community members provided feedback to the teacher. As a result I received almost daily comments on my efforts. If I presented a course or a seminar which people felt was important or enjoyable they responded accordingly. If someone felt I was not doing my best to convey material, this was mentioned in accord with the overall House philosophy of expressing proper concern. The process of taking someone to the group was another example of the feedback process. Just as residents were asked how their work was going, so too I was asked similar questions. Most often they were specific, about people or problems: "Does John speak up in class? You know he is quiet. Do you force people to talk if they are quiet?" Through this questioning process, both staff and residents got a sense of the school and its operation.

The evaluation process was special in its deep commitment to helping an individual. At first the staff made an effort to question me about the school's progress and wanted me to make them aware of any problems. However, as they gradually learned about the program from students and from their own observations, they termed the school a successful and valid part of the Marathon House experience. This information then was passed on to the central office. After six months, I began to hear from visitors from other Houses and from the central office that they felt the program was a success. Although the school program was visited formally only twice during the year, the central office obviously believed the program was a success, since they accepted the communal evaluation. While an outsider's evaluation of the school program might have been helpful, the time that is required to evaluate what is a process rather than a product-oriented program frequently makes the cost of such an evaluation prohibitive.

People have suggested that measures like the college or training program dropout rates should be used to measure the effectiveness of schools like the one in Marathon House. However, neither I nor the central administration saw the school's goal to be the successful completion of such outside programs. The goals were rather to prepare people academically, to give them some minimal sense of what to expect from a job or college experience, and to assist with information about things like how to structure an English paper. If an individual decided, and several did, that college was not what they wanted, then that cannot be viewed as an indication of the school's success or failure. This kind of measure is only marginally significant to the program and reflects one of the tragedies of traditional evaluations: often those running programs like the Marathon House school get caught in the corporate-communal dilemma because they try to remain committed to their complex goals while responding to society's limited and often inadequate performance goals.

Conclusions

This article has tried to show that organizations should be aware of the dilemma they face in attempting to create and implement communal structures and values while simultaneously meeting responsibilities to and depending upon the corporate society. Marathon House, I think, will persist in its belief in the validity of the communal experience for the rehabilitation of drug addicts. As long as society persists in judging the validity of such experiences on the basis of criteria to which the organization is not internally committed, then the dilemma more than likely will not be resolved. Thus this organization, like many similar alternative organizations, will have to be committed to the dual agenda of maintaining internal integrity and external legitimacy. An understanding of the dual agenda can enable those responsible for the internal and external operation of such organizations to create more manageable solutions if in fact they want their organization to survive.

More importantly, the corporate-communal dilemma creates conflict for individuals being served by such organizations. They must make an adjustment to society and develop socially acceptable methods of survival without compromising newly won values and integrity; they must assume responsibility for their actions, without the support and aid of a community, in a society which often does not share these values and behaviors. The organization, therefore, must make every effort to prepare the individual for reentry by making explicit the problems that will be faced—without compromising its values—and by structuring the communal experience into one that is more readily transferable to the larger society.

Despite its problems, which were partially due to its experimental nature, the school in Marathon House was a significant attempt to ease the reentry process and might serve as a model for other organizations faced with the same dilemma. This might be particularly appropriate for alternative schools. Alternative schools arise in part because of their rejection of the large and impersonal aspects of traditional schools. However, in the sense that traditional schools embody the premises of the corporate society, they are "successful" in preparing children for the world they will face. Alternative schools realize that the values they represent may be antithetical to the values of the corporate society. Yet often they are incapable of working out programs that take into account the problems of re-entry.

The Marathon House school had an awareness of the problems that an alternative structure generates for an individual who has to return to the corporate society; it was this self-consciousness that could lead to viable solutions for reentrance. Such a self-consciousness is necessary for alternative schools if they are to work out their own implicit corporate-communal dilemmas.

This article also represents a recognition of the criticism often made of therapeutic communities concerning the difficulties residents face in reentering society. While many of these criticisms are valid, it must also be recognized that for a variety of reasons, it is justifiably attractive for former residents to return to work in such communities. Such work may be far more meaningful and satisfying than the jobs that are normally available to ex-addicts. The individual may lack many of the sophisticated credentials necessary to compete for desirable positions in society, and he or she faces a society where the label "ex-addict" is often more important than any skills or credentials the individual may offer. This labeling process is a pervasive phenomenon in this society and, aside from the moral issues involved, impedes significant attempts by ex-addicts to solve their problems. In this sense, the corporate criterion of success—that therapeutic communities produce graduates who are able to take jobs in the larger society—can be unfair.

Finally, there is a more general point to be made that is applicable to many alternative social service organizations or settings. This argument is simply that organizations that stand at some sort of midpoint between individual-oriented and institutional solutions to social problems—or what I have termed the communal mode of solution—are viable, effective, and worthy of support. There are many arguments for and against individual solutions, such as psychotherapy, and likewise for institutional solutions, such as traditional schools or prisons, and many attempts and support for reforms of these modes. Without an extensive discussion, I would like to point out that there is compelling evidence to suggest that these two modes of solution have dramatically failed their clients. At the very least, some services are more appropriate for some people than others, and alternative structures embodying the communal approach, such as therapeutic communities, should be included in the range of possibilities for support. Of the three modes of service, the communal approach has been the least explored and developed. That the assumptions of the 1960's that led to and characterized many innovative social services have been largely abandoned does not mean that those styles of service did not, cannot, or should not work. Rather, I believe that they should be strengthened and pursued with more care. As there is a diversity of people with a diversity of problems and needs for which no single solution is most appropriate, so too should there be support for a diversity of solutions. The communal approach of Marathon House and similar organizations, while filled with complexities, is a solution whose abandonment would be a tragedy for many individuals in need and for a society that purports to care.

References

Kanter, Rosabeth Moss. *Commitment and Community*. Cambridge, Mass.: Harvard University Press, 1972.

Lamb, H. Richard, and Wilmer, Harry. "Using Therapeutic Community Principles." *Handbook of Community Mental Health Practices*, edited by H. Richard Lamb, Don Heath, and Joseph J. Downing. San Francisco: Jossey-Bass, 1969.

Lennard, Henry L., and Allen, Steven D. "The Treatment of Drug Addiction: Toward New Models." *Phoenix House: Studies in a Therapeutic Community (1968-1973)*, edited by George DeLeon. New York: Mss Information, 1974.

Newmann, Fred M., and Oliver, Donald W. "Education and Community." *Harvard Educational Review* 37 (Winter 1967).

Spiro, Melford. *Kibbutz: Venture in Utopia*. New York: Schocken, 1963.

Sugarman, Barry. "The Therapeutic Community and the School." *Interchange* 1, no. 2 (1970).

Sugarman, Barry. *Daytop Village: A Therapeutic Community*. New York: Holt, Rinehart, & Winston, 1974.

Sugarman, Barry, and Fisher, Nancy. "Job Histories of Marathon House Graduates." *Marathon House Research Reports No. 1*. Providence, R.I.: Marathon House, 1973.

13

Highlander Folk School: A Social Action Community

The Highlander Folk School is a learning and social action community which looks both inward and outward. The inward thrust is toward the creation of democratic learning settings where "teachers" share their particular talents and insights with people in the local area. The outward thrust is toward the identification of social problems, bases of poverty and oppression, which might be ameliorated by the constructive use of information and the courageous effort to act in the interests of the common people. In this latter sense, the Folk School represents a genuine revolutionary tradition: it questioned and resisted laws and customs which were hangovers from the earlier colonial and caste tradition of the South.

One might relate the philosophy and work of the Folk School to the alternative college movement of the late 1960's, when civil rights and the Vietnam War were seen as major problems in the society at large. While there were a number of mass rallies, sit-ins, and *occupations of college buildings, these events generally occurred in well-known traditional colleges. Alternative colleges were more concerned with the creation of intimate and reflective environments for learning. Commonly such colleges (see MacDonald 1972) attempted to create a "learning community" in which teachers and students were on an equal footing and the traditional authoritarian devices such as grades, parietal rules, and academic titles were reduced to insignificance. These institutions, however, were very different from Highlander in at least two ways: they looked inward at the tensions and problems of alienated and affluent youth rather than outward at the oppression of the common people; and the economic base of such institutions rested on the hope of finding adventurous paying students or on persuading college administrators that alternative learning environments were required to meet the needs of some bright but alienated young people who might otherwise be lost to higher education.*

One of the themes not developed in the Highlander selection is the problem of educating the "bad" people. There is a clear orientation toward identifying the oppressors and the oppressed and then finding ways of dispelling the ignorance of the oppressed and making them more efficacious. This assumes that there is still a liberal democratic arena within which political and economic skirmishes are fought out in the interests of the society at large. In the two instances cited, unionization and civil rights, the "good" people made the gains and the "bad" people lost out. Ironically, it may be that both gains were made at the expense of strong local traditions, and that when such local traditions are permanently eroded, broader societal forces (international corporations, centralized governments) will simply overwhelm the local liberal forces represented by places like Highlander. The point on which all locals must agree, perhaps, is that their communities must have a primary influence over their affairs, for it is only under this condition that places like Highlander have any substantial effect.

Highlander Folk School: Getting Information, Going Back and Teaching It

The idea of starting a school to serve oppressed people first struck Myles Horton when he was 22, and then it held his imagination and dedication for life. In 1927, the summer before his senior year at Cumberland University, the Presbyterian Church sent Horton to Ozone, Tennessee, to organize daily vacation Bible schools. While much of the country was enjoying prosperity, Ozone's people were already deep in their own Great Depression. Greed's harvest had exploited and exhausted the natural supplies of timber and coal, and the people who did not leave the region faced extreme poverty and seemingly unending misery. Horton ran the Bible schools, but soon came to feel that memory verses, hymns, and games didn't have much real use in relation to the daily problems faced by the children or their hard-pressed parents.

Nor could Horton learn of *any* school program that was directly related to mountain people and their common problems. Horton decided to do something about the situation. He wasn't certain what to do, so he asked parents of children attending Bible classes to come to church at night to talk about their problems.

To his amazement, they came. Some would walk in the dusk several miles down the hollows knowing they would have to go home in the dark. The things they talked about were basic. How could jobs be found? How does a person test a well for typhoid? Could the stripped hillsides ever grow trees again? Horton's inability to answer

Reprinted by permission from Frank Adams, *Harvard Educational Review* 42, no. 4 (November 1972): pp. 497-520.

most of their questions didn't bother them. Soon, however, they started asking him to find someone who did have the answers. The county agent was helpful. So was a man who knew how to test wells. Once neighbor started talking with neighbor they learned that answers to many of their questions were available right there in Ozone. By the summer's end the people were urging Horton to stay on, and not return to college. Cumberland University became at once unimportant and important. He'd learned that the people knew the answers to their own problems. He'd learned that the teacher's job is to get them talking about those problems, to raise and sharpen questions, and to trust people to come up with the answers. Yet, having been in traditional schools all his life he could not trust this way of learning. He promised to come back when he had something to offer. That fall, he was back in college.

During Horton's senior year, one of Tennessee's leading businessmen, a woolen manufacturer named John Emmett Edgerton, came to Cumberland and spoke against unions. Essentially he said the workers were wrong to think they could decide things for themselves. It was he, Edgerton, and other industrialists, who should determine what was good for the working man. Horton's understanding of the union movement was slight, but Edgerton's speech shocked him. Soon after, Horton went to Edgerton's Lebanon mill to talk with his workers, arguing that they were human beings who should exercise their inalienable rights. His appeal was spirited, but naive; it fell on uninterested, perhaps even fearful, ears. Horton himself was deeply confused and disappointed that the workers didn't rise in rebellion at hearing his arguments. He returned to the campus downcast, only to be greeted by university authorities with orders to stay away from Edgerton's mill. Undaunted, Horton went back, but again to no avail. This time, university authorities threatened him with expulsion.

After a year as student YMCA secretary for the state of Tennessee, Horton was introduced to Dr. Harry F. Ward's *Our Economic Morality* by Reverend Abram Nightingale of Cumberland County, who subsequently urged him to study with Ward at Union Theological Seminary in New York. On being accepted, Horton went to New York, arriving just before the stock market crash, the creation of bread and soup lines throughout the city, and the eruption of much labor strife and violence in the South.

Academic life and Union profoundly affected Horton, too.

Horton recalls that Abbott Kaplan, an urbane northerner, years later told a Highlander fund-raising gathering in New York City: "This little hillbilly fellow wandered up to New York to Union Theological Seminary to get the Word of the Lord. Instead, he ran into Reinhold Niebuhr, who was speaking with almost as much authority as the Lord, and apparently had a greater social conscience."

Niebuhr was just beginning his distinguished career when Horton arrived. He was teaching and writing with biting clarity against any over-simplification of the social gospel. In his course, as later in his books, Niebuhr attacked the uncritical idealism of social gospel advocates and liberal theologians. In response, those he criticized considered Niebuhr a pessimist, noting that even his moral man proved not to be very moral. Such pessimism notwithstanding, Niebuhr's arguments curbed the notion of inevitable progress then rampant in theological circles.

Horton was first drawn to Niebuhr because of his vigorous defense of the working people whose efforts to organize in 1929 were being thwarted across the nation. Niebuhr encouraged Horton in what then seemed just a dream: the idea of a school in the mountains for mountain people. While Niebuhr thought that his student could best accomplish this aim by becoming a minister, he did not withdraw his support in face of Horton's obstinate refusal to accept his advice. In fact, he agreed to help in whatever ways he could if Horton actually got the project underway. As Horton wrote to him as late as 1966: ". . . It was your inspiration and encouragement which provided the reservoir of strength and commitment that still keeps me going."

Horton was also much influenced during this period by the works of John Dewey, Vernon Parrington, George C. Counts, Edward C. Lindeman, and Joseph K. Hart. Lindeman and Hart had both written specifically on adult education, and were among the first to argue that adult education be recognized as a potent agent for social change. Hart, in fact, despaired over the possibility of producing significant change through traditional children's educational programs. He argued that adults must first learn how to live the new social order before trying to teach it. Lindeman's writing, which compared experiences in several countries, prompted Horton to look beyond his own Southern origins. He was only familiar with institutions in Tennessee, but now he began to look around New York and other major cities for models for what he called the Ozone Project. Horton left Union for the year 1930-31 to study at the University of Chicago with sociologist Robert Park and to learn first-hand from the experiences of Jane Addams' Hull House.

His struggle to "get some background" was given still another major push by a Danish-born Lutheran living in Chicago, the Reverend Aage Moller, who encouraged Horton to visit the "Danish folk schools." Horton previously had read about these schools. When the idea first emerged, the Danes were being attacked by Germany. Many Danes were forsaking their customs and even language in order to learn German, and German ways. This was especially true among the Danish upper classes. The first folk school started near the German border in 1844, and had as its major purpose the preservation of the Danish language. Four years later, another school started. It championed the cause of the people in their struggles against the landlords and nobility. A third, started in 1864 soon after Germany had taken southern Jutland, sought to spur the revival of Christianity among the peasants.

In the next thirteen years, some twenty-six folk schools were started; still others came later. The schools were free of government control. They were unencumbered with grades, ranking, examinations, and certifying students. Teaching was primarily limited to the "spoken word," lectures on mythology, Danish history, religion and language. Each folk school had an "emotionally charged" cause and unequivocally took sides on contemporary issues. Anyone eighteen or older could attend. Those who came supported the schools in whatever way possible—work at the school, food from their farms, money, if they had it. They stayed as long as they were able. Music and poetry were used by teachers to engage the students. The lectures were often repeated in the evening for older people who came into the lecture halls from the countryside.

By the end of the summer of 1931 Horton had earned enough money to make the passage. He went to Denmark, learned the language, and studied the trade union movement, the farmers' cooperatives, and the folk schools—many of which were disappointing because they had lost their initial vitality and sense of purpose. But by interviewing many of the older folk school directors he managed to discern four key characteristics that had initially produced the kind of school he had in mind.

First, many of the directors were unconventional educators. They were people on fire with awareness of injustice and the determination to correct it, to awaken the peasants to the misery restricting their lives. Second, the schools, each with its own purpose, sought to evoke among their students, as one director put it, "a picture of reality not as we have met it in our surroundings, but as we ourselves would have formed it if we could—a picture of reality as it *ought* to be." Toward that end, the schools made wide use of poetry and song: a revolutionary spark seemed inherent in these ways of communicating. Third, Horton found, the early schools sought to develop feelings and will more than memory and logic.

Joseph K. Hart best described the fourth characteristic which emerged from Horton's conversations with the older directors: "A folk school in America, as in Denmark, would probably center about a personality of some real teacher; a man who is capable of learning, and who can teach, not so much by his teaching, as by his capacity to learn. America's great lack, at present, is the lack of men of this sort. We have plenty of men and women who can teach what they know; we have very few who can teach their own capacity to learn" (Hort 1927).

Horton now knew what he had to do: get behind the common judgments of the poor, help them to learn to act and speak for themselves, help them gain control over the decisions affecting their daily lives. He left Denmark and returned to New York City, where, with Niebuhr, he began laying plans to fulfill his dream. Niebuhr wrote the first fund-raising letter for the project, which was tentatively called the Southern Mountain School.

Horton's next tasks were to find a staff and a place. He turned to former Union Theological classmates John Thompson, a Tennessean, and James Dombrowski of Tampa, Florida. Both agreed to join Horton before the school's first year concluded, and to help him find other staff people in the meantime. Horton then headed south to the mountains of East Tennessee to find a place. Chance led him to meet Don West, a Georgia native, who also had been to Denmark and was interested in starting a folk school. West had a contract to teach a traditional school in Kentucky that year, but Horton's determination to start a folk school proved persuasive; West broke the contract. They visited Horton's early sponsor, Mr. Nightingale, who knew of a possible place. The house was on Monteagle Mountain, west and north of Chattanooga, and belonged to Dr. Lillian Johnson, the daughter of a wealthy Memphis banking and merchant family. Dr. Johnson, after studying the cooperative movement in Italy, had returned to the South, bought land in Grundy County, built the house, and started a school. Since 1930, however, she'd been talking of retirement and of giving her home to someone who would carry on her ideas of "community betterment."

When Horton and West arrived, Dr. Johnson was shocked as they laid out their plans for a school. Her approach to education and social service was structured and well-planned. The idea of an adult residential school without courses, without a planned curriculum, violated all Dr. Johnson's training and instincts, yet she relented before the insistence of the young men that education ought to be directly useful to the life of the community. She gave them a year's probationary lease, which was later extended indefinitely.

Horton and West moved into the house. They decided on a name which derived from the people, the place, and the school's purpose. In the 1930's, Highland was the popular name for Appalachia. A Highlander was an Appalachian, and, for Horton, folk was a term that had both a positive anthropological and a political meaning. The Highlander Folk School was created.

Grundy County: A Place in Need

The folk school was started in a place where the right to work and the right to live had been a constant struggle. Grundy County's problem could be traced, in part, to the Compromise of 1876 which resulted in the election of Rutherford B. Hayes as President of the United States. Until that year the South was essentially agrarian and characterized by a rigid caste system. While condoning exploitation of Blacks within the region, white Southerners generally were not exploited by industry. However, the Compromise of 1876, engineered by old Southern conservatives and determined Southern industrialists in league with Northern bankers, brought the railroads and industry into the region to take advantage of widespread unemployment and abundant cotton, coal, and timber.

Working people were routinely abused. On August 14, 1892, unemployed Grundy miners, organized by the secretive Knights of Labor, rebelled against the state's practice of leasing convicts to private coal companies. The rebellious miners marched on the huge prison stockade at Tracy City, captured it, and freed 390 convicts under contract to Tennessee Coal and Iron Company, the parent of today's giant U.S. Steel, and then burned the stockade to the ground. The convicts were put on a train and sent to Nashville, as much as a warning to the politicians as to get them out of Grundy. These hapless convicts had been used by mine operators throughout the Appalachian coal fields both as a cheap source of labor and a means to prevent or break strikes.

The next day war broke out between the armed miners and the state militia after 1,500 more convicts were set free at Inman, Oliver Springs, and Coal Creek, all mines owned by Tennessee Coal and Iron. Throughout the early months public opinion remained firmly on the miners' side. By 1893, however, the combined forces of the state and the coal companies had gradually retaken the mines, still using convict labor. But the revolt that started in Tracy City had sounded the death knell of convict leasing in Tennessee. In 1899, the legislature outlawed the practice. (Grundy men still speak with pride of the rebellion of 1892.)

The natural companion of injustice was long-term poverty. In 1938, nearly 80 percent of Grundy's population of 2,250 families were on relief, placing it among the eleven poorest counties in the nation. Most men on the dole were miners and timber workers; on the average, their families survived on monthly benefit checks of $10.26 per person. Men with WPA jobs earned $19.20 a month, less than a nickel a meal for each member of a family of six—provided every cent went for food.

The Wilder Strike: Learning To Learn

Circumstances at Wilder, a bleak valley town over 100 miles to the north of Grundy County, provided a catalyst for Highlander. Horton heard of a mining company that had locked out striking miners at Wilder. He went to see the situation for himself.

Wilder was a company town; coal was its profitable reason for being. The town's few unpainted shacks were company owned. Miners were paid in scrip, good only at the company store, which charged higher prices than independent stores in the region. The company made weekly deductions for rent on the shacks, for a bath house, which didn't exist, and for a doctor, who was infrequently available. No matter how hard or long the men worked in the mines, they couldn't break even, much less get ahead. As their debts piled up, and food at home dwindled, their indignation and desperation mounted. Finally, they struck, without the support of a larger union.

Almost immediately, the company shut off the electricity and took the doors off the houses; it was winter and bitter cold. Horton was told that the company blew up a rotting, unused trestle as a pretext by which they could call on the governor to send in National Guard troops to protect private property. Horton figured that it cost the state more to guard the mines for three months than the company had paid in taxes for twenty years.

The Red Cross, supposedly responding to the emergency created by hunger growing daily in the community, handed out food and flour to the strikebreakers, but not to the strikers who, with their families, were literally starving. The county chairman of the Red Cross was the wife of the mine superintendent.

Having learned as much as he could about conditions in Wilder, and having arranged for students and teachers from Highlander to join in support of the strikers, Horton commenced writing letters to newspapers across the state appealing for food and clothing for the strikers. John Thompson, who had recently joined Highlander, later wrote, "I will never forget the long line of gaunt, haggard, brave people who lined up to receive the scant rations we handed out to last them a week. Each family got a pound of dried beans, a half-pound of coffee, two tins of canned milk (if they had a baby), half a pound of sugar. Those rations saved many lives, but meanwhile many babies had died of starvation."

The strike was led by Barney Graham, a tough mountain man. Nothing the company did seemed to break the strikers' morale. Constant harassment and insults from the National Guard seemed only to deepen the men's resolve to win. The company let it be known that if Horton and Thompson didn't stop bringing food into Wilder, they wouldn't get out alive. There was an attempt to bomb Highlander, the first of many subsequent attempts, and the students and teachers stood armed guard night and day for two weeks.

Horton persuaded Norman Thomas to come to Wilder and speak at a mass meeting for the strikers. His words were stirring, but the *Wilder Blues* written by Ed Davis, one of the strikers, was the hit of the day.

The strike and the violence went on. Barney Graham was shot in the back as he went to fetch a doctor for his ailing wife; once he fell in front of the company store, his head was bashed in by his killers, who then stood guard over his body, refusing to let anyone take it away until the sun set. Other union men's homes were shot into; some were dynamited. One scab was shot and killed; another wounded; six union men were arrested and jailed five months without bail.

Horton was arrested in Wilder, and charged by a National Guard officer with "coming here and getting information and going back and teaching it." It was his first arrest. He was marched off at bayonet point to the officers' quarters, where he was held eight hours before being released.

When the company couldn't break the strike, they started evicting strikers from their rented homes. This action, coupled with the loss of Graham's defiant leadership, broke the strike.

The Wilder strike had a powerful impact on the Highlander staff. The miners' words, songs, and deeds had dramatically illustrated the intense class consciousness of Southern workers. The Highlander staff, most of whom were strongly committed to ideologies, had hoped to kindle the workers' latent revolutionary spirit, but quickly realized that to accomplish this goal, the workers themselves would have to state—one way or another—their own beliefs. Highlander had to learn not to convert, but to bring forth; education not only had to serve the people, but, more importantly, had to be of the people.

Workers' Education: The Highlander Program

Horton's Christmas greetings for 1932 give a good picture of the school in those first days:

Our four regular boarding students from neighboring states have become an accepted part of the local community, and each is in charge of some phase of community activity.

Four regular classes are held each week, with an average attendance of twenty to twenty-five. These classes are: psychology, cultural geography, revolutionary literature, and a course in the study of our present social and economic problems. In addition to those classes, there is a seminar on how social change is brought about. Much of our class discussion is based on information gained by investigation of actual labor situations in the Southern industrial area. Such first-hand information is obtained by both students and teachers. The people of our own surrounding communities are eagerly reading all the books we have and are asking for more. We are fortunate in having the support of our community, many of whom help cut wood and divide their meager food supply with us.

By 1936, Highlander had developed a three-phase educational program: six-week residence courses, extension work, and community activities. Workers who showed promise of becoming organizers or local leaders in the labor movement were selected as resident students, usually by vote of their locals. While the majority came from mills, mines, and farms, a few were college graduates interested in workers' education.

Workers' education in the 1930's usually meant schooling that taught workers reading skills, or some work skill. Highlander, like the Danish folk schools before it, did not disavow teaching basic knowledge, but students at Highlander were not taught to adjust to exploitation. Nor were they expected to become merely good union members. Highlander was teaching that the unions were organized to be controlled by and to serve the members, not the other way around.

The extension program operated in cooperation with the unions and the few farmers' organizations. Highlander students assisted strikers during organization drives. More systematic education work was done through study groups set up by the extension workers (students), often at the picket lines, where songs and group singing techniques were taught, both to spark determination and to build solidarity. Not only did the extension program recruit new students, it also permitted the school to keep in contact with both the labor movement and those former students who were moving up the organizational ranks. In the community activities program, old and young took part in dramatic classes, music lessons, and group dancing. The wide diversity of experiences and geographical backgrounds meant there was much information to be shared among the students participating in the residential programs.

Early Efforts at Desegregation

During the 1930's the staff at Highlander became much more aware of the plight of Blacks in the south and of the shared interests of poor Blacks and poor whites. Too often Blacks had been used as exploited scab labor to prevent the development of better general working conditions.

Even before Highlander opened, Horton had hoped to bring Black and white students together. But, in 1932, the climate was hardly favorable from the point of view of either Blacks or whites. The Scottsboro case, its defendants mostly from nearby Chattanooga, still inflamed racist sentiment. This was aggravated by the U.S. Supreme Court ruling in *Powell v. Alabama* that denial of counsel in a capital case violated the due process clause of the Fourteenth Amendment. The plaintiff, Powell, was a Black.

Thus, Horton was disappointed, but not surprised, when, in answer to his request for help in recruiting Black students, Dr. J. Herman Daves, then teaching at segregated Knoxville College, replied, "At this time we know of no student or graduate of our school who would be a good candidate or who would be desirous of enrolling with you." He added, however, "A number of us are extremely interested in your work."

Try as they might, the Highlander staff failed to attract Black students on any significant scale until 1944. But they persisted, as is evidenced by the fact that about a year after refusing to help find students, Dr. Daves himself, accompanied by his wife, came to teach a course at Highlander. Resident students, including some few from Grundy County, had been studying labor problems and wanted to talk about Blacks in the labor movement. The staff prepared the way by first talking with as many neighbors as possible, and by posting in their irregular community newsletter: "A few students, who have families to support and live in towns where Negroes are unorganized, wanted first-hand information as to how Negro workers could be organized. Following a discussion, several people from the community said that the students should get the Negroes' side."

Dr. Daves and his wife, in 1933, became the first Black people to stay overnight and eat at Highlander. In doing so they violated the State of Tennessee's Jim Crow school law prohibiting Blacks and whites eating together or staying overnight under the same roof. It was a law to be repeatedly flaunted at Highlander.

Throughout the 1930's, Highlander worked to open the labor movement to all working people, regardless of race or sex, and, to this end, they were able to drive an occasional wedge in a closed society's door. The union education program comprised the major part of Highlander's educational effort at the time, and they continually stressed the practical daily damage of discrimination. If the bosses could pit whites against Blacks to keep wages low, then whites had to join Blacks for both their sakes. Eventually these discussions were more and more led by Black labor leaders in the South or college professors.

In 1940, Highlander informed all the unions that it served in the South that the school would no longer hold workers' education programs for unions which discriminated against Blacks. This first paid off four years later when Paul Christopher, regional CIO director and a member of Highlander's board, organized a workshop for the United Auto Workers. It was attended by forty union members, Black and white, from every corner of the South. The workers attended classroom sessions on collective bargaining, the economics of the auto and aircraft industry, and the UAW's postwar plans; while there, they also organized a cooperative food store. After this, Highlander began urging other unions to join the pioneering UAW. Support was soon developed from the Tennessee Industrial Union Council and the Southern Farmers' Union. Others followed.

Highlander found that the common problems which brought union people to Highlander in the first place, plus the informal setting away from home, provided sufficient ground upon which newly-integrated groups could work out their own ways of interacting and relating. One crucially important way Highlander nourished the working out of new interpersonal relationships was through music, usually organized by Horton's wife, Zilphia Horton.

As in Ozone years earlier, Horton found that song and dance sparked people with determination and self-assurance in ways that no other communication could. Moreover, his wife was uniquely gifted in bringing people together through music, and in helping people to express themselves by writing their own music. Perhaps the most striking example is the song brought by two union members from South Carolina that she, with folk singers Pete Seeger and Frank Hamilton, modified. The song was "We Shall Overcome."

Highlanders' Frustration: Fear at the Top

Toward the end of World War II the unions, pledged to no-strike policies for the duration of the conflict, began plans to rapidly expand membership. Those decisions had a local and regional impact. The unions were once again on the move. Highlander reflected this: Horton temporarily took on the job of organizing and developing educational programs for small farmers in Tennessee for the National Farmer's Union; the Tennessee Citizens Political Action Committee was formed at the school in 1944 when sixty delegates, representing twenty-four national unions, gathered; three labor conferences attracted over 280 Southern union delegates to Highlander that year; over 100 students, all sent by their locals, came for month-long resident sessions on labor problems.

These residential students helped run Highlander through a council of workers which was reconstituted each term. In this way, they gained practical knowledge of parliamentary procedures, public speaking, community relations, the making of posters and leaflets, and the writing of news releases and shop papers. In short, how to build a strong local.

Many of the goals shared by Highlander and the unions were attained: union membership increased throughout the South and across the nation; the procedures of the War Labor Board and the "maintenance of membership" clauses added stability to that membership; wages rose, sometimes jumped, and integration of the unions was on the rise. But where, asked Highlander staffers, was the political consciousness of the workers?

Highlanders' early hope that the union movement, especially the CIO, would become a powerful force for social and economic change had dimmed with experience. Any struggle on behalf of the working class had been submerged beneath a bureaucratic struggle for power. By 1949, an organization which had thrived on militancy was fearful of militancy, afraid the bottom might upset the top.

Highlander had joined the union movement when, as John L. Lewis wrote in an introduction to one of Zilphia's union songbooks, "it was a singing army." To many on Highlander's staff and board, though certainly not all, labor's antidemocratic impulse reached its zenith in 1949 when the CIO convened in Cleveland, Ohio, its main order of business to expel ". . . members of the Communist Party, any fascist organization or other totalitarian movement . . . or any person or organization who consistently aided other organizations to accomplish their own purposes rather than the objectives and policies set forth in the constitution of the CIO. . . ." The convention expelled two unions, the United Electrical, Radio and Machine Workers, and the Farm Equipment Workers, for "communism." Also, it withdrew from the allegedly communist-dominated World Federation of Trade Unions.

Believing that the bureaucrats who controlled the unions were using red-baiting simply to preserve the status quo, Horton predicted that ten years would pass before a single top CIO leader left office. He was wrong. It was eleven.

Highlander itself felt the weight of the approaching red purge weeks before the Cleveland convention. The school was notified in July that the union would not hold its usual workers' term at Highlander that year because, "rightly or wrongly, some leaders were of the opinion that at Highlander there exists some left-wing 'communist' influence."

Despite CIO displeasure, Highlander continued its support of the Mine, Mill and Smelter Workers, then one of the last militant unions in the South. The CIO sent out a directive telling locals to stop using Highlander, but Highlander's association with the unions did not end quite yet. There were few enforcement powers in the CIO's constitution, thus their threat of nonsupport was difficult to carry out. In fact, two years after the bitter exchange between the national union hierarchy and Highlander, Horton was asked by the United Packinghouse Workers, an affiliated union, to become their director of education.

Civil Rights: A New Highlander Priority

Horton's work with the UPW was Highlander's final fling with the union movement, however. Developments in the South were as much a reason for the change as disappointment at Highlander with the union movement. By 1950, Grundy County had joined much of the rest of the South in emerging from the worst of its economic ills. Not every Southern worker had a full stomach or a decent paying job, not all their children attended decent schools, but more did than didn't. Since there was little indication that the unions would go beyond these limited attainments, it was time for a shift in Highlander's priorities—away from the union movement and toward interracial progress.

In 1953, Dr. George Mitchell, who headed the Southern

Regional Council in Atlanta and who was chairman of Highlander's board, told the school's annual policy-making meeting: "The next great problem is not the problem of conquering poverty, but conquering meanness, prejudice, and tradition." Highlander could become "a place in which this is studied, a place where one could learn the art and practice and methods of brotherhood." Dr. Mitchell specifically urged them to explore the problems which might occur should the U.S. Supreme Court, before whom the famous *Brown v. Board of Education* was then pending, rule to end segregation in the public schools and/or enforce the separate but equal facilities decision. Consequently, Highlander sponsored two summer workshops for "men and women in positions to provide community leadership for an orderly transition from a segregated to an unsegregated public school system in the South."

To Make the Tongue Work

Two quite separate events in the early 1950's accidentally resulted in what Horton considers Highlander's single most important contribution to the civil rights movement and, broadly, to the field of liberal adult education.

First, in 1953, Highlander received a three-year grant from the Schwartzhaupt Foundation "to increase participation in local and national affairs, in stimulating interest in community problems, and in changing attitudes which limit democracy." In essence, the grant allowed freedom to experiment in adult education.

After two experimental efforts failed, other opportunities arose. In 1955, one of Highlander's students, Mrs. Septima Poinsette Clark, was "let go" by the Charleston School Board. Mrs. Clark had been actively encouraging Blacks to vote. Her second unpardonable transgression was accepting social invitations to the home of Judge and Mrs. Waring, patricians made pariahs by the judge's decision that South Carolina Blacks had a right to vote. After she was fired Mrs. Clark came to Highlander as director of education. It was in this capacity that she introduced the school to Esau Jenkins of Johns Island, South Carolina.

Set off from Charleston by the brackish Stono and Kaiwah rivers, the island was segregated by race in the 1950's, as it had been for some time. It was further divided by tongue—the whites spoke

Charlestonese, a Southern dialect peculiar even to other native-born Southerners, while the Blacks spoke mostly Gullah, a dialect that bore traces of an African Gold Coast language spoken before the days of slavery. Mrs. Clark first went to Johns Island to teach in the 1930's. The island's 3,000 Blacks fished and gardened when they could, but most of the time they worked hard in bountiful fields that weren't theirs. Sickness, illiteracy, disease, and superstition were common. Education was scarce, at least for Blacks. Mrs. Clark was eighteen when she was assigned to a two-room schoolhouse which was badly in need of repair, if not space. Over 130 students, ranging in age from six to sixteen, filled the schoolhouse wall to wall. For her duties, Mrs. Clark was paid $35 a month. Her white counterpart taught three students in a well-furnished, well-kept schoolhouse and was paid $85 a month.

On Mrs. Clark's second visit to Highlander in 1954, she brought along several people from the Charleston area, among them Esau Jenkins. For Jenkins, the immediate problem was literacy education. He told them that "so many people here (on Johns Island) can't read and write and I know this condition because I would have been almost in the same condition if I didn't go back to school." He asked Horton if Highlander would set up night schools for adults "to help them become better citizens."

Over the years, Jenkins himself had tried to do the same, but one man wasn't a school. He operated a bus from Johns Island to Charleston carrying people to their jobs and decided to get a group in the bus in the mornings and teach them how to read the part of the state constitution they would have to read to become registered voters. In this way, in twos and threes, Jenkins had added a handful of Blacks to the voting rolls. But this just scratched the surface.

With the Schwarzhaupt Foundation's money, Horton spent six months visiting Johns Island, listening to the farmers, fishermen, maids, and field hands, in an effort to learn the ways of island life.

Gradually, he learned that the islanders were ill at ease in the state's adult literacy program for some very simple, but not so obvious reasons. For one thing, the adults didn't fit into the classroom chairs. They'd been designed for children. Not only were the adults who attended uncomfortable, but they were called "Daddy Longlegs," and there was just enough deprecation in the nickname to cause embarrassment, just enough embarrassment to cause a prideful man or woman to quit. In just the same way, they were being taught as children: step-by-step; a-b-d-c; "the ball is red"; "New York is a big city." They were being asked to delay reading sentences useful to them until they could read sentences of dubious value to children. It seemed very far from the Constitution. The few who had enrolled just stopped going to classes.

Horton concluded that if Highlander were to respond to the request to "start a night school for adults," then that school would have to be outside the traditional school room and would have to be in a setting, or settings, more familiar to adults. Moreover, the work of learning to read had to be adult work. At the end of three months and thirty-six classes in all, the first fourteen students took the voting test. Eight of them were registered. And before the first Citizenship School ended, its size had more than doubled from fourteen to thirty-seven, just the opposite of the "regular" reading school.

Jenkins later told Guy Carawan of Highlander what happened next:

And then the people on Wadmalaw and Edisto Islands found out later the reason for Johns Island was so successful in registering Negroes. They ask me if it's possible to help them to get an adult school. So the next year when I went to Highlander, when it comes time for immediate problem again, I brought in Wadmalaw and Edisto, and they again say they will help if I can find a place and the teachers. I found the place, and today Wadmalaw registered more Negroes than ever registered in the history of Wadmalaw.

The same thing is happening on Edisto and all over the county. In 1954, in the county, there were 'round five or six thousand Negroes registered. In 1964, almost fourteen thousand. So everybody is jubilant for the Highlander Folk School, who have helped them see the light.

In 1963, seven years after the first Citizenship School began, figures totaled by the Southern Christian Leadership Conference, which by then was running the program, indicated that since they had taken the program over in 1960, nearly 26,000 Blacks in twelve Southern states had learned to read enough to register. SCLC also reported that volunteer teachers were at that time running over 400 Citizenship Schools across the South for over 6,500 adults. In all, Mrs. Clark estimates that nearly 100,000 learned to read and write as a result of the program.

Highlander's role on Johns Island, South Carolina, was that of a catalyst: providing the educational experience, what money was necessary, and recruiting and training teachers. Horton never entered a Citizenship School classroom as a teacher, and, as the idea spread, he discouraged other well-meaning whites from doing so, too. He felt the presence of any white stranger in the classroom altered, even stopped, the naturalness of learning. Citizenship Schools were run by Blacks from the start.

Success Invites Repression: Tennessee versus Highlander Folk

The inevitable happened. Highlander drew fire from Southern white racists. On the celebration of its twenty-fifth anniversary, Labor Day weekend of 1957, about 180 Southerners gathered to renew their friendship, talk about the South, and share their thinking about how Highlander could strengthen its role. Among those that visited were Aubrey Williams and the Reverend Martin Luther King, Jr. Also amongst the crowd was Abner Berry, a writer from the *Daily Worker*, and Ed Friend, an undercover agent for Governor Griffin of Georgia. Berry's unwanted and apparently contrived appearance in many of Friend's photographs—including one of Horton, Aubrey Williams, Dr. King, and Rosa Parks—gave much grist to the anti-Highlander propaganda mill. Undercover agent Friend's report and this photograph, 250,000 copies in all, were subsequently sent throughout the South and the nation by Governor Griffin's Georgia Commission on Education, a tax-funded body he'd set up to root out any deviation from segregation. In an "editorial comment" accompanying the broadside, the governor stated, "It has been our purpose, as rapidly as possible, to identify the leaders and participants of this Communist training school and disseminate this information to the general public. It behooves each of us to learn more of Communist infiltration and the direction of Communist movements. Only through information and knowledge can we combat this alien menace to Constitutional government."

By the first week in October, the slick broadside, which included the photo of Horton, Dr. King, Rosa Parks, Williams, and Berry had been distributed throughout the nation. Shortly, billboards using the photo started appearing across the South, claiming in huge lettering that "King attended a Communist Training Center." Postcards using it still circulate through the mails. Years later, when Horton rejoined the Council of Southern Mountains, a board member, disgusted about Horton's re-election, sent in his resignation on one of them.

Though Governor Griffin subsequently retired, Ed Friend and his undercover work came back to haunt Highlander. He was called to testify against Highlander several years later, and brought along a twelve-minute film he'd made at the twenty-fifth anniversary.

To a degree, Governor Griffin's calumny backfired. The anniversary proved to be Highlander's highwater mark for publicity. *Time* magazine noted the event. The *Christian Century* described Griffin's attack as work "shadowed through . . . distorting prisms . . . sad and sordid enough if it stayed south near whatever paranoid minds nurture such deceit." And on December 22, the *New York Times* carried a statement released by Highlander and signed by Mrs. Eleanor Roosevelt, Dr. Reinhold Niebuhr, Monsignor John O'Grady, then head of the National Conference of Catholic Charities, and Lloyd K. Garrison, former dean of the University of Wisconsin Law School:

The attempt of the Georgia governor's commission to draw from the serious and fruitful deliberations of this gathering sustenance for the efforts of Southern racists to equate desegregation with communism evokes our strong condemnation. This kind of irresponsible demagoguery is obviously designed to intensify the difficulties confronting decent Southerners who might otherwise give leadership in the adjustment necessary for the desegregation which is inevitable. We deem it morally indefensible for any men or group to inflict upon such institutions as Highlander and upon such individuals as the respected leaders, both white and Negro, who attended the Labor Day Seminar, the damage to reputation and position which may result from the wide distribution of this slanderous material.

Highlander's hide proved tougher than the governor expected. And so the Commission on Education turned to other "problem" areas.

Highlander played a significant role in the civil rights protests of the next few years. However, to be consistent with its past and realistic about its present, Highlander had to work behind the Black movement. With perhaps as much gut instinct as analytical insight, Horton realized Highlander could help lay the groundwork for the struggle, but they couldn't much take part in it. They were white and the struggle was Black. Even more important, the leadership was now Black. The people were leading themselves.

Highlander had to figure out ways to respond to those requests for help which moved the social forces in collective directions, while ignoring those which would foster continued individualism.

Specifically to aid the Black movement, Highlander turned the Citizenship School program over to SCLC. As educators, Highlander's staff felt that to continue administering an already established program would hamper their ability to experiment with new approaches. And they believed that a strong educational program linked to a forceful organization would help to build the organization's leadership potential.

There was still another major reason for giving the program over to SCLC in 1960. The year before Highlander had been seriously threatened with revocation of its charter by an investigation conducted by a committee established by the Tennessee state legislature. At the time of the decision, Highlander had been charged with being a place where people engaged in "immoral, lewd and unchaste practices," the scene of "loud, boisterous gatherings," engaging in the sale and consumption of "intoxicating liquor," breaking a 1901 state law forbidding Blacks and whites from going to school together, and, finally, that Horton "operated the school for personal gain." A trial was scheduled.

Shortly after turning the Citizenship Schools over to SCLC, Horton was free to fulfill the roles he thought proper: responding to requests for educational work only when Blacks requested it and fighting for Highlander's survival. Not long after, the State of Tennessee seized the school's property and revoked its charter. The idea and institution were reorganized and rechartered under the present name, Highlander Research and Education Center, Inc., and relocated in Knoxville.

The reorganized institution continued the policy of training community people to become leaders with a major emphasis on helping those interested in the voter registration movement, especially supporting the activities of SNCC in Mississippi. Literally dozens of workshops were run at the Center and in various parts of the South during the next few violent and crucial years of the civil rights drive.

A Glimpse of the Future

By 1964, Horton was trying to get Highlander out of the civil rights movement and back into Appalachia, and to encourage the civil rights movement to become a means by which all suppressed people in America could challenge their oppressors. It was slow work.

Horton foresaw the day when Blacks would tell whites to get out of the movement, to let them run their own show. Yet Horton continued to push the civil rights movement's leadership to go beyond their own concerns and link up with all of the nation's oppressed. The last conversation he had with Dr. King in March, 1968, only days before King was slain, is recorded in a letter he wrote the Reverend Andrew Young upon returning to Knoxville:

I believe we caught a glimpse of the future at the March 14 meeting called by SCLC. We had there in Atlanta authentic spokesmen for poor Mexican-Americans, American Indians, blacks, and whites, the making of a bottom-up coalition . . . .

Highlander continued its involvement by holding annually a five-day workshop where Mexican-Americans, Blacks, Puerto Ricans, American Indians, and whites from Appalachia could get together to talk about common problems. But since 1964, Highlander has been involved primarily in Appalachia, experimenting and evaluating ways to put education to use for perhaps another social movement.

Starting Where the People Are:
The Development of Highlander's Educational Style

While Highlander has attempted to mesh the social and physical setting to make the school a way of life, it was no Utopia in the early years. The staff was young, constantly changing and usually in desperate want of money: thus the pressures and tensions were severe. Petty annoyances often became major sources of friction. Outspoken staff assertions of ideology, coupled with an inability to let the students speak their own minds, sometimes led to difficulties. On the whole, however, the staff tried to live in a way which would demonstrate for the students the sort of new social order they envisioned: one built on brotherhood, democracy, and cooperation. As Horton wrote Jim Dombrowski, before he arrived at Highlander in 1933:

If I understood our purpose correctly, we will all be working at the same job but will be using different approaches. Our task is to make class-conscious workers who envision their roles in society, and to furnish motivation as well as technicians for the achievement of this goal.

In other words, we must try to give the students an understanding of the world in which we live (a class-divided society) and an idea of the kind of world we would like to have. We have found that a very effective way to help students to understand the present social order is to throw them into conflict situations where the real nature of our society is projected in all its ugliness. To be effective, such exposure must be preceded, accompanied by, and followed by efforts to help the observer appreciate and digest what he has seen. This keeps education from getting unrealistic. While this process is going on, students need to be given an inkling of the new society. Perhaps this can be done best by having a type of life that approaches as nearly as possible the desired state. This is where our communal living at the school comes into the picture as an important educational factor. The tie-in with the conflict situations and participation in community life keeps our school from being a detached colony or utopian venture. But our efforts to live out our ideals makes possible the development of a bit of proletarian culture as an essential part of our program of workers' education.

The Highlander staff had begun as rank romantics and idealists. Theirs was a vision of the new workers' world, one where production was for use and need, not profit; where government was of and for the people; where children were well-fed. But the dreams of the Highlander staff did not make room for the people themselves. The people living around Highlander and attending from various parts of the South didn't care about education; they didn't want to build a new society. They wanted food and jobs. To Highlander's young staff, food was just an excuse for communal participation and jobs seemed almost incidental to union-building and cooperative organization. They were at first disillusioned when they proposed a cooperative to grow potatoes, ordered seed potatoes for the planned-for garden, and found that the people ate the seed as soon as it arrived. Slowly, from this and a host of similar experiences—which each staff member had to assimilate himself or herself—they came to realize that if the school was going to teach poor people, the staff would have to start the learning process at that point in their lives where the students were confronted with an immediate problem; moreover, the problem had to be one which they, the individuals or community, not the school, perceived.

In this respect, as far as institutions can, Highlander had to open itself to learning. All the staff had to learn a new tempo of interpersonal relationships, much different than their own middle-class experience. For one thing, the people were reticent and quiet. Only as they understood the people and their way of life could the staff find enough security within themselves to move away from traditional academic methods. Once they stopped trying to teach the way they'd been taught, mutual learning could begin.

Having come to question their own traditions, there was a temptation for the Highlander staff to go all the way, to reject all tradition, even their individuality. "To share their poverty, live in their cabins, assuming that to pick at bed ticks and lice while going hungry is to somehow 'be as one' with the poor is false logic," Horton argued. You could walk a mile in another man's shoes, but you couldn't wear them for life. Horton and others rejected this approach.

There were other "practical" matters to learn before Highlander's effectiveness was fully felt. At one point, soon after the Wilder strike, they were asked to organize an employment agency. At first blush, the notion had appeal. The idea came from the local community, and, if it worked, would be of use to them. However, the staff refused. They said that their goal was to help workers unite with other workers for common strength, not to help a few individuals rise above the rest. An employment agency, as such, would have added little to the community's collective strength, no matter how many individuals advanced because of it. By refusing, they taught something about mutual aid among people, and tried to attack the dilemmas of individualism.

This was one instance among many of the tension at Highlander between individualism and collective action. While the individualistic impulse could come from the students, it was just as likely to arise in the staff. Horton, despite his intellectual commitment to socialism and collective solutions, held to an abiding belief in individualism. Passages he copied as a student from John Stuart Mill's essay *On Liberty* remain in his files today.

He who lets the world, or his own portion of it, *choose his* plan of life, has no need of any other faculty than the *ape-like one of imitation.* He who chooses his plan for himself, employs all his faculties. He must use observation to see, reasoning and judgment to foresee, activity to gather materials for decisions, discrimination to decide, and *when he has decided, firmness and self-control to hold his deliberate decision.*

If a person possess any tolerable amount of common sense and experience, *his own mode of laying out his existence* is the best, not because it is the best in itself, but because it is *his own mode.* (Italics are Horton's.)

Of course, part of the impact of this strain of Horton's thought was positive, for he insisted that students at Highlander establish *their own modes* of existence and share them with the collectivity. This insistence often found fruit first through collective approaches to education. "Peer teaching" was one such method. A worker coming into his own could also help his fellow workers. Horton learned this from Dolf Vaughn, a "blacklisted" miner, who related information to students which they would use, almost immediately, in spite of previous efforts by other staff members to share the same information. Vaughn was a bridge between staff and workers. Formally educated staff members, it turned out, were never as effective in teaching as the people themselves, once they saw themselves as teachers.

At times, when the workers were facing failure and feeling inadequate to make their own decisions, there were poignant displays of the conflict between professionals advising people directly and encouraging them to decide their own fates. The problem was put most clearly to Horton during an extended and bitter strike during 1937 at a cotton mill in North Lumberton, North Carolina. After the strike had begun, Horton moved to North Lumberton to support it.

In spite of the fact that Horton and the local leadership carefully set up committees charged with the responsibility for making decisions about welfare, recreation, or the strike itself, the people weren't experienced in the business of decision making. Horton kept telling them their union would only be as strong as their decisions made it. He rarely took part in committee work. He would make suggestions, point out alternatives, or furnish additional information. He never pushed a committee to a decision. Nonetheless, his suggestions, alternatives, and information carried added weight, especially during the strike's early days.

He was making some progress on this problem during his last weeks in Lumberton. The strike committee was meeting at a moment when it appeared as if the company was going to win. The committee had been unable to reach a conclusion on what steps to take next. There was collective anger when Horton refused to offer a suggestion. "My answer might be better than yours," he said. "Or it might be worse. But it would just be one man's answer. If I make this decision, what will you do when I'm not here and you are faced with tough decisions?"

One man started crying. Another, in desperation, pulled a pistol on Horton.

"You son of a bitch," he yelled, "you are going to tell us what
to do." Horton was too startled to respond instantly. Other committee members got the weapon from their fellow member and sat him
down. Eventually, as tempers cooled, the committee reached a decision on their own, learning, in the process, that they could decide on
issues, and had to. In the end the tactics that were developed were
successful and the union members won the right to an election and a
contract.

Conclusion: The Highlander Idea

Through Highlander's programs, many people have been encouraged to find beauty and pride in their own ways, to speak their own
language without humiliation, and to learn of their own power to
accomplish self-defined goals through social movements built from
the bottom up.

People learn of unity by acting in unity. They learn of democracy by acting democratically. And each time they do these things as
a result of experiences at Highlander they both renew their capacity
to act in these ways again and demonstrate the process of education
in action. Talk about this process distorts, and is one step removed
from the essential element—the people themselves doing. Writing
words about the process is two steps removed. Education at Highlander is a synthesis of person, group, time, place, purpose, and problem. Words and sentences, spoken or written, tend to order this
synthesis and give it logic by making it a sequence, when, in fact, it
cannot be and is not sequential or logical. There are, of course, methods within this context, and it is these methods which Highlander has
been refining with each new experience.

Baffled by education without assignment or examination, without the learned doing the talking and the unlearned the listening,
some critics have described Highlander's residential workshops as
anti-intellectual gatherings where the exchange of anecdote passes for
education. They overlook the fact that Highlander is dedicated to
helping develop the fulfillment of democracy, not to the preservation
of academic discipline. They ignore that what is learned at Highlander is usually tested in real life, under the eye of unrelenting
opponents, not in the classroom under the eye of a tutor.

Highlander changed its focus from workers' education and
union organizing in the 1930's to involvement in civil rights in the

1950's and 1960's and to community organizing in Appalachia in the 1970's. In each stage of its history Highlander has had to combat what can only be termed repression—calumny, accusations, and arbitrary use of the legal system by local and state authorities. This has included harassment by local American Legionnaires in 1935, threats from the "Grundy County Crusaders" in 1940 and investigation by the House Un-American Activities Committee, and prosecution by the state of Tennessee in 1959 which led to the revocation of Highlander's charter and the confiscation of its property.

Highlander has survived, despite arson, arrests, and eviction. And it adjusted, in a changing political climate, to new sets of students and problems. It would be hard to lift out of the historical account of the Wilder strike and Highlander's early days, or out of its later history, a precise set of principles we could call the "Highlander idea." Yet we can make some reasonable judgments. At the least, Highlander can be described as an adult residential center in the South for the development of community leaders among school, church, civic, labor, and farm groups, and for liberal education. And we can say with assurance that Highlander is committed to democracy, brotherhood, mutuality, and united social action. But it is deliberately vague about those governing concepts, letting the people it serves and the times they live in define precisely what they mean. These ideals change as people change and Highlander changes with them.

References

Hort, Joseph K. *Light from the North*. New York: H. Holt, 1927.
MacDonald, Gary. *Five Experimental Colleges*. New York: Harper & Row, 1972.

14

Japanese-Americans: A Modern Ethnic Community

Johnson makes the following points:

1. One of the major burdens of contemporary anthropology is to define "primary human nature" as a basis for understanding pathologies in quality of life in developed or modern societies.

2. The nuclear family as the exclusive primary social unit is questionable. Although it may be the most functionally adaptive family structure in an industrial society, evidence suggests that humans require broader networks of association.

3. The Japanese-Americans in Honolulu are an example of an ethnic or subcultural group who live within "a solidary, supportive system of social relationships [which] makes loneliness quite foreign in the experiential world of a large majority of the population."

The selection deals with the most serious issue for quality of life within small community: What is a reasonable and viable basis of social cohesion? One such basis is ethnicity. While there has been increasing concern about how to maintain ethnic villages within urban centers (based not on material deprivation or social discrimination), there is the constant outflow of people from such villages into outlying suburbs where ethnic and cultural identity is lost. One must ask, perhaps, whether or not the basis of cohesion in ethnic collectivities can be generalized as characteristic of a higher quality of life in any small community. One learns again, for example, of the central significance of kinship relationships. (One cannot have a village or small community if one's children leave the geographic area.) There is also a formal system of mutual obligations to more distant relatives and nonintimate friends. Within the family itself, childrearing does not stress individualism or aggressiveness as desirable traits, but rather conformity to the small group and sensitivity to the feeling of others. Of central importance, of course, is the sense of an ingroup that comes with cultural identity itself.

Perhaps the most interesting aspect of this selection is the concept of modern people living in a three-context world: the nuclear family, the community of neighbors or ethnic "relatives," and the broader corporate world. Johnson suggests that there is no intrinsic psychological dissonance caused by living in two very different cultures, one having a cooperative collective orientation toward the neighborly or ethnic world, and the other having a competitive achievement orientation toward the outside corporate world. This has clear implications for the viability of a world consisting of two very different forms of social regulation: decentralized small communities which have more significant cultural, social, and educational functions than now exist in "mass society"; and broader governmental institutions which might regulate functions related to technology and peace keeping.

Alternatives to Alienation:
A Japanese-American Example

Among the many pieces of contemporary literature on alienation, one must look long for direct contributions from anthropologists. Indirectly, however, the study of primitive society provides the
groundwork for recent theorizing on certain antithetical features of
life in contemporary urban settings. Why anthropologists have rarely
used the concept operationally, particularly in their studies of developing nations, provides an interesting subject in itself, but is beside
the point here. What is of concern is the study of contrasting modes
of social organization, presented by anthropologists, which have generated theories of cultural change that readily lend themselves to the
understanding of processes and states of alienation. In this chapter,
these theories will be examined in the light of empirical data on the
Japanese-Americans residing in Honolulu.

In reading descriptions of primitive society, one comes away
with a highly positive impression of cultural integration and adaptation that has been supposedly irretrievably lost in more complex
societies through the processes of industrialization and urbanization.
In contrast to modern society, the primitive lives in a small, homogeneous society, enveloped in an all-embracing kinship system, with a
strong sense of group solidarity, where sex, age, and family are the
major status determinants. Such a structure creates a highly direct

Reprinted by permission from Colleen Leahy Johnson, *Alienation: Concept,
Term, and Meanings,* edited by Frank Johnson (New York: Academic Press,
1973).

system of social relationships. Political, legal, and economic behaviors are transacted within a system of direct acquaintance and personal knowledge. Robert Redfield (1953) eloquently describes the quality of simpler cultures:

In this condition of humanity, the essential order of society, the nexus which held people was moral. Humanity attained its characteristic, long enduring nature as a multitude of different but equivalent systems of relationships and institutions each expressive of a view of the good. Each precivilized society was held together by largely undeclared but continually realized ethical conceptions. (p. 15)

Stanley Diamond (1963) defines the major task of anthropology today as the definition of primary human nature through the analysis of primitive society, with the aim of better understanding our "contemporary pathology and possibilities." He sees the search for the primitive arising out of a feeling of remorse and loneliness due to the inability of contemporary man to incorporate the organic ties present in simple cultures into modern society. He sees modern man living in a "rationalized, mechanized and secularized civilization [which] tends to produce standard and modal rather than natural varieties of persons. The individual is always in danger of dissolving into the functions of the status" (p. 104). There is, then, a tendency to picture primitive society as a lost Paradise, idealized as a direct antithesis to confusions and alienation present in modern society. The suggestion has been made that man has lost integral parts of himself in the process of his social evolution.

Anthropology has provided descriptive accounts of diverse simple cultures, displaying great variation among them, but showing patterns of stability and cohesion rarely seen in complex, technological civilization. Macroscopic theories of social change have arisen out of these ethnographies which stress the polarity between man's primeval past and his present condition. For example, Redfield's (1953) folk-urban continuum traces the changes in world view from the moral order of the primitive society to the technical order of civilization. Henry Maine deals with primitive society as a status society where the family was the basic unit bound together by sentiment. This is contrasted to the contractual nature of social relationships in modern society where the individual must either mediate for himself or seek technical assistance. Toennies' ideal types of relationships distinguish between *Gesellschaft* (contractual) mechanistic ties, where each individual follows his own rational pursuit of self-interest, and the *Gemeinschaft* (kin-like) organic relationship, bound by an immediate, personal, and moral element. These theories and others have provided a stimulus to students of contemporary society as models of explanation of the current social malaise. However, contradictions have arisen in the form of recent empirical data which have challenged the notion of the existence of a simple continuum between these various polarities. As might be expected, macroscopic theories of social change employing polarities run the risk of oversimplifying complex changes as well as invidiously scaling the value of phenomena (where the simplest are suggested to be "better").

For example, it has been a common assumption among sociologists that the isolated nuclear family is the basic social unit in the United States. As a corollary to this, the nuclear family has been linked to stress-producing socialization practices and segmented extrafamilial relationships (Parsons 1949). Although the nuclear family has been viewed as functional in terms of producing members capable of thriving in a mobile, individualistic society, it has at the same time been held responsible for accentuating the emotional conflicts in the young and intensifying the loneliness of adults. The attenuation of the extended kin relationships is considered to be a serious casualty that has occurred in the process of industrialization and urbanization. Furthermore, Wirth (1964) cites urbanization as causing a mode of life where depersonalization is a common occurrence. It is as if survival in complex urban environments requires the proliferation of fragmented, secondary relationships at the expense of the intimate bonds of family and kinship. "Populations in large numbers suggests individual variability, relative absence of intimate personal acquaintanceship, segmentalization of human relations and their anonymous, superficial, impersonal transitory and utilitarian character" (p. 225).

Such conceptions as these, rather than being used as ideal models on which to base testable hypotheses, have been used by some observers as the reality itself. This use of these concepts has added to the feeling of the inevitability of despair regarding the supposed loneliness and depersonalization of post-technological, urban existence. Fortunately, however, there are some studies of modern urban kinship systems which are stimulating a rethinking and reformulation of these assumptions. Interpretation of these studies has indicated that even in the highly mobile United States, most groups maintain extensive kinship relationships. Although these relationships do not assume the form of corporate groups, functioning extensively in both instrumental and expressive areas (as in simple societies), they nevertheless preserve an emphasis on sentiment and sociability, as well as mutual aid (Winch 1968). Although one cannot completely agree with the statement that the isolated nuclear family is a "myth" (Rosow 1965, p. 341), one must take note of Goode's (1970) extensive data which indicates that "Studies seem to show that no matter what index is used, the family in most industrial nations has not taken on the supposed character of the nuclear family system. The extended kin networks continue to function and to include a wide range of kin who share with one another, see one another frequently, and know each other" (p. 75).

Granted, then, that in studies of the social organization of the city one can detect certain processes which might lead to alienation, perhaps it would be more specific to state that one may also observe various processes of reintegration going on in urban life, some of which operate to alleviate states of alienation. Anthropologists, in their focus on the small group, whether family, neighborhood, or networks of social relationships, have been studying these processes of reintegration in urban areas in Africa. In providing descriptive accounts based on face-to-face relationship rather than the quantitative attitude surveys, anthropologists have shown that although the structure of society changes rather drastically in urban areas and new functions replace the old in the family and tribe, African migrants to the city are by no means cast adrift and without identification (Southall 1961).

The point here is not to deny the vast qualitative and quantitative changes in modern life which can have disadvantageous effects on the quality of human existence; rather, my thesis is that although the structure of modern urban society has produced notable fractionation of economic, political, and legal institutions, the same fractionation of concrete social relationship does not necessarily follow. At the organizational level of day-to-day interaction, functional adaptations can take place among some groups in response to the pressure for disintegration. In other words, there are parallel processes, which, for convenience, can be termed *Gesellschaft* and

Gemeinschaft, operating in a selective and relevant way to guide behavior in various sectors of activity. Therefore, options are open for some whose subculture provides them with supporting modes of organization, reaffirmed by traditional norms and values. For them, alienation is not an inevitable by-product of urbanization, since sources of integration and group solidarity can be found in their cultural backgrounds. The purpose of this chapter is to identify some of these sources of integration in one particular group: Japanese-Americans in Honolulu. . . .

The concept of alienation . . . will be only briefly explained. When I say alienation is virtually absent, I am referring to those forms of social alienation usually considered by sociologists, that is, alienation in terms of separation from other people and in terms of disassociation from cultural norms and values. In other words, rather than experiencing meaninglessness, loneliness and normlessness, the Japanese-Americans avoid being alienated through having a high degree of mutual interrelatedness, a regularized system of mutual expectations, and a stability of role functions over time. The average individual conforms to the social system as his most comfortable alternative, even in a multicultural setting which offers other prescriptions. This is strictly in a sociological sense, however, and refers to social alienation. It must be distinguished from the personal or psychological alienation which can exist among the Japanese, as it does everywhere, for the more marginal individuals.

One explanation given for the relative absence of social alienation among the Japanese-Americans concerns their precedence given to collective value orientation over an individualistic or ego-centered value orientation. The individualistic orientation implies the individual's relative freedom to put his ego-centered interests ahead of the interests of the group. Gratification of personal needs takes priority over one's responsibilities to others. A collective orientation, on the other hand, implies a greater conformity to group demands at the sacrifice of one's personal desires. This is, of course, not an "either-or" situation, but, rather, a direction of emphasis which varies cross-culturally.

The important point is that the collective orientation displayed by the Japanese-Americans in Honolulu facilitates the operation of a solidary, supportive system of social relationships; this makes loneliness quite foreign in the experiential world of a large majority of the population. It is my contention that this high degree of social relatedness, operating in conjunction with a compatible system of norms and values, is derivative from the culture of Japan. This is complementary to, but quite distinct from American culture.

Background of the Japanese-Americans in Hawaii

The Japanese immigrated to Hawaii in large numbers between 1890 and 1910 for the purpose of working as unskilled laborers in the sugar and pineapple plantations. Coming principally from rural regions of Southern Honshu and Kyushu, the explicit goal of virtually all of these laborers was to accumulate sufficient money in a few years to return to their ancestral villages in a state of relative affluence. For a number of reasons, such goals did not materialize. After a few years, many men sent home for brides, usually chosen by their parents, and, consequently, the Japanese family was transplanted to Hawaii. By 1920, the Japanese constituted 42.7 percent of the total territorial population. With the 1924 Oriental Exclusion Act, immigration stopped, and some movement back to Japan and mainland United States occurred. Since that time the in-migration of Caucasians and non-Oriental migrant workers has diminished their relative percentage of the population. The numbers of Japanese declined to 32.2 percent in 1960, and slightly less than 30 percent in 1970. Nonetheless, from 1900 until the last decade, the Japanese have been the dominant group numerically in Hawaii (Lind 1967).

Such large numbers plus the geographical insularity of Hawaii facilitated the retention of traditional institutions, norms, and values. Although the immigrants had little education themselves, they were highly motivated to provide the best possible opportunity for their children. By 1960, they had the third highest median education, 12.5 years, lagging behind only the Caucasians and the Chinese (Lind 1967). The more educated nisei (second generation) no longer were content in the rural occupations of their parents and migrated with the assistance and approval of their parents to Honolulu to continue their education or seek commercial or laboring opportunities. By 1960, 53.5 percent of all Japanese in Hawaii were living in metropolitan Honolulu, increasing from 9.8 percent in 1896 and 22.4 percent in 1920 (Lind 1967).

Despite this high degree of urbanization, the indices of social

disorganization have not risen commensurately. In fact, in comparison to the other ethnic categories in Hawaii, the Japanese portray
impressive signs of social and emotional stability. In 1968, the Japanese-Americans made up only 7.4 percent of all admissions to the
Honolulu Jail (Honolulu Police Department 1968). They had the
lowest rate of illegitimate births (Honolulu Department of Health
1968). In 1960, they ranked lowest in numbers receiving public welfare assistance (3.4 percent) (Honolulu Department of Social Services
1964). Correspondingly, in the area of mental illness they have the
lowest admission rate to public and private mental hospitals (Kimmich 1960). In terms of general health disability, they have the few-
est numbers of days away from work for reasons of illness (Bennett,
Tokuyama, and Bruyere 1963). Finally, they have the lowest outgroup marriage rate (17 per 100 marriages). Of the ingroup marriages, they have the lowest divorce rate, 14 per 100 marriages (Lind
1964).

The Japanese immigration to Hawaii took place during the Meiji
Period, a time when Japan was undergoing rapid modernization and
social change. Because these emigrants mainly originated from rural
areas outside the centers of industrialization, they brought conservative traditions with them. Even today, however, the degree and quality of social change in Japan is the subject of a great deal of scholarly
debate. One point of general agreement relates to the continuance of
a distinctive system of social relationships which stands in marked
contrast to Western cultures at corresponding levels of industrial
development. While the United States has institutionalized individualism as a dominant trait, Japan has continued to stress collectivity
as an organizational factor (Bellah 1962).

In Japan, each individual is closely bound to a series of specific
groups throughout his life. The family is the first of these. In a way
that makes other childrearing techniques appear quite casual, filial
piety, social sensitivity, and vertical loyalties are taught and developed to a very high level of conscious conformity. Other institutions
adopt these same familistic norms, incorporating patterns of paternal
responsibilities to those below the individual, and filial obligations to
those above. These relationships are replicated and reinforced by
public education as well as through norms involving relationships to
peers, friends, and acquaintances. Even the occupational sphere is
within the framework of the simulated kinship organization. For

those in positions of permanent employment, these same themes of loyalty, interdependence, and mutual trust typify the qualities of industrial, commercial, and professional life. Only in a few areas is individualism allowed to develop and flourish. Instead, the Japanese tend to move in a limited social nexus where mutual assistance and interdependent cooperation can be carefully employed. These circumscribed relationships demand that the individual be highly sensitive to his relationship with specific others—the prime requirement being adeptness in reading the cues and responding in appropriate ways (Nakamura 1964). Other important directives patterning behavior (*on, giri* and *ninjo*) are pertinent here and will be discussed later in the chapter. These modes of organization derived from Japan have been singled out here as being significant determinants of the positive integration and stability of the Japanese descendents in Hawaii.

Systems of Social Relationships

The information reported here was collected in 1970-1971 as a collaborative research project with my husband, Frank A. Johnson. As much as possible, subjects were chosen to match the characteristics of the general Japanese-American population in Honolulu. Open-ended interviews were used, ranging in time from two to five hours. In addition, specific questions were asked concerning the relationships within the subject's family and kinship units as well as in his working and friendship associations. Quantitative and qualitative aspects of these relations were specifically sought. The sample included 104 families. Some of their characteristics are shown in table 14.1.

The description and analysis of the social organization of the Japanese-Americans is based on the observation that a high degree of social integration operates in the small group of the individual's day-to-day relationships. The institutionalization of roles for family, kinship, and friendship relations call upon traditional values which stress the collective over self-orientation. The sacrifice of personal interests, in order to fulfill the role expectations of one's closest friends and relatives, is motivated by the internalization of traditional Japanese values. Socialization practices which stress dependency, respect for elders, consideration for others, and compassion promote the acquisition and internalization of these values at an early age. They define

Table 14.1

Subject Population (104 Families)

Generation*	*Nisei*	47%
	Nihan	28%
	Sansei	25%
Age	45-55 years	27%
	35-45 years	47%
	25-35 years	26%
Education (husband's)	College	47%
	Some college	10%
	High school or less	43%
Occupation	Large business or professional	25%
	White collar or small business	50%
	Blue collar	25%

*The Japanese-Americans calculate generation level by labeling the original immigrants, the *Issei,* as the first generation. The *Nisei* are the "second generation," that is, the first generation born in the United States. *Nihan* (a contraction meaning 2½) refers to those subjects who had one parent from the first generation and one from the second. These individuals are either more like second or third generation rather than transitional between these generations. *Sansei* refers to the third generation.

one's adult roles in terms of a moral commitment which transcends personal desires and gratifications. Therefore, at the level of primary relationships, a high degree of social solidarity exists. In these interactions, personal interests and those of the group closely coincide.

As one moves from primary relationships to the more impersonal secondary ones, it becomes increasingly difficult to apply collectively oriented behavior to one's social relationships. For one thing, the system of mutual expectations is less applicable, particularly if one is outside the Japanese-American group. Persons from outside the ethnic community simply do not respond to the cues in a positve or predictable manner. There is less fit between one's role definitions and performance, customarily found in close relationships, and what one faces in secondary, instrumentally-oriented relationships.

Most individuals of second and third generation have a range of acceptable behaviors to call upon, selected from both cultural systems and defined by varying degrees of mutual expectations, affectivity, and moral commitment. There is a gradient in the intensity of response beginning with the nuclear family and progressing outward to the kinship group, the peer group, and the ethnic community. This proceeds with a gradually diminishing use of traditional role behaviors along with less expectation of acceptable responses from others. When one moves outside the ethnic group into the community at large, the individual must draw upon the knowledge and experience he has gained from his partial assimilation to the middle-class American culture (in its particular Hawaiian version). These relationships outside the ethnic group lie largely in instrumental associations: occupational for adults and educational for the young. Here the individual chooses between parallel systems of behavior, one for the *Gesellschaft* or secondary relationships of his work day, another for the *Gemeinschaft* or primary relationships of his leisure time. If given a choice, the great majority of Japanese-Americans in Honolulu opt for the small ethnic-centered group where social alienation in interpersonal relationships or discontinuities from cultural norms and values are rarely experienced.

Social Networks: Who Sees Whom

The term network is used here as a means of describing a map of social interaction. The individual can be conceptually depicted in the center of a collection of friends and relatives. Relationships can be represented by lines radiating from the center. The social field itself is flexible, in the sense that new ties are formed while old ties can be modified or broken. In contrast to the concept of a social group, which has common aims, interdependent roles, and cohesiveness, the network has no external boundaries or, conceptually, no internal divisions (Barnes 1954; Bott 1957). In actuality, most Japanese-Americans make a clear distinction between close relationships, where the ties are cohesive and long-enduring, and other relationships where less solidarity exists. I have called the former the central core of the network, labeled so by the individual's diffuse allegiance to the other members of the network. However, each one in the central core is not necessarily bound to the others with the same degree of allegiance. Hence, the overall unit does not necessarily form a social group in the sociological sense. Within this social network, the quality of the relationship changes as interaction moves from the center to the periphery, as ego's commitment becomes more narrowly circumscribed and more rationalistic.

This theoretical network is concretely observable in daily life. As one observes social groupings on the street, on school campuses, in restaurants, or on the beach, the predominant impression is that the Oriental groups are homogeneous. The occurrence of a mixed group of perhaps Caucasians and Orientals outside of structured situations, while not rare, is less common than observing Orientals clustered by themselves. Even in businessmen's lunch groups where one might expect to find more ethnic mixing, groups are generally ethnically homogeneous. Furthermore, newcomers to the Islands find that they may form few close associations with Japanese-Americans outside the context of public or instrumental situations. Interestingly, this difficulty is encountered by some Japanese from Japan, as well as by Japanese-Americans from mainland United States.

Table 14.2

Composition of the Social Network with Whom One Spends Time

	Percentage of Time
Ethnic determinant:	
Within the Japanese-American community	78%
Outside the Japanese-American community	22%
Kinship or friendship:	
See mostly relatives	47%
Divide time equally between relatives and friends	27%
See mostly friends	20%
See mostly occupation or organizational associates	5%
See few people outside occupation	1%
Other characteristics: geographical and economic determinants:	
Three-generation households	14%
Relatives living in the immediate neighborhood	18%
Economic cooperation in family business	11%
Values emphasized in socialization:	
Collective-centered values	65%
Ego-centered values	16%
Other	19%

The data in this study overwhelmingly support the more impressionistic judgments—namely that approximately 78 percent of the respondents describe their friendships as being predominately with other Japanese-Americans. Those who define their friends as being from mixed groups still show a marked preference for other Orientals. (These ingroup preferences are compounded by a long tradition of Caucasian exclusiveness which exists despite the widespread myth of the Hawaiian melting pot.) However, most respondents state that they have few alternatives because of the time-consuming system of social obligations within their own group, or because of the lack of opportunity to meet others. Permeating most of these discussions is the more subtle theme that the close-knit ethnic network, although confining at times, offers the most predictable and secure environment.

High ingroup preferences are a natural product of a number of social forces: demographic and historical factors, intergenerational continuity in the family system, and well defined ethnic boundaries. Historically, the plantation system clearly delineated ethnic categories into separate residential and organizational units. The transposition of elements of Meiji Japan to rural Hawaii reaffirmed ingroup cohesiveness. Buddhist temples, Japanese newspapers, prefectural organizations, language schools, and esthetic and recreational associations flourished. The resistance of the *issei* to learning English or countenancing the out-marriage of their children reinforced this segregation. Prior to the war, almost all *nisei* children attended Japanese language schools where the inculcation of traditional moral training was encouraged through their texts as well as through the demeanor of the teachers. In pre-war Honolulu, some residential concentration took place, paralleling the conditions on plantations. Although the Japanese-American population is today residentially dispersed, their large numbers and presence throughout the city precludes the necessity of seeking relationships outside their own group for most institutional functions.

In Japan, the psychological focus on a limited social nexus has been described in detail by Nakamura and corroborated by nearly all scholars who survey Japanese culture. This same focus is evident in Japanese-American life in Honolulu. The family supersedes all other relationships; its central significance to the average Japanese-American is indicated by the results of this current study. Excluding their occupational relationship, 47 percent state that they associate predominately with relatives, while 27 percent divide their time approximately evenly between relatives and friends. Twenty percent see friends more than relatives, but, of these, one-half have few relatives in Honolulu and are hence not really exercising any option. Five percent limit most of their relationship to occupational or other instrumental associations. Only 1 percent can be termed isolated in that they see few people outside the nuclear family. In summary, it can be concluded that there is a striking tendency for the Japanese-Americans in Honolulu to associate mainly within their own ethnic group and to prefer relationships with kin.

Family, Kin, and Friends

From a structural point of view, the Japanese-American family is of an isolated nuclear type, if that is defined as being economically independent and residing in its own residential unit (Parsons 1949). The average household size is 4.1 persons (United States Census 1960). In the sample of 104 families reported here, only 14 percent live in a three-generation household, while an additional 18 percent have relatives living in the immediate neighborhood. Economic cooperation in family businesses takes place in only 11 percent of the families. Since this is well below the 74 percent who spend from half to all of their free time with relatives, it can be concluded that the importance of the kinship unit is not simply a consequence of geographical propinquity or shared business concerns; rather, it is connected to cultural patterns which identify the modified extended family as an important locus for primary emotional interaction.*

In defining who constitutes the family, most respondents state that their immediate family is composed of spouse and children, their own parents and siblings, and their families of procreation. In other words, the central core of the kinship unit is not merely the nuclear family of procreation, but is extended to include each

---

*Although statistical verification has not been used to determine the relationship between social class and the ethnic and familial networks, it is apparent from the data and from my personal acquaintance with many respondents that social class is not the most significant variable in assimilation. However, those respondents who remained independent of the kinship unit or ethnic community usually lived on the mainland for an extended period. They could be the professionals with long years of training away from the extended family, but also included are those from other occupational groups who found it necessary to spend some time away.

spouse's family of orientation. This recognition changes as the children in the nuclear family reach adulthood and marry. At that time, the immediate family is usually redefined as the spouse, the parents (if still alive), and the children and their families of procreation. Siblings and their families of procreation usually decline in importance as the descending generation expands. However, certain relationships with favored siblings, aunts, uncles, and cousins may continue on the basis of compatibility and shared interests. Nevertheless, a principle of economy operates in these primary relationships. Because the emotional investment developed in these primary relationships is intense (by comparison with most Caucasian patterns), the numbers held in these relationships are necessarily limited.

At the central core of the network, *Gemeinschaft* relationships find their strongest expression. Bound together by strong feelings of group solidarity, the family, kin, and most intimate friends are seen frequently, almost daily, by many. Mutual aid and sympathy are given unstintingly, in terms of emotional support, advice, child care, homemaking assistance, and financial support on a noncontractual basis. A strong sense of obligation to these selected kin and friends extends over large and unspecified areas. Ideally, conflict must be avoided by each member in upholding mutual respect and consideration. Adherence to these obligations is an expression of a moral commitment of an involuntary, often unconscious nature. Conflicts and controversy, of course, occur in these relationships. Interestingly, such differences are often dealt with through silence, changes in vocal nuance, or through kinesic expression rather than by verbal arguments. Bargains are made implicitly whereby each one agrees to give a little in order to avoid open ruptures and to insure the other's cooperation in the future. (These cultural modes for handling conflict are quite distinctive, but are too complex to be fully discussed here.)

As one moves from this central core to the larger kinship unit, this commitment diminishes in intensity and is supplanted by more formal mechanisms devised to maintain group solidarity. Kin at a more distant level are not considered family; they are relatives. They are seen less frequently and, ordinarily, are not relied upon for frequent mutual aid. Unless one chooses otherwise, obligations to these relatives are narrowed to attendance at large, periodic gatherings on holidays, funerals and memorial services, and other ritualized events of the life cycle.*

At this level of relationship, mutual obligation is formalized into a system of *kosai*, where more formally specified rules apply. Such relationships are similar to close friendships in that obligations are fulfilled in the same reciprocal manner. The amount of contact one has with friends, however, is initially purely voluntary. Also, one can choose one's own friends, although there is pressure (not necessarily verbalized) from the family to seek one's friends within the ethnic community. However, once a friendship becomes established, it assumes many of the nonvoluntary characteristics of the kinship relationships. Close friendships, like kinship relationships, are characterized by periodic meeting and a methodical system of gift-giving. (Friendships can develop an intimacy and intensity that characterize those relationships in the central core of the network. In these cases, the same *Gemeinschaft* principle of nonvoluntary obligatedness and diffuse commitment operates.)

The system of mutual obligations to more distant relatives and nonintimate friends is subsumed under the *kosai*. This is defined by most respondents as their "circle of social obligations." In including relatives and friends, the *kosai* requires that one give gifts of money at funerals, weddings, graduations, births, trips, special birthdays, and illnesses. At marriage, the *kosai* is initially formed by all those who donated at the wedding and continues to expand throughout life to include new relationships. Very careful records are kept of these reciprocal obligations so that one can in the future discharge his obligation through an equivalent gift of money. The most compelling

---

*Japanese-Americans of Okinawan ancestry are grouped with those from Japan proper by the census and by all those outside the ethnic group. They are estimated to make up approximately 15 percent of the Japanese-American population in Hawaii. Although their proportion in my study, 15 percent, is too small for precise comparisons with the other Japanese-Americans, my data and the predominate opinion of the ethnic community indicate that the Okinawans have some distinctive characteristics. For one thing, primary relationships, mutual aid, and economic cooperation more frequently extend over a wider circle of collateral relatives. Second, their ethnic identity as Okinawans is probably characterized by a higher degree of commitment to the entire ethnic group, not just the central core. If this proves to be the case, the definition of the social network would have to be somewhat revised when applied to the Okinawans.

requirement is in the reciprocity of funeral obligations. These obligations are incurred toward all those in his own circle and are even extended to their close family members who often may be outside the range of the giver's actual acquaintanceship. An eldest son, for example, has responsibility in honoring the *kosai* of his deceased parents, particularly in regard to funeral obligations. Hence, throughout adult life, the *kosai* functions as a concrete, formal representation of a family's system of social relationships. This is maintained conscientiously, except in cases of the most serious financial reverses. Although it may consume a relatively large proportion of the family's resources, very few individuals would consider breaking this chain of reciprocities. To do so would symbolize withdrawal from one's social network and, by implication, rejection of his Japanese identity. At the very least it would imply the person's failure to meet his expected obligations and also would directly impugn the reputation of his family.

Lest the *kosai* appear superficially similar to American gift-giving customs, two distinctions should be made. First, the *kosai* is compulsory, in the respect that the individual feels that he is compelled to give in order to maintain his social identity. (Some retired individuals with reduced incomes may reluctantly choose living with a child on the mainland if they cannot afford to keep up their obligations.) Second, the value of the gift of money given on specific occasions is established by relatively inflexible rules, even to the point of allowing for inflation.

At this point, some clarification is needed. Those relationships within the central core of the network are characterized by gift-giving and some formal reciprocity. In this sense, they are part of the *kosai*, but there are far broader implications for primary relationships. These reciprocities are more flexible and spontaneous because they are based on the immediate needs of the receiver and the circumstances of the donor at the time. A high degree of obligatedness and expectation of future reciprocities are established which assume considerable psychological significance. Here one becomes emotionally indebted in his relatedness to the other; this transcends tangible reciprocity. A common example would be an individual who has been sent through college by his older brother. This would generally not be repaid monetarily, but would, rather, generate a perpetual, diffuse obligation that cannot be discharged. In contrast, the *kosai* outside the central core defines the degree of obligatedness more exactly and contractually. This may be repaid in full at the appropriate time, so that the emotional counterparts to social indebtedness do not weigh so heavily upon the individual.

Reciprocal obligation is a highly important element in Japanese culture. However complex it be for the Westerner to grasp, it is essential to understanding the diluted forms in Hawaii, not only in regard to the *kosai* but also in regard to the solidarity of the family.

Japan has been noted as being one of the few cultures which has made a clear-cut distinction between contractual behavior and behavior "undertaken as a result of individual interest or spontaneous feelings" (Sugi 1963, p. 268). In all his vertical relationships throughout life, an individual passively incurs obligations through the benevolence of others (called, *on*). Repayment must be made contractually according to the ethic of scrupulously measured equivalence (called, *giri*) (Befu 1958). At the same time, a noninstitutionalized system for horizontal relationships is present which allows for human desires and feelings (called, *ninjo*). This is concerned with a mutual awareness of others' emotional needs, and a noncontractual desire to satisfy and indulge the other person. In feudal Japan, *ninjo* was subordinated to *giri* in order to reduce conflict between personal desires and the demands of the social system. Hence, relationships were formalized to an astonishing degree (by Western standards) and demanded an acute awareness of loyalties and reciprocities in a hierarchical scheme governing potential action.

In Hawaii, the communication of these social demands is largely inexplicit, and the compelling, direct nature of these demands has been somewhat diluted by the acculturation process. Few Japanese-Americans can distinguish between the compulsory demands of *giri* relationships and the personal, emotional nature of *ninjo* relations. At the same time, there is a diminishing accentuation of vertical relationships at the expense of horizontal ones. Nevertheless, the concept of obligation constitutes the strongest expression of solidarity found in the operation of the social network. The *kosai* represents this reciprocal obligation, but obligations to friends and kin, however arduous at times, can be discharged with *giri*-like components. The element of human feelings receives more emphasis. The proposition that parents should be seen often, loved, and respected is unquestioningly endorsed, but it is no longer a one-way street. Mutual esteem and consideration, plus an awareness of others' needs, bilaterally permeate the parent-child relationship as well as all other primary relationships. The indebtedness is perpetual and diffuse, but has been colored with considerable affective attachment.

Obligation then, rather than being seen as a feudalistic, old-fashioned dictum, has been so permeated with the *ninjo* element that the solidarity of the family and the central core of the network has an internal perpetuation of its own, adhered to voluntarily by its members. The *on-giri* system alone would be nonaccommodative to the demands from the prevailing culture. But through the emphasis on the affectional element, *ninjo*, the mutual awareness of others, pleasing them, and avoiding hurting them, facilitates the nonconflictual functioning of a social network of primary relationships. Furthermore, the obligatory nature of *giri*, as displayed in the *kosai*, is a boundary-maintaining mechanism for one's other relationships. The Japanese-Americans thus have a readily adaptive and modifiable system which has functioned in an integrative capacity in acculturation.

Therefore, the individual may be seen to be surrounded, first, by his immediate families of procreation and orientation, which, along with a few intimate friends, constitute the central core of his social network and the source of his basic security and emotional support. Outside of this central core, he is surrounded by an expanding circle of relatives and friends, usually Japanese, which remain stable throughout life. These latter constitute obligatory relationships in terms of *kosai*, but are voluntary in terms of informal social contact. The central relationships are characterized by a *Gemeinshaft* quality (moral, organic, intimate), while the peripheral relationships are more contractual, although still formalized structurally as "personal relationships." Both types are imbued with a heavy sense of obligation and with a compelling quality resembling *giri*. However, sentiments derived from *ninjo*, particularly at the central core, color these relationships with warmth and security.

In relationships outside the ethnic group, friendships may be formed. Occasionally, such a friend might be incorporated into the central core of the network; more frequently, however, they are not. Those who are met outside the Japanese community, who are seen frequently, are generally met at work, school, or in the neighborhood. Ordinarily, such friends remain on the periphery in terms of some specific mutual area of interest, and are only loosely connected to others within the network. Also, they are not formally included in the *kosai*. Few members from other ethnic groups are included, for they usually cannot understand the inexorable, scrupulous implications of gift-giving and are unlikely to respond appropriately. (With blithe good intentions, Caucasians may easily upset their Japanese-American friends either through failure to reciprocate when given something, or, worse yet, in a rush of impulsive generosity, by giving a friend an expensive or unexpected gift that places the recipient in an impossible dilemma about how to reciprocate.)

One can see clearly that with these systems of social relationships, the individual is never alone, bereft of social support, or dependent only on the scant resources of his nuclear family. Whatever he faces in his occupation or in the impersonal, indifferent world outside, he returns to be enveloped in a close-knit, supporting world at the end of the work day.

Mechanisms for Maintenance of the Networks

One might well ask how such a world is maintained in the face of urbanization, the pressures for assimilation, and the urgency of the contemporary generation gap. Although changes are taking place between generations, and Americanization is increasing, there is a continuity in values underlying the mechanisms of socialization and social control which continue to apply at the level of primary relationships.

In the area of child rearing, a very prominent feature is that individualism, assertiveness, and independence are not singled out as desirable social traits. Instead, the values of conformity to the small group and sensitivity to the feelings of others are traits regarded as desirable and are directly instilled in the child. When asked what they considered the most ideal personality characteristics they wanted in their children, 65 percent of the mothers mentioned traits which can be classified under a collective orientation. Examples are: "To be considerate or compassionate of others," "To think of others before yourself," "To be respectful." Only 16 percent mentioned individualistic or ego-centered traits such as: "To be independent," "To find a life he is most comfortable in," or "All of my children are so different, I can't say." (Other responses from this group fell into categories not directly applicable here, such as "To be happy," "To be serious," or "To study hard.")

This collective orientation clearly incorporates the concept of *ninjo*, discussed above, where one must strive to satisfy another's emotional needs. Another behavioral characteristic, which is complementary to *ninjo*, is that of *enryo*. Although some third-generation Japanese-Americans might not recognize the term, they readily recognize its meaning. Most respondents translate it as "to hold back." More literally, as delivered in admonitions to children, it means "Don't act like a pig" or "Don't be pushy." As a formal category, it includes those traits which Westerners associate with modesty, reserve, and hesitancy to impose on others. As a normative standard, the behavioral correlate to *enryo* is a commonly encountered trait guiding the quality of the Japanese-Americans' mode of interaction.

The emphasis on collective values is not merely ideological, but is concrete and practical in everyday life. The child moves in the *Gemeinschaft* world of his parents. He is included in most of their social activities and is rarely left at home. If he must be left, a babysitter, who comes from outside the central core of the family's network, is quite rare. Most commonly, a grandmother or an aunt is brought in. Except for those who go to college on the mainland or enter the armed services, young people rarely live away from their families until marriage. This collective orientation is reinforced throughout the ethnic community. The child also has the examples of his own parents' behaviors, which exemplify this same ethic. Forces from outside the subculture have yet to interfere significantly with this basically Japanese model.

As with most parents, a serious dilemma centers around the mechanisms of social control in the disciplining of their children. The desire to underplay individualistic gratification of personal desires through stressing respect and consideration for others is coupled with the emphasis on achievement in the broader society. This gives rise to ambivalence, since the parents want their children to compete with the more verbally-assertive Caucasians. Hence, talking back or being disrespectful to parents or elders in general must be negatively sanctioned at home, but most parents realize that this discourages "speaking up" and expressing oneself in school. Therefore, an uneasy compromise is made between essentially contradictory expectations. Nevertheless, such contradictions are not dissimilar to those which the parents faced in their own maturation and from which, presumably, their own parallel systems of social relationships, norms, and values are derived. Such contradictions can be conceptualized as biculturism and testify to the tensions encumbent on the incorporation of two conflictual systems governing certain actions. As in most emigrant groups, the second and third generation display a significant degree of acculturation to the predominant culture, particularly in linguistic and motivational areas for instrumental activities. This in no way (at least in the case of Hawaiian Japanese-Americans) precludes the retention of traditional features of cultural directives which define primary relationships and intraethnic interaction.

There is a "fit," then, between certain of the norms and values learned in the home and the realistic world faced in day-to-day relationships. Hence, a high degree of social solidarity exists at this level. As one moves from these primary relationships, with their unconscious moral commitments, to the Japanese community at large, the uniformity in expectations of reciprocating behaviors continues, but it must be more formally and consciously enforced. The *kosai* is one mechanism illustrating this, but it does not apply to new or casual acquaintances. In its place, a system of etiquette stressing politeness and *enryo* is formalized, where being "pushy," assertive, or too openly competitive is criticized. Such behavior implies that an individual is exhibiting behavior outside the range acceptable to the ethnic group's normative standards.

Furthermore, these more distant relationships cannot always be transformed into sincere and spontaneous systems of reciprocities, however high the sense of ethnic identity may be. For example, Japanese-American politicians complain that they cannot always rely on the "block-vote" of their own people. Others active in Japanese organizations criticize the presence of excessive factionalism and lack of cooperation. Essentially, more ego-centered interests begin to take precedence as one's orientation becomes affectively neutral.

Compromise Between Conflicting Loyalties

In contrast to primitive societies, where instrumental activities are integrated into the kinship system, industrial society is characterized as producing a series of conflicting loyalties between individualistic tendencies, occupational involvement, and family responsibilities. Parsons defines the nuclear family as a compromise between the familial and occupational structures, in that the head of the family, being responsible for only one small, encapsulated unit, is freed to pursue his ego-centered interests, which require social and geographical mobility. In contrast, Japan's bureaucratic system is noted for its paternalistic functions which, rather than undermining the features of loyalty and security in the family, incorporate these into its structure (Abegglen 1958).

In Hawaii, however, Japanese-Americans move in two worlds: the competitive occupational system of the American capitalistic economy (derived from Christian, Occidental cultures) and the close-knit social network of primary relationships (derived from Confucian, Oriental patterns). How then can they compromise ego-centered occupational demands, on one hand, and the highly developed, collective-centered system of loyalties on the other? For one thing, it should be remembered that the *Gemeinschaft* relationships are limited to the central core of the network involving only a relatively limited number of people.

Also, although Orientals are now represented at all levels of Hawaii's occupational structure, such was not always the case. Because of restrictive hiring practices, Japanese-Americans traditionally sought opportunities in the professions, civil service, small business enterprises, and public education, and in many ways were not exposed in their work lives to the pressure for wholesale assimilation to Western culture. In these particular jobs, they became the dominant group; this simplified personal role performance and created little strain in loyalties toward family and subculture. Additionally, with the presence of a sizable ethnic community, the opportunities for establishing and conducting business essentially within their own ethnic community were, and still are, extensive. For all these reasons, then, relatively few Japanese-Americans have been exposed to the "dynamic" and competitive American corporate settings which do in fact demand extraordinary commitment and expect conformity of personal style toward the image of the organization. Furthermore, although this has not been studied systematically, one hears the general assumption that there may be a selective migration of those individuals with stronger ego-centered interests to greater economic opportunities on the mainland. If true, this factor would act to diminish the problem of divided loyalties in the Hawaiian, Japanese culture.

The great majority, however, remain in Honolulu and show little evidence of conflict in regard to exposure to the outside culture. Like the American nuclear family, the Japanese-Americans have considerable conjugal role segregation, with the husband's occupational role being largely divorced from family activities. Although many wives work, their occupation is almost always considered to be secondary and less important, irrespective of the nature of their jobs. The wife is required to be responsible not only for the care of the children and the performance of household tasks, but also for maintenance of the primary and secondary social obligations of the family. She is the instigator and *major domo* of the family's social network, while the husband functions as a participant. It is her responsibility to see that no one is neglected or dropped from the *kosai* because of other demands.

The social network of the average Japanese-American family is maintained on the level of highest priority by the wife and supported by the husband and children in conjunction with their instrumental activities. The fact that conflicting and divisive loyalties do not generally develop results from the only partial assimilation into the American culture and the continuous transmission of Japanese culture to the second and third generation descendents in Hawaii. Rather than being marginal (the plight of many descendents of other emigrant groups) or lost between two worlds with only a fractionated identity with either, the Japanese-Americans in Honolulu possess a very cohesive subcultural identification. They constitute the largest plurality and live in an environment manifesting considerable tolerance of ethnic differences.* Maintenance of traditional norms and values in the individual's private life receives considerable social support, and the effectiveness of the family in the continued

------

*The Japanese attack on Pearl Harbor had a great impact on the Japanese-Americans in Honolulu. For one thing, prejudice against them was blatantly intensified. All Japanese cultural organizations were closed: language schools, clubs, newspapers, and Buddhist temples. However, they never were subject to wholesale evacuation as were their counterparts on the mainland. Furthermore, the success of the *nisei* soldiers in the European campaigns later in the war considerably modified anti-Japanese prejudice. Wholesale rejection by the *nisei* of their Japanese heritage proved to be a temporary phenomenon. Then too, many returning veterans used the G.I. Bill to move into secure middle-class positions from which they occupy leadership positions today (see Murphy 1954).

transmission of their culture reconfirms the allegiance and attachment. In addition, the precedence given to a collective orientation at home, and the necessity for learning the ego-centered orientation in school gives each individual long training in the facility of switching from one behavioral world to another.

Given the high degree of integration found in Japanese-American society, which is attributed to compatibility between normative orientations and the system of ethnic interaction, the possibility comes to mind as to whether they might be alienated from the broader American society. This does not seem to be the case. For one thing, their achievement orientation corresponds closely with the middle-class American pattern (Caudill 1952). Second, the Japanese-Americans are bicultural, living in a pluralistic society where Far Eastern people dominate in numbers, and Caucasians of Northern European origin make up far less than a majority.* As mentioned above, relative harmony and tolerance between groups is the rule of the day. Finally, the lieutenant governor, three of the four congressmen, and 54 percent of the state legislators are Japanese-Americans, by no means an indication of political alienation.

Conclusions

This chapter has been concerned with reporting certain characteristics of Japanese-American cultural life in metropolitan Honolulu in an attempt to display the way in which social alienation may not affect this group. Information abbreviated from a larger study of a hundred and four families residing in the community has been analyzed in terms of their social relationships, their system of obligation, and their dominant values. The experience of personal alienation has been left unexamined; data on experience of this sort are available, but, in interest of economy, are not presented here. Social alienation is defined here as a series of discontinuities in primary and secondary relationships and incompatibility with the prevailing norms and values.

---

*Although the Caucasians of Northern European ancestry (haoles) are a minority group, they nevertheless provide a point of reference signifying the American culture. Whether their life style is accepted or rejected by the individual Japanese-American, the Caucasians represent the "moderns" in a continuum where the polar position belongs to the *issei.*

These conclusions have been based on the large majority who choose a mode of interaction which is seen as derivative of their Japanese heritage. Hawaii is a particularly favorable environment for the preservation of such continuities. Since the emphasis has been placed on systems of social relationships and supporting norms and values rather than on psychological adaptation, no attention has been given to the confining or, possibly, conflicting demands such a system makes on some individuals. As would be expected, the nonconformist has difficulties with the social restraints inherent in such group solidarity. (The fact that few of these individualistic types were encountered in the sample is probably due to eliminating mixed marriages—assuming that the nonconformist is more likely to marry outside the group.) By limiting the sample to families where both parents were Japanese and by choosing "normal" families without social or emotional deviance, an optimal or "rosy" view has been presented. However, much of the research of urban American life is problem-oriented or deriving from social or psychological deviance. These approaches should be counter-balanced with studies relating to integration and positive adaptation to urban life by a modal population. In any case, population statistics on social deviance attest to a low incidence of social alienation in terms of crime and divorce rates, need for public assistance, or mental hospitalization.

The Japanese-Americans have generally been able to preserve the collectively-oriented Japanese values and norms concerned with the regulation of family life. The preservation of a highly integrated central core of relationships is evident in most of the families surveyed in this study. Relationships which are peripheral to this central core are also endowed with an extremely carefully administered series of reciprocal interactions guaranteeing continuity of relationships (*kosai*). The sense of obligatedness to one's family, friends, and relatives is exceedingly explicit and operates to promote security, mutual aid, and reciprocity in social relationships. The affectional characteristic of *ninjo* has also been discussed as cementing relationships within the central core. They have maintained well-defined ethnic boundaries in their social relationships and have been able to create a close-knit social network where mutual expectations and emotional support are complementary. A system of mutual obligations reaffirms these allegiances to a limited social nexus. Furthermore, socialization practices instill a collective orientation in contrast to an ego-centered pursuit of self-interest. For these reasons, most Japanese-Americans have been able to avoid socially alienating experiences characteristic of modern urban society.

References

Abegglen, J. *The Japanese Factory: Aspects of its Social Organization.* Glencoe, Ill.: The Free Press, 1958.

Barnes, J. A. "Class and Committees in a Norwegian Island Parish." *Human Relations* 7 (1954): 39-58.

Befu, H. "Gift-Giving in a Modernizing Japan." *Monumento Nipponica* 23 (1958): 445-56.

Bellah, R. "Values and Social Change in Modern Japan." *Asian Cultural Studies* No. 3 (October 1962): 13-56.

Bennett, C., Tokuyama, G., and Bruyere, P. "Health of Japanese Americans in Hawaii." *Public Health Reports* 78 (1963): 753-62.

Bott, E. *Family and Social Network.* London: Tavistock, 1957.

Caudill, W. "Japanese-American Personality and Acculturation." *Genetic Psychology Monographs* 45 (1952): 3-102.

Diamond, S. "The Search for the Primitive." *Man's Image in Medicine and Anthropology,* edited by I. Galdston. New York: International Universities Press, 1963.

Goode, W. *World Revolution and Family Patterns.* New York: The Free Press, 1970.

Honolulu Department of Health. *Annual Reports.* Honolulu: The Department, 1968.

Honolulu Department of Social Services. *Characteristics of Recipients Receiving General Assistance.* Honolulu: The Department, 1964.

Honolulu Police Department. *Annual Reports.* Honolulu: The Department, 1968.

Kimmich, R. "Ethnic Aspects of Schizophrenia in Hawaii." *Psychiatry* 23 (1960): 97-102.

Lind, A. "Interracial Marriage as Affecting Divorce in Hawaii." *Sociology and Social Research* 49 (1964): 17-26.

Lind, A. *Hawaii's People* (3rd ed.). Honolulu: University of Hawaii Press, 1967.

Murphy, T. *Ambassadors in Arms.* Honolulu: University of Hawaii Press, 1954.

Nakamura, H. *Ways of Thinking of Eastern People.* Honolulu: East-West Center Press, 1964.

Parsons, T. "The Social Structure of the American Family." *The Family: Its Function and Destiny,* edited by R. Anshen. New York: Harper, 1949.

Redfield, R. *The Primitive World and its Transformations.* Ithaca, N.Y.: Cornell University Press, 1953.

Rosow, I. "Intergenerational Relationships: Problems and Proposals." *Social Structure and the Family: Generation Relations,* edited by E. Shanas and G. Streib. Englewood Cliffs, N.J.: Prentice-Hall, 1965.

Southall, A. *Social Change in Modern Africa.* New York: International African Institute, 1961.

Sugi, M. "The Concept of Ninjo." *Paternalism in the Japanese Economy*, edited by J. W. Bennett and I. Ishino. Minneapolis: University of Minnesota Press, 1963.

United States Bureau of the Census. *United States Census of Populations.* Washington: U.S. Government Printing Office, 1960.

Winch, R. "Some Observations on Extended Familism in the United States." *Selected Studies in Marriage and the Family*, edited by R. Winch and L. Goodman. New York: Holt, 1968.

Wirth, L. "Rural-Urban Differences." *On Cities and Social Life.* Chicago: University of Chicago Press, 1964.

15

The Peasant Village: Education To Encourage Cooperative Communal Attitudes

The other settings described in these selections on community have all represented the lifestyles of technologically sophisticated people. This selection is different, exemplifying what has come to be known as peasant society. It is "modern" in the historical sense that it is recent or commonly exists today and is part of a rapidly changing or developing society. But it is very old in the sense that the community contains peasant peoples who are embedded in older traditional cultures. This is the circumstance of peasant societies generally: they have the sense of isolation characteristic of primitive societies, but they have leadership and contact from an outside exploitative urban class. This creates a particular set of problems relating to what we have called the primal and modern tendencies of the human species. The older traditional society, while it is permeated with certain primal characteristics (kinship as a basis of social cohesion, geographic rootedness, a moral or religious orientation),

has gradually eroded before the pressure of modern economic arrangements. Perhaps the deepest and most serious consequence of these arrangements is the sharp division between hopeful "progressive" classes of people and the poverty-afflicted downtrodden. The latter sense that their lives are dependent on those who have political and economic power, and feel that good and bad aspects of life are out of their control. A second consequence of modernity is the feeling that life in the village is dull compared to the glamour and excitement of the city. Television and radio increasingly bring the message of this outside glamour, destroying the peasant's initiative to create excitement, entertainment, and festivity in his own village.

This selection describes several experiments to change the peasant's basic attitudes of selfishness, suspicion of his neighbors, pessimism about the future, and fatalism. The most dramatic experiment is an orphan community, the organization of which is consistent with what Fromm and Maccoby suggest are basic principles of high quality of life for small communities, for example, the principle of unconditional acceptance and the nonbureaucratic spirit. It is significant that these principles also characterize what is perhaps the most successful intentional experiment in microcommunity, the kibbutz. Whether or not peasant communities, which have traditional religious and cultural roots but a harsh economic dependence on modern urban society, can become "intentional," self-directed, and nonexploited is, of course, a critical world question. And, as Fromm and Maccoby point out, this requires a cooperative spirit, a sense of collective destiny which has long been destroyed by colonial relationships. The problem is how these positive characteristics of personality can be regenerated. The peasant's feeling that most aspects of his life are outside of his control, that his neighbor is in competition with him for the goods of life rather than in cooperation with him to create the goods of life, is characteristic of large segments of working class people in all modern industrial settings. What the peasant still has is a community; the modern industrial worker has only a nuclear family and a somewhat magical faith that the larger system will continue to provide material goods and services. In the face of such large-scale problems as pollution, worldwide inflation, and tension between the third world and the industrial nations, there is the possibility that this faith will be shaken, and that modern workers will face the same problem as the peasants: how to cooperate communally to build a higher quality of life at the local neighborhood level?

A Mexican Peasant Village

The setting of the study is a small village, of about 800 inhabitants, in the State of Morelos, about 50 miles south of Mexico City. The village is located in one of the greenest valleys of Mexico, fertilized by underground springs and mountain streams which become rivers crosscrossing the valley. It has a sub-tropical climate, with a dry winter. The average yearly temperature is 72 degrees; it is never cold and seldom uncomfortably hot. For centuries the main crops grown in the area have been sugarcane and rice, and they are also the two major crops of the village, where most of the people are occupied in agriculture. Cane is irrigated from the river and underground springs, and the rains which fall from May to October allow the villagers to flood the bordered rice fields. The climate and relative abundance of water also support the year-round planting of other crops, and the earth is hospitable to the many fruit trees, flowers, and medicinal herbs that can be found throughout the valley.

The Past and the Present

The population of the village is mestizo, meaning of mixed Indian and Spanish ancestry. Before the Spanish Conquest, the area was populated by a mixture of Toltecs and Chichimecs, later joined by Nahuatlaca tribes, especially the Tlahuicas. After 1436, the

Reprinted by permission from Erich Fromm and Michael Maccoby, *Social Character in a Mexican Village* (Englewood Cliffs, N.J.: Prentice-Hall, 1970).

377

Aztecs, led by Moctezuma Ilhuicamina, completed the conquest of the area, making the Province of Tlalnahuac, the present State of Morelos, a part of the Aztec Empire. When the Aztec Empire crumbled, its provinces were quickly incorporated into the new Spanish system. In April of 1521, Hernán Cortés conquered the province after nine days of fighting. In 1529, he received most of the state from the Spanish king as a feudal fief, including 23,000 vassals, and it became the Marquesado del Valle.

Today there is no longer any trace of an Indian heritage in the village. The villagers are children of the Spanish Conquest. Like 90 percent of all Mexicans, they speak Spanish exclusively. Nearby are villages where people still speak Nahuatl and maintain some of the old customs, but the villagers we have studied have lost all cultural ties with the Aztec past. Only place names remain as reminders of prehispanic culture.

Most villagers do not identify themselves with the past, but see themselves as underprivileged, inferior members of modern society. They would like to escape from peasant poverty and participate in the many good things that have been invented to make life more comfortable and enjoyable. Some villagers, especially the new entrepreneurs and the better-off farmers with land, have high aspirations for their children, if not for themselves. They are the ones who see schooling as the means to enter the new industrial society. These peasants are almost completely oriented to material progress and individual profit, and less tied to tradition. They are the richest peasants, the ones who have risen above mere subsistence. For many of the others, the demands of modern industrial society are in conflict with traditional forms, with the love of leisure and fiestas, and with the suspicion of modern forms as corrupting and dangerous.

During the past 50 years, the village has been caught up in a process of rapid change. Before 1910, it was a hacienda. After 1923, it became a community of small landholders (*ejidatarios*). When we arrived in the late 1950's, it had become a society that was of two classes, a small group of landholders and a larger group of the landless.

Today, the spread of communications and new technologies has favored the rise of a new entrepreneurial class and has supported the new ideas and aspirations. In such a period of change, individuals doubt traditional beliefs, many feel hopeless about the future in the

village, and the younger generation seeks models outside of the
family. As the villagers increasingly see life in terms of the consumer
ideals of the city, they become more and more frustrated with the
village which can never satisfy these needs. The villager probably
feels more dissatisfied and hopeless than the villager of preindustrial
times, who did not have the feeling that he could never manage to
buy the commodities that he was told make life worthwhile. Furthermore, as the villagers are attracted increasingly to radio, television,
and movies, they have lost interest in more active forms of entertainment and self-expression. One older villager stated:

In the past the only diversions were musical. They sang and played instruments.
If we wanted any other attractions, we had to invent them. That is why we made
up and performed comedies and dramas and presented them to the public in the
fiestas we used to celebrate. Because at that time there were no movies, there
was no television nor radio, nor electric light. We used to try to add a little more
to the fiestas by organizing theatrical works. Then, afterwards, and with great
enthusiasm, the musical band was organized. After a time, it played very well.
But then—the electricity came. There were radios. There were juke boxes. Television. They brought a movie to show once a week. And then no one was interested. Thus ended the enthusiasm for the band and for the theatrical works.

The result is the growing feeling that nothing offered by the village can compare with the glamour and excitement of the consumer
economy in the city, and that life is hardly worth living for those
who are doomed to the rural backwater.

The present-day village was formed in 1923 at the end of the
Revolution, after the overthrow of the hacienda which had dominated the area for three centuries. The ruins of the hacienda and the
stone aqueduct, as well as some beliefs and practices, are remnants of
the past. But there are many modern influences. Although the streets
are unpaved, the village has worked hard to bring electricity and
piped drinking water into many of the houses. Besides radios and an
increasing number of television sets, villagers have contact with the
urban world through sons and daughters who work in large cities and
through the score of families from Mexico City who have built weekend residences in the village, attracted by its climate and beauty.
Modernization, represented by new industries nearby, paved roads,
and concrete plazas to replace the picturesque tree-filled *zocalos,*
signifies progress for most villagers.

Most of the present inhabitants migrated to the village after the

Revolution, in search of land and new opportunities. The Revolution was a time of great upheaval for the peasants of the area, whether they were fighting on one side or the other, or hiding in terror from both armies. Villagers describe the famine and disease that together with violence took the lives of 23 percent of Morelos during the revolutionary years. It was common for families to be uprooted from their villages, to flee to the mountains where they lived on herbs and grasses. Women were unprotected, as their husbands went off to fight, or were conscripted by the government to join the armies in the north. The fighting in Morelos began in 1911 and did not end until 1920. One can hardly exaggerate the extent of the destruction, especially by the government armies which in 1914 and later in 1916 burned villages and ruthlessly murdered or deported peasants suspected of following the revolutionary peasant leader, Emiliano Zapata. By 1918, with the haciendas in ruins and most of the now-broken families living on the edge of starvation, the great flu epidemic of that year claimed the lives of a quarter of the state's population which had survived the violence of the previous eight years. In 1919, displaced villagers began to return and were joined by thousands of migrants who swelled the population during the 1920's and early 1930's, attracted by the generous land policies of Emiliano Zapata's successors, who were put in charge of the state by the national government of General Álvaro Obregon.

The inhabitants of the village originated from both haciendas and from free villages. Before the Revolution, 38 haciendas in the hands of 21 different proprietors owned 56 percent of the state, including an even larger percentage of the fertile valley land. Twenty-six percent of the land was communal grazing land including mountains, while only 18 percent was held by small proprietors, and this included urban land holdings. The haciendas of Morelos were devoted exclusively to the cultivation of cane, while the small landowners planted corn, garden vegetables, and rice. The identification of cane with hacienda domination, and of rice and vegetables with independence lasts to this day, if not in the conscious minds of the villagers, then in the attitudes associated with the planting of these crops.

The peasants of the free villages owned small plots of land and in some cases shared communal land for planting or grazing. The main reason that the Revolutionary flame burned so intensely in the

State of Morelos was that, in the years preceding the Revolution, many free peasants were losing their lands to the haciendas and being forced into the role of landless peons. One important factor in this development, as Domingo Diez (1967) writes in his history of Morelos, was that the haciendas developed a new method of sugar refining. This combined with the increasing ease of rail transportation made it more profitable to grow more cane and to take over more land from the free villages. Diez writes:

In this year of 1880 the first machinery for setting up the centrifugal method was established in the haciendas. . . . This fact came to radically change the life of the state. To augment their production of sugar, the hacienda owners naturally looked for an increase in the area of cultivation and this had to be, necessarily, at the cost of the free village lands. . . . In a word, one can say there was a complete revolution upon the definite establishment of the modern machinery. The land owners prospered, their cane gave them greater returns, the Government increased its income through taxes, only the (free) villages were obliged to cede their lands and waters. Little by little they were losing out. Some ended by disappearing, and the social disequilibrium intensified, breaking out in the Revolution of 1910. (Diez 1967, p. 130)

From 1870 to 1910, sugar production in the state increased steadily from 8,748,131 kilograms to 48,531,600 kilograms. During this period, the haciendas increasingly took over land from free peasants, aided by the government which abused the law concerning idle lands to justify the haciendas. The primary goal of the Zapatistas, stated in the *Plan de Ayala* of 1911, was return of land that had been usurped by the hacendados.

The dispossessed free villagers were the group that spearheaded the revolution in Morelos. In some cases, families which had held land for centuries were in danger of becoming landless peons. Rather than accept this, they were prepared to defend their property rights with their lives.

Zapata's goals were at first conservative, limited to defending the rights of small property holders. Those peasants whose families had been peons for generations were more likely to have been resigned and submissive, dependent on the hacienda, and unable to imagine another form of life. Only when the government of Victoriano Huerta radicalized the Morelos revolution by treating all peasants as Zapatistas and enemies of the state did Zapata open his army to *peones* (field laborers), and change his revolutionary goals to demand land for all and the abolition of the hacienda. Then, once the haciendas lay in ruins and the old life was gone, the peons' repressed hatred against their former masters added fuel to the explosion. However, there were free villages in which the Revolution was experienced as a threat to a peaceful existence, where no hacienda had encroached on land rights. A group of families within the village we have studied originates from one such village where the inhabitants fought against the Zapatistas.

The Hacienda

Before 1910 all the lands now belonging to the ejidatarios (holders of unalienable land) in the village we have studied were owned by the hacienda which employed them in the cultivation of sugarcane. A small community, no more than 40 to 50 families, lived in thatched huts (*jacales*) outside the hacienda walls. Some villagers were able to rent land from the hacienda, paying for it by sharecropping and labors (*faenas*) for the hacienda. A very few were small entrepreneurs, such as the muleteers (*arrieros*) who contracted to carry cargo from the village to the outside and back. The arrieros were particularly independent and brave individuals who constantly risked attack from bandits during their journeys. It is interesting to note that two of the five entrepreneurial villagers we encountered are sons of arrieros.*

Almost all of the villagers were dependent on the hacienda. While some of the employees worked as foremen (*mayordomos*) or supervisors (*capatazes*), the majority were field laborers (peones), who lived in total subjugation to the hacienda. Life for the peon was hardly distinguishable from slavery. Unlike the feudal manor, the hacienda offered no guarantees or legal protection to the peon. The hacienda made its own law. Those who were rebellious would be whipped and possibly expelled from the hacienda, from then on blacklisted in other haciendas. A peon who stole from the hacienda might have been executed.

---

*It is also interesting that Emiliano Zapata was both a small landholder and had worked as an arriero. Known for his independence and incorruptibility, he was chosen by his village as a leader to defend small landholders from the haciendas.

The peon lived in perpetual fear of being beaten or of losing his source of livelihood. He learned to bow his head before his masters, to smile at small favors, to show abject submission. Even then, there was practically no hope for bettering oneself. Given the peon's poverty and perpetual indebtedness, there was no way of acquiring land, which in any case was scarce; and the hacienda owners or their managers (since some owners lived in Europe) had no interest in educating the peons who were for them most useful as submissive parts of an agricultural machine.

The peons were usually paid in kind, by land use or grazing privileges. The small sum of money due them seldom reached their hands, but went toward paying the account in the hacienda store (*tienda de raya*) where debts accumulated by fathers were inherited by their sons. Chained by these debts, most peons could not leave the hacienda even if they could imagine working on the outside, and, furthermore, they were fearful that life elsewhere might be worse. In return for total obedience and hard work, the hacienda saw to their subsistence and tranquilized them with cheap drink, occasional fiestas, and spectacles.

When the Revolution finally began to speak to the peons of independence and hope, the submissive, receptive attitudes moulded by centuries of hacienda life were not easy to erase. Once the peon became a landowner, he was not only psychologically handicapped for the postrevolutionary world, but he also lacked the training and experience to administer his land, to take account of costs and credit, and to consider problems of marketing. In adapting to the hacienda, the peons had become submissive and dependent and they did not have either the character or the knowledge essential to a free peasant. It will be seen that the peasants with character structure adapted to hacienda life have great difficulties adapting to the present-day circumstances.

Aside from these special historical influences, most villagers are subject to the present conditions of life which are similar to those of peasant societies throughout the world. For those who are fortunate enough to have land, cultivation is largely done by the same rudimentary methods which were in use centuries ago. The plots are too small to justify mechanized agriculture. The villager, like most peasants, is dependent on the city to buy his products and set the price, and he is powerless to influence the conditions that determine his profit and loss. Vulnerable to exploitation, the peasant distrusts, often with good reason, all those from the urban world. At the same time, he is dependent on the city, not only for markets, but also for the consumer goods he wants and the cultural stimulation he cannot create for himself.

The Inner Life of the Villagers

The villagers we have studied have many of the qualities described in accounts of peasants in other places and times. They are selfish, suspicious of each others' motives, pessimistic about the future, and fatalistic. Many appear submissive and self-deprecatory, although they have the potential for rebelliousness and revolution. They feel inferior to city people, more stupid, and less cultured. There is an overwhelming feeling of powerlessness to influence either nature or the industrial machine that bears down on them. Here are some dreams which are shared by many villagers and typical of their feelings.* One man's dream expresses this feeling: "I dreamt that I was in bed in my house with all my family, all in bed, when I saw a train, an engine that came over all of us. On seeing the engine, I jumped from the bed, yelling to the one driving that he stop his machine and not crush us all." Other dreams express helplessness against animals or the inability to defend onself against attackers.

The peasant villager suffers from poverty and frustration. Many dream of riches, but are fearful that the dream itself will cause them bad luck. It is dangerous to hope. A woman of 32 years dreamed "that I found a little money. I asked myself what I'd do with it. Then I told my husband I'd found money and that I would give it to him so that he could work by himself without anyone ordering him around. I woke up happy, but at the same time I was disillusioned because it was not true. After this dream my husband failed in his harvests." A grown man remembers a dream provoked by hunger when he was a child. "I was five years old and asleep in my bed of straw when I began to dream I was eating a piece of bread. I took some delicious bites, because I felt the sensation of hunger. Suddenly I saw I was finishing and I gave a hard bite. I awoke and what I was biting wasn't bread but the fingers of my hand."

---

*These dreams are taken from over 150 dreams we have collected from villagers.

Dreams of women, especially, express the sense of being worn down by burdens, childbearing, and the heavy, constant work that prematurely ages the peasant woman. A woman of 30 said, "Sometimes when I am sleeping, I feel that I am carrying a heavy and cold burden, and that my feet are being pulled down. I want to cry out and I cannot. I am frightened. I think it must be ghosts or dead people that want to take me to the cemetery." She feels that the burdens of the past and present are dragging her to an early grave.

The villager's world is hard and frightening. As many nightmares (*pesadillas*) show, there is a constant struggle against death. A man of 40 dreamt "that I was in bed and that death (*la muerte*) came. I felt I was seated in the bed, and it touched me and I cried out: 'Hija de la chingada! You are death.' And I gave it a blow in the head, knocked it over, and heard the bones hit the floor. I awoke frightened, looking for the bones, but I did not see anything." This dream symbolizes the reality of constantly fighting against hunger and disease. The villagers take pleasure in the conquest of death, even though they know that they will lose in the end.

The peasant's dreams express a sense of living in dirt, with the constant danger of infection from parasites and other diseases.* The dreams also reveal the wish to escape, to fly above the dirt and poverty, but the dreamer usually falls back into the mud. Even in dreams the peasant feels little hope.

Despite the shared misery of peasant life, deep friendships are rare, and the villagers spread gossip about each other which is often damaging and not always true.† An extreme distrust and fear of

---

*Studies done in the village by Professor Francisco Biagi and his collaborators from the Medical School of the National University of Mexico discovered that over 90 percent of the villagers are infected with intestinal parasites. After the study, Dr. Biagi instituted a campaign for treatment and prevention of parasites. Dr. Adan Graetz had the idea for instituting the study and helped in setting it up.

†The use of gossip as a source of information is an ambiguous method. Certainly some gossip is true, but some other is not. To be able to know when one is dealing with either true or false gossip is exceedingly difficult. It would seem that a piece of gossip can be believed when all or the majority of the villagers believe it, but this assumption is by no means correct. It is notorious in small and large groups that a rumor will be believed by many, and yet the many, under the influence of suggestion and their sadistic pleasure, may be as wrong as only one individual may be. Not more trustworthy is the old maxim that "where there is smoke there must be fire"; or better, perhaps, if there is fire, it might be

others, based in part on experience of being cheated or betrayed, limits the possibility that the peasant will open himself fully to others. Throughout life the closest emotional tie of the villager usually remains with his mother. . . . The dream of an old man, age 80, expresses distrust which persists throughout a lifetime, even though in this case the distrust proved to be baseless. In fact, the dream itself was remembered by the dreamer as "evidence" against a potential friend. "A long time ago I had a dream that made me feel very bad. At that time I was 14 years old. I was still young. I dreamed that I was standing in the street, and an individual that was my friend came over. Then without any motive, he stabbed me here in the breast where the heart is. Upon taking out the knife, I saw blood flowing out into a pool. I woke up frightened and nervous. I don't know why I dreamt that. He was a friend. Afterward he was even a *compadre* [a ritual co-parent based on being the godfather to a child or another important ritual role such as a godparent to a marriage]. There was never a single difficulty between us."

Mistrust, pessimism, and maliciousness are one side of peasant life. The villagers are also concerned about living a good life, about being good people. They are ashamed and unhappy about their egoism, the lack of trust and cooperation. Some of the villagers, those who are more active and productive, measure themselves in terms of Christian teachings. They would like to have faith in their fellow man, to love their neighbors, but their experiences and their own character make this difficult. To understand the inner life of the peasant, one must understand the constant conflict between cynicism and hopelessness on the one hand and faith, often a childlike faith, on the other. This is the same conflict that Huizinga (1950) describes as characteristic of peasants at the end of the middle ages in Europe, and it is sometimes expressed in the villagers' parables and sayings (*dichos*). Some of these sayings are almost identical to the ones Huizinga quotes. The medieval peasant said, "He who serves the common weal is paid by none for his trouble," and "No horse is so well shod it never slips." The Mexican villagers with good humor and resignation will say that "He who works in a soap factory should be

---

in the one who spreads the gossip rather than in his object. Considering the value of gossip one is reminded of Spinoza's saying: what Peter says about Paul tells us more about Peter than about Paul.

prepared to slip," and "He who walks with the wolves will learn to howl." There are many stories and sayings to illustrate the dangers of trying to help the community.

Furthermore, despite the peasant's submissiveness, one is struck by his dignity and sense of self. The peasant knows who he is and has few illusions about himself. In his dealings with other peasants, he values both the forms and substance of respect. Villagers refer to a family head as *Don* José or to a married woman as *Doña* María, using the Spanish designations of nobility in their normal form of address. Although the peasant humbles himself before powerful individuals, it is often the case that a villager will leave job and risk starvation rather than accept a personal insult.

There are also unique satisfactions in being a peasant villager in Mexico. One of the most important is the sense of rootedness, of living in a small village where each person knows everyone else. While gossip is sometimes hostile, it is also a means of filling out one's knowledge of a common world. In our studies comparing the villagers' modes of thinking with those of urban Mexicans and Americans (Maccoby and Modiano, 1966, 1969), we found that the villager is more concrete, descriptive, specific, and less abstract or generalizing in his mode of ordering experience. The difference in modes of thought reflects differences in the demands of culture on cognition. In the industrial world, time is money and value is constantly converted into abstract terms. People must learn ways of approaching tasks rather than specific operations, so that as methods are continually modernized individuals will not have to learn them from scratch. The industrial world demands an approach to experience that is abstract, functional, and flexible. The peasant world does not make these demands. Methods of work have remained the same for centuries. Rather than seeking to understand abstract operations, the peasant is interested in the significance of concrete experience. He is concerned about the changes in the weather. He observes the state of a plant or an animal with a careful concern for its health and illness. He is extremely perceptive in observing the emotions of others and is often accurate in judging character, especially in those he has known for a long time. The villager spends his life learning to know a few things deeply. His knowledge is concrete and nontransferable, which is a reason that many peasants feel totally lost and helpless if they are uprooted. They have not learned the modes of thought and abstract principles which are useful in the industrial world, but what they have learned about their fellows and their physical world gives them a satisfaction of being related to their surroundings, of feeling at home. The peasant has a strong sense of the nontransferability of experience, even from one peasant village to another, and he will explain the lack of knowledge or strange conduct of someone who was not born in the village by saying "He is not from here" (*No es de aquí*) even if the person has spent his whole adult life in the village.

The Mexicans tell a story about a man from the city who arrives in a small peasant village, looking for a house on *Calle Revolución*. He asks a peasant standing by the road how to find the street, and the peasant answers that he does not know. "What?" says the city man, "You live in this tiny village and don't even know which street is *Calle Revolución*? You must be very stupid." "That may be," says the peasant, "but I'm not lost."

In terms of the comforts of modern society, and even in terms of the peasant's own aspirations, his life offers little pleasure in comparison with the hardship, scarcity, anxiety, and constant frustration. The Revolution gave the peons freedom and land, but today the growing population means that three-fourths of the men are again landless. Yet, one is struck by the villagers' good humor, their hospitality and tact, their realism and relatedness to life, and their ability to respond, despite suspiciousness and pessimism, to new opportunities.

As we shall see, one cannot easily generalize the villagers' attitudes and responses. While modes of thought and culture are held in common, significant variations in socioeconomic class and individual character influence important differences in behaving and experiencing life.

Possibilities for Change: Character and Cooperation

What are the possibilities for the future of the village? The most likely possibility, if the social and economic conditions remain the same, is that the current trend will continue. The new entrepreneurs will further consolidate their control over the village. The ejidatarios will increasingly become dependent on them as middlemen and as political leaders. The landless either will leave for the cities or, since good jobs are scarce and they are not qualified for them, many will continue to work as day laborers.

If conditions remain the same, this will mean that most villagers will live their lives in poverty and that there will be no alleviation of their hopelessness and alcoholism. Various suggestions have been made by experts concerning how to better the situation of villagers in Latin America and throughout the world. In the light of our findings, we shall consider three such proposals.

1. It has often been proposed that the peasant be given technical training to use more modern agricultural methods and to learn new skills (e.g., handicraft, poultry-raising) that will increase his income. Such training is often of value, especially to those peasants with larger land holdings and some capital. However, it is only a limited solution.

New technology requires different attitudes on the part of the peasant. . . . To be more than minimally effective, technical training must be combined with change in the character structure of the peasant.

Such a change could be accomplished to some extent through entirely different methods in schooling. (A most impressive and ingenious program for peasant education which not only conveys knowledge, but affects the whole personality is that of Freire (1968), who experimented with his program of alphabetization of adults with peasants and urban workers first in Brazil, and then in Chile. Freire's method can be applied to the education of children as well as adults. But so far there are only a few groups experimenting with it in this way.) As far as the rural school system in Mexico is concerned, it is saddled with very traditionally oriented teachers, and unless one could bring in a sufficient number of teachers who know how to stimulate interest and activity, nothing much can happen. Another way of influencing character would be to change the traditional socioeconomic system of the village in the direction of a greater amount of cooperation and initiative, but this too is a remote goal under the given circumstances.

Furthermore, one could think of an integrated program of

cultural stimulation. Attempts in this direction were made under President Lazaro Cardenas, but later petered out. Nevertheless, as we shall indicate later in this chapter, we think that while the difficulties are great, serious efforts in the field of education, cultural stimulation, and cooperative methods—if they went to the roots and were integrated in a new system of life—would have a significant effect.

Another way of changing the peasant's deep-rooted emotional attitudes has been suggested by David McClelland (1961) who proposes a method of training villagers to have a higher "need for achievement." He suggests that individuals with this need are more likely to become entrepreneurs who will adopt and develop new methods and create new industries.

But the facts indicate that entrepreneurs do not solve the village's economic problem. A few entrepreneurs have prospered, but they do not raise the general economic level. In fact, their prosperity is gained at the cost of others. Lacking resources for large-scale economic activity, they become middlemen, money lenders, and storekeepers. While they may employ others as day laborers, the result is to increase the dependency and powerlessness of the landless.

Thus, it seems to us that changes in peasant attitudes in the direction of making more of them small-scale entrepreneurs rigidifies a new class structure and increases misery for the majority. The question which will be considered further in this chapter is whether peasant attitudes can be changed in a way that favors both economic development and life-centered values.

2. Albert O. Hirschman (1967), an economist specializing in problems of development, cautions that new programs must take account of the peasant's cognitive attitudes which often block economic development. He suggests that development projects be of two types: those that are "trait taking" and those that are "trait making."

A "trait taking" project is built by taking into account the existing traits and does not demand that the peasant change in any way, while a "trait making" project is one which demands that the peasant develop new traits. It requires more from him than does his normal work. In responding to the demands of an exacting job, an individual must develop new traits in order to maintain the project.

We agree with Hirschman that trait making projects are desirable. We want to stress, however, that it is important to be aware of which traits one wants to make, those of the entrepreneur type of modern farmer or those of the productive-cooperative type. As is clear from our overall discussion, we do not think that all psychological traits which serve to speed the process of economic development are desirable from a human standpoint.

3. Programs of education, trait taking, and trait making alone leave certain problems unsolved. Even if the peasant were to increase his earning power somewhat, he would still remain economically powerless in relation to the city, unless he were able to cooperate with other peasants in buying and selling. A cooperative movement which fits this requirement has begun in Mexico under the direction of CONASUPO and has bean achieved in other countries such as Sweden in a more extensive and systematic form.*

However, an even stronger cooperative movement would be necessary to prevent the trend in this village and others toward a new class stratification, to protect the small independent peasant from the entrepreneur. A cooperative organization, such as the Israeli kibbutz, or some of the cooperative ejidos developed in the Lagunilla area, allows for greater differentiation of work, a high level of technology, and more rewarding work for the landless peasants. To organize this type of cooperative ejido on a large scale requires changes in the system as well as the support of the government which would have to buy or expropriate the land for these projects and provide the technical leadership.

In considering this third alternative, of a strong cooperative movement, we must keep in mind the fact that peasants throughout the world are extremely individualistic and suspicious of others. When cooperatives are introduced by outside agencies, they almost always fail, even when they promise the peasant greater profit, more power in the market, and new technical training. The kibbutzim comprise a special case, since they were founded not by peasants, but by urban intellectuals, motivated by the ideals of socialism, who set

---

*An example of a trait-making project which also has increased peasant cooperativeness and his economic and political power is Danilo Dolci's project in Sicily. One aspect of the program is the construction of a dam which requires new skills and traits on the part of the peasants. Dolci has found that he needs not only to train villagers technically, but also to make them aware of their passiveness, fatalism, and submissiveness before their attitudes and work habits change.

out to create an agricultural community which would maximize not
income but the quality of life for its members. In contrast, failures
have been reported in cooperative peasant projects in Latin America,
Italy, and India, as well as in many communist countries.* The question remains, however, whether the peasant will inevitably reject
cooperative projects or whether their success depends on more adequate methods of introduction and structure.

In this chapter we shall consider the villagers' attitude toward
cooperative activities as it relates to character. Then we shall report
experiments which demonstrate ways of developing cooperative projects and cooperative attitudes.

Cooperation in the Village

In the recent past the village has sporadically organized cooperative enterprises which have lasted only for brief periods. A cooperative store prospered only so long as it was supported by strong-
minded and respected rural schoolmasters. A rice growers' cooperative which promised the ejidatarios higher profits as well as
protection against loss collapsed as individual members became suspicious that they would be cheated by the others and fail to receive
their proper share. In both cases these cooperatives benefitted a large
group of villagers at the expense of the entrepreneurs whose gains
were threatened by the projects. Those who stand to lose from the
cooperative have the natural tendency to play on the suspicions and
fears of the villagers that the cooperatives will cheat them, that the
ideals of cooperatives hide new forms of domination from the outsiders.

Public works projects rather than cooperative enterprise are the
kind of activity in which the villagers do work together successfully.
The leaders of the village, all of them richer peasants, have organized
movements to bring electricity and piped drinking water to the village. As we have already described, these "modern" entrepreneurs,
oriented to the market economy and away from traditional practices,
succeeded in doing away with the most costly fiestas and collected
money to build a school. For most villagers the concept of "coop-

---

*Yugoslavia is a notable exception.

erating" (*cooperar*) means contributing money for such public works, or if they are not rich enough, donating their labor to clean the ditches or fix the roads (*faenas*), always with the hope that the authorities or some rich patron who wants to be governor will also "cooperate" in return for the village's gratitude and political support.

Foster (1967) suggests that, traditionally, the richer peasant spends part of his wealth on fiestas, musical bands, masses in the church, and food for the others who in turn are expected to give him the respect due such a generous individual. In this way, the rich also try to avoid the envy of the poor. In the village we have studied these traditional practices are being replaced by more modern practices, but the goals of gaining respect and avoiding envy remain the same. Since the richer villagers consider money spent on fiestas and fireworks as wasted, they prefer to put money into building a new road that will bring more tourists and weekend residents to spend money in the village or a new school that will give their children a chance to better themselves. In supporting these public works projects, they emphasize their own public-spirited, "cooperative" attitude in order to make the case that they are using their wealth for the community benefit. To visitors they express the wish that the village were more truly cooperative instead of being so egoistic and divided. In fact, they justify their leadership by organizing the others only for projects which promise profit for themselves, and they are the first to withdraw from the institutionalized cooperatives.

By making a show of "cooperating" more than others, they also try to soften the envy of the poor. Here is another example of how misleading it would be to judge character on the basis of stated ideals. Most villagers will state that they favor cooperation, and they may even cite the cooperative ideology of the Mexican Revolution, but their character and their actions contrast sharply with this ideology.

One notable exception to lack of cooperative activity is that villagers will join together to oppose a common enemy. They have worked together against a neighboring village in a struggle over water rights. And a number of villagers banded together to oppose an ejidatario who tried to use for himself what they considered to be communal land. But these cooperative groups dissolved as soon as the struggle had ended.

Anticooperative Attitudes

While the few entrepreneurs are likely to oppose any cooperative effort which might limit their own opportunity to make money (a credit union would compete with their money lending, a buying or selling cooperative would limit their activities as middlemen), this does not explain why many of the nonexploitative, traditional peasants are opponents of cooperatives.

It is our conclusion that the reluctance of these villagers to put effort into maintaining cooperative ventures, even when they promise them material gain, is influenced in large part by attitudes rooted in the hoarding character and in the traditional sociopolitical orientation. These attitudes must be taken into account in any form of cooperative planning.

First, the peasants distrust each other and are afraid that both fellow villagers and outsiders will steal from them if they have the opportunity. Sometimes these suspicions have been justified, but even when they are not this intense distrust and fear of being robbed are understandable in terms of the hoarding character syndrome. The hoarding individual's security system is based on protecting himself and his possessions. His fear is that others will take what he has, and he is constantly on the lookout for thieves. A small incident or evidence of dishonesty which might seem unimportant to another type of person is enough to convince him that his fears are justified.

The peasant's willingness to work jointly for public works projects contradicts the above only apparently. The hoarding individual can contribute small sums for public works despite the risk that they will be stolen, because it is a small sum, and it is only a one-shot affair. Furthermore, to exclude himself from public works would mark the villager as an egotistical person and do harm to his standing with others.

In contrast to the productive-hoarding peasant, the passive-receptive villager might remain in a cooperative with the hope that others will give him something, but he is too irresponsible and inactive to contribute to the venture. It is a telling fact that, comparing the 14 men who first opposed the rice cooperative with those who remained in it, the ones who left first were those with productive-hoarding characters, while those who stayed were passive-receptive ejidatarios.

Second, the hoarding peasant has a strong sense of private property, and feels happier and more secure when he has his own piece of land and feels that he depends on himself alone for his livelihood. It is difficult for him to take part in a cooperative which appears to threaten his security in controlling private property. The original followers of Zapata were willing to die rather than lose their land. For the hoarding individual, his property is part of himself. The more property he has, the more of a man he feels that he is. This does not mean, however, that it is not possible to organize cooperatives which respect the peasant's wish for private property, from which he can withdraw if it is not to his advantage to remain.*

Third, we have observed that the productive-hoarding peasant does not like to take orders and is at the same time unhappy about telling others what to do. The first trait is related to the compulsive need for independence and the obstinacy that is part of the hoarding character. The second trait is related to the productive-hoarding person's fear of having to reciprocate. He feels that if he asks something of another person then he owes that person something in return. In a complex cooperative project, tasks must be allocated and someone must be responsible for their completion. Many peasants who have the capacity for leadership and are themselves responsible are unwilling to demand such discipline from others, because they do not want to feel under obligation, and also because they are sensitive to the dislike others feel in taking orders. As they see it, why should someone risk the

---

*One of us (Maccoby) visited such a peasant cooperative in Yugoslavia where individuals maintained legal possession of their plots but worked together in a cooperative in which they bought seed and sold their produce as a unit, divided labor according to different skills (e.g., tractor driver, bricklayer, expert on poultry, etc.), and received profits in terms of differential work and the amount of land contributed to the cooperative. Although decisions were made by a board of managers according to requirements of scientific agriculture, the members of the cooperative could replace the managers by vote at any time. It was proven to the peasants that they profited more by belonging to the cooperative than by remaining independent. However, some peasants were allowed to apply for limited membership in the cooperative for the purpose of buying seeds and selling produce only, while farming their land by themselves. In this way, the Yugoslavians made it clear that the peasant was not forced to join the cooperative, and he could wait until he was convinced that full membership would be beneficial to him.

enmity of others for a project which is, in any case, unlikely to succeed?

In the village the more productive peasants sometimes accept positions of responsibility but most do not want to be considered as leaders (*lideres*), a word which has a strong negative connotation throughout Mexico suggesting exploitative bosses. They are aware that the villagers distrust all leaders and suspect them of using their positions to get what they can from others. In fact, those who have accepted leadership roles complain that they always end up making enemies. Some villagers refuse to accept posts in the village government, and there was even a case of a villager who became sick with a psychosomatic back ailment on being chosen comisariado ejidal. Consciously, he considered that he could not refuse the responsibility. The ailment, which allowed him to avoid taking office, resisted both medicines and curings until another man was chosen in his place. The reluctant villager, no longer faced with a conflict between duty and desire to avoid trouble, got better shortly afterward.

When a villager does accept a position of leadership, he hardly ever tries to force others to comply with their legal obligations. Although by law all heads of families must attend the assemblies called by the ayudante or pay a fine for absence, the authorities never attempt to collect the fines. If a villager refuses to "cooperate" on a project, he may be asked to contribute once or twice, but if he expresses strong opposition, his refusal to cooperate will be respected. The loose political structure of the village allows an individual to refuse to go along with the majority as long as his behavior does not imply an attack against the majority. While this type of political structure avoids conflict, it minimizes the possibilities of organizing the villagers for many kinds of cooperative activities.

Once in a while a charismatic individual, like the two schoolmasters in the late 1930's who organized the cooperative store and other cooperative activities, will animate and stimulate the villagers to forget their fears and work together, but the cooperative spirit lasted only so long as the teachers remained. It was not possible to institutionalize their charisma.

There is always the danger that a cooperative project introduced by outside authorities who provide leadership may be treated as a semifeudal setup, requiring submission to new patrons in return for favors. Anyone who tries, as we did, to create cooperative projects runs up against the peasant's attempt to place him in the category of hypocritical do-gooders seeking admiration or political support. And if the outsider does not want this, the villagers think he must be seeking to exploit them in some other way. It is deceptively easy to fall into the role of patron, cushioned by the flattery of the village and by the feeling that only in this way can anything get done.

Often outside authorities are convinced that their projects will benefit the peasant and they are taken in by the seeming submissive acceptance of the new plan. But this "submissiveness" is generally a way of avoiding conflict, and the peasants have no intention of following through. By not taking account in their plans of peasant suspiciousness, the authorities ignore the need to construct conditions which reassure the hoarding individuals. Such conditions would demand knowledge of the peasants' attitudes, as well as patience and ingenuity to change them. Many well-intentioned projects are constructed on shaky foundations. They may last as long as the outside authorities remain and the peasant feels it is worth his while to please them in return for benefits, but as soon as the authorities leave, many peasants automatically withdraw behind their walls.

Possibilities for Cooperation

Yet, well-structured cooperative projects could be profitable for the majority and benefit the village as a whole. Cooperatives for buying and selling would give peasants more power against the markets and the middlemen. Cooperatives based on the division of labor would allow individuals with talents outside of agriculture, masons, mechanics, and artisans, to specialize and develop their abilities and would be an alternative to developing large farms under the control of entrepreneurs. The question remains whether the peasants' attitudes and character structure are insurmountable obstacles to the construction of institutionalized cooperative projects. Our study cannot provide a definitive answer to this question, but before citing our own experimental evidence, we want to give two examples which demonstrate that peasant individualism and suspiciousness can be overcome to a great degree, if a project is well organized. The Mexican government's CONASUPO program is an example of a project that has been successful, because it has built-in safeguards that take account of the peasant's suspiciousness. Beyond these experiments, the orphanage *Nuestros Pequeños Hermanos* (Our Little Brothers) is an example of another possibility of changing the peasant character by organizing a community on the basis of cooperative, life-oriented principles. Our own experience with a boys' club suggests the possibility of achieving higher levels of cooperation in villages such as this one by educating the peasant to become aware of irrational attitudes in himself, especially those having to do with traditional authority.

The CONASUPO program (*Companía Nacional de Subsidios Populares*), until recently directed by Professor Carlos Hank Gonzáles, has two major goals. The first is to guarantee a fair price to the peasant for his harvest, and the second is to make available consumer goods to the peasants and the city workers at the lowest price possible, which is done through a network of CONASUPO stores which undersell private retailers while still making a small profit.

CONASUPO and the agencies that preceded it began by offering to buy the peasant's harvest (corn, grain, rice, beans, etc.) at a guaranteed price, paid in cash, and avoiding all bureaucratic procedures. The price was usually above the one private buyers would pay. The price was set both to protect the peasant from speculators and exploiters and to encourage the planting of crops which were either needed for national consumption or which could be exported by the government. It was expected that CONASUPO would provide a minimum price which would protect the peasant but not affect the possibility of a higher price being offered by private buyers. If there was an overproduction of certain crops, the government would store or export the surplus.

It was soon discovered, however, that many peasants were unable to transport their produce to CONASUPO centers. Speculators who owned trucks were still able to take advantage of the small farmer, buying his harvest at low prices and then transporting it to CONASUPO centers. The speculator benefitted, but the average peasant did not. CONASUPO was willing to send trucks to the villages, but it ran up against the problem that most villages lack storage facilities, and that peasants did not want to store their grain in a common warehouse for fear that they would be cheated out of their proper share.

The response of CONASUPO was imaginative and ingenious. A cone-shaped silo, based on a colonial model, was designed. It was cheap to make from local stones or brick, simple and beautiful, and extremely practical for protecting grain from animals and dampness.

(The cone shape solved the problem of roofing materials which are often not durable and disintegrate during the rainy season.) Together with the offer of a loan for building a cooperative silo, CONASUPO proposed a system that protected individual property rights, demonstrated a way of making a greater profit, and offered safeguards against stealing.

A peasant who would act as a CONASUPO representative would be chosen by the village to be in charge of weighing the corn, grain, or whatever the village harvested. He would be sent first to a CONASUPO school to be trained in methods of judging the quality of the produce. Weight and quality would be recorded, with a copy remaining in the peasant's possession. This employee (and CONASUPO offered to train any peasant interested in learning) would be subject to discharge by the village assembly at any time. Furthermore, CONASUPO representatives would periodically visit the village to check on the operation.

As a way of guaranteeing to the peasant that he would profit by selling to CONASUPO, the village was told that they could keep the money loaned to build the silo, if they did not in fact benefit from the system after the first harvest.

Finally, as a dramatic safeguard against theft, the silos were sealed with three different locks, and the village was told to choose three men to hold the separate keys. Hence the silos could be opened only in the presence of all three. Most villagers were convinced that, while one man would probably be dishonest, and two might join forces, it would be unlikely that three men would conspire to rob the rest of the village, since that would demand too much cooperation. This was an ingenious way of trait taking, using the villagers' suspiciousness to reassure them.

The first step in instituting the CONASUPO system in a village is for the representative to speak to any assembly and explain the program. If possible the peasants are invited to visit other villages where the system has been established. The CONASUPO representative then rates the village's reaction, whether it is "very interested," "moderately interested," or "uninterested." There is a follow-up only when the village is very interested, but increasingly villages, which on their own have observed the success of the system and the profits to the participants, have petitioned for help in building a silo and instituting the CONASUPO system.

By instituting conditions that overcome peasant suspiciousness,

CONASUPO has succeeded in creating a minimal system of cooperation with clearly demonstrable benefits for the peasants and safeguards against their fear of being cheated. Rather than attacking the hoarding character or traditional authority, it gives those with this character the chance for more effective organization; in other words, it does not change character but rather behavior. That the negative traits of the peasant character, such as extreme distrust and egoism, can be changed by a radical reorganization of social and cultural conditions is demonstrated by an orphan community under the direction of Father William Wasson in Cuernavaca, Morelos, called "Our Little Brothers and Sisters."

Around 1954, Father Wasson started a home for orphans, some of them young adolescents already with prison records. This home developed into an institution, or rather a community, that now comprises about 1000 boys and girls from the ages of 3 to about 20, living in Cuernavaca or in a branch of the institution in Mexico City. The boys and girls come from the poorest classes, from families in which the mother has died, and, in about 80 percent of the cases, in which the father has abandoned his children. Considering these conditions, one would expect a great many behavioral difficulties—either destructiveness or sexual problems—since they are prevalent among children and adolescents of the poor in Mexico as in many other countries. But contrary to such expectations, no major behavior problems exist among these children. There are practically no cases of violence in the sense of serious physical assault against either another member of the community, teachers, or outsiders, nor are there any serious sexual problems, in spite of the fact that the boys' dormitories are not far from those of the girls, and the kind of supervision is such that secret meeting would not be impossible. What is remarkable, however, is not only the absence of major behavioral problems but the presence of a spirit of cooperation and mutual responsibility. The boys and girls feel themselves to be members of the "family" and are proud of this membership, although this family is not based on the common tie of blood and is so large that it exceeds the limits of what could even be called an extended family. It is actually a community with life-centered values, characterized by a spirit of cooperation and responsibility.

The following is but one example of this spirit. "From time to time benefactors write and ask the boys to pray for them or some other person in trouble or seriously ill. For the boys the praying takes a special form: instead of kneeling to pray, they do a special act of kindness. Sometimes this takes the form of helping a friend or a stranger, volunteering to clean some place, or any little thing that takes a bit of extra time and consideration."* In fact, even aside from the Catholic character of the institution (although no boy's religious activities are controlled and no pressure is exerted to make him go to Mass or confession), the personality of the director expresses his sincere love for the children and his fellowman, and makes his teachings credible—teachings centered around the command to love one's neighbor, and the evil of selfishness and egotism.

It is interesting to study the conditions under which boys and girls coming from peasant stock not different from the people we studied in the village could change their attitudes in essential areas, especially those of cooperation versus selfishness and suspiciousness. Following are the most important principles which seem to us to be responsible for making this change possible.

1. *The principle of unconditional acceptance.* No child once accepted in the community is ever expelled, for whatever reason. There is nothing the child or adolescent can do which could lead to expulsion. This principle is carried so far that even when they are through with high school (the institution has a high school of its own, which is actually one of the best in the region) they are not forced to leave the community, but can go on to study at the university provided they devote as much time as their studies permit to working in the community. Even if they do not study, there is no fixed time limit by which they are forced to leave. This situation expresses the principle of motherly love which is unconditional, and which never excludes a child, regardless of what he may have done. Children are also not given away for adoption, in spite of many pressures in this direction.

2. This motherly principle of unconditional acceptance is balanced by the paternal principle of demanding from the child *respect for the rights of others and fulfillment of his obligations to the community in accordance with his age.* And what is done to enforce

---

*This, like the next quotation, is from a personal communication from Mrs. Robert Conti, wife of the Director of the adolescent group.

obedience to this demand in cases where the children violate or flout it? It is true that mild forms of punishment, mainly the withdrawal of certain privileges or spankings, are used. But these disciplinary measures are so mild that they would certainly not deter strong destructive or asocial impulses. The fact is that such impulses hardly ever manifest themselves, and hence there is no need for stricter disciplinary measures. In fact, the disciplinary measures are of relatively small importance for the control of behavior in comparison with what the institution produces, an atmosphere of solidarity and realism, with an absence of threat or any kind of brutality. It should be added that if any behavior problems arise they are "talked over" in a realistic, friendly, yet unsentimental manner.

3. Another principle which seems to us of great importance is that of the extensive participation of the children, especially the adolescents, in the *management of their own affairs*. Every two weeks a "house director" is appointed in the unit of boys who attend secondary school. "This boy assumes complete charge. He assigns boys to their various chores: sweeping, cleaning classrooms, mopping halls, dorms, and windows. He also makes out the work staff for the kitchen, and *he* appoints any overseers. The boy in charge sees that bells are rung for Mass and breakfast, that study hall is on time and everyone present. He is the 'acting director'; if he sees that someone is not doing his job, he finds out why. The boys he appoints for kitchen duty plan the meals and cook them. They also make out the shopping lists and give them to the boy in charge of buying. Washing of clothes, ironing, and mending are done by each individual boy in his own spare time. Also, making his bed and keeping his locker clean. The boy in charge will see that the dorms are clean and neat. Very few need to be reminded of this duty."

The children cultivate their own vegetable garden and take care of the animals (chickens, cows, ducks, pigs). Aside from cooking, they also bake their own bread. While the system of participation, formally speaking, goes on under the general supervision of the director of the adolescent group, and does not constitute a co-participation in which formally the children have equal voice with the administrative staff, practically speaking they are independent and take responsibility for the management of the affairs with which they have been entrusted. It must be added that this system functions very well, and that there are no difficulties, for instance, arising in the self-management of the kitchen and other departments. We believe that this degree of responsibility and self-management is very important for the understanding of the low degree of aggressiveness and the spirit of cooperation which exists.

4. In relation to this, another factor must be mentioned which is crucially important. In spite of the fact that this is a rather large institution, it is conducted in a *nonbureaucratic spirit*. The children are not treated as "objects" to be managed by a bureaucracy, but are loved and cared for as individuals by Father Wasson and his assistants, in spite of the fact that by now they number 1000. This tends to show that where a loving attitude is genuine, it becomes credible and that what matters is not the amount of time that is spent with children, but the atmosphere which is created. Characteristic of this nonbureaucratic spirit is, for instance, the fact that in contrast to most Mexican school children, these children do not wear uniforms, and also the fact that the rooms are not numbered but instead are given names.

5. Another factor of considerable importance is the *degree of stimulation* which the children receive. There is a folkloric dance group, a mariachi band (string instruments and trumpets), and children play individual instruments too. All this was first taught by a music teacher who came from Mexico City, but now the older children teach the younger. The children also learned to make their own costumes, and the boys as well as the girls enjoy sewing. There is a carpentry shop, and there are classes in painting, sculpture, and ceramics. There are good soccer and baseball teams; a library of books and records is being developed, again under the supervision of older boys. The richness of stimulation compares well with that of a good high school or junior college attended by children from the middle and upper classes. In an institution attended by the poorest children in Mexico it is unique.

We have mentioned the five principles which in our opinion make it possible to have the remarkable results in behavior and attitude and to some extent in character which this institution shows. It is important to stress that these various principles form a unity or, as we might say more technically, a system. Many attempts for change are made on the erroneous belief that a certain symptom has a certain cause, and that if one changes *the* cause, one cures the symptom.

This kind of thinking is based on a linear model of cause and effect. Stimulated by the progress in the natural sciences, and to some extent in the social sciences, it has become ever more clear that one cannot change a symptom by changing *the* cause which produces it. This is precisely so because every symptom is part of a system in which every factor is related to every other factor in such a way that if you change one factor you have to change all, or at least many others. Any system shows such a tremendous inertia and resistance against change precisely because it is so completely integrated that it has the tendency to continue in its particular structure. However, while on the whole one cannot cure one defect by changing its "cause," it is possible to change the system if one creates another set of conditions which in themselves have a systemic character and can produce a change in the system as a whole. To give an example, if one would apply the principle of unconditional motherly love and acceptance only, children would probably react in such a way that would make it impossible to conduct a large-scale institution. The situation would be different in a relatively small group, but even then we believe the motherly principle has to be complemented by the fatherly principle of realism and responsibility. On the other hand, if one employs only the principles of realism and responsibility without the motherly principle of unconditional acceptance, one creates a hard, bureaucratic structure which may force children to behave dutifully, but which at the same time will create a great deal of antagonism which, while repressed at the moment, will cause havoc in the child and, on the whole, lower the level of his energy and inner freedom. If the two principles however, are fused, something new emerges which results in changes that each of the two principles by themselves could not achieve.

The two other features characteristic of the conduct of this institution are also important as part of the new system. The principle of self-management and the nonbureaucratic spirit stimulate a sense of responsibility, rather than enforcing a sense of duty by the use of threats and rewards. Eventually, the active intellectual and artistic stimulation intensifies the productive elements in the character of the members of the community; hence the hoarding and receptive tendencies are changed from their more negative to their more positive qualities. Or, to put it another way, the atmosphere of the community tends to dry up the destructive and suspicious elements in the personality and to feed the loving and cooperative elements. As a result those who have more negative traits than the average do not express them, because they would lose the respect and affection of their peers.

Needless to say that the success of the community would have been impossible without the authenticity and strength of Father Wasson's personality but this probably makes the difference between success and failure in many intentional and other communities, especially those in which most of the members have not developed a critical and independent attitude. As is to be expected in a traditional Catholic institution, the element of stimulating critical attitudes toward authority seems to be absent in this community, except in an indirect way in that the children can compare the reality of Father Wasson's attitude with both sadistic-authoritarian conditions and the ideological unreality to which they have been exposed all their lives.

The Village Boys' Club

Can individuals living within a village such as the one we studied develop more cooperative behavior? With the aim of seeking the answer to this question experimentally, the study introduced cooperative projects to observe the reactions to them, and to discover whether and which new methods of achieving cooperation could be instituted. The first attempt was a cooperative chicken-raising venture which ended with some of the richer villagers selling the community chickens. They claimed the money was needed to pay for school expenses, but most of the villagers had their doubts that the profits were used for this purpose. The second experiment was organized more carefully. The study formed a Boys' Club with the help of volunteers from the American Friends' Service Committee. The club, including about 20 boys ages 12 to 16, started by planting hybrid seed corn on land belonging to the school which was loaned by the village school committee, based on the agreement that the boys would get half of the profits with half going to the school. Later the club started raising chickens for egg production; milk-producing goats, Jersey Duroc pigs, and a cow were given by an American organization, the Heifer Project, to the club which paid only the transportation of the animals from the United States.* The aim of the club was to teach the boys new methods of farming and animal raising, to give them the opportunity of earning some money by their work, and to stimulate a sense of responsibility and an experience of cooperation.

At first the club suffered from the lack of cooperation characteristic of community development projects. The boys treated the study as a new patron which could bring unheard-of riches to them. They took no initiative in feeding the animals or in caring for the crops, but waited for orders from the bosses. The village boys did not believe they would ever receive the profits, and some took eggs, milk, or tools to compensate themselves for their work. When they became convinced that they would receive the income from the sales of produce, each began to accuse the others of laziness or irresponsibility, of trying to get more than his work deserved. In response to the discontent of those productive-hoarding boys who did more work than the others, we introduced a system of *bonos* or credits for the number of hours worked. At the end of the month half of the profits were reinvested, and the rest were distributed to the boys in proportion to their work. This resulted in greater satisfaction and harder work from the more productive members, but the boys still depended on the orders of the "authorities" and they would not take personal responsibility.† A schedule had been made indicating the days each boy would feed the animals, collect the eggs, milk the cow and goats, clean the pens and the chicken coop. But if one boy forgot his chores or did not feel like doing them, the others would neither pressure him nor do the chores themselves, even though they knew this negligence endangered the animals and the whole project. The more responsible boys did their work, but they were increasingly discouraged by setbacks due to others' irresponsibility. At this time,

---

*Our total contribution for materials to build a chicken coop and buy feed and tools was about $400, which was supplemented by other donations from Mr. Dewey Lackey (chickens), the Heifer Project directed by Mr. Paul Stone, and CARE directed by Mrs. John Elmendorf.

†The Boys' Club was organized and supervised at first by Dr. T. Schwartz. After he left the village this work was taken over by Maccoby, who was in constant contact with the boys, while the daily work was supervised by AFSC volunteers who moved to the village.

they felt unable to do anything about the situation. They were reluctant to pressure anyone else to comply with community obligations. Furthermore, they considered our study as the owners of the animals, and when their companions neglected tasks, their reaction was a passive discouragement with the expectation that the "patrons" would eventually assert authority and save the project.

The club had begun on the wrong basis for a cooperative venture, because the boys had received too much as gifts, and they did not feel they had earned anything by their own work. We first had to overcome the idea that we were rich patrons who would continue to feed the project. After some of the boys had begun to work and to feel a sense of ownership and after the system of bonos had been introduced to divide profits according to the amount of work done, the projects still remained in danger, because many of the boys did not work if the supervisors of the study left the village for a day or two.

At this point we instituted a weekly discussion of two hours with the aim of making the boys more conscious of these anticooperative attitudes so that they could see for themselves how they sabotaged their own possibilities for greater profit.

At first the boys blamed their neglect of the animals on lack of time and lack of knowledge, but they soon recognized this as a rationalization, since they had plenty of time to play or to sit around the plaza, and they avoided learning what we were eager to teach them.

What blocked their energy and self-development were the submissive-authoritarian attitudes which marked the peasants' relation both to government authorities and potential patrons. Each boy felt his only bond within the club was his tie with us, the patrons. Despite the new system of profits based on individual work, the boys still saw their fellows as rivals who were trying to get as much as they could from the club with as little work as possible. Even in our meetings, when one boy spoke to another, it was to accuse him, never to support him. When the boys spoke to us, they always sounded guilty, as though they feared that whatever they did we would be dissatisfied.

During the first meetings most of the time passed in painful silence. We asked them to say what was on their minds but we refused to follow the pattern they expected, to lecture them and give new orders. At one meeting no one spoke for an hour until finally one boy, the bravest and most responsible of the group, admitted that he had been thinking of going to a dance that had just begun. But he was afraid to say it, sure that the "patron" would be angry. The boys were told that we did not want to schedule meetings conflicting with dances and that they were free to go, but it was suggested that they talk some more at the next meeting about the fear of saying what was on their minds.

Discussions at the next meetings centered on the ever-present guilt that each boy felt before his parents and any other authority. The boys had been taught that to anger the authority for whatever reason meant punishment. Therefore, with parents, with employers, or with us, it was better to remain silent, to do what one was told to do, and hence to avoid any initiative. It was suggested to them that this attitude was the way a peon felt in the hacienda, but that it no longer was necessary for them to be this way. Indeed, with such a fearful and submissive attitude, they would be peons in their souls and never feel like free men; by accepting the idea that the right thing to do depends on another's judgment, they could never develop their own sense of right, they could never be the masters of their own activity, and they would always be more interested in escaping punishment than in the work they were doing.

After this meeting there was a surge of initiative and responsibility. We suggested that the Friends' Service Committee volunteer, who was living in the village supervising the work, leave for a few days to give the boys a chance to work on their own and then to examine the results. At the next meeting the boys were asked how they had managed by themselves, and they all turned their eyes sheepishly to the floor. This reaction was quite surprising to us since in fact they had done a good job by themselves, but they were unsure the authorities would be satisfied. They were unable to decide for themselves whether their actions were good or bad. Traditionally, authorities in their village show their approval by not scolding or punishing. Seldom do they stimulate children to feel satisfaction in a job well done. This attitude of always expecting failure is common to peasants in Latin America; Hirschman (1967) makes the significant suggestion that for many Latin Americans success is disconcerting because it demands a radical change in one's view of the world.

At this point, we tried to interest the fathers of the boys in the club so that when we left they would support the project. The club had now become a small business with valuable animals and some 350 chickens which produced 220 eggs a day. But we had failed to reckon that the parents were likely to feel, fatalistically, that like every other cooperative enterprise begun in the village this one would fail. Naturally the parents' point of view, well known by the boys, weakened their confidence.

In a last attempt to enlist the support of the parents we asked the ayudante municipal to call a meeting. When the parents heard about the difficulties the boys had in cooperating, and the losses due to negligence, they were all for giving up the club. Their immediate response was to express the characteristic self-deprecation of the peasant. "These boys are just egoistic," one father said. "You should move the club to a village that will appreciate it." "Why do you waste your time?" another asked. "These boys are not worth it." We assured the fathers that the boys had done a great deal, and that we would not leave until the club was financially solid, but privately we wondered how the club would carry on without help from the older generation and how the boys who were present at the meeting would react to their fathers' fatalism and lack of hope.

At the next reunion the boys were asked what they had thought of the meeting. By this time the group of boys who came to these discussions had shrunk from twenty to a hard core of six of the older boys who always came and one or two others who came from time to time. One boy said the meeting seemed fine. He was immediately challenged by the others. "What do you mean, fine?" one said. "They have no interest in helping us, they think we are no good, and they want the club to end." This boy and the others realized they could expect no support from their parents, and they decided they could do without it. "Already we know more about chickens than they do," said one boy, "and we have learned how to market the eggs. Even if they were to help, they would only order us around and take the profits."

This discussion marked the turning point in the boys' attitude. After this discussion the boys began for the first time to cooperate in setting a day in which each one took the others' animals to pasture. Before this, they had refused even to keep their goats in the same pen, even though this was necessary for breeding purposes. Each one carefully kept his own goat at home. Now they decided to build a roof for the goat corral. They demanded that others cooperate or leave the club. Those older boys who had before shunned leadership in order not to seem to put themselves ahead of the others accepted the fact that if they did not lead, nothing would be done. They organized a dance to raise money; and, taking advantage of the Mexican love of lotteries, they sold chances on a pig, realizing a greater profit from the lottery than they would have made in the market. They began to think of new projects, such as fixing up a village bath house, long run down by disuse, and charging a few cents for soap and a shower. They petitioned and received village approval for the project.

Shortly afterwards, three years after it began and after a year and a half of the discussion meetings, the study withdrew from the village and the boys' club continued to prosper under its own steam for over a year, which in itself is remarkable for such a project. However, the boys had grown older and were no longer able to spend time at the club. By this time one productive-hoarding boy had gone away from the village after passing examinations to enter officers' training school. Another of the same character type was attending medical school. A third was playing football professionally. Another of the boys who had at the start been typically receptive and passive was now taking a technical training course at a high school in a nearby city. Another boy from a fatherless family whose receptive traits had become more positive was taking a course in horticulture and was organizing a rock band in his spare time. Another boy with an entrepreneurial character had gotten papers to work in the United States. Only one of the original group, a very intelligent but, at the start, extremely rebellious and mother-fixated boy, was working as a day laborer, and he was trying to find a job in a newly-opened factory. Thus, one result of the club was to stimulate the development of more productive traits and a new sense of possibility in the boys, rare among peasants, to train themselves for more demanding and rewarding work.

The boys then decided that it was necessary for them to prepare a new generation to take over the club, but they found themselves stymied by the same lack of cooperation that had characterized the beginnings of the project. Finally a group came to discuss these difficulties with us. One of the boys remarked that he now understood what we must have felt with them, their irresponsibility, egoism, and rebelliousness. But he did not know how to change this behavior in the new members and asked that we hold meetings for the younger boys just as we had done for them. This was not possible, and it became evident that the club could not continue. With regret the boys sold the communal animals and the club was closed, some of the boys keeping the animals they had earned, to raise at home.

The aim of the project was experimental, to see first of all whether the young people could respond to a new opportunity and, second, to help the boys become conscious of deeply-rooted attitudes that made responsible cooperation impossible.

The first barrier to cooperative work was the feeling on the part of the more productive boys that the others would take advantage of them. This was solved by the trait taking bono system which gave greater profits to those who worked more. The second barrier was the attitude of defeatism and fatalism which was shaken by the experience of managing the club successfully during our planned absence and then analyzing the inability to feel satisfied and hopeful about it. The third obstacle was the authoritarian mode of relation which made the boys submissive to the new patrons and at the same time rebellious when they were away. The authoritarian mode of relation implied an egoistic, suspicious, and hostile attitude toward each other and a lack of responsibility for the communal enterprise.

The decisive and most important point in breaking through the authoritarian-submissive attitude was the meeting in which the boys criticized their fathers; this was not an emotional, "rebellious" criticism. It was a criticism in which they saw the fathers realistically, as they were; and they saw, furthermore, that the authorities were stifling their chances to grow. This intellectual and affective insight was the crucial point in changing their attitude. Although we did not plan this confrontation, we had prepared the boys for their new awareness that their submissiveness and fear of punishment made them passive and unable to judge for themselves, that they had been irresponsible because they were unable to respond to life. While before they could react only to commands, their new awareness produced a new kind of responsiveness. After the confrontation with the fathers, one of the boys opened the next meeting by saying: "Now I know what you mean about the difference between fear and the ability to respond.

Before I always fed our cow because I was afraid that my mother would beat me if I didn't. But last week I looked into the cow's eyes and for the first time I realized she was alive and that if I did not feed her she would die, and I knew that I would never again forget to feed her."

How shall we describe the weekly discussions which were an integral part in the process of dissolving authoritarian attitudes? Were they psychoanalysis? Or group therapy? Not in the usual sense. The boys were not encouraged to talk about their personal problems or private hangups; no one complained about not receiving enough love from his mother; neither was there a discussion about individual goals in life, although some of the boys came to talk about these privately. There were three essential factors in the effectiveness of the discussion group:

1. The boys were trying to respond to a new possibility (reality) which would allow them to do interesting work with animals and gain material profit. They could see that their attitudes limited their efficiency, and they wanted to change them.

2. The discussion group offered the boys a way of critically analyzing both their work and the psychology of the villagers. In part the discussion group was a type of educational seminar very different from traditional village schooling, or, for that matter, conventional education throughout the world.

3. The whole study, including the village doctor and the supervisors of the club, had created an atmosphere of trust and confidence that contrasted sharply both with the authoritarian and fatalistic atmosphere of the home and the expectations concerning outside authorities. The boys had the emotional support first from us and later from each other, to confront authority. But we also made it clear that we respected their right to remain as they were. We did not push them to confront authority. Unlike group therapy, they did not have to work through a "transference" of their fear of authority with the group "leader," because they "worked through" the real thing with their parents.* Nevertheless there was an element of psychoanalysis

---

*Such a confrontation rarely happens without outside support. We know of an isolated village, Cuauhtenco, in the State of Tlaxcala, in which a strong spirit of cooperativeness prevails. One of us (Maccoby) who visited the village

in this session: but not in the conventional way. Here the analysis was restricted to one problem, the attitude toward authority, and not carried out with conventional methods but by explaining a good deal about the problem of authority. Even so, the decisive break-through might not have happened had it not been for the fact that in the meeting with the fathers they saw the clear proof of what had been told to them before. This session had a cathartic quality; the various pieces of their own experience and our explanation "gelled," as it were, and a real, though limited change occurred in their character structure.

The result was increased productiveness and cooperativeness and increased independence as shown by the subsequent careers followed by most of the boys. It is also notable that the boys did not become resentful and vengeful toward their parents. They did not blame them for their troubles, but rather took the realistic attitude that they had to become independent. They saw their parents more clearly and decided, *"así son"* (that's the way they are), and "we must be different."

Similar methods of opening the peasant's mind, of broadening his consciousness, have been described by Danilo Dolci in his work with the Sicilian peasant and by Paolo Freire with the Brazilian peasants and urban slum dwellers. Both men have described how the passivity, submissiveness, and egoism of the peasant can be overcome

---

(with Ed Duckles of the AFSC) was struck by the uncharacteristic peasant cooperativeness and asked whether the village had always been this way. The village leaders, all of them young men in their late twenties, replied that up to five years ago the village had been run for centuries by the old men, and that in those days there was little or no cooperation. Then a rural school teacher had encouraged a group of young men, the present leaders, to dig a well, since the village had no supply of water, except what was collected during rains or imported. Using the crudest methods, they began to dig with shovels, scraping the earth out and, as the well became deeper, raising the earth in baskets mounted on handmade wooden pulleys. The elders ridiculed them, saying they were fools and that if water were under the ground it would have been found centuries before. But they persisted and found water at about 300 feet. Their achievement exploded the traditional authoritarianism, overturned the authority structure, and made them the leaders. They then demanded cooperation from other villagers in digging more wells, building a road to the village, and instituting a cooperative weaving project. The result has been to increase both hope and prosperity in the village.

when he becomes aware of these attitudes and when he begins to think creatively about his culture and himself.

The experiment demonstrated that the development of critical awareness about reality, in this case especially about traditional authority, leads to a transformation of character, to greater activeness and responsiveness, which also resulted in greater cooperativeness among the boys. How such critical awareness can be furthered on a large social scale is a political and cultural problem of such dimensions that it transcends the scope of this study. Our experiment tends to confirm the thesis that not hate nor accusations, but radical critical thought which dissolves paralyzing illusions, is the way to change the peasant's traditional submissiveness and passivity.

Does the experience of the orphanage contradict our findings about the crucial importance of critical thinking? We do not think so, mainly because the case of the orphanage consists only of young, hence more malleable people. It is guided by an extraordinary personality in whom love for children is completely real. Such personalities are exceedingly rare, and all the more so since it is necessary that they also have great practical and organizational talent. In a sense, the orphanage is a life-oriented traditional community, more like the ideal medieval village than the modern world.* Eventually, the village is led by authoritarian men oriented to material gain who dominate a majority of submissive, passive people, and use this domination to continue the existing village system. Without the awakening of the capacity for critical thinking, the social structure will hardly change. On the other hand, in the orphanage there are no obstacles of an economic or social nature to be overcome. There are no problems of law, scarcity, modes of production, or exploitation by one class of another.

However this may be, we have given the example of the Pequeños Hermanos not because we want to recommend it as a solution of the peasant problem, but because we believe it is relevant for two reasons: first, because it shows to what extent children and adolescents are capable of undergoing important changes when adequate

---

*To what extent the adolescents who graduate from the orphanage will sustain the cooperative spirit they show as adolescents remains to be seen; one might suspect that they may adapt too well to a competitive, alienated society, precisely because their critical attitude has not been sufficiently awakened.

methods are employed; second, because the methods employed—even without their particular religious frame of reference—show that changes must be brought about by introducing a number of new conditions which are interrelated, these being a spirit of unquestioned human acceptance, unsentimental realism, stimulation, and active responsible participation. By comparing the principles employed in the boys' club and those in the orphanage, it can be easily recognized that they are very similar, except in the point of assisting critical thinking.

As far as the special problem of adolescents is concerned, Father Wasson's methods show that neither the principle of letting adolescents act out and thus "get rid" of their aggressiveness, nor that of threats of punishment is adequate to cope with actual or potential aggressiveness: making life interesting, stimulating activity, and a group spirit which does not admire violence or force all have an effect that neither indulgence nor threats can produce.

In short, what this experiment shows is that, given a new set of conditions, the traditional peasant character can to a considerable extent undergo changes, and traditional peasant behavior can change from antagonism and selfishness to cooperation. The main problem is to find those new conditions which in a systemic way are able to bring about these changes. And this is only achieved by an organization of social life that is conducive to an increase in the productive elements of the character structure.

References

Diez, Domingo. *Bosquejo Historico Geografico de Morelos*. Cuernavaca: Editorial Tiahuica, 1967.

Foster, George. *Tzintzuntzan: Mexican Peasants in a Changing World*. Boston: Little, Brown, 1967.

Freire, Paulo. *Educação e Conscientização*. Cuernavaca: CIDOC, 1968.

Hirschman, Albert O. *Development Projects Observed*. Washington, D.C.: The Brookings Institution, 1967.

Huizinga, Johan. *The Waning of the Middle Ages*. London: Penguin, 1955.

Maccoby, Michael, and Modiano, Nancy. "On Culture and Equivalence." *Studies in Cognitive Growth*, edited by J. C. Bruner et al. New York: John Wiley & Sons, 1966.

Maccoby, Michael, and Modiano, Nancy. "Cognitive Style in Rural and Urban Mexico." *Human Development* 12 (1969): 22-23.

McClelland, David C. *The Achieving Society*. Princeton: D. Van Nostrand, 1961.